The Theatre of Medieval Europe

This volume brings together the work of thirteen internationally recognised scholars of early drama to give a comprehensive account of recent findings in the field. While reflecting the large body of research on English drama, the book widens the focus of its survey to represent the continental theatre of the period, with a succession of essays covering France, Italy, Spain, Germany, central Europe and the Low Countries. In addition, it deals with Latin musical and liturgical drama, and addresses both the archival and stage-oriented aspects of theatre research. In reviewing the subject in this way, the collection not only offers an account of recent discoveries across a range of countries and types of drama, but also suggests the comparative and interdisciplinary ground on which these areas of research may increasingly come to meet and cross-fertilise one another in the future.

A major feature of the book is its authoritative chronological and fully indexed bibliography, which should serve as an invaluable guide to the most significant contributions in the field.

The Theatre of Medieval Europe
New Research in Early Drama

edited by

ECKEHARD SIMON

Professor of Germanic Philology
Harvard University

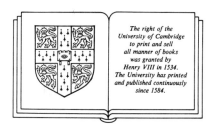

The right of the
University of Cambridge
to print and sell
all manner of books
was granted by
Henry VIII in 1534.
The University has printed
and published continuously
since 1584.

CAMBRIDGE UNIVERSITY PRESS
Cambridge
New York   Port Chester   Melbourne   Sydney

Published by the Press Syndicate of the University of Cambridge
The Pitt Building, Trumpington Street, Cambridge CB2 1RP
40 West 20th Street, New York, NY 10011, USA
10 Stamford Road, Oakleigh, Melbourne 3166, Australia

First published 1991

Printed in Great Britain at the University Press, Cambridge

British Library cataloguing in publication data
The Theatre of medieval Europe: new research in early drama.
– (Cambridge studies in medieval literature; 9)
1. Europe. Theatre, history
1. Simon, Eckehard
792'094

Library of Congress cataloguing in publication data applied for

ISBN 0 521 38514 8 hardback

CE

To the memory of
Stanley Jadwin Kahrl (1931–1989),
colleague and friend

Contents

vii

Contents

Contributors

David Bevington, University of Chicago
C. Clifford Flanigan, Indiana University
Andrew Hughes, University of Toronto
Alexandra F. Johnston, University of Toronto
Stanley J. Kahrl, late of Ohio State University
Alan E. Knight, Pennsylvania State University
Hansjürgen Linke, University of Cologne
David Mills, University of Liverpool
Eckehard Simon, Harvard University
David Staines, University of Ottawa
Sandro Sticca, State University of New York at Binghamton
Elsa Strietman, University of Cambridge
Ronald E. Surtz, Princeton University
Glynne Wickham, University of Bristol

Preface

This volume gathers together thirteen papers reporting on medieval drama research since the 1960s prepared for a conference convened by the Committee on Medieval Studies of Harvard University, 9–11 October 1986. The scholars participating were kind enough to read the papers in advance. At the meeting they were then joined by some local medievalists to discuss each report in detail. The discussion was taped so that the editor might use it in devising instructions for revision. As they enter the present volume, then, as a guide to research, the papers bear the imprint not of one but of a team of editors for whose help I am most grateful.

Although five of the chapters are devoted to English drama, it was not this field that prompted the editor to persuade a reluctant Committee to sponsor a conference. Scholars of English drama have been talking to each other since the 1950s, not only in seminars at MLA meetings and the Kalamazoo International Congresses but in journals such as *Research Opportunities in Renaissance Drama* and *Medieval English Theatre*. It seemed to me, however, that they have done this largely without the rest of us. This conference, then, was intended to help scholars of continental drama to join the conversation and to encourage all of us to begin looking over national fences.

It also seemed time to bring in the harvest. Research on medieval theatre has enjoyed enormous growth since the 1960s, and not only in England and North America. So it seemed appropriate to take stock, to see where we stand, to share our concerns and to suggest where we might go from here. The editor suspects that a major new direction will be to study European drama as a comparative field, signalled by the productive meetings of the International Society for the Study of Medieval Theatre. The present research reports, tied to a bibliography, may perhaps serve as a guide for the work to come.

The title of this book is a kind of headline to be placed over drama research since the 1960s. 'Theatre' suggests what has been most innovative and productive about this scholarship: the discovery that medieval drama was primarily theatre, that performance went far beyond the text. How this revolution began is told in the introductory essay by Glynne Wickham, the scholar first to mount the barricades. Wickham's *Early English Stages*, appearing since 1959, is both manifesto for and companion to this period. As will be discussed below, work to understand medieval drama as theatre has taken two directions. One has been to mine archives for theatrical activities, and is exemplified by the Toronto project 'Records of Early English Drama'. The other has been to put on modern performances of medieval plays and thus to examine them as works of the stage, as living theatre.

Moving to the subtitle, 'early' addresses the concern that this drama can be called 'medieval' only if we grant the term a long afterlife. In virtually all countries, as the conference debate made clear, medieval plays continued to be performed alongside the new theatre of the Renaissance and the Baroque periods. 'Early drama', then, designates a tradition of European theatre lasting some 800 years, from the tenth to the eighteenth centuries. With 'medieval Europe', lastly, the main title voices the hope that scholars might find it rewarding to study the drama of 'their literature' in the light of what was being staged in the countries around them.

By 'countries' we should, of course, not think of European nations as they exist today. The geography of medieval drama was one of languages. It thus often differed from the political map. For the present volume, we therefore need to explain what chapter-headings like 'France', 'Spain' and 'Germany' actually mean.

The plays of France, as Alan Knight notes, were mostly written in the French of the north. But there is a substantial number of texts written in Old Occitan (Provençal), the dialect of southern France, resembling Italian and the Catalan of Spain. In the twelfth century, plays in (Anglo-Norman) French were performed in England and in the thirteenth we find French drama at the courts of southern Italy and Sicily (Adam de la Halle's *Robin et Marion*, for example). Later on, these courts become home for Aragonese theatre from Spain.

To paraphrase Ronald Surtz, Spain did not exist. What we have is drama from four indigenous regions (Catalonia, Castile, Portugal, Aragon), remarkably different in history and traditions. Plays in German were written in such outlying regions as Latvia, Bohemia, Hungary, Romania and northern Italy (Trent, Friuli). The German plays of towns along the Lower Rhine, although linked to the south, were written in a dialect little different from early Dutch. Dutch drama, again, was found not only in today's Netherlands, but in the provinces of Flanders, Brabant and Limbourg of present-day Belgium. Language geography is further discussed in the five chapters on continental drama in this volume.

While providing more coverage than some, our survey cannot claim to be complete. A few regions are missing and we do not report on the research done on certain Latin pieces. The paper on Spain omits Portuguese and Aragonese theatre because in medieval times these were not major traditions. The same can be said of Scandinavia where the earliest vernacular play dates to the 1470s. More serious is lack of coverage for the Slavic drama of Eastern Europe. As Glynne Wickham reports, interesting work is being done in Poland, for instance, on Corpus Christi and Passion plays. It should be

Preface

noted, however, that the Czech drama of Bohemia is heavily dependent on German plays. For some early texts in Byzantine Greek, there is still no evidence to determine whether they were in fact staged drama.

Equally debatable, much research notwithstanding, is the theatrical status of dialogues in the manner of Terence written in the tenth century by the Saxon canoness Hrotswitha (or Hrotsvit) of Gandersheim and the so-called 'elegiac comedies', produced in the twelfth century in centres of learning along the Loire River. These are marvellous pieces, in lively and witty Latin, and one wishes they were plays. Much recent research on them has been done by Italian scholars and Sandro Sticca gives us a brief account. The consensus at the conference was, however, that these texts were not written for the stage.

Throughout medieval Europe, Latin drama was sung not spoken. But this was evidently not the case for Hrotswitha's playlets and the *comoediae*. That must have made them something entirely different, a different genre, as it were, from the oratorio-like Latin drama of the time. One doubts, therefore, that the authors thought of them as staged drama. Hrotswitha scholars face the additional hurdle that medieval theatre, painful as it is to state these days, was 'for men only'. This was not a matter of conscious discrimination, of course, but of social convention. By the thirteenth century, to be sure, liturgical plays were sung by nuns in some convents and fifteenth-century civic records occasionally mention women in minor parts. But from the Winchester Easter play of c. 975 to Shakespeare and beyond, theatre was the province of men.

As a learned canoness related to the reigning emperor, Hrotswitha would have been indignant at the suggestion, I think, that she and her fellow nuns, like minstrels at a banquet, should act out this Christian answer to Terence. The monastic schools, we remember, read Terence for his Latin. Terence the playwright and the Roman stage were unknown.

The same can be said of Hildegard, the learned and powerful twelfth-century abbess of Bingen on the Rhine. It is gratifying to see our age rediscover Hildegard's poetry and her great visions. And her so-called *Ordo virtutum* – involving vices, virtues and the devil – may in fact be the first morality. But it is poor sociology to claim, as music performance groups like *Sequentia* do, that Hildegard and the nuns of Bingen would have staged the *Ordo* in the convent cloister.

These remarks reflect the engagement with which this question was debated at the conference. But we actually spent most of our time discussing the reports themselves, especially important findings new to most of us. Hansjürgen Linke surprised us with the news that German scholars had for some years known of a second manuscript of the *Ludus de Antichristo* (see the bibliography, no. *78*), a political Antichrist play of the 1160s from the Bavarian abbey of Tegernsee. Alan Knight shared his discovery, at Wolfenbüttel, of a large corpus of religious plays from the city of Lille. Like some cycles of north English towns, these plays were performed on pageant wagons. Wagons were also used for Corpus Christi plays put on at the cathedral of Toledo. Among the more unexpected items, Ronald Surtz pointed to records from Catalonia mentioning Jews as participants in Christian theatre.

Also much discussed was the state of research in each field and the vast differences in the rate of progress. A century ago, scholarship on medieval drama was flourishing in France, Italy, Germany and the Low Countries. During the first half of this century, however, the field lay largely dormant. It was, curious to note, the early sixties that saw a common resurgence of drama research in these countries. Yet much of this newer scholarship remains unknown to those working on English drama. Sandro Sticca observed that virtually no one outside Italy reads the important work done at centres like Viterbo. Except for publications on Latin drama, German scholarship is largely ignored as well and most of us were surprised to learn how many plays Spain produced and how much research is in progress there.

England is clearly the most 'developed country'; its research economy is booming. For every lone scholar toiling away on liturgical drama or music, on French or German plays, there are whole teams of professors and graduate students plowing and re-seeding the English field. Our volume reflects this situation, of course, in devoting five papers to early English drama. These permit a much more detailed discussion of the state of research than is possible for our correspondents from the continent. In introducing research little known to most, they must often confine themselves to listing the work done and adding brief comments. One hopes, on the other hand, that much of what David Mills, for example, has to say on editing English plays will be useful to editors of continental texts. For Church drama, Clifford Flanigan had reviewed research since 1965 in a major article published in 1975–6 (bibliography, no. 36). In their present papers, he and Andrew Hughes are therefore able to concentrate on work done since the early 1970s. As an authority on music and liturgy, Hughes casts a critical eye on Church drama research done mostly by scholars without training in musicology. This is clearly a field where most work remains to be done.

The glories of Marlowe and Shakespeare may explain why research on English drama is so far ahead of any other field. But it has probably more to do with the large number of English departments (and their size) in Great Britain and North America. The nineteenth century organised our discipline along lines of national languages. For medieval literature this created a vast discrepancy between what we have and what we study. The number of plays written in Latin or German, for example, is easily ten times that of what survives from England. For German-speaking central Europe we now have about 160 religious plays and a few new ones seem to come to light every year. The leading civilisation in drama – as in practically all medieval culture – was France. The total corpus is now estimated at about 220 religious plays, 70 moralities and about 150 farces. Modern editions, as Alan Knight notes, exist for less than half of these. Many lengthy Passion and saint plays lie dormant in manuscripts. Here is a country, then, where many an emigrant from the overgrazed fields of England could find a happy home.

One other question we debated and which the correspondents wished the editor to address was 'When does medieval drama end?' I mentioned this at the beginning when I explained why we are using 'early drama' in the subtitle. Our colleagues in English were quite spirited in pointing out that 'medieval' was not the appropriate term for the theatre we are studying. The adjective is little used by them. Since the work of Glynne Wickham one speaks of 'Early English Stages'; Toronto's archival project is called 'Records of Early English Drama'. A 1987 collection of conference papers on European drama is entitled *Early Drama to 1600* (see the 'Recent works' section of the bibliography).

From the English perspective, this view makes good sense. Drama written in English starts very late, at the end of the fourteenth century. The same is true for plays in Dutch: the Van Hulthem collection dates from about 1410. And leaving aside a twelfth-century Magi play linked to France, vernacular theatre in Iberia begins even later. Yet the chronology is more 'medieval' for other traditions.

When the first English plays appeared, Latin drama had been around for four centuries. The first French-language plays were written in the twelfth century. For the thirteenth, we have a few semi-dramatic Italian texts and several fairly substantial Easter and Passion plays in German. In the continental context, it seems to me, it is therefore still more appropriate to speak of *medieval* drama.

But the question is directed more at the end than at the beginning. And here there can be no doubt that the end of the Middle Ages does not mark the end of medieval drama. This holds true for all of Europe.

The great cycle play of Chester was last performed in 1575, and thus at a time when London already had a professional theatre. Throughout the sixteenth century, as David Staines notes, the older religious cycles and morality plays were performed side by side with Tudor and Elizabethan drama. It is widely accepted that Marlowe and Shakespeare were familiar with some forms of medieval drama, notably with the Vice figure popularised in moralities. While the idea of continuity has come under question, as David Bevington points out, England is still different from France and Germany in that the new playwrights (of the Tudor period) actually worked with their medieval heritage.

Only in Spain is the continuity more pronounced. The medieval theatre of Castile leads without break into the Golden Age of the seventeenth century. In sixteenth-century Catalonia, as Ronald Surtz reports, religious plays were still sung in the manner of Latin liturgical drama. Some Easter plays continued to be performed until the nineteenth century. The *Misteri d'Elx*, celebrating the Assumption of the Virgin, is still being staged in the town of Elche. While its performance practices, replete with lifts and pulleys, may not be entirely medieval, some manuscripts do in fact date back to the seventeenth century and the play itself is attested since the early 1500s.

For England and Spain, then, the term 'early drama' is fitting because it suggests a productive continuity between the old and the new. Elsewhere, clearer lines of demarcation can be drawn. In Italy, there is a fairly sharp break in 1539 when Pope Paul III forbids the staging of *sacre rappresentazioni* in Rome. These pageants had by then become fairly baroque spectacles. French Renaissance playwrights, as Alan Knight observes, made a conscious break with their medieval past: 'Racine has no medieval roots' (below, p. 151). But ignoring it does not mean that the old theatre did not continue. French morality plays were, in fact, performed continuously from the fourteenth to the seventeenth centuries. In Paris, the staging of Passion plays was officially prohibited in 1548. But it is the nature of such decrees never to reach the provinces. In villages of Savoy and the Dauphiné, Passion and saint plays were put on until the eighteenth century.

In German central Europe, the same holds true for those southern provinces where the Reformation did not take root. In Bavaria, Swabia, some Swiss cantons and in Austria, especially the Tirol, the medieval plays of Easter, Corpus Christi and Christmas continued to be staged in towns like Bolzano up to 1700. The famed Passion play of Lucerne, last performed in 1616, can in fact be viewed as a public affirmation of medieval faith. While we do have a few Passion plays written by Protestant authors, in most towns medieval plays disappear from the records as Lutheranism is adopted. Oberammergau, despite its popularity, is not a true relic from the medieval past. While parts of the oldest Passion play were taken from sixteenth-century texts, what one sees today has little to do with medieval theatre.

In the Low Countries, the effects of the Reformation were felt somewhat later. But the conflicts it brought eventually put an end to the old theatre produced, in happy competitions, by urban guilds known as *Rederijkerskamers* (Chambers of Rhetoric). In the south, the religious wars of the 1570s and 80s prevented the guilds from meeting and in the north, as Elsa Strietman has noted, Calvinistic church councils eventually prohibited theatre of all kinds.

The point of the discussion here reviewed was not, of course, to quibble over the use of 'medieval' and 'early'. The important issue was to establish that no form of medieval literature survived longer than the drama. The reason for this is that medieval drama was not really literature, as we understand it, but theatre. It was a pervasive, ubiquitous and tenacious form of popular culture. On this note, I return to the title of this volume: *The Theatre of Medieval Europe* signifies the most productive turn that research since the 1960s has taken.

The work on medieval theatre, as I have noted above, has been carried out on two different fronts: on the stage and in the archive. Studying medieval plays through modern productions began in England in the early 1950s. As Stanley Kahrl relates in his lively and personal account, the movement took hold in North America in the early seventies, mostly on university campuses, with Toronto leading the way. At international meetings, one hears from colleagues that performing medieval plays has caught on with student groups in France and the Low Countries as well. Little of such activity, on the other hand, is being reported from Italy, Spain and Germany.

England has remained in the lead and medieval theatre enjoys substantial academic support at universities such as Bristol, Leeds, Lancaster and Cambridge. In modernised form, medieval plays have made it to the London stage and onto television. Since 1979, these performances have been documented in *Medieval English Theatre*, a journal edited at Lancaster University that vigorously promotes medieval drama as living theatre. Some French and Dutch plays have joined the repertory. The movement is being led by a new generation of scholars whose ways are more informal and who easily mix with student actors and 'citizen spectators'. In his new book *Playing God* (bibliography, no. *136*), John R. Elliott has now written the history of modern medieval theatre.

Some of the theatricals one sees are no doubt governed by the same happy spirit that dwells in such neo-medieval groups as the Society for Creative Anachronism active on American college campuses. And in service to a sterner muse, some continental colleagues will, one suspects, continue to raise an eyebrow or two. But as Stanley Kahrl makes clear, the method is sound. Medieval drama was not meant to be read. That is why our students have always found it so boring. It was meant to be heard and seen. Theatrical effects, however, cannot really be imagined: they must be reproduced and observed. The language of stage symbolism is mainly visual. Andrew Hughes sums this up succinctly when stating that 'scholarship is *never* complete until the result has been seen in practice: on the boards...' (below, p. 61). It is perhaps significant that this statement comes from a musicologist. When we think of medieval music, we think of performance, not of reading notation.

As a medievalist, one must be grateful that at least some of what we study is beginning to enter the popular imagination, that *The Second Shepherds Play*, *Everyman* and *The Play of Daniel* have become almost as much part of our repertory as, say, *The Trojan Women* or *Oedipus Rex*. A director conversant with scholarship can no doubt give authentic shape to a performance. Anyone who has seen Toronto's Poculi Ludique Societas perform will agree. And when watching such a play, the trained eye can see effects of medieval stagecraft that no one reading the text could have imagined. When at Toronto's York Cycle of 1977 Christ was played by twelve quite different men, which pageant-wagon staging makes necessary, the effect was to humanise the role, to make Christ into suffering Everyman.

What we must remember, however, is that we are only conducting an experiment. We are not really able to re-create a medieval performance. Perhaps the resurgence of research we are now witnessing will eventually result in a poetics of the medieval stage, a historically accurate dramaturgy. But at this point we really do not know whether a stage effect we find meaningful, powerful or moving was intended by the playwright or was perceived as such by the townspeople who came to watch.

Preface

Such doubts will lessen the more we combine the stage with the archive, the more those scholars direct modern performances who are doing the best research into the historical record. The return to history is the most promising trend in recent scholarship. The flagship is Toronto's 'Records of Early English Drama', a research group founded in the mid-seventies by Alexandra Johnston. REED has by now engaged dozens of scholars to search the archives of Great Britain for evidence of theatre, minstrelsy and entertainment. How rich these first harvests have been, Professor Johnston shows in her fascinating 'All the world was a stage' (chapter 7, below). The results go beyond theatre history. When the work of many volumes is complete, much of the social history of England between 1400 and 1700 will have to be rewritten.

We have always suspected that the plays we have represent only a fraction of what medieval playwrights produced. But such losses befell other types of literature as well. The REED searches are beginning to suggest, as David Mills puts it, that 'dramatic activities uncontained by text were the medieval norm' (below, p. 65). That is to say, much of what was spoken and acted on the medieval stage never existed as a formal text and hence was not written down. But we must know this kind of theatre in order to reconstruct how the plays we have were staged. Archival research will show the way.

Nothing like the REED project exists so far for continental Europe. For France, Italy and the Low Countries one still has to rely on documentation assembled in the last century by antiquarians and local historians. As useful as some of these old histories of theatre 'in our town' still are, systematic archival work remains to be done. Given its splendid heritage, one can only imagine what lies hidden in the archives of France. Here are gaps that call for scholarly action, especially from those with historical training.

What scholars heeding the call can discover is shown by the German records recently published by Bernd Neumann (bibliography, no. 565), who spent fifteen years mining German archives. While no single scholar can cover all sources (consider the thirty-five or so researchers engaged by REED), Neumann's pioneering effort is fundamentally changing our understanding of where and how German drama was performed. The records mention types of plays previously unknown. Regions for which not a single text survives were actually dappled with theatre of all kinds. In fact, Neumann proposes the thesis that, in late-medieval times, every town had theatre; every town no matter how small had at least one play.

The social implications of this are profound. Theatre played a central role in late-medieval town life. Drama was the only form of 'literature' practiced in churches and market squares, on the streets and in houses. Poems, romances and chronicles were heard in several dozen courts by perhaps a few thousand members of the gentry. Theatre, however, was for everybody. It was, in today's parlance, a mass medium, whether used by the Church for instruction, as a way to put one's town on the map, to raise money or for merry sport at Carnival and May revels. The archival work will continue to show, in sum, that medieval theatre was an important form of popular culture. It was a popular culture that spanned seven centuries and was so ingrained in custom and civic rite that, as I have noted, it far outlasted the age that created it. Viewed as popular culture, medieval theatre would seem to be an ideal field for interdisciplinary studies.

To promote such work and to foster comparative study of European drama was, of course, the reason for convening our conference and producing this volume. What, in conclusion, are the prospects for such work? It will be difficult to find good academic homes for it. Departments and institutions of literature, here and abroad, are surrounded by the traditional language fences. Theatre institutes are few – only two at German universities, for instance – and they tend to cater to the modern stage. Hopes turn once again to the English departments of Great Britain and North America, with their flocks of talented doctoral students. It might be possible to return to older standards of foreign-language proficiency. Then perhaps the important scholarship published in French, German, Dutch, Italian and Spanish will not continue to pass by unread there. Until such time, we will need large-scale surveys, that is, detailed histories of Latin and continental drama written in English.

The vision of professors and graduate students of English reading several foreign languages will perhaps provoke a smile. But making scholarship accessible is only half the problem. What about the plays themselves, many written in obscure regional dialects? It is hard to imagine someone in English spending years learning, say, Middle Low German just in order to read the Easter play of Redentin. So a realistic first step, the conference agreed, is to start translation projects making major plays available in English. Such a program, as Sandro Sticca reported, has now begun at the State University of New York at Binghamton under the auspices of its Medieval Center. Elsa Strietman and Robert Potter are making rapid strides in translating Dutch plays.

The signs are encouraging. At conferences from Viterbo to Lancaster, in journals like *Comparative Drama* and *Research Opportunities in Renaissance Drama* scholars have begun talking over the national fences. There is much to be gained all around.

As the volume goes to press, it is a pleasant task to be able to thank at least some of those who helped with this project: Harvard's Committee on Medieval Studies for sponsoring the 1986 conference, and the thirteen scholars who cheerfully took on the somewhat thankless task of writing about the work of others and who, with unruffled spirits, acceded to the host of demands made by an unyielding editor. I am grateful to Paula Nicholas for feeding the bibliography into the office computer and to Susan Deskis for

Preface

reading proofs and producing the index. We all owe thanks to Cambridge University Press and its literature editor, Kevin Taylor, for accepting our research survey into its 'Studies in Medieval Literature' series and to Maureen Street for copy-editing a typescript of divers hands with judicious care.

Eckehard Simon
Cambridge, MA
5 January 1990

Note on the bibliography and system of references

To call the list of titles on pages 253–90 a *complete* bibliography would be a considerable overstatement. As we noted at the 1986 Harvard conference, a complete scholarly bibliography for just a single area, such as German drama, would take up *all* the space available here. A more appropriate title might therefore be 'Reading list' or 'Working bibliography'. For what is listed here are the works which the thirteen scholars contributing to this volume felt, in their collective judgement, to constitute the most significant publications on medieval drama since the early sixties. In an age of seemingly endless bibliographies (what *not* to read is the question), we thought that a selective bibliography would perhaps be more useful. A number of titles not included may be found in the 'Notes' at the end of most of the chapters that follow.

The bibliography, then, was assembled and arranged by the editor from listings submitted by the contributors. It is thus by origin a reference section to the chapters below, where the authors cite the works by means of the italicised number preceding each title in the bibliography. A few late additions made it necessary to generate new entry numbers through the suffix '*a*' (e.g., *9*, *9a*). (As we go to press we are appending a section of 'Recent works' in order to bring the bibliography up to date.)

So that the bibliography might also be used independently of the chapters reporting on research, we grouped the entries into traditional sections and subsections, starting with 'European drama' (general), 'Latin Church drama' and 'Music', and then moving by country from England to the Low Countries. Within each section, the sequence is chronological, suggesting a basic history of research. In cases where works were published in the same year, however, they appear in the alphabetical order of their authors' names.

Several headings were chosen for ease of recognition rather than strict accuracy. As was noted in the Preface, modern geography has often little to do with the map of medieval Europe. By 'Germany', for instance, we mean 'drama in the German-speaking countries of central Europe'. Subheadings such as 'Other religious plays' are obviously more convenient than scholarly. In the same spirit, abbreviations have been kept to a minimum. The bibliography is followed by an index which lists the names of all the authors (and editors) cited in alphabetical order.

Abbreviations for journals and series

CD   *Comparative Drama*
EETS   Early English Text Society
LDF   Leeds Texts and Monographs: Medieval Drama Facsimiles
LSE   *Leeds Studies in English*
MLN   *Modern Language Notes*
MLQ   *Modern Language Quarterly*
MP   *Modern Philology*
RD   *Renaissance Drama*
REED   Records of Early English Drama
RORD   *Research Opportunities in Renaissance Drama*
RR   *Romanic Review*

Introduction: trends in international drama research

GLYNNE WICKHAM

Set the task of charting for this volume the most significant advances in the research work undertaken during the past twenty-five years relating to theatre in the Middle Ages, I regard it as advisable to start by trying to establish an historical framework against and within which to measure recent developments. It is thus without further apology that I shall retreat from the present and recent past deep into the nineteenth century in order to supply a *raison d'être* for regarding the past quarter-century as a period possessed of some significance of its own rather than as just an arbitrary, if convenient, time-span to validate the organising of this volume. Against the background of this introductory survey, covering landmarks of international interest in the dramatic literature and theatre practice of the Middle Ages from their demise late in the sixteenth century until the middle of the present century, I shall then proceed to examine four particular areas of study in which I believe major advances to have been made in previously accepted criteria for critical evaluation: records; performance; centres for research, colloquia and journals; and, finally, historical and critical analysis.

FACTS AND THEIR INTERPRETATION, 1700–1960S

As a start, it is useful to recall that, from the early years of the seventeenth century until near the end of the eighteenth, knowledge of medieval dramaturgy and its accompanying stagecraft slowly waned as interest in it, from both a scholarly and a practical viewpoint, crumbled everywhere in Europe under the weight of the advancing neo-classical Enlightenment. Dismissed as a product of Gothic outlooks on life, and thus as barbaric, memorials of it retreated into the custody of libraries and municipal and parish archives for the better part of two centuries.

When recollections of it were stirred out of this long sleep by the Romantic Revival, they returned at the hands of antiquarians and archaeologists in the early years of the nineteenth century overpainted with both the roseate tints of the Romantic imagination and the darker stains of continuing Protestant distrust of the Roman Catholic Church and all its works, both in Britain and in much of Germany. The result resembled a visit to a kind of zoo in which the artistic endeavours and customs of a vanished era were resurrected as curiosities for leisured gentlemen and ladies to gaze at, and to ponder in their libraries. Three fine English examples of this process exist in Joseph Strutt's *The Sports and Pastimes of the People of England* (first published in 1801); in William Hone's *Ancient Mysteries Described* (1823); and in Thomas Sharp's *A Dissertation on the Pageants or Dramatic Mysteries anciently performed in Coventry* (1825).

Just as important to future pronouncements on the nature and quality of medieval drama was the steady increase in the editing and printing of metropolitan and provincial civic records, not only in Britain but also in France, Germany and other continental countries, many of which contained isolated facts and figures relating to dramatic performances in churches, guildhalls, convents and market squares. This process was further strengthened and accelerated by the foundation of Societies – historical, literary, philological and philosophical – whose members dedicated themselves to a more systematic approach to the recording and transmission of surviving evidence: the Percy Society, the Camden Society and the Early English Text Society may suffice as examples. Thus, by the end of the century, a large enough corpus of factual documentation had become available to scholars to encourage attempts to impose some form of order upon the random assortment of play texts (some in Latin, some in vernacular languages), of records of histrionically oriented folk games and dances and of payments to actors and to craftsmen for stage-gear and for time spent in rehearsal and performance recorded in Treasurer's Accounts.

An important stimulant to the undertaking of such tasks arrived in 1888 with the discovery of Johannes de Witt's sketch of the Swan Playhouse in London (*c.* 1596) which led directly to the earliest practical attempts to revive at first Elizabethan and Jacobean plays and then medieval ones, in conditions resembling those depicted by de Witt, stripped of all Victorian pictorial clutter. In this respect the founding by William Poel of the Elizabethan Stage Society in 1894 must be regarded as at least as significant to future research as, say, the publication of L. Petit de Julleville's *Les Mystères* (2 vols., 1880) or H. Deimling's edition of *The Chester Cycle* (for EETS, 1892).

The first major assaults on Everest – if I may so describe the double task of trying to impose order on, and to abstract sense from, the mass of documentary evidence by then available – were made in four different countries between 1891 and 1906. First, from Italy, came Alessandro D'Ancona's *Origini del teatro italiano* (2 vols., 1891), next from Germany, Wilhelm Creizenach's *Geschichte des neueren Dramas* (3 vols., 1893–1903), then in England, Sir Edmund Chambers' *The Mediaeval Stage* (2 vols., 1903 [9]), and then from France, Gustave Cohen's *Histoire de la mise en scène dans le théâtre religieux français du moyen âge* (1906). Nothing could ever be quite the same again; for here were set the groundrules by which all subsequent scholars engaging in research into medieval drama and stage conventions would have to live. The plain fact is that all four works remain, nearly a century later, essential basic reading for today's aspiring M.A. and Ph.D.

students; and if that is not remarkable enough, what is still more astonishing is that these books were largely written as a leisure-time occupation. There is a lesson here for us to which I will return in the concluding section of this chapter.

With that said, it remains to observe that all four of these scholarly giants laboured against several serious obstacles, the worst of which was the still substantial gaps in the factual data available to them. As those of us who have sought to impose order upon historical narrative know well – whether that pattern be theological, political, social, economic or aesthetic – when confronted either with a baffling lack of concrete evidence, or with only slender or ambiguous bits of quasi-documentary evidence, we find it difficult to resist speculative judgements that fit the desired pattern and so allow the narrative to proceed with some semblance of logical progression. The pattern chosen, moreover, normally reflects an outlook coloured by the personal prejudices and predilections of the author. To this extent the four cornerstones to which I have referred, and upon which scholarly opinion in the first half of the twentieth century grounded its attitudes to medieval drama, were still deeply dyed in what we now recognise to have been Victorian approaches to the Gothic past. To some students medieval drama remained 'naive', 'quaint', 'primitive' and dead beyond recall; to others it resembled a monolithic structure which, despite organic evolutionary growth along sound Darwinian principles, was even less accessible to the public at large than the Greek or Roman plays; to yet others (most notably to Protestants and scientific humanists) such claims as it could muster to regain contemporary respect arose directly from its secularisation once it had been transferred from the hands of the clergy to those of peasants and artisans. In one way or another all these prejudices have stuck, and continue to surface from time to time even in the 1980s, as anyone who teaches the subject will know from the experience of answering students' questions.

Inevitably, in the wake of these four major 'histories', there had to be a breathing space for scholars to digest their conclusions and to allow time for some of the still substantial gaps in factual knowledge to be filled by further research before any serious questioning of these conclusions could begin; in scholarly terms of reference that breathing space lasted for nearly half a century which, perhaps surprisingly, brings us to within a decade of the 1960s.

This period of consolidation, however, also heralded two important advents, one international, the other specifically American. The first was the growth of learned, quarterly journals which accorded space to interpretative articles about medieval plays and stagecraft; the second was the publication of Karl Young's *The Drama of the Medieval Church* (2 vols., 1933 [31]). Both of these developments provided launching pads for new departures; yet notwithstanding the innovative and monumental grandeur of Young's work, it served in two vital respects to confirm existing prejudices. It did so by reinforcing the traditional (if rather indeterminately defined) divisions

3

between text and music, as also between Latin liturgical drama of the tenth, eleventh and twelfth centuries on the one hand and vernacular religious drama of the fourteenth, fifteenth and sixteenth centuries on the other, leaving that of the thirteenth century suspended in a kind of limbo from out of which it still awaits rescue today.

Thus by the outbreak of World War II, scholarly opinion in the West, concentrated as it then was in university departments of language and literature, had come to regard the reappearance of dramatic literature in Christian Europe as a strictly literary phenomenon rather than either a theological or a musical one, and thus as a subject as readily divisible into compartments as, say, philology, with a clear-cut beginning, middle and end. The first of these three sections could conveniently be defined as 'Latin liturgical drama', starting with the earliest version of the *Visitatio Sepulchri* (stripped of course of its music) and ending with expanded versions of the *Ordo Prophetarum* and the *Officium Stellae* and loosely linked to Latin offices for Easter and Christmas. The second section, despite the lack of any substantial texts relating to post-Easter offices, was described as 'transitional drama', starting with the assumed aggregation of all existing plays into complete Latin liturgical cycles, followed by translation into vernacular languages. The third section could then be labelled 'vernacular drama', beginning with the transfer of responsibility for texts and performance from churchmen to laymen, a process held to account for the advent during the fifteenth century of morality plays, saint plays and moral interludes, and to end with the collapse of all religious drama under the combined pressures of economic recession, anticlericalism and humanist alternatives of neo-classical origin. Lest it be supposed that I am still discussing events in some distant past, let us all recall that this simple, evolutionary view of the birth, growth and demise of medieval drama was being broadly reiterated as recently as 1955 by Hardin Craig in his *English Religious Drama of the Middle Ages* (*105*). And so too was the view that the vexed areas of folk drama, civic pageantry and courtly entertainments (vexed because both were so ill-equipped with texts) could be hived off from the mainstream of medieval and early Renaissance drama as lacking any serious claim for study in departments of language and literature.

What then confronts us as the real revolution in academic attitudes that has taken place since the end of World War II is the steady erosion of these artificial sectional divisions, accompanied by a growing determination to replace them with more sensitive approaches to, and reappraisals of, the actual processes of development and change. If, then, there is any meaningful subdivision to be made between the first and the last two decades of the forty-year period 1946–86, I submit that the key to it lies in the words 'erosion' and 'reappraisal'. Naturally, some measure of reappraisal had to accompany the erosion of the old beliefs, but, no less self-evidently, the process of erosion must have progressed to a point where the results had become obvious if reappraisal was to advance much beyond speculation.

Introduction

And this is where I think separation of the nature and quality of the research work in medieval and Renaissance drama undertaken between 1945 and the 1960s on the one hand, and that engaged in during the past two and a half decades on the other, becomes a meaningful proposition.

It so happens that 1946 was the year in which I myself entered upon this scene as a graduate student at Oxford, so from that time forward I can at least speak from first-hand experience. In the following sections of this chapter, therefore, I shall try to maintain the distinction that I have just made between 'erosion' and 'reappraisal' both after and before c. 1965 without, as I hope, distorting or diminishing the respective achievements of either the first or second halves of what, historically, has unquestionably been a single era of accelerating change. Both processes began with the publication of George Kernodle's *From Art to Theatre* in 1944 (*9a*), followed by H. C. Gardiner's *Mysteries' End* in 1946 (*104*). Between them these two American books, written during the war years, set up a large question mark above the most fundamental dogma of orthodox academic opinion both in North America and in Europe. Could it be – so both authors appeared to ask – that medieval drama was *not* a self-contained literary and artistic entity, born either by immaculate conception or by committee resolution relating to the presentation of the Eucharist c. 975 and dying from exhaustion derived either from obesity or from sterility some six hundred years later? Kernodle, by first insisting upon adopting an aesthetic approach, and by then imposing its values upon the visual aspects of dramatic art during the fifteenth and sixteenth centuries, succeeded in opening up for young students of my generation new vistas of approach to medieval drama: Father Gardiner, by insisting that medieval drama was deliberately murdered by its enemies in the course of the Reformation and Counter-Reformation rather than dying of natural causes, did as much to make the continued segregation of 'medieval' from 'Renaissance' drama an untenable proposition. These were the first wide cracks to appear in the seemingly well-shored-up edifice of the received account of the historical development of medieval drama.

A third yawning gap in credibility was shortly to appear following Sir Tyrone Guthrie's revival of Sir David Lindsay's *Ane Satyre of the Three Estaitis* at the Edinburgh Festival in 1948, and the first full-scale production of the York cycle at York in 365 years by E. Martin Browne in 1951. Audiences and critics alike who witnessed these performances were astonished. In an almost literal sense, those who had come to gaze, even to mock, stayed to pray. Once more, therefore, nothing could ever be quite the same again where critical appraisal of medieval dramaturgy was concerned: for the speed and efficacy of the stagecraft had proved to be as compelling and convincing as was the power of the spoken text to stir imaginations and to move hearts to both laughter and tears. Such plays could no longer be dismissed as historical curiosities: rather did they cry out to be reassessed as living theatre. In short, medieval drama had at last escaped from the enforced custodianship of librarians, archivists and dons, and had returned to audiences drawn from all walks of life. The edifice of received academic pronouncements upon it was not yet in ruins, but it was crumbling fast.

So much then for an historical context for this research survey – a long and curious story briefly sketched. With that behind us and, as I trust, some measure of agreement about its central features, we can now move with greater safety into the more treacherous rapids of contemporary scholarship. As I have already stated, I believe the dominant characteristic of the period from 1945 to the 1960s to have been the systematic erosion and demolition of all doctrine relating to medieval drama that could no longer stand up to either detailed critical analysis or to the equally exacting test of theatrical revival, and that of the period from the 1960s to the present day to have been methodical reappraisal, based upon supplementary factual evidence within a wider time-frame that is leading towards a rebuilding of the old edifice both on more stable foundations and refaced, with most of the original, decorative features that were formerly missing now restored. To divorce these two processes altogether would however be wrong, since that could only be to the detriment of an accurate understanding of where we stand now: for many of the speculative, but cautious, reinterpretations of artistic and literary achievement during the Middle Ages that were postulated in the 1950s and early 1960s have in fact been corroborated in the work of scholars during the 1970s and early 1980s, and much of the strictly factual materials unearthed during the earlier period provided the data needed to lead to some of the critical conclusions reached in recent years.

RECORDS

Arguably, the most important single development in research over the past twenty-five years respecting medieval drama has been the renewed onslaught on the orderly unearthing, transcribing, editing (frequently re-editing) and publishing of records, spearheaded by the Malone Society through its continuing series of 'Collections'. Giles Dawson's edition of *Records of Plays and Players in Kent* appeared under this imprint in 1965 (*138*) followed in 1974 by Stanley J. Kahrl's *Records of Plays and Players in Lincolnshire* (*139*). Flanking these invaluable provincial facts and figures lie *Dramatic Records in the Declared Accounts of the Treasurer of the Chamber, 1558–1642*, edited by David Cook and the late F. P. Wilson (1962 [*137*]), and the no less valuable *Dramatic Records in the Declared Accounts of the Office of Works, 1560–1640* (1977 [*140*]), transcribed by F. P. Wilson and checked and edited by R. F. Hill. The principal burden, however, of providing up-to-date scholarly editions of English records has shifted since 1975–6 to Canada and to the team of young scholars based at the University of Toronto, led by Alexandra Johnston and funded initially by the Canada Council.

Records of Early English Drama was launched, as JoAnna Dutka observed in her first *Newsletter* under that imprint, for the specific purpose of systematically locating, transcribing and publishing all surviving civic and ecclesiastical records pertaining to medieval drama in Britain. This effort to co-ordinate the interests and labours of scholars previously working in isolation in Canada, the USA, Australasia and Britain has already enriched us with volumes on York, Chester, Coventry, Newcastle, Norwich, Cumberland, Westmorland, Gloucestershire and Devon (with more to follow), each of which now possesses the authority of a standard text. As the editors have been the first to admit, all of them have been helped by a small army of English archivists who, since 1945, have been patiently restoring, cataloguing and conserving such municipal and parish records as survived the wartime air-raids and accompanying damage from fires, fire-fighters and rehousing, thereby making the editorial tasks of locating and transcribing records easier than it had ever been before. Since 1945 other, more isolated items of factual record have been discovered in legal documents and school libraries and subsequently published in an expanding number of journals (see pp. 12–13, below).

In France, similar endeavours, pioneered by Jean Jacquot at the Centre Nationale de la Recherche Scientifique in Paris, have led to the publication of the *Collection Le Choeur des Muses* starting with *Fêtes de la Renaissance I*, published in 1956. Unlike the Canadian enterprise which has restricted itself to records of English drama, this one has been conducted from an international standpoint and has substantially augmented contemporary comprehension of Burgundian, German and Spanish drama of the sixteenth century and earlier, as well as French. It is to this initiative that we owe Elie Konigson's superbly organised volume, published in 1969, on the Passion play at Valenciennes in 1547 (*335*).

Nevertheless it has to be admitted that we still lack any continental European equivalent to the Toronto enterprise covering municipal and parish records in France, Italy, Spain or any eastern European country. For German-speaking central Europe, a major collection of archival records, by Bernd Neumann, has just appeared (1987 [*565*]). Beyond the lack of adequate funding there are other obstacles of which not the least is language. The USA, Canada and Britain, possessed as they are of a common language, can muster several Roman legions of medievalists, and from their ranks can assemble several cohorts of specialists in medieval drama. That is not the case in any single continental European country. Isolated enthusiasts exist everywhere across the map from Portugal to Poland, as they have done for the past hundred and fifty years or more; but numerically they scarcely add up to more than a platoon in any one country; consequently they lack the vocal power to make their claims for funding heard in the corridors of their respective Ministries of Education whose officials everywhere control university finance.

A ray of light on the horizon is to be seen in the prospectus recently issued by the Cambridge University Press for a sixteen-volume *Theatre in Europe: A Documentary History*. Two whole volumes in this series (nos. III and IV) are to be devoted to the Middle Ages in Europe, but it is unlikely that either of these volumes will be published before 1994. Meantime, I wish to transfer attention to play production, more specifically to theatrical revivals of medieval plays.

PRODUCTIONS

Within the purview of this survey, I recall four events which attracted wide attention at the time, and which I still regard as outstanding. The first of these is a revival of the entire Cornish *Ordinalia*, presented by my own Department of Drama at Bristol University and directed by the late Neville Denny in the ancient earthwork 'Round' at St Piran, near Perranporth in Cornwall, in 1969. It was followed shortly after by the publication of Markham Harris' new translation of the Cornish text into English. The second is the broadcasting of the Chester cycle on British television, directed by Jane Howell, in 1977. The third is the first production in North America, also in 1977, of an entire English cycle (York) on the campus of the University of Toronto organised by Alexandra Johnston. The most recent is the production, again in Britain, of *The Mysteries*, a wide-ranging compilation and free adaptation of medieval religious plays from several sources scripted by Tony Harrison, directed by Bill Bryden and presented by the National Theatre in 1984, and again in 1985 at the Lyceum. And to this group of four, I must append a fifth, albeit from the years 1958–60: this is Noah Greenberg's revival of *The Play of Daniel* (*Ludus Danielis*) in January 1958 at the Cloisters in New York City, followed in 1960 by my own revival in his version of it for the Carmel Music Festival (with singers from the San Francisco Opera and Stanford University conducted by Sandor Salgo). The impact of both productions on their East and West Coast audiences was comparable to that of Sir Tyrone Guthrie's production of Sir David Lindsay's *Ane Satyre of the Three Estaitis* in Edinburgh in 1948 and the first production of the whole of the York and Chester cycles in York and Chester respectively in 1951.

What these previously unimaginable events have proved is that medieval drama can once again be taken seriously by the public at large: it is no longer the preserve of antiquarians, archaeologists, philologists and other academics. Indeed, it is even providing a source of fresh inspiration for today's young playwrights who now borrow its stage conventions and stagecraft without self-consciously realising that this is what they are doing!

How did this come about, and what lessons can it offer us? In answering this question, I must again revert briefly to the nineteenth century and to the discovery of the de Witt sketch in the library of the University of Utrecht in 1888 which led directly to the founding of the Elizabethan Stage Society by William Poel in 1894. That is our *fons et origo* where stage production is concerned, since it was Poel himself who led the long process of experimental revival with his production of *Everyman* in 1901 in a double bill with the Chester version of 'The Sacrifice of Isaac'. His example was swiftly followed by his disciple Nugent Monck whose 1909 production of the 'Passion Play' from the N-Town cycle was brought to an abrupt end with his arrest for violation of Britain's blasphemy laws!

To us this may seem as incredible as it is now laughable; but the effect of this police action, instigated by the Lord Chamberlain, was to make it dangerous to risk reviving any medieval play in Britain for presentation to a paying audience in which either *Deus Pater* or Christ Himself appeared onstage in a speaking role. In this way, advancing scholarly research became divorced from continuing experimental revival for another forty years: only in 1951, and then only as a concession to the Festival of Britain, were these laws relaxed to allow the York and Chester Cycles to be produced – a concession linked more closely by the Government to the revival of tourism than to interest in the revival of medieval drama! Even in 1959, I myself had to answer to the Lord Chamberlain for permitting a performance of Bernard Shaw's *Black Girl in Search of her God* to be presented by a Belgian company at an international student festival in Bristol without his permission. Permission to proceed was only granted three hours before curtain-up, and then only because I had apologised and supplied a written promise that the performance would be conducted throughout in French! Not until 1968 were these archaic powers of censorship abolished.

While in a general sense (and despite the obstacle of stage censorship while it lasted) the driving force behind twentieth-century efforts to revive medieval plays has been British, considerable momentum was added to it, at first in Germany and France, and then in North America. A unique thread of continuity surviving from the first half of the seventeenth century was preserved in Germany in the revival every ten years of the Passion play in the Bavarian village of Oberammergau, where the right to participate is still jealously guarded as a matter of family pride and regarded as an act of devotion rather than as a professional or commercial enterprise. Nearby, in Austria, Max Reinhardt's production of Hugo von Hofmannsthal's adaptation of *Everyman* (*Jedermann*), presented in front of the Minster at Salzburg (1912), proved to be popular enough to be repeated as an annual event, dropped only during the years of the two World Wars.

Another important innovation during this period was the formation in France by Gustave Cohen of Les Théophilians, a group of student actors based at the Sorbonne and dedicated to the revival of French medieval plays; this company then took these plays on tour both in France and abroad during the summer vacation.

Cohen's example was copied in the 1960s by John Leyerle at the University of Toronto where he founded the Poculi Ludique Societas, and also in England in the University of Bristol. These initiatives led, during the 1970s, to the creation of a company describing itself as The Medieval Players based at the Universities of London and Cambridge.

A factor common to all these enterprises from the founding of the Théophilians to the present day has been a determination to abide as faithfully as possible by the original stage directions, and thereafter to employ the test of performance both as a new tool for the advancement of research and as a new dimension to critical appreciation. This has brought us to a point where performances of medieval plays ranging from cycles to single moralities, saint plays and interludes are so frequently on offer to the public as no longer to occasion surprise; nor do the large audiences who pay to attend these performances continue to regard the plays themselves as 'quaint' or 'naive' in a pejorative sense. Indeed, most of these productions are now formally reviewed and catalogued, thanks to the efforts of John Elliott Jr and G. K. Hunter who, since 1967, have been recording and publishing them annually in *Research Opportunities in Renaissance Drama*.

What the precise results of this extraordinary re-emergence of medieval plays in performance over the past twenty to thirty years has been is difficult to assess; but what is certain is that the new opportunities which have arisen to present, criticise and discuss these plays as dramatic art, instead of simply as texts, have led everywhere to an enriched appreciation of them, and to a new-found seriousness in the study of their stage directions, both explicit and implicit. In other words, the effort and skills needed to recover the visual iconography and the musical factors which originally accompanied both the devising and execution of these plays have led scholars to devote far more time and energy in recent years to the dramatic and theatrical, rather than strictly literary, qualities of these plays. The truth of this proposition becomes apparent on even the most cursory perusal of recently published bibliographies.

Richard Southern's *The Medieval Theatre in the Round* (1957 [*122*]), T. W. Craik's *The Tudor Interlude* (1958 [*242*]), Alec Harman's *Medieval and Early Renaissance Music* (Fairlawn, NJ: Essential Books, 1958), M. D. Anderson's *Drama and Imagery in English Medieval Churches* (1963 [*110*]) and V. A. Kolve's *The Play Called Corpus Christi* (1966 [*151*]) set the tone of the new criticism; to this shortlist I might add at one end the first volume of my own *Early English Stages* (1959 [*107*]) and at the other Sidney Anglo's *Spectacle, Pageantry and Early Tudor Policy* (1969 [*251*]). This sudden widening of research horizons has resulted in as many dissertations, articles and books being devoted to stage crafts as to texts and their interpretation during the 1970s and 1980s. This development has in turn had an effect upon the terms of reference laid down for editors of records. References to and payments for tournaments, civic pageants, mummings, disguisings, entertainments, triumphs and folk games have all come at last to be regarded as meriting inclusion alongside those to plays and players, and this enrichment of the primary evidence now available to young scholars has served greatly to extend our understanding of medieval attitudes to the aesthetic, social and political precepts of dramatic art in addition to the more familiar theological and literary considerations.

Perhaps an even more significant aspect of this development is what it has achieved during the past two decades in bringing students from many different academic disciplines, for long isolated from one another, together again through recognition both of interests shared and of interdependence upon each other's specialist skills. In short, even in Academe itself, medieval drama no longer belongs to departments of language and literature alone, but numbers art historians, musicologists, social and economic historians, theologians and folklorists amongst its votaries. And that observation leads me directly to the next section of this chapter.

RESEARCH CENTRES, CONFERENCES, COLLOQUIA, NEWSLETTERS AND JOURNALS

I have already spoken about the sense of isolation that characterised virtually all research work relating to the Middle Ages until shortly before the outbreak of World War II. It was still a factor that I had to contend with when I entered this area of study in 1946 as a graduate student at Oxford; for even that prestigious university found it impossible to provide me with a member of its English Faculty willing to supervise a thesis devoted to examining possible links between medieval pageantry and the stage. That takes some believing now; but the fact is that when first Nevill Coghill and then Helen Gardner withdrew from this task on the quite reasonable grounds that they felt unable to offer adequate bibliographical advice, the Faculty found itself obliged to farm me out to Professor Donald Gordon at Reading University – a rescue for which, in the event, I have had cause to be grateful ever since. Four years later, it proved almost as difficult to appoint appropriate specialist examiners, but since the university could not farm out that duty, it recruited Percy Simpson and F. P. Wilson who, as outstanding Renaissance scholars, at least knew something about the theatre and were leading authorities on sixteenth-century dramatic literature.

I've risked including this personal anecdote because it serves to highlight one of the most striking changes that has overtaken study of medieval drama in recent years. Today it is unthinkable that such a problem could arise in any major university in Britain, North America, Germany or France. The establishment of centres for the study of medieval civilisation on an interdisciplinary basis has both accelerated interest in and occasioned a deeper understanding of medieval drama in ways scarcely imaginable even as recently as 1950. Toronto, Kalamazoo and Binghamton, Leeds, Bristol, Cambridge, Lancaster and York, Paris, Perpignan, Amsterdam, Nijmegen, Cologne, Berlin, Rome and Viterbo now trip off the tongue as centres where scholars of many nationalities can expect to meet to share progress reports, develop fresh insights and consolidate, through debate and subsequent correspondence, the critical evaluation of common interests: it is even becoming possible to anticipate the presence of individuals from eastern Europe and Japan.

These direct, face-to-face encounters, moreover, have been supplemented by the rapid growth of journals and newsletters which serve to keep scholars in touch with each other between such meetings, as well as to provide a much richer variety of openings for the publication of short articles and book reviews than ever existed before, and to persuade publishers that a wide enough market now exists for a continuing supply of new books on many aspects of medieval drama and theatre to appear in their catalogues. Indeed, it can confidently be claimed that at no other time outside the past twenty to thirty years has the bibliography of the subject been augmented so swiftly and so widely, a matter to which I shall return in the final section of this chapter.

Meantime, it is necessary to draw attention here to the advent in recent years of the journals that now find their way regularly into university libraries and into the collections of individual scholars, and among these a special accolade must be accorded to *Research Opportunities in Renaissance Drama*, now edited from the University of Kansas by David Bergeron. Although originating some thirty years ago from Northwestern (the earliest volumes being rare and prized collectors' items), and despite having had to eke out a peripatetic existence between 1971 and 1975, it has acquired, since establishment at Kansas, a degree of authority previously accorded only to *Speculum* and *Medium Aevum*, and has become an imperative on any self-respecting library's periodical purchase-list.

Later into the field have come *Comparative Drama* (Western Michigan University, 1966), the tri-quarterly *English Literary Renaissance* (University of Massachusetts, 1970), the bi-annual *REED Newsletter* (Toronto, 1976) and, most recent recruit of all, *Medieval and Renaissance Drama in England* (ed. J. Leeds Barroll III and Paul Werstine, AMS Press, New York, 1984) – all North American. Europe, for reasons already glanced at, has failed to produce many directly comparable new journals, but that does not mean that the numerically much smaller groups of scholars who there devote time and energy to medieval drama lack adequate outlets for the publication of their research. Shortly after the end of the Second World War Professor Heinz Kindermann launched *Maske und Kothurn* from Vienna (1954), published quarterly: while this periodical embraces all aspects and periods of theatre history, it has nevertheless always provided scholars writing in German with a standing invitation to contribute articles on medieval drama, and to review both German and foreign-language books devoted to it. Similarly, in France, *Cahiers de civilisation mediévale* was launched from Poitiers in the 1950s, to be followed up in the 1960s by *Cahiers Elizabéthains* centred on Toulouse, Montpellier and Bordeaux: both can be regarded as specialist supplements to the long-established *Revue de l'histoire du théâtre* published from Paris. From Switzerland came *Theatre Research/Recherches théâtrales*, launched from Berne in 1958, which, being bilingual in format, was open to contributors of all nationalities.

In Britain, a similar pattern of post-war development becomes discernible with the appearance in 1946 of the first number of *Theatre Notebook*, now celebrating its forty-fourth year of continuous publication, followed in the early 1960s by *Encore, New Theatre Magazine* and *Theatre Quarterly*. In 1975 *New Theatre Magazine* (published from Bristol University) was merged with *Theatre Research/Recherches théâtrales* to become *Theatre Research International*, edited from Glasgow University and published by Oxford Journals. Not to be outdone in this respect, Cambridge University Press, in 1984, launched *New Theatre Quarterly*, now known as *NTQ*.

A striking difference between European and North American practice, implicit in the titles of the journals, is the much sharper distinction that has traditionally been observed in all European countries between dramatic literature and theatre history. This separation is unquestionably derived from the fact that in the universities of all European countries for the past three hundred years, dramatic literature (if studied at all) was confined to schools of language and literature. Theatre history was hived off as irrelevant and left to the erratic care of the professional theatre schools (*conservatoires*) and to amateur *savants*, including archaeologists, bibliophiles and eccentric enthusiasts. One such, we should not forget, was Sir Edmund Chambers.

This situation only began to change radically with the inauguration of departments of drama, speech and drama and theatre arts in America in the 1920s and 1930s. Britain did not follow this example until 1947, and then only at Bristol University, until the 1960s when that experiment came to be more generally imitated. Where new journals were concerned, America thus took the lead at an early date with the launching of the *American Educational Theatre Journal*, followed later by *The Tulane Drama Review* and *Drama Survey*. The significance of these new journals lay not so much in the contribution that they made as outlets for the publication of specifically medieval research as in what they did to develop the idea of performance criticism, and thus to stimulate the revivals of medieval plays that I have already discussed, in both Britain and America.

The ultimate reward of this extension of horizons is thus to be seen in the 'Consensus of Medieval Drama Productions' and 'Consensus of Renaissance Drama Productions' which formed so useful a feature of *Research Opportunities in Renaissance Drama* through the 1970s and in the pages of *Medieval English Theatre* (originally a newsletter, now a journal), founded in 1979 by Meg Twycross and Peter Meredith conjointly from the Universities of Lancaster and Leeds (both of which were by then possessed of flourishing drama departments).

Between the two World Wars, continental Europe compromised on the issue of recognising drama as an academic discipline by admitting schools of theatre history, at graduate level only, into a minority of its many universities, a process extended only hesitantly after 1950. Cologne, Munich and Stockholm were among the pioneers, followed by Berlin, Paris, Lyons, Copenhagen, Amsterdam, Venice and Vienna; but elsewhere – especially in Italy, Spain, Portugal and Eastern-bloc countries – scholars with research interests in medieval plays and theatre history still remain isolated, both from one another and from contact with scholars who share their interests beyond their own frontiers. Nor has it been easy for them to achieve what the existence of drama departments elsewhere has so manifestly encouraged – the revival of medieval plays; where this has been achieved, responsibility for the initiative has usually lain with groups of students in departments of language and literature, guided and supported by an enthusiastic member of the faculty along the lines laid down by Professor Cohen at the Sorbonne when creating Les Théophilians.

While, clearly, contributors to this volume can rejoice on helping to arouse this degree of interest in medieval drama when contemplating the vast improvement in scholarly apparatus that frequent international conferences, the founding of new journals and the revival of so many plays represents, may not the time have come for us to ask ourselves whether there is really room or justification for yet more? Indeed, even during the past decade, I have myself become conscious of a decline in the significance of many of the communications presented at these conferences by fledgling graduates, and have begun to wonder whether the motivation accounting both for the presence of some of these individuals and for the nature and quality of the topics accepted by the organisers for discussion has not become more closely geared to academic career ladders than to any genuine concern for the advancement of the subject. While medieval drama may still be a more open field than many others, is it altogether outrageous to suggest that we may be approaching a point where the near obligatory M.Litt. and Ph.D. thesis has come to exercise a dangerous tyranny over an area of humane artistic endeavour that originally existed as much to entertain as to educate?

In my view these dangers are not imaginary, but real. For the past twenty to thirty years students have everywhere been gaining admission to our universities with standards of literacy that would have shocked such founding fathers of our discipline as the D'Anconas, Creizenachs and Cohens at the start of this century. We have thus started to reap the harvest from this seed-corn, especially in departments of English and drama, in the recruitment of staff who, lacking training in either a sense of historical chronology or a knowledge of theology, and unable to read any play text or related document in a language other than English, are nevertheless required to teach medieval drama and theatre. I am being both hard and provocative, but deliberately so, since many of the students I have endeavoured to teach in Canada and the USA since 1970, as well as those in Britain, have fallen by the wayside because they had been so inadequately prepared for the journey on which they had so optimistically embarked, or succeeded only by taking recourse to very expensive and time-consuming correctives. In short, if these problems of relatively recent origin are to be resolved before they overwhelm us during the next two decades, a concerted effort will have to be made, especially in English-speaking countries, to redefine the qualifications now required of students seeking admission to this area of graduate studies.

Introduction

I turn finally, with some relief, to the achievements of more recent scholarly research. This, as I have endeavoured to make clear in earlier sections of this chapter, is something that cannot be wholly contained within the convenient time-span of the past twenty-five years, for just as the visible blooms and foliage of any healthy plant are directly dependent on the root-growth put down earlier, so the most fruitful research undertaken and published within that time grew out of roots put down in printed form during the previous two decades. Indeed, sufficient time had passed by the 1980s for it to become possible to question some of the theories advanced in the 1940s and 1950s by such founding fathers of the new criticism as H. C. Gardiner, Richard Southern and T. W. Craik, and among those now deemed questionable I might include myself! That is not a wholly new experience since my memory is long enough to recall being severely taken to task in *Speculum* by Hardin Craig for what he regarded in 1959 to be the mischievous nonsense printed in Volume I of my *Early English Stages* (*107*).

Happily for me, others have since thought differently – more especially about those extensions of medieval theatrical horizons which that book, however tentatively, suggested might repay more serious attention: tournaments, disguisings and civic pageantry, costume and scenic iconography, political allegory and, above all, the survival of many aspects of medieval dramaturgical precepts into both courtly and popular drama of the Renaissance. My own examination of the subject, given a self-imposed 600-year time-span, was, to say the least of it, cursory, especially where Latin liturgical drama and folk drama were concerned; so these areas of study also invited more methodical research and, as I'm equally happy to say, have received it, not least in Volume III of *Early English Stages* (1981 [*126*]) which discusses every known English play written from the tenth century to 1576, and attempts to describe a style of both visual and verbal theatrical iconography which was consistently transmitted and extended, generation by generation, throughout that period.

This observation leads me directly to O. B. Hardison Jr's *Christian Rite and Christian Drama in the Middle Ages* (1965 [*46*]), the first major critical advance on Karl Young's *The Drama of the Medieval Church* (*31*) in thirty years; alongside it, I place Richard Axton's *European Drama of the Early Middle Ages* which, although published nearly a decade later in 1974 (*18*), succeeded in raising the question of the probable coexistence of a vigorous secular drama grounded on late-Roman and early-medieval precedents, and examined the likely impact of this tradition on Christian religious drama.

No less outstanding as works of reappraisal derived from the erosion of previously held beliefs were V. A. Kolve's *The Play Called Corpus Christi* of 1966 (*151*) and Stanley Kahrl's *Traditions of Medieval English Drama* (1974 [*119*]), each of which served to open up the aesthetic and doctrinal tenets *separating* chanted Latin liturgical drama of the tenth, eleventh and twelfth

Glynne Wickham

centuries from spoken vernacular drama of the fourteenth, fifteenth and sixteenth centuries to a point where continued belief in some logical, evolutionary pattern of organic development by accretion from the earlier into the later theatrical form became impossible to sustain. Two other blows for emancipation from deferential homage to received traditions' at this same time were delivered by David Bevington and Sandro Sticca with the publication respectively in 1962 and 1972 of *From 'Mankind' to Marlowe: Growth of Structure in the Popular Drama of Tudor England* (214) and of *The Medieval Drama* (2), an edition of the papers read in 1969 at the Center for Medieval and Early Renaissance Studies on the Binghamton campus of the State University of New York. *'Mankind' to Marlowe* not only reinforced both Father Gardiner's thesis in *Mysteries' End* (1946 [104]) and T. W. Craik's conclusions in *The Tudor Interlude* (1958 [242]), but added new fuel to the growing belief that continued segregation of medieval from early-Renaissance drama for no better reason than syllabus and timetable convenience, was misguided, artificial and no longer acceptable. Sticca's volume reawakened interest not only in contemporary thinking about French, German and Italian religious drama, but also in the music which had originally accompanied the texts of all Latin liturgical plays. William Smoldon's 'The Origins of the *Quem queritis* and the Easter Sepulchre Music-Drama, as Demonstrated by their Musical Settings' (85), printed as the concluding essay to that book, was as startling and refreshing then as was the work on medieval music which John Stevens and Alec Harman had published during the previous decade.

Three other books published during the 1960s warrant special mention in this survey: David Bevington's *Tudor Drama and Politics* (1968 [249]), Sidney Anglo's *Spectacle, Pageantry and Early Tudor Policy* (already remarked upon on p. 10, above) and David Bergeron's *English Civic Pageantry 1558–1642* (1971 [116]). These books between them served to prove beyond all further doubt that henceforth students of medieval and Renaissance drama would have to devote as much attention to the visual, iconographic dimension of both courtly and popular dramatic entertainment as to strictly literary considerations: they would also have to acquire a command of the history of the political, religious and social life depicted in medieval and Renaissance plays, pageants and masques to recognise topical allusions and emblematic figures chosen to circumvent stage censorship, a lesson signposted by Alois M. Nagler, in an Italian context, in *Theater Festivals of the Medici, 1539–1637* (1964 [393]). Yet another tool of indispensable use to scholars which appeared that year was Harbage and Schoenbaum's *Annals of English Drama, 975–1700* (112). This extension of horizons continued into the 1970s in the direction of moralities, saint plays and entertainments as represented by Robert Potter's *The English Morality Play* (1975 [225]), D. L. Jeffrey's article 'English Saints' Plays' (1973 [207]), together with Frances Yates' *Astrea* (1975 [259]) and Jean Wilson's *Entertainments for Elizabeth I* (1980 [281]); and to this list I would like to add

Introduction

Rainer Pineas' *Tudor and Early Stuart Anti-Catholic Drama* (1972 [254]),
if only as the first mild corrective to the hitherto uncritical acceptance of
H. C. Gardiner's conclusions.

If the majority of these books were products of American scholarly
endeavour, I am sure that all contributors to this volume would wish to
express thanks to British publishers for their remarkable courage, faith and
perseverance in funding the transmission of so much research on medieval
and early-Renaissance drama into printed form during the past three
decades. Without that help both British and American scholars might well
have found it as difficult to bring the fruits of their labours to public notice as
is still frequently the case today in the universities of continental Europe.

Taken collectively, this flowering of extrovert work in pursuit of reappraisal
has led to a spate of critical reassessments of medieval plays, particularly the
English cycles. Here, Eleanor Prosser was the first to look seriously at their
theological basis in *Drama and Religion in the English Mystery Plays* (1961
[149]), an examination extended to embrace literary considerations by Rosemary Woolf in *The English Mystery Plays* (1972 [153]). Jerome Taylor and
Alan Nelson in that same year published a volume of articles under the title
Medieval English Drama: Essays Critical and Contextual (100), which was
followed a year later by another volume of essays, edited by Neville Denny,
entitled *Medieval Drama* for the series Stratford-upon-Avon Studies (3).
Here we find language, imagery, music, characterisation and stagecraft, folk
custom, saint plays, disguisings and medieval notions of comedy and tragedy
all demanding attention; and that attention they have duly received in many
articles published in journals since 1974. Another line of development may
be seen in the appearance in readily accessible modern editions of a wide
range of Tudor interludes, credit for which lies largely with Peter Happé,
E. T. Schell, J. D. Shuchter, J. H. P. Pafford, Mark Eccles, J. A. B. Somerset, R. M. Benlow, Ian Lancashire, Alan Nelson and Richard and Marie
Axton. In short, by the time the REED project was launched in 1975, the
width of the spectrum that the words 'medieval drama and theatre' had come
to represent since 1945 had been firmly established on stronger and broader
foundations.

Understandably, throughout the period under review, American and
British scholars have largely chosen to interpret the words 'medieval drama
and theatre' to mean English drama and theatre. Why, I have to ask, did so
few of them undertake to concern themselves with the rich resources of
records and texts surviving in other European countries?

Not since Grace Frank published *The Medieval French Drama* in 1954
(283) has any serious attempt been made to assess the literary and theatrical
qualities of an archive of medieval plays, stage directions, financial records
and graphic materials which, at least where morality plays, saint plays,
Passion plays and farces are concerned, is infinitely richer and more varied
than the surviving English heritage can offer. Is it not time that this neglect
was halted? Not since Kernodle published *From Art to Theatre* in 1944 (9a)

Glynne Wickham

has any British or American scholar researched the archives of the Dutch and Flemish 'Chambers of Rhetoric', or translated and collated the articles printed by Dutch and Belgian scholars since then to produce a significant book in English. Alone among British and American scholars, Gordon Kipling has set himself the task of checking and analysing another rich source of continental medieval records, those from Burgundy (1977 [646]). This same neglect of German, Swiss, Italian and Spanish drama is, alas, no less obvious, with only an occasional voice, like those of Sandro Sticca, Ronald Surtz and Kathleen Falvey, raised to direct attention to these areas. A more substantial corrective arrived with the publication of William Tydeman's *The Theatre in the Middle Ages* (1978 [25]); but still the resources of eastern Europe remained unexplored. Having had the good fortune myself to visit Poland on several occasions between 1965 and 1975, I am aware of the work being done on Corpus Christi and other religious plays in that troubled country, and most of us are aware that drama flourished, at least from the thirteenth century onwards, both to the north-east in Livonia and to the south in Hungary and Bohemia; yet few of us know where or how to gain access to the results of this research. Nor are Eastern-bloc countries lacking in graphic illustrations of these performances. One such picture – beautiful in its own right – appears as Plate 4 in Volume III of my *Early English Stages* (*126*), a version of the *Visitatio Sepulchri* now in the Art Gallery at Cracow; another, this time from the ancient Hungarian capital city of Estergom, depicts Christ's burial and Resurrection, carved and painted on a huge three-dimensional pageant wagon, or 'tabernacle' dated *c.* 1485, now housed in the Museum of Christian Art, which is printed in colour in my *A History of the Theatre* (1985 [30]). Is it unique?

I do not need to labour this point any further since there are other contributors to this volume who will both make it more forcefully and supply correctives to this perspective. For those British and American scholars who read French and German, several books have become available in recent years which are well worthy of note. These include, in order of publication, Elie Konigson's splendid account of the Passion play at Valenciennes in 1547 already referred to (1969 [335]) and his broader 1975 study *L'Espace théâtral médiéval* (*21*); Theo Stemmler's *Liturgische Feiern und geistliche Spiele* (1970 [12]); Jacques Chocheyras' studies on religious theatre in Savoy and Dauphiné (1971 [286]; 1975 [289]); and, recently, Jarmilla P. Veltrusky's *A Sacred Farce from Bohemia* (Ann Arbor, 1985). To these important European offerings we have even seen added a Japanese assessment of English morality plays in Sumiko Miyajima's *The Theatre of Man* (1977 [229]). The brightest prospect for the future, however, lies in the recent establishment of the International Society for the Study of Medieval Theatre (with bases in Toronto and Barcelona), a body ideally equipped to carry the modest beginnings represented by the publication of this volume forward to another grand stretching of our horizons to match that achieved a century ago.

PART I

Latin drama

Medieval Latin music-drama

C. CLIFFORD FLANIGAN

Major difficulties confront anyone who wishes to survey the scholarship on medieval drama, especially on the so-called liturgical drama. One can, of course, go to the library, use the standard bibliographies to generate a listing of everything published on the subject, read and digest these pieces of research and then simply report on the present state of the question. But if someone really were naively to undertake such a simple procedure, he or she would immediately recognise how imprecise the designation 'medieval Latin drama' is. In a survey of scholarship on the liturgical drama published over a decade ago (1975–6 [36]), I discussed more than 100 items, only twelve of which were listed in the annual 'definitive' bibliographies published by the Modern Language Association. The primary reason for this seeming lack of attention to the medieval music-drama is that the MLA bibliography is devoted to literary studies, but much of the work undertaken on this subject has been carried out within the framework of other disciplines, especially musical history and liturgiology. The standard bibliographies in these areas must therefore be consulted. When one attempts to undertake this task and bring together the work of scholars in disparate academic disciplines on what might appear to be the same subject, new difficulties arise, however. There is, first of all, the extremely unfortunate fact that literary scholars usually fail to consult the work of their musicological counterparts; similarly, few historians of music are known for their enthusiasm for literary scholarship. A more fundamental problem is that different disciplines operate by different and often incommensurate paradigms, so that the issues which engage the literary scholar in the study of the Latin music-drama are often of little interest to musicologists; of course the opposite is true as well. The professional student of the liturgy is usually somewhat informed about literary scholarship and generally aware of musicological studies relevant to his discipline, but since basic journals and handbooks on the history of the liturgy are often absent from large academic libraries in the United States, liturgical studies have generally had little impact on the way that either musicologist or literary scholar has thought about the music-drama, though, as we shall see, this situation is beginning to change.

Of course, all subject matters raise these kinds of interdisciplinary issues, but few do so with the same intensity as the medieval Latin music-drama. In naming literary studies, musicology and liturgiology we have by no means

C. Clifford Flanigan

exhausted the disciplinary interests in our subject, for palaeography, art history, monastic history, historical theology and the history of Christian spirituality are self-evidently also concerned with it. So are economic and political history. Given such a broad range of disciplinary interests, no survey of scholarship can be complete, least of all the one that follows. But it is of fundamental importance that we acknowledge at the start the importance of viewing the Latin music-drama from a number of disciplinary perspectives if we are ever to find a way of understanding these texts from a genuinely historical perspective, one which takes its point of departure from, but is not limited by, the disciplinary configuration of knowledge near the end of the twentieth century. This acknowledgement is particularly important since in this volume the subject of Latin music-drama has been split into literary and musicological treatments (this chapter and chapter 3). This fragmentation has been necessitated by the limits of expertise in contemporary academia, but it must be forcefully stated that the exclusion of musicological scholarship in this article must not be taken to justify any consideration of the Latin music-drama which ignores its musical aspects.

Modern scholarship has subsumed a number of different medieval performance practices under the term 'liturgical drama'. On the one hand is the relatively small number of highly developed literary and musical forms, mostly of the twelfth and thirteenth centuries, which are readily recognised as drama, as the term has been defined since the Renaissance. On the other, there are brief musical and verbal texts preserved primarily in medieval liturgical books which record practices, mainly for Easter and Christmas, that were part of the ritual cursus of monasteries, cathedrals and parish churches. In theory, scholarship has rarely distinguished between these two forms of performance, and this lack of differentiation has encouraged a great deal of speculation – much of which seems highly problematic in the light of recent work – about a unified history of drama in medieval Europe, a history which is supposedly fragmented only by its later division into national literatures. Often generic distinctions were mistakenly confounded with techniques of historical periodisation, so that the 'simple' ritual texts were said to be early, while the 'more developed' texts were thought to represent the final stages of the 'development' of the drama; as much recent work has confirmed, such a view is a gross oversimplification. In practice, however, the division between texts which were narrowly tied to liturgical performance and more elaborate 'literary' ones whose relationship to the liturgy is more problematic has been upheld in scholarship; except for attempts to write the history of medieval drama, books and articles on the Latin music-drama have tended to be devoted to one or the other genre. Significantly, the studies devoted to the more ritual-like texts are almost always historically conceived, with their goals being the elaboration of dramatic history. In contrast, studies of the more elaborate 'literary' dramas generally give little attention to dramatic history and instead turn their attention to specific textual details, and to issues of local production, often with the aim of providing a literary interpretation. These more specific studies, however, have been quantitatively overwhelmed by attempts to make historical sense of the huge number of Easter texts and the much smaller number of ritual enactments of the Christmas story which survive to us. Fittingly, then, we shall first turn our attention to those studies which give the place of privilege to the Easter texts centering on the *Visitatio Sepulchri*, the medieval enactment of the biblical account of the visit of three women to the tomb of the resurrected Jesus. In the account that follows, I will be less concerned with offering a comprehensive and balanced report than with highlighting certain theoretical and historical issues which either have played a persistently important role in past scholarship or which seem to me to be of crucial significance for future studies of the Latin drama.

I

Until the late nineteenth century, scholars seemed content with merely collecting and editing examples of the *Visitatio*. The most significant of the earlier collections of these texts, that published by Carl Lange in 1887, made little attempt to account for their history or development, though it did offer significant perspectives on the textual history of the form.[1] By the turn of the century, however, various accounts of the origin and development of the Latin drama became available. In the Anglo-American world, the most influential of these was E. K. Chambers' *The Mediaeval Stage* (1903 [9]). Like other scholars of his time, Chambers believed that it was the task of scholarship to accumulate 'facts', and that facts possess an intrinsic value that interpretations of them lack. Hence his book is a massive compendium of miscellaneous information about various forms of insular and continental medieval performance practice which Chambers, by his own admission, could not wholly digest. Chambers' 'facts' were mostly of late, in contrast to early, medieval origin, and favoured popular in contrast to ecclesiastical institutions; these limitations undoubtedly affected his interpretations. His interests were far broader than the Latin drama, but his conclusions in this area were to have enormous significance. Chambers argued that a genuine ludic impulse existed among the half-pagan ordinary people of the Middle Ages rather than in the Christian rituals imposed upon them. Chambers reluctantly admitted that the 'liturgical drama' was of ecclesiastical origin, but believed that in its earliest form it was 'a mere spectacle', and that it acquired more value and appeal when it 'broke the bonds of ecclesiastical control' and appealed to a 'deep-rooted' native instinct; thus '*officia* for devotion and edification' gave way to '*spectacula* for mirth, wonder and delight' (9, II, p. 69). Though modified in a number of ways, Chambers' views continue to govern a great deal of scholarship, including that which claims to be strongly critical of them. At least Chambers acknowledged that 'the Church' (and here too, in its viewing of the Church as a monolithic institution, Chambers' work anticipates that of his successors) was the site of

23

C. Clifford Flanigan

the origin of the drama. Others, like Robert Stumpfl, Oscar Cargill and Roy Pascal, viewed the modern drama as wholly 'pagan' in its origins.[2] Even as recently as 1961 Benjamin Hunningher argued, on the basis of illustrations in liturgical books, that the *Visitatio Sepulchri* was enacted by non-ecclesiastical performers, an assertion rapidly set aside by Helena Gamer.[3] It is frequently claimed that the massive evidence published by Karl Young in his *The Drama of the Medieval Church* (*31*) put to rest this fascination for the non-ecclesiastical in the writing of the history of the medieval Latin drama, but this is hardly the case, as one can see from the sophisticated use made of it, in the light of contemporary literary theory, in Rainer Warning's *Funktion und Struktur* (1974 [*16*]); a version of Warning's notions about the medieval drama has appeared in English in his article 'On the Alterity of Medieval Religious Drama' (1979 [*26*]). Warning admonishes us not to equate unquestioningly the institutional function of the medieval Latin drama with its 'official self-conception'. He sees the relationship between the Church's liturgy and the religious drama as 'a rivalry of two institutions which the church ultimately settled in its own favor [only] after several centuries of toleration' (*26*, p. 267). Such a view suggests that we may be on the verge of encountering new forms of what at the present moment seem old-fashioned arguments about the 'pagan character' of medieval Latin drama.

If such ideas do seem old-fashioned, however, it is due in large part to Karl Young's monumental *The Drama of the Medieval Church*, published in 1933 (*31*). Though Young's book has rightly been criticised on many counts, it remains the most influential and the most significant book in the entire field of medieval Latin drama studies.[4] The importance of Young's book is twofold. In the first place it offered meticulously edited texts of all the examples of liturgical plays known up to the time of its publication. Secondly, the interpretative commentary which Young wove around his texts set the direction for the study of the medieval Latin drama for the next forty years. The influence of Young's interpretative model is all the more remarkable because Young offers no consistent argument through the whole of his two long volumes; in fact, he often assumes the guise of a positivist who merely comments on what he assumes are the 'self-evident facts' about the texts that he presents. Nevertheless, with such comments Young persuasively established his assumptions about his subject matter. Among the most important of these is a claim boldly inscribed in his title. For Young, and for most of his successors, the medieval Latin drama is indeed the drama of the Church; its content is churchly, and it was solely ecclesiastical institutions which fostered and controlled its performance. Although, as we have seen, some recent studies have sought to reach beyond Young and minimise the role of the Church, on the whole there seems little reason to take issue with Young on this point. But for Young the drama occupied a peculiar and problematic place in ecclesiastical practice; the drama took its point of origin from the liturgy, yet at the same time, Young insisted, ritual and drama are essentially different practices. Indeed, Young sought at every

24

turn to draw strict lines of demarcation between liturgy on the one hand and drama on the other, largely on the basis of impersonation. In drama, he insisted:

the performer must do more than merely represent the chosen persona; he must also resemble him, or at least show his intention of doing so. It follows, then, that the dialogue and physical movements of those who participate in the liturgy will be transformed from the dramatic into drama whenever these persons convey a story and pretend to be characters in the story. (*31*, I, pp. 80–1)

On the other hand:

The impossibility of there being impersonation in the liturgy of the Eucharist arises from the fact that since the early Christian centuries this rite has been regarded as a true sacrifice. The central act is designed not to represent or portray or merely commemorate the Crucifixion, but actually to repeat it ... The celebrant remains merely the celebrant, and does not undertake the part of his Lord. He is only the instrument through which Christ acts. The Mass, then, has never been a drama, nor did it ever directly give rise to drama. (Ibid., p. 85)

This insistence on the difference between two practices which even Young recognised as strikingly similar is the most questionable claim in Young's great opus. Such a claim runs counter to the understanding of ritual in the work of seminal anthropologists and historians of religions like Emile Durkheim, Victor Turner and Mircea Eliade. It also runs counter to the conception of liturgy as it has been developed in contemporary liturgiology. Young was able to navigate the apparent contradiction between his claim that the drama arose in the liturgy but was not of the liturgy by arguing that the trope to the Introit in the Easter Mass, rather than the Easter Mass itself, was the point of origin for the drama. That the musical and verbal text of this trope, the famous *Quem quaeritis*, is closely associated with subsequent Easter enactments within the Latin liturgy is a claim that few would care to dispute, even today. But Young's assumption that a trope is only 'paraliturgical' and not 'authentically' liturgical is, from the present standpoint of the study of the medieval liturgy, a highly suspect claim. For Young tropes are 'deliberate, and perhaps unsanctioned, literary additions to the authorized liturgical texts' (*31*, I, p. 178). Recent students of the medieval liturgy, however, view tropes as closely tied to the ritual texts which they gloss, and have thus tended to undercut the neat dichotomy on which Young's distinction is based.[5] Indeed, our knowledge of troping has been significantly altered by the 'Corpus Troporum' project at the University of Stockholm, which is attempting to publish the verbal texts, with textual variants, of the entire repertory of early-medieval tropes. Several volumes have already appeared and several more are in preparation.[6]

Whatever one might think about the precise nature of the relationship between the *Visitatio Sepulchri* and the trope, no student of the drama can afford to neglect these trope editions, nor indeed other important editions of medieval liturgical texts. Such an observation, obvious as it is, points to one

C. Clifford Flanigan

of the greatest sources of misinformation and misunderstanding in the study of medieval Latin drama: because students of literature are convinced that they are dealing with literary texts, they often fail to accord detailed attention to liturgical studies. This neglect has led to unsubstantiated speculation and widespread and often uncritically repeated misinformation. Anyone with serious interests in medieval Latin drama simply must orient himself in the world of medieval liturgical texts and the present state of the study of the medieval liturgy; as Thomas Campbell's 1981 survey has shown, this great desideratum is finally beginning to be realised.[7] Though from the perspective of a decade and a half I recognise many oversimplifications, I nonetheless offer my own early attempt to study the relationship between the *Quem quaeritis* trope and the *Visitatio Sepulchri* as a possible example of drama scholarship which takes liturgiology seriously (1974 [*61*]). A major though somewhat derivative study of the verbal texts of the Easter dramatic offices which takes its point of departure from liturgical scholarship is Blandine-Dominique Berger's *Le Drame liturgique des Pâques du xe au xiiie siècle* (1976 [*64*]). More exciting, and more exacting, since unlike most studies chronicled here it takes seriously both the verbal and the musical elements of the *Visitatio Sepulchri* and related texts, is Susan Rankin's examination of 'Musical and Ritual Aspects of *Quem Queritis*' (1985 [*99*]).

Young's book had such a pervasive effect on Anglo-American and most continental scholarship that the three decades that followed its publication saw little work that could be regarded as anything more than a filling of the small gaps left in his edifice. The exceptions to this rule were a handful of specialised monographs, of which the most distinguished were perhaps Solange Corbin's study of *La Déposition liturgique du Christ au Vendredi Saint* (1960 [*56*]) and Richard Donovan's exploration of *The Liturgical Drama in Mediaeval Spain* (1958 [*445*]). This latter book was of special importance since it demonstrated the pervasiveness of Latin drama in a geographical area in which it was earlier hardly known.

II

The relative stagnation in medieval Latin drama studies in the 1940s and 1950s was sharply brought to a conclusion with the publication of O. B. Hardison's *Christian Rite and Christian Drama in the Middle Ages: Essays in the Origin and Early History of the Modern Drama* in 1965 (*46*). Hardison's book sets out a number of related claims, among the most important of which are the following:

1   Late-nineteenth- and early-twentieth-century bias against religion caused almost all scholars of the Latin and vernacular medieval drama to underplay religious and liturgical elements in their work and to place apparently peripheral 'secular' elements at the centre or near the centre of their inquiry.
2   The earlier fundamental studies of the medieval Latin drama were based on a tacit acceptance of the model of evolutionary development adapted from the

biological sciences; the unacknowledged acceptance of this paradigm by scholars caused them to arrange and describe texts in a linear and regular order which, as they themselves acknowledged, contradicted the surviving manuscript evidence.

3　The study of the Latin drama must be grounded in an understanding of the early-medieval ritual; thus Hardison offers an extended summary and paraphrase of the commentaries of Amalarius of Metz, the most influential Carolingian student of the liturgy, and he offers Amalarius' allegorical interpretation of the liturgy as a model for understanding the *Quem quaeritis* dialogue.

4　Contrary to Young's claims, the *Visitatio Sepulchri* ceremony did not develop out of the *Quem quaeritis* trope to the Easter Introit; the drama has its origins in the Vigil Mass of Easter.[8]

5　The vernacular dramatic traditions were not the products of a logical development out of complex plays in Latin, but had their beginnings in a tradition separate from the liturgy.

As should be apparent, Hardison's study had a twofold aim: to criticise the then widely accepted scholarly tradition in medieval drama studies which was based on Chambers' book and Young's revision of it (and which had recently been restated in Hardin Craig's synthesis of 1955 [*105*]) and secondly to replace this view with a radically different understanding of the early development of the Latin and vernacular drama. In the former aim, Hardison succeeded beyond any reasonable expectation. The brief first chapter of his book so thoroughly devastated the received tradition that almost no one writing on the drama since the appearance of *Christian Rite and Christian Drama* has disputed its claims. But Hardison had considerably less success in persuading others to his own position concerning, for example, the importance of the Easter Vigil or the relevance of Amalarius' writings for the history of the medieval drama. Though the present chapter is hardly the place for taking up these issues – some of which have in fact yet to be considered in a major way – it must be candidly admitted that Hardison's speculations are often not solidly grounded and that they sometimes manifest a surprising lack of knowledge of both musical and liturgiological scholarship. But such reservations can in no way diminish the inestimable influence which Hardison's work has rightly had on all subsequent medieval drama scholarship.

Though Hardison's book took issue with Young's conclusions at every turn, he did not challenge the assumption made by Young and earlier generations of scholars that the question of the origins of the Latin drama was central and decisive. In fact, the question of the origins of the music-drama has continued to vex a number of more recent critics. Perhaps the most important of these is Johann Drumbl, who first in a seminal journal article (1979 [*52*]) and then in more elaborate monograph form (1981 [*53*]) has put forward a significant variation of Young's claim (still accepted by most scholars, Hardison notwithstanding) that the 'origins' of the *Visitatio Sepulchri* are somehow tied up with the *Quem quaeritis* introit trope.

C. Clifford Flanigan

Drumbl's claims are exceedingly complex, and cannot possibly be summarised within the scope of the present chapter. Yet because his work is the most serious recent attempt to explore the historical origins of the *Visitatio*, and therefore demonstrates in an exaggerated way the assets and liabilities of this form of scholarship at its best, it is worth addressing at least some of the methodological issues that Drumbl's work raises.

What is of fundamental importance for our understanding and evaluation of Drumbl's work is that like Young, and like Helmut de Boor (see below, pp. 32–4), Drumbl assumes that tropes and the *Visitatio* ceremony which he believed developed from them are paraliturgical phenomena that can be set apart from the 'authorised' liturgy. This view allows Drumbl to regard the *Visitatio Sepulchri* in the *Regularis Concordia* – where it makes its first known appearance – as an unessential adornment to the Easter liturgy, and to seek its origin in some continental quasi-liturgical, essentially literary, practice. Since there is no direct evidence for a *Visitatio Sepulchri* text which pre-dates the one in the *Regularis Concordia*, Drumbl's inquiry inevitably turns to questions about sources of other texts in the *Regularis*. Historians of monasticism have generally assumed that many of the practices advocated there are derived from houses participating in the Lotharingian reforms in Ghent.[9] Drumbl, evoking the most unlikely of arguments, however, insists that the text of the *Visitatio* in the *Regularis* stems from the Benedictine house at Fleury and that, despite the fact that monastic houses which were part of the Cluniac movement never included the *Visitatio Sepulchri* among their practices, its probable author was Odo of Cluny or someone who wrote under his direction.

Drumbl goes on to ask why the new ceremony was composed for the precise moment in the liturgical cursus in which we encounter it in the *Regularis Concordia*. The reason is to be found, if I understand Drumbl correctly, in a reform of the Easter procession in France in the ninth century, a reform which limited the route of the procession to the interior of the church, whereas earlier it had encircled the entire complex of monastic buildings. This new processional practice, Drumbl claims, created a need for a new ceremony. Odo thus composed the *Quem quaeritis* chant in order to fill an 'open space' in the Easter cursus. But when this piece of liturgical poetry passed over to other, non-French, communities which had not experienced the reform of the Easter procession and hence did not require a piece in order to fill in a newly vacant moment in the cursus, these changed the text and inserted it, often with some difficulty, into their pre-existing communal rites. This explains, in Drumbl's view, why the *Quem quaeritis* text survives in three different forms, as processional piece, as trope to the Easter Introit and as a dramatic ceremony performed before the singing of the *Te Deum* at Easter Matins.

Ultimately Drumbl's claims must be judged by historians of monasticism, though it must be admitted that on the surface they seem to be marked by an astonishing improbability.[10] It is certainly true that the *Quem quaeritis* is preserved in tenth- and eleventh-century sources in a number of different positions in the liturgy. But as David A. Bjork has shown in an article of singular importance (1980 [92]), the division between those which situate the chant before the Mass and those which incorporate it into Matins is neither haphazard, as Drumbl suggests, nor chronological, as Hardison supposed. It is geographical. As a general rule, to which there are, of course, exceptions, the dialogue was sung at Mass in southern France, in Catalonia, in Italy and in a few East Frankish locales such as St Gall, Rheinau, Heidenheim and Minden. It was sung at Matins across northern Europe, in England, northern France, the Rhineland and in most of the East Frankish territory. It is possible, of course, to integrate this observation into Drumbl's scheme, but it certainly calls into question the claim that monastic houses included the new composition in their observances because they found it attractive, but were presented with the difficulty of finding a place for it since its creation was unmotivated by local circumstances.

Even more important than these historical issues are the tacit theoretical assumptions which underlie Drumbl's work. Of all the authors scrutinised in this chapter, Drumbl has in many ways most taken seriously the new orientation in liturgical drama studies which has gradually emerged since the appearance of Hardison's book. Drumbl's work is steeped in liturgiological scholarship and in the history of monasticism. It is extraordinarily informed by continental scholarship, though it shows important lacunae in Anglo-American criticism. But apart from its historical claims, Drumbl's book fails in part because it continues to accept some of the same working hypotheses which governed earlier medieval drama scholarship.

In the first place, like Hardison and Young, Drumbl completely ignores the musical aspects of the *Visitatio Sepulchri* and writes as if only the verbal text is significant. As long as literary scholars continue this arrogant practice, we are not likely to make much progress in the study of the Latin *music*-drama. Related to this observation is another troubling methodological presupposition which governs Drumbl's work, just as it governs the work of most other historians of the *Visitatio*: Drumbl deliberately sets out to prove that the *Quem quaeritis* dialogue was from its moment of origin a piece of liturgical poetry rather than an ordinary ritual practice. It is this ambiguous quality which, according to Drumbl, enables the dialogue to have a continuing place in literary history rather than merely in liturgical history. Thus in many ways Drumbl's work returns us to Young's views about the 'paraliturgical' and the line of division between liturgy and drama. But this distinction is extremely questionable both historically and theoretically. The fact remains that, with a few exceptions, the *Visitatio Sepulchri* offices are preserved in liturgical books, and nothing in those manuscripts justifies the separation of these few lines of liturgy from their immediate context. Nothing in the *Regularis Concordia* text, for example, would substantiate the claim that the practitioners of the *Visitatio* rite inscribed there regarded it as a piece of paraliturgical poetry or (even more unlikely) as an incipient drama;

C. Clifford Flanigan

such questionable claims can only be made in the light of the future use of the *Quem quaeritis* dialogue of which they possessed no knowledge. Though claims like Drumbl's about the origins of the 'liturgical drama' have been repeatedly advanced in the name of 'objective history', they seem more likely the products of the presuppositions of literary studies – itself a decidedly non-medieval institution.

Drumbl's work offers somewhat of a variation on the mainstream accounts concerning the 'origins' of the medieval Latin drama. A few writers have offered more strikingly different perspectives. In a series of articles Catherine Dunn has pointed to the drama-like multiplicity of voices in the Gallican liturgy, especially in its recitation of saints' lives.[11] One is never certain whether Dunn is pointing to these Gallican practices as the actual starting point of the medieval drama, or if she merely wishes to point to drama-like factors which were present in the liturgical environment out of which the *Visitatio Sepulchri* emerged. If the former is her aim, her argument does not, at least in its present form, seem convincing. In any case Dunn provides us with important information about early-medieval cultic practices, and her writings always display a keen sensitivity to the spirit of the liturgy which is too often lacking in medieval drama scholarship. Like Dunn, I have also pointed to the significance of the Gallican liturgy for an understanding of the drama-like qualities of the Carolingian rite (1974 [50]), but I have emphasised the paradoxical manner in which the *Quem quaeritis* dialogue appeared only when the Roman rite, the most 'undramatic' of all the Western liturgies, was imposed on Gallican churches.

Quite in contrast to such quests for the beginnings of the drama in liturgical practice is Leonard Goldstein's 'The Origin of Medieval Drama',[12] an essay which uses the work of the turn-of-the-century Cambridge school of anthropology to argue for a drearily orthodox Marxist interpretation of dramatic history which is remarkable only for its unremittingly doctrinaire voice and its unforgivable ignorance of post-World War II scholarship. It is truly regrettable that more viable Marxist readings of the Latin music-drama have not been forthcoming, for it is certainly true that virtually all of the scholarship recounted in this survey takes little or no account of the socio-economic institutions in which the liturgy was practised and the drama was born, and this is a lack that really must be addressed.

Several scholars have dealt with the relationship between the visual arts and early-medieval liturgy and drama. Despite its title, Carol Heitz's *Recherches sur les rapports entre architecture et liturgie à l'époque carolingienne* (1963 [57]) is primarily concerned with liturgical piety and the way that it gave rise to cultic practices like the *Visitatio Sepulchri*. Heitz's main subject is the emergence of a new christology in the Carolingian period which emphasised the human rather than the cosmic Christ, and the way that ecclesiastical architecture and ritual gave expression to this new emphasis. His work is somewhat speculative, but highly stimulating, and deserves far more attention than it has thus far received. More comprehensive, but perhaps less academic since its concerns are more with play production than with dramatic and liturgical history, is Fletcher Collins Jr's *The Production of Medieval Church Music-Drama* (1972 [34]). Collins examines in detail medieval visual representations of the subject matters of the repertory of the mostly later and developed music-dramas and on this basis speculates on the settings and costumes used in the original productions of these plays. The book is a joy to look at and always enlightening to use, but it is based on a far too easy equation of visual artifact and liturgical and dramatic practice, one which seems mostly unaware of, for example, the enormous role played by iconography in the medieval visual arts.

A book of extraordinary interest is Pamela Sheingorn's *The Easter Sepulchre in England* (1987 [66]). Sheingorn's study primarily consists of a catalogue of all known Easter sepulchres in England, but it also offers a rich bibliography and an extended essay on the history of this architectural fixture and its place in religious life. I know of no account elsewhere which captures as this study does the way that liturgy, spirituality and everyday life as it was lived in concrete material existence were intertwined in the medieval period. Much of Professor Sheingorn's material stems from the later Middle Ages, a period to which *Visitatio* studies have given little attention (even though the vast majority of our surviving manuscripts stem from this time), and it is therefore especially refreshing to learn from her documentation how vital ceremonies connected with the sepulchre were then.

III

We have thus far reported on studies that touch on the *Visitatio Sepulchri*, but of at least equal importance are new editions of this and other music-dramas. Fletcher Collins Jr has provided us with a controversial performing edition of a number of the more elaborate plays, mostly from the Fleury Playbook (1976 [44]). More significant is the appearance of six volumes of Walther Lipphardt's *Lateinische Osterfeiern und Osterspiele* (1975–81 [43]). The great achievement of Lipphardt's edition, which includes all known Latin materials associated with the dramatic rites of Easter, is that it more than triples the amount of material edited in Young's two volumes. And rather than ordering by logical type, as Young did, Lipphardt arranges his material according to manuscript provenance. Often a number of versions of the *Visitatio Sepulchri* from the same church or diocese are included, arranged by date, and this makes it possible to see how the 'same' text was preserved and at times altered. Thus Lipphardt's work enables us to sketch the history of liturgical and dramatic practices within a local community. In this regard the appearance of Lipphardt's work is very good news for the scholarly community. Unfortunately, there is also some bad news. Lipphardt's book reproduces only verbal texts. Thus Lipphardt, who was himself a musicologist, perpetuated the grave misconception that the *Visitatio* is primarily a literary phenomenon and only secondarily a musical

C. Clifford Flanigan

phenomenon. There is even more to regret about Lipphardt's work. It is becoming increasingly apparent that much of the transcription that underlies this edition was done hastily and carelessly. In some cases it seems unlikely that Lipphardt even saw the manuscript which he edited.[13] A volume of corrections is apparently planned, and when it appears it should be judiciously used with the original six volumes. But surely everyone working on the Easter drama must be indebted to Lipphardt, and the final word here about this great resource cannot be a negative one. Whatever its limitations – and they are certainly formidable – Lipphardt's edition opens up a seemingly limitless number of new possibilities for exploration, possibilities which surprisingly have not been exploited in the decade throughout which these volumes have been available.

As remarkable as the appearance of the many new Easter liturgical offices and plays in Lipphardt's edition is the appearance of two major attempts at producing a textual history of this material. Young had proclaimed that the Easter material was too rich and too complex ever to be submitted to the traditional efforts of a textual historian. This observation, he believed, justified the 'logical' arrangement of material in his book, rather than an arrangement that reflected manuscript date and provenance. But in 1967 Helmut de Boor produced his monumental *Die Textgeschichte der lateinischen Osterfeiern* (47) in which he demonstrated that it was possible to arrange the Easter offices and plays in an order which makes sense of their temporal and geographical places of origin and which allows one to write a tentative textual history of the growth and transformation of traditions associated with the *Quem quaeritis* dialogue. It is of course not possible to recount here the details of de Boor's work; it will, however, be useful to consider briefly some methodological issues which arise out of it. In the first place, like so many other scholars of the Latin music-drama, de Boor carried out his work entirely on the basis of the verbal text. It is clearly not desirable – and in fact bound to lead to serious errors – to establish textual affiliations on the basis of only one half of the evidence available for many (though certainly not all) of the exemplars. Happily Diane Dolan avoided this one-sidedness in her study of the musical and verbal texts of *Le Drame liturgique de Pâques en Normandie et en Angleterre au moyen-âge* (1975 [86]), a book which, as its title indicates, proceeds on a limited geographical plane.

To this reservation it must be added that de Boor's work was based on certain theoretical assumptions which, if questionable, nonetheless are of great interest. At the foundation of de Boor's enterprise is the distinction, which runs back in German scholarship at least as far as Carl Lange, between *Feier* (liturgical celebration) and *Spiel* (play). By *Feier* de Boor means 'All that is intended for use in the framework of ecclesiastical ritual'; *Spiel*, on the other hand, means 'a text which is out of place in the liturgical realm, regardless of whether it was written in Latin or the vernacular, whether it was written by clerics and presented inside the church or was produced with the cooperation of the laity in an outdoor place' (47, p. 5). Elsewhere de Boor tells us that in the *Feier*, in contrast to the *Spiel*, 'the clergy do not represent sacred figures; they "fulfill'" them, they become them' (p. 9). With such statements de Boor seems to break decisively with older literary paradigms and to employ the language of liturgiology to locate the *Visitatio* in a set of assumptions far removed from Young's demarcation between ritual imitation and dramatic impersonation. But matters are not, unfortunately, so simple. If de Boor rejected Young's belief in the centrality of impersonation, he accepted his distinction between the liturgical and the paraliturgical; tropes and *Feiern* are not liturgical objects in the strictest sense of that term according to de Boor. Indeed, he claimed that it was possible to write a textual history of the Easter tropes and offices only because they occupied an anomalous state somewhere between 'authentic' liturgy and 'art'. Such phenomena, he claimed, 'live within the liturgy', but are not indispensable to it. This peculiar position, de Boor argues, gives them a 'freedom of movement' which the official liturgy does not possess. Because of this freedom, the *Visitatio* could be altered in different ways; it could be abbreviated or expanded or otherwise changed in order to make it fit the special needs of different occasions. It is this openness to change, according to de Boor, which makes a textual history of the *Visitatio* possible. On the other hand, this freedom puts the ceremony in constant danger of being transformed into a drama. For de Boor, the history of the *Visitatio Sepulchri* consists of its taking one 'chance' after another in this direction. For example, in the inclusion of the race of Peter and John to the tomb in the Type II *Visitatio* (this system of categorisation of *Visitatio* types goes back to Lange and also provides the basis for the arrangement of the materials in the first volume of Young's book), a 'chance' is taken in allowing the *Feier* to become more historical and hence less liturgical. And in the Type III office, in which Christ Himself appears, de Boor sees the complete overstepping of the boundaries which separate *Feier* from *Spiel*.

This interpretative paradigm is highly suggestive, but it is also problematic. In the first place, it is governed by a philosophical essentialism which grants items an essence apart from the way that they are regarded by their users. Left out of de Boor's scheme is any consideration of how the participants in the Easter offices understood them. Secondly, though de Boor acknowledges the correctness of Hardison's critique of the evolutionism underlying earlier studies of the music-drama, he remains a victim of this way of understanding the history of the *Visitatio Sepulchri*. While he can imagine a *Feier* becoming a *Spiel*, he makes no mention of the possibility of a *Spiel* becoming a *Feier*. For de Boor, history apparently moves relentlessly in one direction. However, despite my reservations about de Boor's appropriation of earlier scholarship's notions of the paraliturgical, its essentialism and its evolutionism, I believe that a rethinking of his methodological assumptions offers as yet unrealised opportunities.

Probably the same cannot be said for the details of de Boor's textual history, however. Michael Norton is presently in the process of producing a textual history of most of the same material treated by de Boor, but for the first time on the basis of both verbal and musical texts. Norton has been working on this project already for several years. Not surprisingly, given its enormous scope, his work is still in a somewhat preliminary stage. In a recent lengthy article (1987 [65]), Norton has published some of his initial findings as well as his present understanding of the methodological assumptions which underlie Young's and de Boor's division of the Easter offices and plays into three stages. Since such work is the product of painstaking observations of details, it cannot be summarised here. But it is apparent that much of de Boor's work will need to be revised in major and significant ways. Norton has, for example, offered persuasive evidence against the claims for a unified Type I and Type II *Visitatio*, and against the very existence of a Type III form. Though one might wish for a greater awareness of the theoretical issues at stake in this project, it is easy to recognise that Norton's work promises to be among the most significant in the entire area of medieval Latin drama studies in the next decade. It seems likely that, once it is complete, we will need to rethink much that the scholarship of the past century has assumed about the *Quem quaeritis* Easter dialogue in its various forms.

IV

The *Visitatio Sepulchri* texts are by no means the only form of medieval Latin music-drama. Closely related to them is the much smaller number of Christmas texts which centre on the question addressed to the shepherds, *Quem quaeritis in praesepe?* There are obvious similarities between the Easter and Christmas *Quem quaeritis* dialogues, and older scholarship tended to regard the Christmas texts as wholly modelled on their earlier Easter counterparts. Indeed Theo Stemmler (1970 [12]) made this similarity one of the bases for his claim that the same fundamental typology underlies all of the plays in the repertory of medieval Latin music-dramas. There has been surprisingly little written about the Christmas plays, and what little has appeared has tended to play down the parallels between Christmas and Easter texts. Recent investigations of the Christmas texts have been undertaken by James M. Gibson (1981–2 [63]) and Thomas Campbell[14] and though each approaches the texts from a different perspective, they both come to strikingly similar conclusions: that the content of these *officia* is directly tied to the liturgy for the season, and that most of them – to adapt the vocabulary employed above – can best be regarded as *Feiern* rather than *Spiele*. Thus the groundwork has been established for more detailed investigation of the Christmas offices, but thus far no substantial studies of them have appeared.

When we move beyond the Christmas texts to the rest of the repertory, we are confronted with a small number of often elaborate religious plays which have a great diversity of subject matter. In contrast to the 'simpler' category of texts thus far discussed, each of these plays must be regarded as an *unicum*, even if on occasion some affinities can be discerned with other surviving texts. Some of the most interesting and telling work in the entire field of medieval music-drama studies has been done in attempting to specify how these plays are different from the more strictly liturgical offices for Easter and Christmas. For example, building on de Boor's methodological assumptions, Theo Stemmler (1970 [*12*]) marches through the whole of the music-drama repertory deciding whether and to what degree each of these plays qualifies as *Feier* or *Spiel*. He argues that plays closely connected to the liturgy, such as the *Visitatio Sepulchri* and its Christmas counterparts, lack a logical or narrative structure, while texts like the Beauvais *Daniel*, for example, or those in the Fleury Playbook, manifest a tight and logically controlled chain of episodes. In fact, for Stemmler it is precisely their characteristic logic and appeal to everyday experience that marks such texts as genuine plays with little ritual (but much dramatic) significance. Somewhat similar conclusions are reached by Hans-Jürgen Diller (1973 [*118*]) who offers an elaborate account of how such 'genuine' plays emerged from a wholly liturgical context. The moment of transformation comes for Diller when the character Herod appears in the *Officium Stellae*. What is important about Herod in Diller's scheme is that he has no liturgical function; he is merely a biblical character who acts in opposition to the divine, something that does not occur in the Easter or Christmas offices where the chief characters are conceived of as Christians and are regarded by the ritual logic which governs them as representatives of the medieval worshippers celebrating the rite. Thus those texts which are genuine plays appeal to their audiences emotionally, while liturgical texts have as their basis the type of bonding which characterises – and constitutes – a ritual community. Diller notes the importance of elaborate and unrestrained emotional expression in the laments of Rachel in the Innocents play and of Mary Magdalene in a number of full-scale Easter plays, and compares this form of dramatic expression with the much restrained and ritually motivated sense of grief expressed by the women in the *Visitatio Sepulchri*.

Wilfried Werner's perceptive study *Studien zu den Passions- und Osterspielen des deutschen Mittelalters in ihrem Übergang vom Latein zur Volkssprache* (1963 [*542*]) is wholly based on the macaronic use of Latin and vernacular German in selected Passion and Easter plays, but makes a similar point about the centrality of the human and the emotional in the elaborate Latin plays of the twelfth and thirteenth centuries. Building upon a distinction firmly established in German scholarship, Werner claims that it is the emergence of peculiarly human concerns, in which, for example, the Virgin Mary is portrayed as a suffering human being, that marks the transformation from *Feier* to *Spiel*. This generic shift is related to a pervasive shift in European piety in the early thirteenth century when confidence in the early-medieval hierarchical ('gradualistic') world order is said to have been shaken. Werner finds it significant that the need for the vernacular expression of human emotion was first felt in Passion plays, which were themselves the

C. Clifford Flanigan

product of that shift in piety, and which emphasised above all the humanity of the suffering Jesus.

An entirely different perspective on the transformation of liturgical office to dramatic enactment is offered by Rosemary Woolf in the opening chapters of her study on *The English Mystery Plays* (1972 [*153*]). Woolf asks 'to what extent this development was itself stimulated by a conscious knowledge of and reflection upon the art of drama' (p. 25). To deal with the question she considers 'a ragbag of scraps of evidence of widely different kinds', such as the growing interest in Roman drama in the twelfth century, and the attempt to imitate this genre in the production of elegiac *comoediae*. She also points to discussion of theatre and drama in the learned literature of the period, especially in glosses and encyclopaedias. Her tentative conclusion is that the production of at least some of the most elaborate Latin music-dramas was affected by a new understanding of drama and theatre in Europe. One piece of evidence in favour of her hypothesis is the appearance of the antique and secular term 'ludus' in liturgical books to designate ritual enactments which in earlier manuscripts were termed 'ordo' or 'officium' (though these more traditional terms certainly continued in use through the end of the Middle Ages).

Drawing upon Woolf's work, as well as that of scholars like Stemmler and Diller, I have argued (1985 [*40*]) that discussion of the classic question of the differences which separate liturgy from drama needs to be based more firmly on manuscript study than has thus far been the case. I also insist that such study needs a theoretical basis to be convincing and that perhaps the most useful one for this purpose is that offered by reception studies and reader-response theory. According to this paradigm, texts are not intrinsically rituals or dramas; they are granted their generic identity neither by their moment of origin nor by their authors' intentions. It is an audience's (or reader's) perception of a text, and the use put to that text, which confers generic identity on it. That means that the distinction between office and drama, between *Feier* and *Spiel*, is always a fluid one. If the performance of a text that earlier had been widely understood as a ritual is perceived as a dramatic one, then for that performance what was ritual has 'become' a drama. But having 'become' a drama, it need not always remain so, for a drama perceived as ritual then 'becomes' a ritual. From this perspective, the ritual/drama dichotomy needs to be addressed in terms of what we can learn about the 'horizons of expectations' (the term is taken from Hans Robert Jauss' programmatic essay 'Literary History as a Challenge to Literary Theory'[15]) which successive audiences brought to these texts rather than from an identification of any supposedly intrinsic and permanent characteristics which the texts possess. Whether Latin music-drama scholarship, which remains for the most part cautious and conservative, is ready to explore such a possibility is an open question.

Having reviewed the important general discussion about the generic identity of the longer plays, we can turn our attention to studies of specific plays and groups of plays. The most extensive collection of medieval Latin music-dramas is the so-called Fleury Playbook, now manuscript 201 in the Orléans Municipal Library, though its original provenance continues to be a point of contention. This collection is well known not only for its singular significance in the history of European drama, but because of the famous productions in the 1950s and 1960s of *The Play of Herod* (actually a compilation of two separate Fleury texts) by the New York Pro Musica, productions which initiated the by now relatively common practice of re-creating medieval music-dramas for modern audiences. This entire collection, consisting of ten plays, has been photographically reproduced and joined to a collection of essays (1985 [*39*]) devoted to general issues concerning the manuscript (Flanigan on the relationship to other manuscripts containing plays, David Bevington on performance practices, Thomas Campbell on the thematic unity of the playbook, Clyde Brockett on the musical coherence of the manuscript, Fletcher Collins on its provenance) or to specific plays (Kathleen Ashley on the Lazarus play, Miriam Anne Skey on the Herod), and a concluding essay by Cynthia Bourgeault on 'Liturgical Dramaturgy and Modern Production'. Most of these essays include bibliographies, and so this handy collection readily serves as a guide to further study of the Fleury collection. Of the interpretative essays devoted to texts in Orléans 201 published elsewhere, special mention should be made of Robert Guiette's brief 'Réflexions sur le drame liturgique' (1966 [*32*]) which, in addition to providing an insightful characterisation of Latin music-drama in general, offers an interpretation of the Slaughter of the Innocents play which deserves to be ranked as one of the most sensitive readings of any play in the entire repertory. Important for the study of the Fleury Saint Nicholas plays, as well as for the texts in the Hildesheim collection, is Charles W. Jones' *The Saint Nicholas Liturgy and its Literary Relationships (Ninth to Twelfth Centuries)* (1963 [*58*]).

The *Ludus Danielis* from the cathedral school at Beauvais is one of the best known of all Latin music-dramas, yet strangely there has been little written about it; Jerome Taylor, however, has provided a useful but eclectic interpretation in his 'Prophetic "Play" and Symbolist "Plot" in the Beauvais *Daniel*'.[16] Wulf Arlt (1970 [*60*]) has given us a marvellous edition, with extensive textual and musical commentary, of the entire manuscript in which the play is contained, a manuscript which sets out the liturgy for all of the services for the octave day of Christmas at Beauvais. Arlt's edition provides us with a rare opportunity to see a Latin music-drama in its context, which here is a liturgical cursus of incredible splendour and of great literary and musical ingenuity. Even a superficial glance at this liturgy, which includes many processions, hymns, sequences, tropes and tropes of tropes, with texts drawn from both biblical and classical sources, will put to rest the often repeated claim that the music-drama was a relatively rare 'paraliturgical' addition to a fixed and authorised liturgy. Rich and elaborate as the *Daniel* is, it is no more so than the liturgical celebration in which it was embedded.

C. Clifford Flanigan

The number of Passion plays in Latin is quite small, but the genre has received a great deal of attention from Sandro Sticca. His work on *The Latin Passion Play: Its Origins and Development* (1970 [69]) sums up a number of his earlier pieces. In this book Sticca has a twofold aim: in the first place to call attention to the Montecassino Passion play, which appears to be older by more than a century than any other extant Passion play, but which until recently has been unjustly neglected. Sticca's edition of this text is included in his volume. Secondly, Sticca wishes to call attention to the way in which the Passion play developed in ways different from the Christmas and Easter offices. It is generally acknowledged that the Passion plays have not 'descended' from the liturgy; Young and others found their origins in the poetic laments of the Virgin Mary over the Crucifixion and death of her son. Sticca prefers to see the plays as growing directly out of the Gospel narratives, under the influence both of certain rhetorical practices and, more importantly, the affective and emotional piety of the High Middle Ages. Sticca has elaborated and developed his perspective in his study of *Il Planctus Mariae nella tradizione drammatica del Medio Evo* (1984 [74]), which is primarily devoted to the place of the *planctus* in medieval spirituality. Both of Sticca's books are informative and have the advantage of including extensive bibliographies which give attention to studies produced on the continent that have been overlooked by many Anglo-American scholars. Robert Edwards has also published a study of the Montecassino play (1977 [70]), but aside from providing an English translation of the text, his monograph seems little more than an elaboration on Sticca's work.

Michael Rudick is one of the few recent critics to attempt to make sense out of the two dramatic texts about the Passion in the *Carmina Burana* manuscript.[17] Centering his attention on the *Ludus Breviter de Passione* he argues that the play is essentially an amplification of the major themes of the Palm Sunday liturgy and may have been intended for performance on that day. More recently, Thomas Binkley and I have jointly reconstructed the verbal and musical texts of the *Carmina Burana*'s longer Passion play, a work which was previously believed to be marked by many textual cruxes. This project was made possible by the recognition that the entire play is nothing but a pastiche of verbal and musical quotations of pre-existent liturgical elements; its author's skill lay not in creating new lines, but in arranging elements already close at hand. This discovery foregrounds the centrality of liturgy for the entire Latin music-drama repertory, even for those texts better characterised as dramas than as liturgical *officia*. We are preparing an edition of the play based on this discovery. A preliminary account of the play's recovery can be found in Thomas Binkley, 'The Greater Passionplay in the *Carmina Burana*: An Introduction' (1982 [72]). In many ways the *Carmina Burana* plays have close affinities to the liturgical and dramatic traditions from the great Augustinian house at Klosterneuburg. The long and elaborate *Ordo Paschalis* from that institution has been submitted to an extensive analysis by Richard Blank.[18] Blank's study is virtually unknown, even in German circles, and that is to be regretted, since it offers one of the most extensive and sensitive readings ever afforded a Latin music-drama.

This brief survey of recent studies on individual plays and groups of plays can only indicate some of the directions of the current interpretation of the music-drama. It by no means exhausts the materials available. If we look back over this material, along with the more general studies which have also been touched on here, we will be able to arrive at a few generalisations about the present state of medieval Latin drama scholarship. Some of the issues which concerned the earliest generations of students of this material more than a century ago continue to be central in the current discussion, above all questions about origins, about historical development and about the distinction between ritual and drama. In this regard Young's great compendium, itself a culmination of earlier work, remains influential after more than fifty years. But in other respects the manner in which we think about medieval Latin music-drama has shifted radically in the last quarter-century. Claims about the evolutionary development of medieval drama from Latin to vernacular, from simple to complex, once universally accepted, are no longer accepted by anyone. Just as important is the way that the study of the liturgy, as that area has been defined both by Christian liturgiology and by the social sciences, is playing an increasingly important role in drama scholarship. Finally there are other developments which are unfortunately not yet widespread, but which are definitely afoot, that give great promise for redefining music-drama scholarship and for making substantial advances in areas in which previous generations of scholars were baffled. The most important of these is the grudging recognition that the liturgical drama is a *music*-drama, and that to emphasise text over music, or music over text, is to distort in a fundamental way the object under study. There can be no doubt that in many respects our view of the Latin music-drama is significantly different from what it was a generation ago. It may be that we are at last on the verge of grasping its function within the larger configurations of medieval culture. If the scholarship of the next generation enables us to arrive at such an understanding, then we shall have finally moved beyond the foundations which the pioneers of Latin music-drama scholarship established.

NOTES

1 Carl Lange, *Die lateinischen Osterfeiern: Untersuchungen über den Ursprung und die Entwicklung der liturgisch-dramatischen Auferstehungsfeier* (Munich: Stahl, 1887).
2 Robert Stumpfl, *Kultspiele der Germanen als Ursprung des mittelalterlichen Dramas* (Berlin: Junker and Dünnhaupt, 1936); Oscar Cargill, *Drama and Liturgy* (New York: Columbia University Press, 1930); Roy Pascal, 'On the Origins of Liturgical Drama', *Modern Language Review* 36 (1942): 369–89.
3 Benjamin Hunningher, *The Origin of the Theater* (Amsterdam and The Hague:

C. Clifford Flanigan

Martinus Nijhoff, 1955; New York, 1961); Helena Gamer, 'Mimes, Musicians, and the Origin of the Mediaeval Religious Play', *Deutsche Beiträge zur geistigen Überlieferung* 5 (1965): 9–28.

4 For a discussion of the significance of Young's work from the perspective of more recent scholarship, see C. Clifford Flanigan, 'Karl Young and the Drama of the Medieval Church: An Anniversary Appraisal' (1984 [*38*]).

5 See, for example, Paul Evans, 'Some Reflections on the Origin of the Trope', *Journal of The American Musicological Society* 14 (1961): 119–30, and *The Early Trope Repertory of Saint Martial de Limoges* (Princeton: Princeton University Press, 1970); Richard Crocker, 'The Troping Hypothesis', *The Musical Quarterly* 52 (1966): 183–203; Heinrich Husmann, 'Sinn und Wesen der Tropen veranschaulicht an den Introitustropen des Weihnachtsfestes', *Archiv für Musikwissenschaft* 16 (1959): 135–47; and Alejandro Planchart, *The Repertory of Tropes at Winchester* (1977 [*90*]).

6 Ritva Jonsson, ed., *Corpus Troporum*, 5 vols. to date, Studia Latina Stockholmiensia (Stockholm: Almqvist and Wiksell International, 1975–).

7 Thomas P. Campbell, 'Liturgy and Drama: Recent Approaches to Medieval Theatre', *Theatre Journal* 33 (1981): 289–301.

8 Hardison elaborated further on this point in his 'Gregorian Easter Vespers and Early Liturgical Drama', in *1*, pp. 27–40.

9 On the sources of the *Regularis Concordia*, see Dom Thomas Symon's edition, *Regularis Concordia: The Monastic Agreement of the Monks and Nuns of the English Nation*, Nelson's Medieval Classics (London: Oxford University Press, 1953); the definitive study of the Lotharingian reforms is Dom Kassius Hallinger's *Gorze-Cluny: Studien zu den monastischen Lebensformen und Gegensätzen im Hochmittelalter*, Studia Anselmiana 22, 24 (Rome: Herder, 1950, 1951). On the relevance of monastic history for the study of the Latin Easter drama, see Hallinger's 'Die Provenienz der Consuetudo Sigiberti: Ein Beitrag zur Osterfeierforschung', in *Mediaevalia litteraria: Festschrift für Helmut de Boor zum 80. Geburtstag*, ed. Ursula Hennig and Herbert Kolb (Munich: C. H. Beck, 1971), 155–76.

10 For a cautious, but generally more positive, assessment of Drumbl's work than the one offered here, see Anselme Davril, 'Johann Drumbl and the Origin of the *Quem quaeritis*' (1986 [*55*]).

11 'Voice Structure in the Liturgical Drama: Sepet Reconsidered' (1972 [*35*]); 'Popular Devotion in the Vernacular Drama of Medieval England', *Mediaevalia et Humanistica* n.s. 4 (1973): 65–8; 'French Medievalists and the Saints Play: A Problem for American Scholarship' (1975 [*51*]); 'The Saint's Play as Mimesis: Gallican Liturgy and Mediterranean Culture', in *102* (1984), 13–27.

12 Leonard Goldstein, 'The Origin of Medieval Drama', *Zeitschrift für Anglistik und Amerikanistik* 29 (1981): 101–15.

13 For a cogent statement of this problem, see the review of Lipphardt's book by Hansjürgen Linke (1983 [*45*]).

14 Thomas P. Campbell, 'The Liturgical Shepherds Play and the Origin of Christmas Drama', *Mosaic* 12 (1979): 21–32, and 'Why Do the Shepherds Prophesy?', *Comparative Drama* 12 (1978): 137–50.

15 In Hans Robert Jauss, *Toward an Aesthetic of Reception*, trans. Timothy Bahti, Theory and History of Literature 2 (Minneapolis: University of Minnesota Press, 1982), 3–45.

16 *Comparative Drama* 11 (1977): 191–208.

17 Michael Rudick, 'Theme, Structure, and Sacred Context in the Benediktbeuern "Passion" Play', *Speculum* 49 (1974): 267–86.

18 Richard Blank, *Sprache und Dramaturgie. Die Aischyleische Kassandraszene, das Osterspiel von Klosterneuburg, Machiavellis 'Mandragola'*, Humanistische Bibliothek, Series 1, Abhandlungen (Munich: Wilhelm Fink, 1969), 69–129.

3

Liturgical drama: falling between the disciplines

ANDREW HUGHES

Of the several issues that inspired the production of this volume, it was easiest to address the question that asked what was lacking in the available material dealing with medieval – in this case liturgical – drama, and it was correspondingly easy to identify what was needed to advance our knowledge. In a few words, what is needed is the production of comprehensive reference tools enabling the user to find information conveniently, and the consolidation, sifting and assessment of the work done within the last century.

The bibliography on the topic is huge. One might ask, in fact, how students could be given a reasonable reading list, even in a seminar devoted specifically to drama. To absorb in detail even the basic literature that is taken for granted – the works of Young, Chambers, Coussemaker, de Boor, Hardison, Corbin, Lipphardt, Smoldon and others who are cited in every other footnote of more recent work – would be itself a Herculean task. My bibliographical search for this article was from about 1976 to the present: Clifford Flanigan's articles of 1975 and 1976, listed in the bibliography (*36*), deal with the field up to 1975. One of the most urgent undertakings, then, is to provide a comprehensive reference tool: an annotated bibliography, supplemented by a convenient and usable list of the 600-odd surviving dramas with information about sources and editions, and whether or not the chant is included.

Another need just as urgent is to provide for the non-expert, whether student or experienced scholar, a basic introduction and survey, readable and shorn of the medievalist's obsession with manuscripts, Latin terms, multi-syllabic German words, liturgical jargon and footnotes. For example, in the English literature of the past half-century rarely is there an explanation of the difference between the Type I and Type II drama, a difference made clear in Tables 1 and 2 below. This introduction, like the reference tool, however, must be produced by someone expert in a great number of fields that are themselves vast in size and vastly complex. The most recent publication that promised to address most of the required issues, by William Smoldon, is, unfortunately, still not adequate; I shall discuss it in detail later.

In order to deal with liturgical drama of the Middle Ages, expertise is required not only in the literature and liturgy and drama of the period, but also in the music that is an essential part of the text; in the art and manuscript studies that support the work in those areas; in such matters as the oral and written transmission by which the texts and chants were passed from source to source; and in the practical considerations that arise when a drama is actually mounted, and that may in the Middle Ages have affected the text in use and thus its position in the transmission. Knowing that expertise in so many esoteric disciplines will be hard to find in a single person, few will be surprised at the lack of appropriate texts and tools.

Few will be surprised either to learn that there are serious deficiencies in the tools that do exist. In earlier decades, musicologists often ignored the need to work with non-musical evidence, neglecting literary and liturgical matters. Conversely, the literary scholar often ignored liturgical and almost always ignored musical evidence. I see no signs that the improvement in recent musicological work has been matched by a corresponding change in other disciplines. We now know from the work of such scholars as Leo Treitler, Richard Crocker and John Stevens that the full import of medieval texts that are sung cannot be known without observing whether the musical notes or notation confirm, deny, clarify or modify literary judgements. The failure of scholars in other fields to take musical evidence into account has resulted in some seriously flawed conclusions, some of which I shall discuss. The effects of ignoring the music, which is required for performance, are perhaps more noticeable in drama than in other literary fields because to achieve its full impact drama must be performed. To the need for reference tools and an introduction, then, I would add the urgent need to persuade scholars that learning to cope adequately, if not expertly, with medieval music is as essential as, and no more difficult than, learning to cope with medieval codicology or rhetoric or philosophy, or whatever discipline one has to master in order to treat every aspect of the subject. In this task, it is for the musicologists to provide the necessary tools for learning: I would concede that this task they have not fulfilled.

Like most scholars of the drama, I am not equally expert in all the required fields. What I bring to this topic, then, bears not on the details, but on the broad aspects of liturgy, music and manuscripts, and how they have been dealt with. My own research over the past decades has concentrated on precisely these three areas. It is clear that liturgical drama is merely one other facet of that research into literary and musical composition for the late-medieval liturgy.

The nearly monolithic liturgy of recent centuries, standardised by printing and the Council of Trent, has left a false impression of medieval circumstances. Although rubrics may vary from church to church, the standard texts of the services, especially on the oldest and holiest of days, were more or less and always have been immutable. But the Council of Trent eliminated nearly everything but these texts. Items of late-medieval origin, new offices, tropes, sequences, suffragia – devotions that typically consist of a processional chant, a hymn and a prayer – and many other similar semi-liturgical accretions existed in quantities so vast as to threaten to overwhelm the basic liturgy. They and their chants, and the organisation of the books in which they are found, are characterised by endless variety, in small and large detail. The liturgical drama is just such a text. The variability of its texts and rubrics, and the methods by which they were transmitted, have been important issues in liturgical drama, bearing significantly on the view of the drama as an oral or written phenomenon. Until recent decades, when sequences and tropes were comprehensively edited and made the object of concentrated study, only the liturgical drama had been investigated with any thoroughness. Even now, late-medieval offices, the largest repertory of all, remain virtually unknown. It is easy to understand, then, why research into medieval drama has often failed to take the liturgical and musical context adequately into account. For drama, as used to be the case for music, this failure may result in scholarship based on inadequate foundations. Some reservations outlined here must eventually be addressed in detail elsewhere.

Liturgical dramas, which shall be my chief concern, are transmitted in liturgical manuscripts. Frequently, the dates of these manuscripts cannot be or have not yet been established certainly within a span of a century, and occasionally within as much as 200 years. What does 'tenth–eleventh century' mean? In the absence of distinctive illumination, the handwriting and notation are not reliable guides for these sources, which preserve traditional styles long beyond their disappearance in other kinds of manuscript. It is my opinion that the assignation of a place and an ecclesiastical Use for most liturgical manuscripts has not been sufficiently established. The trouble lies in a grossly inadequate perception of the word 'origin' or 'provenance' for liturgical books. Three things, confused even by liturgists and cataloguers, must be isolated: the place where the physical book, its notation and its script originate, that is to say, (i) the scriptorium, or where the book is 'from'; it is not necessarily the same as (ii) the place whose Use the book follows, whose Use the book is 'of'; nor is it necessarily the same as (iii) the destination, the individual church or owner the book is 'for'. In addition, the location where the manuscript now is must be distinguished from these three designations: what the French *de* or German *aus* or *von* mean in this context often cannot be determined. 'Provenance', technically referring to the place of origin, is normally used to mean the destination, although some scholars reserve it for the general history of a manuscript from its origin to the present day. When scholars refer to a liturgical play by its origin or provenance, they mean its destination, assuming that the play is for the same place the book is for. Sometimes, the destination is determined by where the book is from, using script, illumination or notation. But St-Gall notation, for example, tells us only that the book was written in a scriptorium where that style was normal, or by a scribe working elsewhere but trained in that notation, and writing for one of the many places where it was familiar. It does not *necessarily* indicate that St Gall was the place where the book was used, although that *may* be a reasonable inference. Nor does it give us accurate information about date, since the notation was used for some five centuries, as the information given for St Gall MSS 381 and 384 reveal (*43*, VI, p. 420). Sometimes the destination is determined by the Use the book follows. But, for example, the rites of Paris were followed at Quimper, some 300 miles distant; the Use of the Sainte-Chapelle in Paris was ordered for the collegiate chapel in Bari in the fourteenth century (*43*, VI, p. 220). And surely we do not believe that the Sarum Ordinal was *necessarily* intended for use only at Salisbury: it is equally relevant, at least in its broad principles, to many other institutions that follow the Use of Salisbury. Often the destination is determined by considering the feasts within the book. But we lack comprehensive lists of places where saints were venerated. One cannot seriously doubt that the play assigned to Paris in the Noted Breviary, British Library Add. 37399, is for Paris, but it is not certainly established. The book has *Incipit ordinarius … secundum … Paris* and *secundum usum Paris*, telling us only that the Use of Paris was followed. The feasts of Saints Genoveva and Denis suggest Paris. But Denis is almost universally celebrated. St Genoveva seems a secure bet: but apart from being celebrated at several churches within Paris itself (Ste-Geneviève and St-Victor and elsewhere) her feast is found at least in books for Quimper, ?Autun, ?Auxerre/Bourges, ?Meaux and Bavaria/Austria (?Metten), and in the Breviary for Philippe le Bon. Without additional information, such as the style of the initial letter opening the feast or the presence of other feasts to the same saint – the translation of the saint's relics, for example – one cannot be sure. Mostly we simply do not have sufficient information about these matters to make inferences safely. One has only to think of the recent change in assignation of the *Carmina Burana* (and presumably the plays it includes) from Benediktbeuern to Seckau, and more recently still to South Tirol, still not acknowledged in some literature on drama; no responsible scholar would nowadays assign the famous set of Aquitanian manuscripts to the abbey of St-Martial in Limoges, which seems to have been partly a repository created by an acquisitive librarian. Similarly, any attempt to localise the Fleury Playbook is premature: in the case of that famous manuscript the only reason for claiming its use at Fleury is that it was once there (a quite strong indicator), to offset which one might state that its musical notation is not that of other Fleury manuscripts of later periods. For reasons already stated, the presence of Saints Nicholas and Lomer in the book is of little help.

Lists of dramas with their destinations appear in Lipphardt (*82*) and Hardison (*46*). These and the discussions in de Boor (*47*) are explicitly based, with uncritical acceptance, on Young's seminal publication of 1933 (*31*). Young must often have relied on nineteenth-century catalogues; Leroquais' monumental cataloguing work with French liturgical books was still largely in press, and is limited to France.[1] None of these lists can be used easily by the scholar not familiar with the field, in any case, because they often omit the library and shelf-mark, so that the alleged destination *de facto* becomes the future reference. Although Smoldon's list (1980 [*93*]) does give shelf-marks, it includes only sources with music, accepts the dates and places of the

45

other scholars and is so full of inaccuracies as to be unusable. The descriptions of manuscripts in the *Corpus Troporum* series, and in standard and supposedly authoritative works such as *Corpus Antiphonalium Officii* and *Le Graduel Romain* are inadequate.[2] David Bjork comments: 'the actual origin [destination?] of many of these sources is unknown, and ... the attributions and dates given here and in the [secondary] sources cited are often only inferences or estimates' (*92*, p. 8). But in 1981, twenty-one years after the publication of his earlier lists, Lipphardt published the sixth volume of his monumental set of editions (*43*). It includes some 300 pages describing the manuscripts, in which the place of origin and place of destination are distinguished, when necessary. Lipphardt assigns many sources to a destination with reasonable certainty, on good evidence from the manuscript, which he often cites. Unfortunately, to use Lipphardt's catalogue to find the source of the plays, one must have all six volumes to hand.

When one considers the exact location and date of a drama, then, a second thought about the evidence for those identifications would seem to be wise. Obviously, too, the results of any attempt to group dramas that relies on only these two criteria would require a second thought. When the evidence supplied by the chants for localising, dating or comparing dramas is ignored, the results become suspect. Consider this text:

> Pastor cesus in gregis medio
> pacem emit cruoris precio
> letus dolor in tristi gaudio ...

Many sources give 'precio / o letus dolor'. The extra *o* in the third line is clearly an error, since it damages the metre. It can easily be explained. So too can the vocative *o* in

> Quem queritis in sepulcro, o christicole.

Smoldon is the sole scholar to have come near to the explanation, with a practical, mundane solution, but seems not to have understood what occurs in these situations, and continued to include the superfluous vowel. He says:

> the 'o' sound was there from the start – in performance. When it came to writing down something that was a matter of memory it sometimes got lost, [because] it formed ... a continuous sound from ... 'sepul-*chro*'.
>
> (*85*, p. 143; compare *93*, pp. 80–1)

This is almost the reverse of the facts. In the *Pastor* text cited above, the end of 'precio' is extended with musical notes, a frequent occurrence at the ends of phrases. Under such notes, especially if they were on a new line, the scribes were likely not to lose something but to repeat the vowel (sometimes many times) as a convenience for the singer:

> precio o o o

Here the extension is rather short so that only a single repetition of the 'o' was necessary. In this situation a musically literate scribe preparing a manuscript with the chant might introduce the 'o', even if it were not in his exemplar. Such an addition is not an error. But it certainly confuses the comparison. Deprived of its music, the repeated vowel cannot be explained. A later scribe not literate in music and preparing a manuscript without chant might copy the unnecessary second 'o' as a vocative particle. This addition is an error. A manuscript with the extra vowel could have been copied from a source identified as a member of a group defined precisely by the *lack* of the extra vowel: in this case, the manuscript with the extra vowel would belong to the group defined by the lack of the vowel. The reverse situation could also occur. The separation of sources into groups on the basis of the presence or absence of the vowel therefore immediately falls. Some weeks ago, I was only vaguely aware of this allegedly significant variant in the *Quem queritis* nucleus, and was astonished to find that it has formed the basis for extravagant theories about various respectful forms of address (rightly scorned by Smoldon), and the basis for separating traditions of the drama. Certainly it is legitimate, with *Quem queritis* as with *Pastor*, to separate sources in this way, but only if the additional musical information and the possibility of a musically literate scribe is taken into account with every example. To make later discussions clearer, Table 1 shows the two earliest versions of the Type 1 *Visitatio*.

TABLE I.

(a) Type 1 *Visitatio*, 3-line dialogue (the St Gall MS 484 seems to be the earliest source).

- Quem queritis in sepulcro, christicole?
- Jesum Nazarenum crucifixum, o celicole.
- Non est hic, surrexit sicut predixerat: ite nunciate quia surrexit de sepulcro.

(b) Type 1 *Visitatio*, 5-line dialogue (the fourth and fifth lines vary) (the Aquitanian MS, Paris BN lat. 1240, seems to be the earliest source).

- Quem queritis in sepulcro, o christicole?
- Jesum Nazarenum crucifixum, o celicole.
- Non est hic, surrexit sicut ipse dixit: ite nunciate quia surrexit.
- Alleluia, resurrexit dominus hodie: resurrexit leo fortis Christus filius Dei.
- Deo gratias dicite eia.

I am quite certain that the sentence without the vocative 'o' was the original, in which case the Aquitanian source would already be a copy. In this case, then, a knowledge of music and how liturgical scribes transmit musical texts came together, quite by chance, with a knowledge of the liturgy sufficiently wide to know how these circumstances work.

In sources that have the vowel, we must now decide how the music provided for it can be accommodated; such an exercise might call for the first phrase to cadence in a different place, musically and textually. As has been pointed out by David Hughes (*88*, p. 280, n. 12), even a slight knowledge of music would force a similar adjustment of these lines, which are misleadingly laid out in Young, even though his punctuation seems correct (*31*, I, p. 443):

Qui condonasti	Magdalene gravia
Peccamina;	per te vita perfruar perpetua

Lipphardt, the musicologist, lays them out differently, but also errs in breaking the line after 'gravia': presumably, on page 1676 of Volume v of his editions (*43*), in which the music could not be included, he forgot to consult the notation:

Figure 1. Part of Mary Magdalene's lament (see David G. Hughes, 'The First Magdalene Lament of the Tours Easter Play' [*88*]).

It is a small point. So are many points that scholars have used to categorise the repertory. Consider the much more commonly occurring line:

Alleluia resurrexit Dominus hodie resurrexit leo fortis...

To my knowledge, every scholar except Susan Rankin places punctuation or a new line after 'Dominus'. This division is undoubtedly correct in some cases, because a rubric or an initial letter determines the issue. Often, however, there is no indication one way or the other, except in the chant, where the motive that sets 'hodie' corresponds to a late-medieval chant cadence:

Figure 2. *Quem queritis*, line 4, from the Winchester Troper (Oxford, Bodleian Library MS 775) (see Susan Rankin, 'Musical and Ritual Aspects of *Quem quaeritis*' [*99*]).

If minute distinctions are used to identify groupings of texts, these musical details are matters unsuspected by the textual scholars. Sometimes the observation of the size of letter in the original manuscript can help the determination of such details. The arrangement of initial and capital letters on the page normally signifies something about the hierarchy of the items within the day, within the service and as subsections of other items. Judging by my recollection of dramas, in Tropers – books that contain texts extending the strictly liturgical items – the beginning of the *Visitatio* is signalled by a large letter, but in other Office books by nothing special, so that it continues as a normal item of Matins, on the level of one of the responsories, for example. This kind of evidence may tell us something about how independently the drama was regarded in certain books, perhaps about its status as a trope or an independent ceremony, and about its gradual emancipation from the liturgical context.

Perhaps also concerned about the uncritical acceptance of place and date, Helmut de Boor in his *Die Textgeschichte der lateinischen Osterfeiern* of 1967 (47) tries to eliminate the prior evidence of place in order to reassert it as a conclusion of his analyses in the form of regions, dioceses, individual churches or monasteries with which the dramas can be associated. He seems constantly aware of the uncertainty, or at least changeability, of assignations (see, for example, his conjecture concerning Reims, Paris and Chalons, pp. 105–6): commenting on this book, Planchart cites some regional characteristics that seem to be inaccurate (90, I, p. 238, n. I). Since de Boor's work seems set fair to be the basis of much future scholarship, it must be discussed in some detail. De Boor distinguishes the dramas from the liturgy, which he thought was uniform, claiming that because they are literary and variable one can construct from them a textual history (47, p. 10). But he rejects rubrics as being too variable and too specifically concerned with particular places. Later, however, de Boor seems to stress the *stability* of dramas as literary rather than oral texts that are consciously uniform constructions because they originate in scripture and dogma (pp. 16–17). All of this seems a rather muddled set of premises on which to build a history of the texts by new methods. De Boor is undoubtedly right to set aside conventional methods of textual analysis as not suitable (pp. 1 and 14). He cites Creizenach, Chambers and Young on the matter (p. 15). Creizenach's comments are particularly pertinent:

it would be a vain endeavour to set up a stemma of dependencies and relationships ...
and certainly would require proof for all the different and widely distributed places
and times of origin. (my translation, from de Boor)

But the inadequacy of dating and localising is not the most important reason that conventional textual analysis fails. Here we return to the premises that de Boor was surely seeking: the distinction is not between literary drama and fixed liturgy, but between fixed literature and text written for live performance. Both liturgy and liturgical drama fall into the latter category. Musicologists, some of whom are knowledgeable about, even if not intimately concerned with, live performance, have come to recognise that it is the fact of performance that makes conventional analysis impossible. At least one writer on drama has skirted the topic.[3]

Andrew Hughes

Some special features that make problematic the application of textual criticism to music have obscured the real difficulty. Textual criticism was devised for the study of texts that medieval scribes were concerned to copy as accurately as possible, because they were important for the preservation of the culture. Such texts are monuments, and do not change except by errors of transmission. Musical or dramatic texts, on the other hand, were for practical use, for performance. The conditions by which they are transmitted, and what happens to the text once it has been copied, are quite different from that of the poetry of Ovid, or the *Consolation of Philosophy*. In musical manuscripts it is certain, for example, that the scribes sometimes exercised a good deal of discretion in what they copied and how, and that later users sometimes made additions and real changes as well as corrections, as a result of the practical needs of performance. To cite another much-debated detail, in

> Quem queritis in sepulcro, christicole?
> Jesum Nazarenum crucifixum, o celicole ...

the substitution of the singular 'celicola' for the plural is used to distinguish textual traditions. This change may be no more than the initiative of a scribe who knows the limitations of his local performing group. Changes of this kind, which cannot be predicted, and which sometimes can hardly be described systematically, render conventional textual criticism impotent. So de Boor rightly rejects conventional analysis as resulting in 'an inextricable tangle', and claims the tangle comes immediately loose when the pursuit is to isolate regional groupings rather than detailed stemmas, a gross rather than minute distinction, allowing the scholar to avoid the problems of place and date (47, p. 19). This is splendid. Unfortunately, the analysis itself comes loose immediately since de Boor relies heavily on the presence or absence of the vocative 'o' as one of his criteria for grouping, without considering the musical context. Planchart points to different mixtures of the two groupings (90, 1, p. 238). In fact de Boor says, almost in the same breath, 'text and music form an inseparable unity' and 'I shall deal only with the words.'[4] How can a serious scholar make such a statement? Despite his refusal to pursue a detailed stemma, de Boor attempts 'to realise an organised text history' from 'minute analysis of text structure' (47, p. 20). But this attempt fails, too, as soon as we read that no manuscripts will be consulted, and that the analysis will be based on editions by Lange (1887), N. C. Brooks (1908/9) and Young (1933 [*31*]). It is inconceivable that any analysis of texts in their smallest detail, 'minimalen Einzelheiten' (47, p. 19), can be done adequately without minute examination of the original manuscripts.

De Boor's premises seem muddled; his misconception of the context casts doubt on his methods; he ignored the scribal evidence of the manuscripts; he relied on editions lacking adequate apparatus recording variants. His work should perhaps now be reconsidered, especially taking into account Walther Lipphardt's recent, more scholarly editions.

Although in de Boor's work there is in fact little evidence of the minute analysis that could confirm it, he is surely correct in accepting written transmission as the normal practice, and rejecting oral transmission (*47*, pp. 16–17). The transmission of late-medieval offices and of dramas seems similar in that some elements are used, some rejected and occasionally all are rejected (*96*, p. 229). But in the core of the drama, as de Boor shows, the texts are either drawn from or can be adapted easily from readily available liturgical texts (*47*, pp. 28ff.). Can we then ever really know whether transmission took the form of a real text, or merely the idea of the drama, its general shape and the scriptural source for its texts? Let us consider what used to be called the 'abbreviated form' of the drama, a form accepted by Hardison (*46*, p. 197), and rightly demolished on liturgical and musical grounds by Smoldon (*85*, p. 145). In this kind of witness, *incipits* give the source and general shape of the play, just as Ordinals do for the liturgy: completion of Ordinal *incipits* is governed by the presence of canonical texts in other books; completion of the drama, however, is governed only by the general process of adapting the scriptural source. If this process were really at work, it would damage the concept of 'a text'. Furthermore, any process of adaptation brings the possibility of scribal initiative that makes any kind of textual analysis very risky. It is possible, it seems to me, to make a case not for oral transmission but for a kind of extemporised realisation, and we may be reminded of many modern scores that give hints in the form of musical notes (textual *incipits*) as to what the performers are to do, perhaps with a set of verbal instructions (rubrics). Very few of the *incipit*-witnesses also have the musical *incipits*: I found four in Lipphardt (*43*). Alejandro Planchart says:

To my knowledge, the only one of the kernel verses [of the drama] that is given in an abbreviated form in any of the actual chant books is the second ... which does appear in a shortened form in [two manuscripts]. (*90*, I, p. 237, n. 3)

We have at last come to understand liturgical drama as music-drama. But if its chants were new compositions that could not be sought in readily available books, they must have been transmitted in full. In incipit dramas, the *incipits* make complete sense textually, and nonsense musically. If they are valid, then, they imply either a quite different musical setting, which the evidence of those that do have music belies, or spoken performance. It is difficult to imagine that there could ever have been spoken performance. Given the failure of many scholars to note in reference books and manuscript catalogues whether music is present or not, it is difficult to pursue this point.

Let us pass now to the state of research into the musical aspects of liturgical drama, and especially to studies that concern concepts of text, transmission and the identification of place. One cannot ignore William Smoldon's comprehensive survey, *The Music of the Medieval Church Dramas*, published posthumously and after many years of delay in 1980 (*93*). Smoldon was capable of extraordinary insights. His knowledge of medieval music, liturgy and chant would have been unsurpassed in his day. But he was

Andrew Hughes

not able to benefit from the liturgical and palaeographical knowledge that has accumulated recently. Despite the reviews of several musicologists cited in the bibliography (94), I shall, sadly, endorse my own review and these comments from Alejandro Planchart's review: the book is 'dangerously misleading' and 'a scandal'. Unfortunately, at least one recent important publication implies that later work should 'build upon' Smoldon's foundation (*The Fleury Playbook* [39], Introduction, p. xix). But Smoldon's one enduring and essential lesson seems *not* to have been learnt: any study of the drama that sets the music aside is scholarship that ignores half the evidence. He would have agreed in adding that, with few exceptions, to ignore the music in a study of any text that has a musical setting will result in half-complete scholarship.

My attempt systematically to assemble a bibliography of significant research into the music of medieval drama in the past ten years resulted in very little return: important contributions emerged through references in other work. In 1984, Robin Wallace suggested that the role of music has recently been overemphasised (98). But what the music does not contribute to the drama as a drama, or to emotional expression, or to characterisation, or to the declamation of the text, must be balanced by a recognition that plainsongs and melodies based on plainsong carry with them many layers of symbol and liturgical context that we cannot possibly now penetrate. In an article described by Flanigan as exemplary of the finest musicological writing, 'free of ... jargon, and expressed in a manner that students of literature can understand' (36, 1976, p. 122), John Stevens exposes the 'expressive fallacy' and confirms that chant 'brings to the drama from outside a wealth of association and meaning' (84, p. 30). A more interesting point raised by Robin Wallace is that even in the earliest, tenth-century, manuscripts of liturgical drama the pitches of the chant are more accurately represented than in other contemporary manuscripts where the notation is merely a reminder to one who already knows the melody. The use of such a notation implies that the chant was outside the standard plainsong repertory, could not be found in plainsong books and would thus need a fixity of transmission. In his review of Smoldon's *The Music of the Medieval Church Dramas*, Alejandro Planchart also refers to the stability of the melodic tradition of *Quem queritis* in its earliest stages (94, p. 121). A written transmission for the complete chant is implied. It is hardly possible that the chant was transmitted in written form without its text, and to assess how the stability of the melodic tradition relates to variability of the textual tradition we need an analysis of the kind that Michael L. Norton has done for the Type II *Visitatio* (see below). The Stage II drama, as it was called by Lange in 1887, is defined by the presence of the apostles' scene after the core sentences, whether or not other additions are present. De Boor, however, relies only on the different form the core sentences take, whether or not the apostles' scene is present. (See Table 2.)

Liturgical drama

TABLE 2. A Type II drama (one form).

- Quis revolvet nobis ab hostio lapidem quem tegere sanctum cernimus sepulcrum?

Core:
- Quem queritis, o tremule mulieres in hoc tumulo plorantes?
- Jesum Nazarenum crucifixum querimus.
- Non est hic quem queritis, sed cito euntes nunciate discipulis eius et Petro quia surrexit Jesus.
- Ad monumentum venimus gementes; angelum Domini sedentem vidimus, et dicentes quia surrexit Jesus.

Apostles' scene:
- Currebant duo simul et ille alius discipulis precucurrit cicius Petro et venit prior ad monumentum. Alleluia.
- Cernitis o socii ecce lintheamina, et sudarium et corpus non est inventum in sepulcro.

For a paper delivered at the annual meeting of the American Musicological Society in Vancouver (1985), Norton issued a 44-page handout: 'The Type II *Visitatio sepulchri*'. The outline just given is from page 3. The remainder of this paragraph summarises the handout. Norton first outlines the modal structure of the drama, placing each item into a category on the basis of various musical characteristics, then comprehensively lists detailed melodic variants, arranging them in related groups. He co-ordinates these two groupings (by modal characteristics, and by melodic variants) with the various arrangements of the texts, including only gross variants of words and word order, much as de Boor does. The lists are ordered by 'provenance' (destination?). They confirm that all sources of the same 'provenance' are related. The last table is ordered according to geographical subgroups, to show that they, too, are related, but the musical evidence shows that some sources are more closely related than the textual evidence alone reveals. Norton shows fairly convincingly that the dramas in Augustinian institutions reformed by Archbishop Conrad of Salzburg share characteristics not found elsewhere. Setting aside reservations about the identification of destination, we must accept this kind of complex research, co-ordinating textual and musical evidence, as necessary for some purposes.

Of the chants and texts of the Type II setting, only *Currebant duo simul* is liturgical: an antiphon. As far as we know, all the others are newly composed. Norton discovers some unique musical settings. To research text and chant in conjunction, then, we need to identify and distinguish Vulgate texts, liturgical texts and newly composed texts, and to correlate them with chants drawn from plainsong, newly composed and unique chants and chants newly composed but adapted from non-liturgical tunes traditional to the drama. Only for France and England has this kind of careful comparison been done, in a Cambridge dissertation by Susan Rankin (97). Believing that previous studies have quite neglected the reuse of old (what she calls traditional) material, Professor Rankin says:

For each ceremony it must be established what is *old material*, already extant at the time of composition ... and what is *new material*, newly composed for that particular ceremony ... it is not sufficient to know if ... the same words were used in another ceremony, or even if they were based on the Vulgate, for it must also be known whether those words had already been set as the text of a liturgical chant ... If the text can be shown to be that of a liturgical chant, rather than to have been drawn directly from the Vulgate, and the liturgical melody is not used, then reasons for the rejection of the melody must be sought.   (*97*, pp. 3–8; cf. *96*, pp. 230 and 231)

In an article on the Peregrinus plays, Clyde Brockett does not distinguish the liturgical sources from the Vulgate, and claims the plays are independent ceremonies because the items and their melodies derive from liturgical models (*91*). But Professor Rankin shows that a body of shared, traditional, melodies in these plays demonstrates their relationships (*97*, pp. 275–8).

An adequate catalogue of liturgical dramas would include (a) the scriptural source of the texts, (b) the actual texts, (c) the source of the music and (d) the actual music. And let there be no mistake: for the source of the music, the *Liber Usualis* will not suffice. Nor, in all likelihood, will any of the available published facsimiles. A local chant book must be found so that its contents and variants can be compared with the version of the play. Hence one can insist on the need to identify the destination of the play correctly and precisely. The determination of what is a significant variant and what is error demands that the scholar be saturated in liturgy and chant.

The difficulty in acquiring extensive knowledge of these two fields is one reason for the paucity of musical interest in the topic. Another is that there seems to be not much to say about the music, at least for the musician. As in that tiny but extraordinarily beautiful repertory of thirteenth-century songs with English texts,[5] one can do little except describe each piece individually, usually in the driest and most uninteresting of musical terms. One of those English songs, the 'Prisoner's Song', is related musically and textually to the *planctus ante nescia*, and although rather vaguely perhaps even to the Cividale *planctus Mariae*.[6] Musical research can trace relationships of this kind. With tunes of the drama that are plainsongs, one can outline the minute differences in detail from version to version; one can compare tunes that are newly composed with the plainsong repertory as a whole, or with other liturgical repertories, given an adequate knowledge of those other repertories. In fact, Susan Rankin, working from the drama, especially in Normandy, and I, working from new offices of the late Middle Ages, some of which originate from Normandy, independently came to the conclusion that the new melodic compositions of drama and office ought to be compared. But musicology still lacks a comprehensive method for describing melodies, let alone comparing them, and such activities at present contribute little to what we can see in the first few moments of assessment.

In the published version of her doctoral dissertation, Diane Dolan makes a thorough and interesting survey of the historical and cultural context of the institutions, mostly monastic, which the plays of England and France are said to have been for (*86*). As one might suspect, many visits, dependencies, transfers of abbots and abbesses and the like can be documented. But very few contribute directly to a knowledge of how the ceremonies were transmitted. Dr Dolan's book does analyse the chants: she claims, for example, that a chant in the Dublin source derives from that of a source generally agreed to be associated with Rouen; despite the obvious differences at the beginning of the tune, Dr Dolan asserts the relationship because 'aucune autre rédaction anglo-normande du jeu de Pâques n'a la version de Rouen: *Ubi positus fuerat.*' (See Figure 3.)

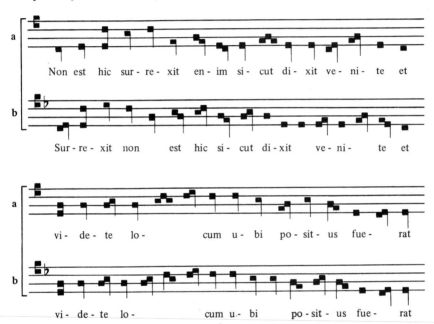

Figure 3. Paris BN MS lat. 904 (a) and Dublin, Archbishop Marsh MS Z.4.220 (b) (see Diane Dolan, *Le Drame liturgique de Pâques en Normandie et en Angleterre au moyen-âge* [*86*]).

As is evident even to one who does not read music, that particular phrase is certainly not musically identical. Nor is it by any means very distinctive: it is, in fact, merely a very common way of setting the final line of text in a tune in this mode. The whole tune, in fact, resembles quite closely many antiphons of newly composed offices of the late Middle Ages. The one in Figure 4 is very similar to tune (b) in Figure 3.

That the Dublin tune is said to derive from the Rouen tune, rather than the reverse, is based solely on the putative dates of the sources, the former cited merely as fourteenth-, the latter as thirteenth-century. The physical appearance of the script, notation and other features of these manuscripts allegedly from different centuries is so similar that, lacking other evidence, I would not

Andrew Hughes

Greg - or - i - us or - tus Rome/   e se - na - to - rum san-gui - ne/...

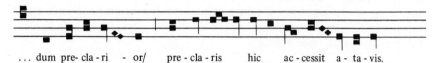

... dum pre- cla - ri - or/   pre - cla - ris   hic   ac - cessit a - ta - vis.

Figure 4. Matins antiphon 1: Office of St Gregory, composed in Alsace by Bruno, Bishop of Toul (Pope Leo IX), c. 1049 (Switzerland, Fribourg Kantonal Library MS L322).

pursue very far any theory based on the relative ages of these tunes. Nevertheless, the Dublin version seems later, on the basis of musical analysis. The change in textual order coincides with a change in the melody. Dealing with the origins of the core sentences and the low-lying melodies that precede 'Non est hic', Susan Rankin points to a reinforcement of the text caused by the rising fifth: the higher pitch asserts that 'something important is happening' (99, p. 191). What is important is that 'He is not here'. The modification in the Dublin source suggests another compositional sophistication. The association of the word 'surrexit' with the rising fifth is surely coincidental. Of more interest is its removal from pitches that are musically unstable and weak to assertive and stable pitches strongly centred on D and A, perhaps to strengthen 'He is risen' rather than 'He is not here'; the latter phrase is used in the Dublin version to round off this grammatical clause, set to a chant phrase that is in late-medieval style rather than like conventional plainsong, so that the meaning of the text is highlighted by deliberate change. In an article published in 1976 (88), David Hughes, in his usual direct and splendid way, deals with music, although only with a single item in a single play: speaking of 'a purposeful revision of a piece originally rather looser in structure', he shows, as I attempted to show with 'Non est hic', how a tune can be manipulated to strengthen subtle points of textual emphasis.

In an article of 1985 already cited (99), Professor Rankin convincingly uses musical analysis to show that the original core of the Easter drama probably consisted not of the three-line dialogue, but of the larger form involving five elements (see Table 1 above, p. 47). In a more recent article, without knowing of Rankin's work, Anselme Davril comes to the same conclusion from purely textual evidence (55). Rankin elegantly demonstrates that the musical shape of the five lines, within each phrase and, more importantly, in the overall structure, 'forms a coherent and balanced structure' (p. 191). Accepting these conclusions, I would tentatively put forward a somewhat new view of what the *Quem queritis* is. The following paragraph, then, is an excursus for which further supporting evidence must be sought. It

56

Liturgical drama

demonstrates once more, however, how musical and liturgical information can contribute essential clues.

Is the five-element core of the *Quem queritis*, quite simply, an imitation of a liturgical responsory? A typical medieval responsory and verse has this form, where the significant musical units are identified by capital letters, and the text by lower case (the marks ' and '' modifying letters indicate variants, and further variants):

R.	intonation sung by	solo	Aa
	continuation, by	chorus	Bb
V.	(normally two halves)	solo	Cc
			Dd
R.	repeated, by	chorus	Aa
			Bb

Sometimes (I do not know how early this practice can be traced) the musical phrase D is related to B, giving AB CB' AB. In Easter time, a brief *alleluia* (x) is often appended, thus: ABx CB' ABx. In the five-element drama (see Table 1 above, p. 47), the third and fourth lines consist of parallel half-lines, and the musical form as demonstrated in Susan Rankin's analysis is:

1, 2	AB
3a, b	CB'
4a, b	DB''
5	E

A and B are musically related: B, B' and B'' are similar in range, and melodically alike at one or two striking points. C and D share the distinctive high range differentiating them from the low-lying melodies of A and B, as described earlier. Let us now collate what we have with the *Quem queritis* text.

Responsory	Drama			Responsory	Drama
R.	A	A	*Quem queritis . . .*	solo	(Angel)
	B	B	*Jesum Nazarenum . . .*	chorus	(three Marys)
	x		*alleluia* omitted (because the cause for rejoicing has not yet been heard?)		
V.	C	C	*Non est hic . . .*	solo	(Angel)
	B'	B'	*ite nunciate . . .*		
R.	A	D	*Alleluia resurrexit . . .*	chorus	(three Marys)
	B	B''	*resurrexit leo . . .*		
	x	E	*Deo gratias . . .*		

Substituting D in the drama where A repeats in the responsory can be explained by the need to repeat the joy of 'Non est hic' at 'Alleluia', so that sentence D takes the high melody characteristic of C in the drama. Where the responsory text would repeat at AB, the drama text continues. These seem slight modifications, easily managed by a skilful arranger. The feature that drew my attention to the possibility that the tune was related to a responsory was the beginning of D, and to some extent C: the alternation of the pitches AGAG so prominent here must have been heard as the beginning of the responsory tone (that is, the conventional melody for responsory verses, to which C corresponds in this scheme; see Figures 5a and 5b, below). The tune combines modes 1 and 2 (sometimes called Dorian and Hypodorian), not unusual in the later Middle Ages. This combination can be explained by the need for a low pitch that forces 'Quem queritis' to rise in a musical question, whereas 'Non est hic' and 'Alleluia' require the higher pitch. Nearly all the individual musical phrases in the drama can be found in late-medieval responsories without much difficulty, including a resemblance between the 'Deo gratias' phrase and 'alleluia' terminations:

Figure 5a. Quem queritis dialogue, from the Winchester Troper (Oxford, Bodleian Library MS 775) (see Susan Rankin, 'Musical and Ritual Aspects of *Quem quaeritis*' [99]).

Liturgical drama

COMPARE PHRASE A

R. Iam   pu- e- ri - le   de -   cus

St Arigius: mode 2 responsory, phrase 1, Paris, BN MS lat. 908

COMPARE PHRASES C AND B RESPECTIVELY

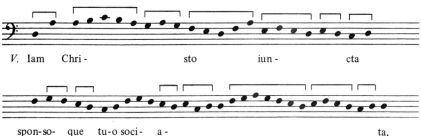

V. Iam   Chri -   sto   iun -   cta

spon-so- que tu-o soci- a -   ta.

St Catharine: verse of Matins responsory 9, mode 1, Switzerland, Fribourg,
Kantonal Library MS L322

COMPARE PHRASES D AND C

   etc.

Tone for verses of responsories in
mode 1

COMPARE PHRASE E

(i)   (ii)

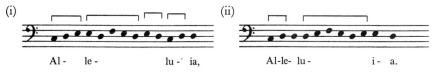

Al - le -   lu -´ ia,   Al-le- lu -   i- a.

(i) St Peter of Tarentaise: alleluia termination ending Matins responsory 6, Karls-
ruhe, Landesbibliothek MS Licht 15
(ii) Office of the three Marys: alleluia termination of Matins responsory 2, Mainz
Diösesanbibliothek Kodex E, cited in James Boyce, Cantica Carmelitana: The
Chants of the Carmelite Office (unpublished New York University Ph.D. thesis,
1984), vol. II, p. 274).

Figure 5b. Phrases of responsories of late-medieval offices.

The possible significance of this resemblance to a Matins responsory for the origin of this form of the drama hardly needs emphasis. Before leaving this excursus, which requires more extensive treatment, I must acknowledge Smoldon (*93*, p. 89):

the first and most obvious fact is that the dialogue is a repetition in dramatic form of the scene portrayed by the [preceding] responsory [*Dum transisset*].

In a most stimulating article concerned with the origins of the core sentences, Type I, David Bjork compares the wide dissemination of Roman liturgical material with the very local distribution of Frankish compositions such as tropes, and points to the universal manifestation of the *Quem queritis* in the Frankish realm. He concludes:

One thing a study of the dissemination of Frankish chant can tell us is that *Quem queritis* was not written at St Gall or at St Martial or in northern Italy, for what characterizes the pieces written there is that they seldom circulated outside their own regions ... The prevailing routes of transmission led from the North of France to the South; from the Rhineland into Germany and Switzerland; across the North of Europe; into England from the North of France; into Spain from the South of France; and into Italy from the nearest quarter ...
    Chant scholars are slowly reaching a consensus that neither St Martial nor St Gall ... warrant their reputation as the preeminent musical centres of Frankish civilization ...   (*92*, pp. 14–15)

An important contribution, published in 1976, is Timothy McGee's assignation of the Type I *Quem queritis* dialogue to the Collecta ceremonies before Easter Mass, another piece of evidence freeing the sentences from their single status as a trope: this, too, is not an examination of the music but of the ritual and liturgical context. Professor McGee concludes that the dialogue probably originated in the Carolingian world of Aachen and Metz (*89*).

    Concluding her dissertation (*97*, pp. 293–9), Susan Rankin outlines the history of the drama thus: in the tenth and eleventh centuries the essential core sentences, whether of three or five lines, were cultivated, and the chants of this nucleus were newly composed. One might now suggest 'adapted'. This is Type I (following older practice, she calls it Stage I). Some ceremonies, mostly from Germanic repertories, have the apostles' scene, which uses a liturgical antiphon. This is Type II. From the late eleventh and into the twelfth century, French and English repertories mostly add an opening or internal lament or *planctus*, and the Mary Magdalene scene in general. This is Type III. In her article discussing the Mary Magdalene scenes in detail (*96*), Rankin carefully distinguishes between items drawn from the liturgy, traditional versions that appear in several or numerous dramas but not in the liturgy and newly composed pieces, showing that new composition was preferred and, indeed, that chant melodies, if they were available, were rejected. New composition made it possible to realise modal and stylistic unity with the surrounding items. In fact, because its set of texts and melodies was transmitted *en bloc* the Mary Magdalene scene may have been composed by one person at one time (*96*, p. 250). Concurring with de

Boor's analysis of the texts, she suggests that this group of melodies was composed in Normandy in the late eleventh century. Eleventh-century Normandy was also the home of a school of liturgical composers, a few known by name, who were responsible for some nineteen new offices, two of which became a standard part of the Romano-French liturgy. This situation 'seriously calls into question the claims of St Martial and Fleury to preeminence in the composition of liturgical dramas in France' (97, pp. 298–9).

For the original ninth/tenth-century ceremony, McGee suggests the Carolingian courts, and Bjork emphasises the importance of the north. For the origin of the eleventh-century Type III ceremony, Susan Rankin stresses Normandy. My own experience with the parallel repertory of ninth/tenth-century offices leads me to the region of Metz and the Rhineland, where we have evidence (including a few named composers) for lively cultivation of composition and music theory; for eleventh-century offices, the evidence points to Normandy. Where are St Gall and St Martial? At the outset, I had no idea that the issue of geography would constantly return. Reservations about the assignation of place for the manuscripts therefore become more urgent, although I advocate only more caution.

It is extremely difficult to work in detail with this repertory, since the sources are so numerous and so scattered. And there is no avoiding the issue that one must work with the originals, or facsimiles of them: almost no published editions are adequate for research. As for editions that do not include the music, Clifford Flanigan generously says 'we must be grateful for what we have' (36, 1975, p. 83). Sometimes, as apparently was the case for the musicologist Walther Lipphardt, the omission of the music can be attributed to the publisher. His series of six volumes editing all the plays known to him is now complete, with an extensive catalogue of the manuscript sources, and comprehensive but not annotated bibliography: textual corrections and a commentary are to appear soon in a three-volume appendix. Scholarly transcriptions with the chants of all French and English plays may be found in Rankin's Cambridge dissertation (97).

In considering such minute details of scholarship, one must keep in mind the relative value of discussing how many angels – 'celicole' or 'celicola' – can stand at the end of a line. When directing actual performances, I am extremely conscious that scholarship is *never* complete until the result has been seen in practice: on the boards, necessity always reveals something about the texts or chants that could never be imagined in the abstraction of a study. Issues of performance of drama have hardly reached the musicological community other than through the books of Smoldon and Collins (93 and 34). The latter, Fletcher Collins' publication of a number of Latin plays with the music, is not so much an edition as an interpretation designed for performance, quite legitimate and bound to be extremely useful, but tending to reinforce the view that there is a single correct way, especially a correct rhythmic way, to perform medieval drama, an attitude we in music have been fighting for years to eradicate with respect to medieval music in general. Cynthia Bourgeault, of course, is quite correct when she says that 'there are

Andrew Hughes

any number of items ... whose metrical patterns are so pronounced and regular that even when left [unmeasured] they tend to fall into rhythm',[7] but there are also thousands of metrical texts from the period for which rhythmic performance of their chant would be difficult to sustain. Opinions on this and most matters of musical performance remain merely opinions. Hence the desperate need for editions, with the chants transcribed in a neutral manner, or, even better, facsimiles of the original sources.

In this rather critical assessment of the state of the research, I question a quite large body of scholarship. I should end, then, by reiterating that I have researched only a few accessible details: a general experience in related areas causes me to be somewhat alarmed at what has been done, and the future prospects for improvement. Up to the present, it seems to me that research into liturgical drama, falling between so many disciplines as it does, has suffered from incomplete assessment of all the evidence. It is impossible for one person to be expert enough in all fields. The value of interdisciplinary conferences and publications such as this one can therefore hardly be stressed sufficiently.

But incorrect details of localisation, dating, transmission and the like can be submerged in the overall sweep of the evidence. Some fields of research endeavour are so large that preliminary, tentative and partial results must be accepted: after a century of drama research the overall picture is no doubt reliable.

NOTES

1 Victor Leroquais, *Les Sacramentaires et les Missels manuscrits des bibliothèques publiques de France*, 4 vols. (Paris, 1924); *Les Bréviaires manuscrits des bibliothèques publiques de France*, 6 vols. (Paris: Protat Frères, 1934); *Les Psautiers manuscrits latins des bibliothèques publiques de France*, 3 vols. (Mâcon: Protat Frères, 1940–1).

2 *Corpus Troporum:* a series of editions of tropes published in the series 'Acta Universitatis Stockholmiensis: Studia Latina Stockholmiensia' (Stockholm), general editor, Ritva Jonsson; René-Jean Hesbert, ed., *Corpus Antiphonalium Officii*, I: *Manuscripti 'Cursus Romanus'*, II: *Manuscripti 'Cursus Monasticus'*, III: *Invitatoria et Antiphonae*, IV: *Responsoria, Versus, Hymni et Varia*, V: *Fontes earumque Prima Ordinatio*, Rerum Ecclesiasticarum Documenta, ser. major, Fontes 7–11 (Rome: Herder, 1963, 1965, 1968, 1970, 1975); *Le Graduel Romain* II: *Les Sources*, ed. by the monks of Solesmes (Solesmes: Centre National de la Recherche Scientifique, 1957).

3 Stephen Orgel, 'What is a Text?', *RORD* 24 (1981): 3–6.

4 P. 2: 'Mein Buch isoliert die Texte der Osterfeiern und beschäftigt sich nur mit dem Wort ... [obwohl] Text und Musik eine untrennbare Einheit bilden.'

5 E. J. Dobson & F. Ll. Harrison, eds., *Medieval English Songs* (Cambridge and New York: Cambridge University Press, 1979).

6 Cividale, Museo Archeologico Nazionale, MS CI, fols. 74–76ᵛ: text in *31*, vol. I, pp. 506–13.

7 'Liturgical Dramaturgy and Modern Production', in *39* (pp. 144–60), p. 157.

PART II

English drama

4

Modern editions of medieval English plays
DAVID MILLS

Editions of medieval plays take many forms – 'definitive' editions for scholars, anthologies and teaching texts for students and general readers, facsimiles, modernised versions, performance-texts, abridgements and so on. Each has its own functional value and scholarly worth. But all in some measure manifest the great power that an editor wields to determine the text that is read, to direct the response of the reader or performer, to set the focus and course of criticism and even to influence our idea of what 'medieval drama' means. Student readers in particular may not always recognise the ways in which the editor's selective principles of 'typicality', or 'literary excellence', or 'evolutionary progression', or 'structural coherence', stated or undeclared, can shape an anthology or edition. Assumptions about the nature of drama, the mode of production, the kind of theatre for which the text was 'intended' and the supposed expectations of a medieval or modern audience often direct practices of emendation or other forms of editorial intrusion. A publisher, too, may unobtrusively control the shape of an edition by imposing upon it commercial considerations of cost, length, format and readership.

Additionally, living within a book culture, the modern reader may forget that dramatic activities uncontained by text were the medieval norm, and that such activities provided a complex frame of reference for the appreciation of minority, text-centred drama. By isolating a written text for discussion, we are often privileging an 'authorised and official' form of drama over the less closely regulated 'popular' dramatic activities. Indeed, from one viewpoint the medieval play text can be regarded as a vehicle for the containment and thematic direction of potentially anarchic dramatic activities. Little attention has been given to this 'political' aspect of the play text – the extent to which it is descriptive, in loosely setting limits to the action and in offering some explanation of what is occurring visually; and the extent to which it becomes prescriptive, seeking to contain the action more narrowly until control of the textual content or possession of the physical playbook itself becomes part of Tudor centralism and censorship.

Above all, we should recognise that a 'play-book' is an anomalous form, occupying a position intermediate between a literary text – a purely verbal creation manifested in manuscripts and printed books – and a dramatic action – a visual creation of movement, colour and sound intended for a

65

collective viewing audience. An edition constantly challenges its reader to construct imaginatively the performative circumstances of its text.

From the late eighteenth century the Romantic imagination found the Middle Ages a useful point of appeal for native English values, unrefined passions and popular culture. In the early nineteenth century this interest was met by a number of book-clubs formed with the aim of making previously unpublished texts available to subscribing members, often at high cost. Some of these clubs (for example the Surtees Society, founded in 1834, or the Camden Society of 1838) are still productive, and the products of all are on the shelves of our longer-established libraries. They include the first full editions of our older plays – Thomas Sharp's *Digby Plays* (Abbotsford, 1835), James Raine and James Gordon's *Towneley Mysteries* (Surtees, 1836), James O. Halliwell's *Ludus Coventriae* (Shakespeare, 1841) and Thomas Wright's *Chester Plays* (Shakespeare, 1843 and 1847).[1] But the emphasis was upon access rather than accuracy and, in the absence of any consistent editorial philosophy, the editions are uneven and unreliable.

The impetus towards the modern edition of the medieval play came through the interest in comparative philology in England in the second half of the nineteenth century. The links between this linguistic interest, the work of the Philological Society and its project for a 'New English Dictionary on Historical Principles', and the energising influence of F. J. Furnivall have been well documented.[2] In 1864 the Early English Text Society (hereafter EETS) was founded as a utilitarian venture to serve the project by publishing accurate texts that provided evidence of early language and manners. Play texts formed an important component of the Society's early output and, remarkably, some of these old editions remain as our only 'standard' texts to this day, still awaiting replacement by modern editions with different priorities. Such are George England's *Towneley Cycle* (*165*), for which A. W. Pollard provided side-notes, and Katharine S. Block's *Ludus Coventriae* (*177*). Hardin Craig found little to add to his *Two Coventry Corpus Christi Plays* (1902) when he revised it in 1957 (reprinted 1967).[3] Other editions, which are still on library shelves, have been subsequently superseded – the *Chester Plays* of Hermann Deimling (1892) and the mysterious 'Dr Matthews' (1916), which was reprinted as late as 1967; Furnivall's *Digby Plays* (1896) and, with A. W. Pollard, *The Macro Plays* (1904); L. A. Magnus' *Respublica* (1905); R. L. Ramsay's *Magnyfycence* (1908); and Osborn Waterhouse's *Non-Cycle Mystery Plays* (1909).[4]

Ian Lancashire (*124*) has discussed the manifestations of what he terms the 'Victorian distaste for medieval drama' in these early editions and his essay should be read by all who are compelled to use them. Here I would emphasise two consequences of the Society's work that seem particularly important for the development of the subject. First, the play texts published by the Society have created an impression of the kind of drama comprehended by the vague term 'medieval', in contrast to non-EETS texts which are vaguely felt to be 'Renaissance'. The foundation of the Malone Society in 1909 for the exact reproduction of English play texts printed before 1640[5] – now less precisely stated as 'reprinting of documents referring to drama and plays of the Renaissance period' – may have sharpened this perception, for the EETS now defines its purpose as 'printing of English texts earlier than 1558'. This limit accommodates plays such as *Respublica* or *Magnyfycence*, but the Society's output of early Tudor plays is very restricted; W. W. Greg re-edited *Respublica* in 1952 (reprinted 1969) for EETS, but Paula Neuss' edition of *Magnyfycence* (1980) was published in the Revels Plays series and Medwall's plays – never edited for the Society – appear in the Tudor Interludes series, edited by Alan H. Nelson (*263*).[6]

Secondly, the Society's editions presupposed a specialist readership whose principal requirement was a conservative transcription allied to fairly light modern punctuation. Furnivall countered a protest from Hermann Deimling in his *Chester Plays* edition about this conservatism by commenting:

As our members are more or less accustomed to faithful prints of MSS., we like as little change in MS. habits as is needed for the understanding of the text. Our books are not meant chiefly ... for girls and boys. (p. xxix)

The – to modern eyes – forbidding-looking texts of these early editions were accompanied by a scanty apparatus of notes and glossary, together with brief introductory descriptions of the manuscripts and their language. Other information was included at the discretion of the individual editor – and of Furnivall himself! – and varied considerably. Pollard's *Towneley* introduction deals mainly with the supposed three stages of the cycle's development, and was written under the influence of evolutionary theories of literature. Deimling's *Chester* introduction deals with the relationships among the four cycle-manuscripts (he was unable to locate the fifth and earliest!) and ignores entirely the performance history of the cycle attested in guild- and civic records, whereas Craig's *Coventry* edition gives major place to performance records. By the time Katharine Block came to edit the N-Town cycle, W. W. Greg had delivered his Sandars Lectures on 'Bibliographical and Textual Problems of the English Mystery Cycles',[7] and the introduction to her edition shows the influence of his rigorous quasi-scientific approach, as she marshals textual variants, watermarks, stanza-forms, structural features and source material to establish the complex process by which the extant manuscript was put together, and its implications. Her bibliographical sophistication contrasts with the irritatingly conservative transcript of the accompanying text.

A different kind of edition from those of the Society was produced by Lucy Toulmin Smith in her *York Plays* (1885).[8] Miss Smith had acquired her father's historical and social priorities working with him on records of English guilds[9] and saw the cycle as a social as well as a literary document.

Her introduction draws upon the civic records of drama at York both to establish a performance history for the cycle which covers content and production, and also to suggest the wider context of civic drama within which the cycle was located. Still wider comparisons with other cycles and related texts are drawn, and a modern notation is offered for the music in the cycle. Although the self-evidently erroneous manuscript order of the plays is retained, editorial titles, scene divisions and stage directions are supplied. Where York and Towneley have plays in common, the Towneley text is printed for comparison at the bottom of the page. In a passage duplicated in the plays of the Masons and the Goldsmiths, Miss Smith omits the Masons' section as 'unnecessary to print it twice over', but supplies the necessary collation. With its appendices comparing the contents of the English cycles and listing plays and places in Great Britain, this edition offers its readers a wide and helpful range of material for interpreting the text and anticipates some priorities of more recent editions. Reissued in 1963, it was only recently superseded as the standard edition of the York cycle (see *163*).

The new critical perspectives of the 1960s brought keener awareness of the deficiencies of the older editions and gave impetus to the production of new, more accessible editions. Since the mid-60s the EETS has replaced a number of its older editions with new ones – *The Macro Plays* (*217*), *Non-Cycle Plays and Fragments* (*205*), *The Chester Mystery Cycle* (*190* and *203*) and those plays formerly included under the title of 'The Digby Plays' (*211*). Richard Beadle re-edited *The York Plays* for a commercial publisher (*163*). New editions of Towneley by A. C. Cawley and Martin Stevens, York by Arthur Brown *et al.*, and N-Town by Stephen Spector are in preparation for the Society. Some foretaste of the Towneley edition is given in Cawley's 1958 anthology (discussed below) and the more recent edition of the *Talents* play (*174* and *175*).

Two major features distinguish these new editions from their predecessors. First, they are bibliographically and textually more reliable and consistent. Furnivall, with characteristic insouciance, had silently added the plays of *Christ's Burial* and *Christ's Resurrection* from Bodley MS e Museo 160 to the plays of MS Digby 133 in his so-called *Digby Plays*, and had relied upon the somewhat inaccurate copying of George Parker for his text, leaving a number of misconceptions and errors to be corrected by the later editors. The 1982 edition presents the plays in the Digby 133 sequence, unlike its predecessor; it removes Furnivall's tendentious division of *Mary Magdalen* into 'Parts' and 'Scenes' but does insert location indicators such as '[Jerusalem – Pilate's Palace]'; and it offers the two plays from e Museo as independent plays whereas Furnivall had presented them as two parts of one play.

Second, the new editions supply a much fuller apparatus. S. J. Herrtage's glossary to Furnivall's *Digby Plays* occupies just eleven pages, while that in the 1982 edition occupies fifty-two and separates words from names. Though not providing a complete glossary, the new edition does include

Modern editions of medieval English plays

'special contextual meanings' and words 'disguised orthographically'; it significantly does not include the etymologies of the earlier glossary, suggesting a changed perception of the concerns and capabilities of the reader. While Furnivall provided no notes, the new edition has thirty-six pages of notes dealing with textual, source and staging problems. In place of Furnivall's anecdotal ten-page introduction, the new edition's ninety-one pages of introduction treat each play individually, offering a detailed apparatus of versification and language; but additionally consideration is given to sources and there is an account of the character and staging of each play, uniting literary and dramatic concerns and implying that some users may be considering practical performance. An extensive bibliography is also provided.

The 1982 Digby edition is about mid-way in an editorial spectrum. The modern heir to the EETS's philological tradition is Norman Davis' *Non-Cycle Plays* (*205*), a more extensive collection than its predecessor, which provides an introduction to each play that concentrates upon bibliographical, textual and linguistic matters, and glossaries of Anglo-Norman, of names and of 'unfamiliar' English words and senses; it introduces performance history for the Norwich Grocers' play and an appendix on the music of the Shrewsbury Fragments, but is otherwise unconcerned with production matters. At the other extreme, Richard Beadle (*163*) simply refers his readers to existing studies on the language, versification and sources of York, concentrating – as Miss Smith's 'heir' – on the character of the manuscript and the performance history. He corrects errors in Miss Smith's transcript and also the errors in the manuscript sequence which she reproduced. Unlike her, he does not introduce editorial directions into the text. Beadle had the advantage of the REED work on York's drama-records in his account of the performance-history of each play (*142*). At the overlapping section of the Masons' and Goldsmiths' plays, he is able plausibly to reconstitute from production records what was in effect a single play 'partly with the help of evidence not accessible to Miss Toulmin Smith'.

The 1982 Digby edition aspires to be multifunctional and to reach an audience of more diverse interests than the readers of Furnivall's edition – an audience of whom fewer prior assumptions can be made. But as an edition expands beyond the narrowly textual, so the limits of inquiry become progressively less clear and the problem of reconciling the editorial process with performance history and production becomes more difficult. The scholarly edition today is consequently fuller, more diverse in content and takes correspondingly longer to bring to press than its predecessors. As scholarly editions have widened their appeal, so they have begun to incorporate features characteristic of texts for the 'non-professional reader'. The length of many medieval plays and the complexity of editorial apparatus make them seem daunting research projects to young scholars, and unattractive commercial propositions to modern publishers. We all have good reason to be grateful to EETS for its continuing willingness to produce large editions at affordable prices.

David Mills

In these circumstances, however, is it always necessary or desirable to publish the plays of a single manuscript, such as Digby 133, as a collection rather than individually? This question may be particularly apposite in the case of two 'cycle' manuscripts – the British Library's Cotton Vespasian D VIII (N-Town) and Huntington 1 (Towneley) – which have been described as compilations or editorially constructed manuscripts employing the organising framework of a play cycle. Peter Meredith has suggested that the N-Town manuscript was produced to create 'an all-inclusive play adequate to anyone's needs' (*128*, p. 21) and that 'the matters that the N-Town manuscript raises are related to revision – turning a heterogeneous collection of plays into a homogeneous whole' (p. 20). The consequences of this view are seen in his edition of *The Mary Play* (*185*), abstracted from the manuscript as an originally independent play and reconstituted in its earlier form by relegating to appendices 'later' revisions – part of 'Joseph and the Generations', 'Joseph's Trouble' and an alternative ending. The introduction and notes focus on bibliographical and textual problems and draw upon source material. This is a scholarly edition in paperback form with conservative transcript, page-foot collation and full glossary. Yet its priorities are very different from those of Miss Block, and the 185 pages needed for the 1,596 lines of 'core-text' offer an apparatus on a scale that would be prohibitive for an edition of the whole manuscript.

The Towneley manuscript has traditionally been regarded as the official register of Wakefield's play cycle, although this identification is now challenged. But such a view does not preclude its function as a descriptive account of available plays or as an anthology compiled perhaps for local use from scattered local resources. The stylistic heterogeneity of the text, its borrowings from York, its duplicated episodes – notably the two Shepherds' plays and the 'Dicing for Christ's Cloak' – are suggestive, though not conclusive, indicators of this possibility (*176*). A. C. Cawley's anthology of plays attributed to the Wakefield Master (*166*) is indicative of the ways in which this collection may be broken down into subgroups. Recently, he and Martin Stevens, co-editors of the projected EETS edition of the manuscript, have abstracted the *Talents* for independent editing as 'an anomaly' and 'a later addition' (*174*), publishing a conservative transcript with glossarial/translation notes, together with a critical survey and interpretation by Cawley (*175*).

If indeed some texts took their final shape only in the process of preparing our extant manuscripts as the scribe, or his director(s), sought overall coherence for their text, the manuscript assumes the status of a printer's copy text, the final version before a book is set in print. Moreover, its value as an index of performance history and production becomes problematic and great caution must be used when evaluating any staging diagrams or stage directions it contains. While, for example, the extensive stage directions of the N-Town 'Passion Play' may describe performance, they may equally reflect an unachieved ideal or be a stimulus to the reader's imagination.

This possibility anticipates the situation of the later printed play, intended as much or more for reading as/than for actual performance. *Everyman*, though dramatic in form and pre-Reformation in focus, is a close translation of the Dutch play *Elckerlijc* and the opening in Skot's print: 'Here beginneth a tretise', may indicate its status as a reading rather than an acting text, perhaps accounting for some of the unique features which set this play apart from other English 'moralities' (*213*). After John Rastell's publication of Henry Medwall's *Fulgens and Lucres* (*c.* 1512) the play book becomes as much literary as dramatic in function.

There is a case for regarding a civic register such as the British Library's Additional 35290 of the York cycle as a different kind of manuscript from the N-Town and Towneley manuscripts – one which might be modified according to production circumstances, which possibly bore traces of past revision and change, and might contain a variety of equally valid 'authorised' forms of the cycle for different purposes or for use at different times. But even here the descriptive function of the Register is uncertain and its relation to actual performance doubtful. Complaints in the York records and on the Register itself about 'unregistered' material suggest that the practical concerns of 'producer' and performers might not always coincide with the controlling intentions of the officially authorised text.

FACSIMILE EDITIONS

The facsimile edition of a medieval play manuscript is a recent phenomenon. Traditionally, the textual scholar worked directly with original materials (or employed an assistant), and although photographic technology had made facsimiles possible by the start of this century, costs were high, definition poor and the public demand for texts requiring specialist palaeographical skills probably low. As technology developed, the interested scholar without access to the manuscripts would probably purchase a microfilm, since it was cheaper than a photograph and could show finer detail by transmitted light. The black-letter page of the early printed book reproduced better on the printed page and became the concern of the Malone Society. Yet in 1907–8 the *Macro Plays* were offered by J. S. Farmer in three volumes of the Tudor Facsimile Texts Series,[10] a subscription series that included facsimiles of printed play texts such as *Everyman*.

Since 1960 the resurgence of interest in medieval drama and improvements in the quality and cost of facsimiles have promoted the facsimile edition as a useful tool in the 'back-to-basics' approach in which a close description of the visible evidence of the manuscript was an essential prelude to editorial decisions and to critical judgements. The facsimile thus belongs to the same impulse which led REED to publish accurate plain transcripts of drama records as the neutral bases for research.

The first modern facsimile – David Bevington's 1972 *Macro Plays* (*219*), which initiated a new series by the Folger Library – was in part intended to protect the manuscripts from further wear by reducing the need to consult them. To facilitate the photography, the Library disbound the manuscripts and, in reassembling them, corrected an error in the gathering of *The Castle of Perseverance*, thereby destroying the sequence of page numbers in the manuscript. Bevington arranges the plays 'in probable chronological order', thereby further dislocating the correspondence with Furnivall's edition. The quality of reproduction is high, with variations in tone registered clearly, and the user is assisted by the provision of facing plain transcriptions and page-foot collations and textual notes. In the transcript of *Wisdom*, words are supplied as necessary from the Digby version. For the textual scholar, the introduction has a section on ownership and textual matters (including a comment on the relation of the Digby and Macro versions of *Wisdom*). But additionally Bevington has an introductory section in which he provides the reader with an overarching critical context; the plays become the starting point for a discussion of the origin and early history of the English morality play, including matters of staging and characterisation.

This approach, which seems to envisage a wide readership, is very different from that of the Medieval Drama Facsimiles Series launched in 1973 by Leeds Texts and Monographs, which addresses more narrowly the specific textual interests of the scholar. Its General Editor, A. C. Cawley, describes the aims of the Series in its first volume as 'to complement the Early English Text Society editions of medieval English plays, and to encourage the study of the primary documents for medieval English drama' (*188*, p. iii). The introductions to the volumes in the Series have been written by editors of the EETS or equivalent edition and access to that edition seems presupposed of the reader. Hence there is no transcription or collation, and reference is by folio and line (which has to be counted on the appropriate folio by the user). The introductions are textually and bibliographically descriptive – literary-critical material is not admitted. The presentation is starkly sectionalised, with extensive marshalling of references.

The series is reasonably priced (for facsimile), paperbound and photographed in black and white with the occasional colour frontispiece. Since individual pages are not tonally adjusted, rubrication and marginalia do not always register clearly. The manuscripts are reproduced in their original dimensions with the exception of Chester HM2 which, without explanation, appears in reduced form. Photographic quality varies, from Chester's Bodley 175, printed from microfilm, to York's British Library Additional 35290, splendidly photographed. Eight volumes have so far appeared in the series: Chester manuscripts Bodley 175 (*188*), Huntington 2 (*196*) and Harley 2124 (*201*), the manuscripts of Towneley (*170*), N-Town (*182*) and York (*164*, with the 'Ordo Paginarum' section of the York Memorandum Book), the Digby and e Museo manuscripts of the *Digby Plays* (*208*) and manuscripts of non-cycle plays (*210*). Two other volumes – the Coventry manuscripts, introduced by Pamela King, and individual manuscripts of cycle plays – are in preparation.

Modern editions of medieval English plays

Access to facsimiles of two antiquarian copies is offered by *REED News-letter*: Henry Bourne's 1736 printed text of the Newcastle Shipwrights' play of *Noah's Ark* (*209*) and John Kirkpatrick's transcript of the Norwich Grocers' play of *The Fall of Man* discovered in 1972 and not available to Davis for his EETS edition (*212*). Though important documents, these transcripts perhaps have less to reveal about the nature of the text than the medieval manuscripts, but are symptomatic of the same scholarly concern with original sources.

Editors tend today to ask questions of their manuscripts that are certainly different and hopefully more powerful than those of their predecessors. They resist – even react against – tacit assumptions that the text is primarily a guide to the language and customs of a past age or that there is a necessary connection between the performance and textual histories of a play. Issues such as the date of original composition or the successive layers of revision, featuring prominently in early editions, are now acknowledged rather as conventions of editorial introductions. The facsimile edition signals the extent to which attention now concentrates upon the character and purpose of the extant manuscript and the need to scrutinise it minutely for the evidence which it may contain.

ANTHOLOGIES

The 'image' of medieval drama that a new generation of students receives is largely conditioned by the kind of texts they use. When, in 1890, A. W. Pollard produced his play-anthology, *English Miracle Plays, Moralities and Interludes*,[11] he directed it towards 'the many lovers of literature unable to make the subject their special subject'. His anthology addressed the two problems that still determine student editions – the prohibitively high cost of full and scholarly editions and the need to offer students an adequate linguistic and critical framework. Pollard provided thirteen 'specimens of pre-Elizabethan drama', abridged and – with the exception of Chester material from the Huntington manuscript which Pollard had transcribed – taken from scholarly editions; other material was added in appendices. The modern student would notice many differences from today's anthologies: the conservative text, the glossary of 'unusual forms', the mere forty-seven pages of notes. One suspects, however, that the extensive introductory essay expounding an evolutionary thesis of drama development was widely influential. Strong overseas sales encouraged the Oxford Press to commission a second edition and the collection was kept thereafter in print and revised to its eighth edition in 1927. New scholarship, such as Chambers' work, was progressively assimilated, and the 1904 edition included illustrations from early art. Still a standard teaching text in the 1950s, it was actually reissued in 1961.

In 1909, encouraged perhaps by Pollard's success and by the interest in early drama generated by William Poel's revival of *Everyman*, Ernest Rhys

David Mills

edited *Everyman, with Other Interludes* in the popular Everyman Library, including a random group of seven cycle plays together with Bale's *God's Promises*. It was reprinted seven times in the next fifteen years. In 1956 this volume was replaced by A. C. Cawley's *Everyman and Medieval Miracle Plays*.[12]

This last anthology has become an established classroom 'standard'. In addition to *Everyman*, it offers a reconstructed skeletal cycle of fourteen plays, allowing a better sense of cycle form. Presentation is attractive – a modern-spelling edition based on scholarly editions or (for the Towneley material and *Everyman*) Cawley's work on original manuscripts, an apparatus of side-glosses and footnote translations on the same page and editorial indications of locations, settings and action. The editor is uncompromising in his defence of the subject: 'There is no longer any need to be hostile ... or to be patronizing or squeamish [about such drama].' Each play has its own headnote, and the brief introduction encourages appreciation of the inherent qualities of the plays rather than presenting them as examples of a wide-ranging thesis. Sensitive to the needs of the beginning student and, importantly, leaving space for the teacher, this edition was to become an attractive introduction to the early drama for many of the 1960s scholars.

Pollard's American counterpart, J. M. Manly's two-volume *Specimens of the Pre-Shaksperean Drama* (1897–8),[13] had the aim of 'helping the student to follow the fortunes of modern drama through its strange and interesting nonage'. The anthology was flawed by the inaccuracy of its texts and particularly by the absence of a projected third volume of notes, glossary and descriptive historical essays, but it is a huge collection which was reprinted as late as 1967, presumably to meet the new demands for student texts. David Bevington's *Medieval Drama* (*19*) replaces this anthology and typifies the modern attitude to the subject in offering 'Medieval Drama as an artistic achievement in its own right' in place of Manly's condescension. It is a course-book, sectionalised from 'Liturgical Beginnings' to 'Humanist Drama', with accompanying essays and headnotes to its sixty-four pieces. Particular attention is given to the plays as drama (the N-Town 'Passion Play' is offered with possible 'theatre-in-the-round staging', for example), and this concern continues in the editorial directions to the texts. Textual accuracy is guaranteed by checks against manuscripts or photographs, and conservative spelling is adopted. Latin and French texts appear in the original with accompanying translation, and side-glosses and page-foot translations accompany the English texts. The cycles are represented by a reconstructed cycle of banns and twenty-seven plays. The chronological limits of Manly's anthology now translate into a series of generic categories. The book offers students a wide selection and a positive line of approach to the whole subject.

In England, Cawley's anthology suggested further developments. The same editor went on to provide two editions which offered more detailed and scholarly apparatus, perhaps for students ready to progress beyond the first anthology. In 1958 he published his excellent edition of those Towneley plays assigned by stanza and style to 'the Wakefield Master' (*166*), and in 1961 a new edition of *Everyman* (*213*). Both offer an insight into the semantic problems of the texts and discuss issues of source and content while insisting on the plays as drama. His Everyman anthology was complemented in 1976 by Glynne Wickham's *English Moral Interludes* (*227*) in the same series and format with a strong insistence upon the plays as drama validated by the editor's practical experience. 'Interlude' is stretched somewhat to include *Mankind*. Peter Happé has edited two important paperback anthologies containing extensive and helpful introductions and conservative texts based on editions but collated with manuscripts/facsimiles, and with editorial stage directions. *English Mystery Plays* (*120*) offers a thirty-eight-episode reconstructed cycle which, by duplicating episodes from different manuscripts, encourages comparisons and contrasts. *Four Morality Plays* (*230*) brings into revealing juxtaposition four long allegorical plays, not readily accessible even in scholarly editions.

The subject has been fortunate in that scholars of the stature of Bevington, Cawley and Wickham have recognised the importance of teaching anthologies as a means of introducing students to the plays and to current scholarly thinking. But each selection has its own underlying assumptions, and while some plays are regularly anthologised, others are – for various reasons – largely neglected. Perhaps anthologies should cede priority now to other enterprises. There is urgent need for student texts of complete cycles and the longer plays at prices which students – and their teachers! – can reasonably afford. Moreover, teacher and student might have more choice if the contents of large manuscript anthologies were published as separate plays or groups. Above all, we need accurate and clearly glossed texts with good bibliographies, dispensing with elaborate introductions and notes to reduce price; a more exploratory critical approach might well result.

THE EDITIONS OF THE CHESTER CYCLE: A CASE-STUDY

In the 1960s R. M. Lumiansky and I began collaboration on a scholarly edition of the Chester cycle for the EETS to replace the Deimling–Matthews edition. This project has already generated a series of studies and editions in a research programme which is still on-going, and it therefore seems appropriate to use it as a case-study to give focus to the general issues raised above, though I would emphasise that our procedures are not necessarily typical of or applicable to editions of other medieval plays.

Chester's editorial problem differs from that of other cycles because the text of the full cycle is evidenced in five manuscripts and there are also three manuscripts/fragments of single plays extant. We therefore had a choice of manuscript (see *204*). In 1892 Deimling chose as base the latest cycle-manuscript as representing the older and better textual tradition; the British Library's Harley 2124 was written in 1607 by three scribes, the principal being James Miller, a scholar with 'editorial' tendencies. The practical disadvantage of this choice was that the 1607 text differed considerably from the others in particular readings and also lacked a number of long passages present in the other manuscripts (*189*), so that a large number of 'majority' readings, together with those extended passages, had to appear in page-foot collation, making the structural implications hard for the reader to assess. We felt that there was no means of assigning priority or superiority among the manuscripts, and therefore we sought as base text the version that enabled the clearest and most convenient presentation of data for the reader's assessment. For us, that meant the fullest possible version with the largest number of supported readings, so that page-foot collation was minimised and divergencies could be expressed, as far as possible, as 'omissions' rather than 'additions'. Whereas the latest manuscript had fewest supported readings, the earliest – Huntington 2 of 1591 by Edward Gregorie, not available to Deimling – had the most. Though it lacked the first play, we preferred to supplement this loss from the 'runner-up' – George Bellin's 1600 copy, now Harley 2013 – rather than increase the overall complexity of apparatus by adopting a different base manuscript. Our intention from the outset was therefore to present data accurately, clearly and 'neutrally', though we hope that our readers recognise the inevitable subjectivity of even the lightest editing. For example, we elected to list 'significant' variants, meaning by 'significant' 'a variant which affects the meaning of the text'; but that distinction involves subjective judgement. Variants might affect rhyme or the syllabic structure of a line; but in noting such instances we employed no preconceived notion of metre. All the extant cycle manuscripts either ignore the eight-line stanza which predominates in the cycle or reduce it to quatrains; we elected to restore the stanza-division. Punctuation, too, however light, imposes a personal reading on the text, and even a collation term such as 'omission' has a tendentiously censorious ring. But our intention was to free the edited text from subjective value-judgements and theories of origin and transmission in order to permit a closer analysis of it as a record of change at a later point in the editing process.

A consequence of this pragmatic approach was that many of the preliminary considerations of bibliographical and textual evaluation could be postponed until the text and its variants were in place. This in turn affected the pattern of our edition, since the cycle was too long to be accommodated in edited form in a single volume. We were enabled to present the text with its variants conveniently in a single volume, together with manuscript descriptions (*190*). We then planned to provide an apparatus of notes and glossaries specific to that text in a second volume and to draw together internal and external evidence about the cycle in a third volume which would deal with textual and source problems, survey the evidence for the cycle's performance history and offer a specialist analysis of the music. Here, however, commercial considerations overtook the academic project. Though the publication of the text-volume predicated the publication of the apparatus, the material for the remainder of the edition proved too extensive for the EETS to accept.

Modern editions of medieval English plays

Accordingly, a truncated apparatus of notes and glossary (without a Latin or names glossary) was published by the Society (*203*), and the material intended for the third volume was substantially redrafted and published separately in the form of a collection of essays (*200*). Though a reader's sense of the wholeness of the editorial process has perhaps been dissipated by this format, the three volumes, each with its own *raison d'être*, form part of a single editorial impulse centring upon the text. The presentation emphasises the distinction between the descriptive assembly of data and the various stages in its evaluation.

The text aspires to be an accurate transcript of the base manuscript, with some spelling normalisations such as 'F' for 'ff' and 'v' for consonantal 'u'. The three single-play manuscripts were excluded from collation and printed in appendices together with four major divergences in Miller's manuscript. We did not wish to emend the text in any way, since such intrusion involved subjective notions of priority, but EETS insisted upon emendation in a number of specified instances 'where the Hm reading seems palpably non-sensical'. We reluctantly acceded to this requirement, still feeling that material from the later apparatus was being used to shape the text received by the reader.

Even before our first volume appeared, we were fortunate to be involved in the Leeds Facsimile project and have, together or singly, introduced facsimiles of three Chester manuscripts (*188*, *196* and *201*). Facsimiles of the three single-play manuscripts are in preparation, and I would hope that all the cycle manuscripts, together with banns and other material, might be made available in time. I can attest the value of the discipline of close description imposed by this series upon its editors, and I am reassured that readers of our edition can verify or query our readings and descriptions for themselves.

In our second volume our concern was semantic: what did the words mean? Variants among the manuscripts offered meaningful choices which could be evaluated lexicographically, taking account also of the opinions of previous editors. Selective use was also made of known sources, such as *A Stanzaic Life of Christ*, and of obvious analogues such as the Vulgate Bible (knowledge of whose content can no longer be assumed of readers), the *Historia Scholastica* and the *Glossa Ordinaria*, suggesting both the meanings of passages and also the degree of invention in the text. The notes are, therefore, a mixture of the textual and linguistic, the contextual and the critical.

The *Essays* volume offers a still wider and more individually intrusive evaluation of the bibliographical and textual issues discussed piecemeal in the notes. Analysing the patterns of variation, we characterised the lost common exemplar of the extant manuscripts and the practices of the individual scribes, rewriting the textual history of the cycle and discovering in the manuscripts a record of underlying change – their exemplar had embodied alternatives and choices. At this stage we introduced performance history, aided by L. M. Clopper's study of the cycle's development (*192*) and his

David Mills

REED volume of Chester records (*141*). In our account of the cycle's development and staging and of its individual plays, we also provided edited transcripts of the relevant documents for the reader's convenience. These included the pre- and post-Reformation banns; two scribes preface the cycle with the latter, and Deimling printed Bellin's 1600 transcript at the start of the text; but their connection with the extant cycle is debatable and we felt that they should be printed separately as evidence of performance history. Though the studies of external and internal evidence were separated, they concurred in their demonstration of the underlying instability of the cycle text. The apparatus was completed by a descriptive classification of stanza-forms and an essay on music by Richard Rastall.

In our edition we have sought to involve the reader in the editorial process by displaying clearly the possibilities and problems that the text contains, and by signalling the stages in our own processes of appraisal. Among our greatest satisfactions have been the renewal of critical interest in the cycle that followed the publication of our edition, and the appreciation of its values as practical theatre, notably at Leeds (see *202*), at Toronto and at the 1987 Chester Festival.

From the beginning Robert Lumiansky insisted that the main priority after the publication of the scholarly edition must be an edition for students in modern spelling with accompanying linguistic apparatus. Such an edition is now in preparation. Moreover, it is obvious that the editorial process must extend beyond the establishment of the text, for beyond our third volume lie further essential studies: the topographical, social and economic factors that shaped the production; the political and theological background which the cycle addressed and in which it developed and was suppressed; the sources and models which its authors adopted; and the continuing exploration of its literary and dramatic values. As the study widens its scope, so the need for the REED collections of Lancashire and Cheshire records and for new editions of sources such as the *Stanzaic Life* becomes more urgent. Editing is now a collective scholarly enterprise that resists the specialist circumscriptions placed upon it by the past.

Moreover, those extending explorations, radiating out from the manuscript text, will in time seek out the deficiencies of our current edition and will provide the impetus to re-edit the old texts yet again.

NOTES

1 T. Sharp, *Ancient Mysteries from the Digby Manuscripts. Preserved in the Bodleian Library* (Oxford and Edinburgh: Abbotsford Club, 1835); J. Raine and J. Gordon, *The Towneley Mysteries* (London: Surtees Society, 1836); J. O. Halliwell, *Ludus Coventriae: A Collection of Mysteries Formerly Represented at Coventry on the Feast of Corpus Christi* (London: Shakespeare Society, 1841); T. Wright, *The Chester Plays*, 2 vols. (London: Shakespeare Society, 1841-7).
2 See W. Benzie, *Dr. F. J. Furnivall: A Victorian Scholar Adventurer* (Norman: Pilgrim Books, 1983).

3 H. Craig, *Two Coventry Corpus Christi Plays*, EETS Extra Series 87 (London: Oxford University Press, 1902; 2nd edn, 1957).

4 H. Deimling, *The Chester Plays*, vol. I, EETS Extra Series 62 (London: Oxford University Press, 1892) and 'Dr Matthews', vol. II, EETS Extra Series 115 (London: Oxford University Press, 1916); F. J. Furnivall, *The Digby Plays*, EETS Extra Series 70 (London: Oxford University Press, 1896); F. J. Furnivall and A. W. Pollard, *The Macro Plays*, EETS Extra Series 91 (London: Oxford University Press, 1904); L. A. Magnus, *Respublica 1553: A Play on the Social Conditions of England at the Accession of Queen Mary*, EETS Extra Series 94 (London: Oxford University Press, 1905); R. L. Ramsay, *Magnyfycence: A Moral Play by John Skelton*, EETS Extra Series 98 (London: Oxford University Press, 1908); O. Waterhouse, *The Non-Cycle Mystery Plays, Together with the Croxton Play of the Sacrament*, EETS Extra Series 104 (London: Oxford University Press, 1909).

5 See F. P. Wilson, 'The Malone Society: The First Fifty Years: 1905–56', *Collections IV* (London: Malone Society, 1956), pp. 1–16.

6 W. W. Greg, *Respublica: An Interlude for Christmas 1553 attributed to Nicholas Udall*, EETS Old Series 226 (London: Oxford University Press, 1952); P. Neuss, *Magnificence: John Skelton*, Revels Plays (Manchester: Manchester University Press, and Baltimore: Johns Hopkins University Press, 1980); A. H. Nelson, *The Plays of Henry Medwall (263)*.

7 K. S. Block, *Ludus Coventriae or the Plaie Called Corpus Christi*, EETS Extra Series 120 (London: Oxford University Press, 1922); W. W. Greg, 'Bibliographical and Textual Problems of the English Miracle Cycles' (the 1913 Sandars Lectures), *The Library*, 3rd ser., 5 (1914): 1–30, 168–205, 280–319, 365–99 (and, as a separate publication, London: Alexander Morning, 1914).

8 L. Toulmin Smith, *York Plays: The Plays Performed by the Crafts or Mysteries of York on the Day of Corpus Christi in the 14th, 15th and 16th Centuries* (Oxford: Clarendon Press, 1885).

9 Toulmin Smith, L. Toulmin Smith and L. Brentano, *English Gilds, their Statutes and Customs*, EETS Old Series 40 (London: Oxford University Press, 1870).

10 J. S. Farmer, *The Tudor Facsimile Texts* (London and Edinburgh: T. C. and E. C. Jack): *Wisdom* (1907), *Mankind* (1907), *The Castle of Perseverance* (1908).

11 A. W. Pollard, *English Miracle Plays, Moralities and Interludes: Specimens of the Pre-Elizabethan Drama* (Oxford: Clarendon Press, 1890; 8th edn, 1927).

12 E. Rhys, *Everyman, with Other Interludes* (London: J. M. Dent, and New York: E. P. Dutton, 1909); A. C. Cawley, *Everyman and Medieval Miracle Plays* (London: J. M. Dent, and New York: E. P. Dutton, 1956; rev. edn 1974).

13 J. M. Manly, *Specimens of the Pre-Shaksperean Drama*, 2 vols. (Boston and New York: Ginn and Co., 1897–8; repr. New York: Dover Books, 1967).

5

The English mystery cycles

DAVID STAINES

Opening before God's creation of the world and closing after His final judgement of mankind, the mystery cycle is a sequential drama that flourished in many English towns and cities during the fourteenth, fifteenth and sixteenth centuries. Usually performed in one location on scaffold stages or in procession on movable wagons, the cycle was a major and often annual creation of its community, an expression of civic pride and piety, each individual pageant or play being the responsibility of one craft or religious guild. And the cycle is both a unique English play, bearing little direct connection with continental drama, and a unique product of the later Middle Ages, developing within an intellectual milieu that also witnessed the creation of *summae*, universal chronicles and other encyclopaedic forms.

Of the four extant English mystery cycles, the oldest is the N-Town cycle, a sequence of forty-one plays compiled in a manuscript dating from no earlier than 1468. Among its distinctive features is a group of five plays about Mary, actually a separate and self-contained composite Mary play, and a Passion sequence that is a single play from a separate manuscript incorporated by the scribe into the compilation. The N-Town cycle employs the two forms of staging, the movable wagons and the scaffold stages.[1]

Unlike the N-Town, the York cycle, the second oldest cycle, has an acknowledged home, the city of York, whose forty-eight plays were committed to manuscript around 1477. The plays, which were performed on wagons, had been presented for about a century before this time and continued through the mid-sixteenth century. Despite the suppression of the plays, as late as 1579 the City Council of York was still eager to stage them.[2]

The thirty-two plays of the Towneley cycle survive in one incomplete manuscript from the late fifteenth or early sixteenth century. Because the cycle shares five pageants from the York cycle, 'Pharoah', 'The Doctors', 'The Harrowing of Hell', 'The Resurrection' and 'The Last Judgment', the Towneley, often regarded as originating in Wakefield, seems to have borrowed these plays and adapted others from the York cycle.[3]

Once considered the oldest cycle, the Chester cycle is now known to be the latest of the extant cycles. Unlike the other cycles, which survive in only one manuscript, the Chester survives in full in five manuscripts, none of them compiled before 1591. It originated in a Passion play that was performed in one fixed location on the feast of Corpus Christi. Sometime before

1521 the play was shifted to Whitsuntide. Then came the decision to perform it in more than one location, and the ultimate result was a twenty-four-play cycle that was presented on movable stages over a three-day period. The final performance of the cycle took place in 1575.[4]

Like all of early English drama, the mystery cycles first became a subject of scholarly attention in the mid-nineteenth century, and modern understanding of the cycles has been determined by nineteenth-century critical assumptions that only the last three decades have begun to question and, in many cases, to reject. As an undergraduate at the University of Toronto in the mid-1960s, I was first exposed to the mystery cycles in a third-year Honours English course, 'Drama before 1642'. We noted 'The Second Shepherds' Play', paused at *Everyman*, then began our course with the dramas of Kyd, Marlowe and Shakespeare. More than a century ago, A. W. Ward's monumental three-volume *History of English Dramatic Literature* affirmed that 'The direct connexion between the clergy and the miracle-plays continued, if not quite to the last, at all events till the period when those plays were about to be superseded by the beginnings of the regular drama.'[5] Our undergraduate course was relentlessly – though perhaps unconsciously – taught in this nineteenth-century tradition where 'the regular drama' demanded study and the earlier anonymous works by supposedly narrow-minded clerics were dismissed.

That same academic year, 1965–6, a graduate seminar in medieval drama at the University of Toronto led to the formation of the Poculi Ludique Societas, a theatre group dedicated to producing early English plays.[6] The juxtaposition on the same campus of one course on early drama that bypassed the medieval period and another that created the Poculi Ludique Societas as a student-led response to the appeal of that period's plays appropriately images the transition in critical thinking about early English theatre that occurred in the 1960s.

B. J. Whiting's graduate seminar in medieval drama at Harvard University in 1968 confirmed the transition. Using A. C. Cawley's edition of *The Wakefield Pageants in the Towneley Cycle* as its major text, the seminar included oral reports on all major critical studies. We explored the accepted tradition in criticism, reporting in detail on E. K. Chambers, Karl Young and Hardin Craig, and we also became aware of the new thinking, the revolutionary investigations of Glynne Wickham, O. B. Hardison Jr and V. A. Kolve. The criticism of this transition period revealed the fundamental contributions made by nineteenth-century scholars but also exposed the limitations of their work. And the criticism showed clearly that modern appreciation of the cycles has been shaped by nineteenth-century attitudes. As a consequence, early English drama became the centre of unprecedented critical interest, as Glynne Wickham observes:

Research of the past three decades has greatly enriched our knowledge both of liturgical-music-drama and of the vernacular Cycles and Moralities: indeed it might be fair to claim that more books have been published since the end of the second

David Staines

World War on these aspects of English dramatic literature – Shakespeare, of course, excepted – than on any other. (*134*, p. 101)

The purpose of this essay is to explore the critical transition in the light of its historical antecedents and then to examine the various approaches to the English mystery cycles that dominate contemporary criticism.

The first editors of the mystery cycles found no adequate designation for this distinct yet seemingly un-unified form. The Surtees Society's edition of the plays in the Towneley manuscript, the first publication of all the plays of one sequence, appeared in 1836 under the title of *The Towneley Mysteries*.[7] Five years later, J. O. Halliwell edited the *Ludus Coventriae* and appended the subtitle, 'A Collection of Mysteries'.[8] *The Chester Plays*, published by Thomas Wright between 1841 and 1847, received the same subtitle, 'A Collection of Mysteries'.[9] Equally perplexed by the proper appellation for the groups of mystery plays, subsequent editors and critics assigned various terms: 'the Chester, Coventry, or Towneley series',[10] 'the whole series of plays',[11] 'sequence of Mysteries ... series of Mysteries',[12] 'English *Collective Mysteries*',[13] 'sets of Miracles or Miracle-plays'[14] and 'the other sets of Mysteries – the Towneley, Chester, Coventry, and Lord Ashburnham's York one'.[15] In their failure to find an adequate or acceptable designation, editors suggested their own inability to comprehend the cycle form.

English dramatic criticism inherited the term 'cycle' from French criticism, in particular the pioneering studies of Marius Sepet. His influential work, *Les Prophètes du Christ* (1878), depicted the development of medieval drama in an evolutionary pattern: a reading from the Christmas Matins grew into the Latin Prophets play, which in turn underlay the Old Testament plays 'dans le grand cycle dramatique du quinzième siècle'.[16] The latter phrase refers to the large sequence of plays that Sepet regarded as the climax of medieval drama, the continental Passion plays and the four extant English cycles.

For Sepet, a cycle was primarily a cluster of stories centred around one main event; his use of the term was a direct consequence of the denotation of 'cycle' in a romance context where individual romances were categorised according to their central figure, be it Arthur, Charlemagne or Godfrey of Bouillon. Each liturgical drama revolved around the feasts of Christmas and Easter, and each holy day became a centre of dramatic presentations.

In the related use of 'cycle' as the designation for the long sequences of plays, Sepet implied that such sequences were simply the amalgamation of separate dramas. The English mystery cycles brought together the Christmas cycle of Nativity plays, the Easter cycle of Resurrection plays and assorted Old Testament stories. The series of Old Testament scenes culminated in the Prophets plays, which became an epilogue to these stories and a prologue to the New Testament stories. Only the strict chronology of the sequence of events offered any semblance of unity among the individual plays. In borrowing the term 'cycle' from romance criticism, therefore, Sepet inherited the pejorative connotation that a cycle lacked any unity beyond the presence of a central figure or event and the natural unity inherent in chronology. Furthermore, Sepet relegated medieval drama to a comparatively minor place in the history of world theatre, concluding that, despite all the inherent disorder and confusion of medieval drama, a Shakespeare would appear out of this formless background.[17]

In her introduction to the first publication of the Brome 'Abraham and Isaac' in 1884, Lucy Toulmin Smith introduced 'cycle' into the vocabulary of English dramatic criticism:

Five English plays on the subject of Abraham's Sacrifice are known, the Brome MS. gives a sixth, and no two are alike. Each of the four great collections of Plays, the Chester, York, Towneley, and Coventry, includes it; one is also found in a separate form at Trinity College, Dublin ... The play may in some instances have been performed separately, independently of the great cycle in which it formed a part, when complete in itself as in the York or Dublin MSS.; the fact that it is sometimes found in detached manuscripts would seem to indicate this. Even at Dublin, however, we know from the city records that the play of 'Abraham and Isaac, with their offering and altar' was performed by the weaver's company, as one of the Corpus Christi plays.[18]

'The great cycle' is synonymous with 'four great collections of Plays' and 'the Corpus Christi plays'. In borrowing the term 'cycle' from French criticism, Smith employed it to designate more clearly than it had done before a distinct genre; the other sense of 'cycle' as the classification of plays that revolve around a particular event did not assume major importance in English criticism. A cycle, therefore, could be any sequence of plays, and the emphasis fell on the sequential pattern rather than on some central event.

Smith went on to edit *The York Plays* (1885), and her introduction often used 'cycle' to designate the four extant groups of mystery plays as well as similar groups that survive only in fragments. Her enumeration of the places where medieval plays were performed in England differentiated between individual plays and plays that formed part of a cycle.[19]

After the publication of *The York Plays*, editors accepted and confirmed Smith's terminology. Although the next edition of *The Chester Plays* (1892) avoided the term entirely, the 1897 edition of *The Towneley Plays* used the term often to designate the four great sequences of English mystery plays, and twenty-five years after Smith's first employment of the term, an edition of plays that did not form part of any larger sequence appeared under the title, *The Non-Cycle Mystery Plays*.[20]

Adoption of the term 'cycle' confirmed two beliefs about the medieval stage. First, a cycle was a gathering together of individual plays. There was no internal unity to the gathering, for the Darwinian theory of evolution stood implicitly behind the understanding that a cycle came into being at the moment when individual plays grew or came together. The English mystery cycles were thus seen as a climactic moment of evolution, medieval drama having evolved slowly and naturally from the *Quem quaeritis* trope in the

David Staines

Easter liturgy through the Latin liturgical drama into vernacular plays that formed the basis of the cycles.[21]

Behind the view of cycles as mergers was the understanding that medieval drama existed in a dim world of its own, remote from 'the regular drama' of the Elizabethan period. Ward, the most influential critic of the mystery cycles in the nineteenth century, defined their negligible literary value:

> The writers of these plays ... could not for a moment mistake the audiences for whom they wrote. This by no means implies an utter absence from this body of literary remains of the graces and charms of composition. As a whole their literary talent may be said to surpass their dramaturgic skill, although even of this evidence is by no means wanting. But these graces and charms ... may fairly be described as the result of accident ... the historic sense – the sense of what is correct – was as completely wanting in these plays as a sense of what was fitting; but the anachronisms of the Middle Ages do not puzzle us as much as their improprieties, more especially as the jester in these plays as elsewhere thrusts himself forward with loud laugh or protruded tongue, often at the most critical points in the action ... the grossness of many passages in these plays is manifestly of indigenous origin, and points to the slow progress of aesthetic culture rather than to an absence of moral sentiment.[22]

The nineteenth century thus closed with little research on the cycles themselves as dramatic art. At a time when later periods of English drama were being carefully and perceptively investigated, A. W. Pollard could write about the English mystery cycles: 'So little attention has as yet been devoted to these plays, that the relations of the different cycles to each other, and of the different parts of the same cycle to the whole, have as yet been very imperfectly worked out.'[23] And the twentieth century opened with the publication of E. K. Chambers' *The Mediaeval Stage* (1903) where the cycles were again seen as the final step in an evolutionary ladder 'from liturgical office to cosmic cycle' (*9, 11,* p. 124). So monumental was Chambers' compendium of information that his views on the mystery cycles, themselves simply reiterations of nineteenth-century attitudes, continued to dominate criticism through the first half of the twentieth century.

In *English Religious Drama of the Middle Ages* (1955), Hardin Craig accepted unquestioningly the critical position of the nineteenth century. The cycles were gatherings of individual plays: 'When the major groups, such as those belonging to Christmas and to Easter, were united, there may have been gaps to be filled, and there may have been at that time a considerable amount of anonymous new composition in order to complete the all-inclusive drama that extended from the Fall of Lucifer to the Judgement Day' (*105,* p. 7). The technique of the plays 'was inevitably naive and firmly conventional ... This drama had no theory and aimed consciously at no dramatic effects, and, when it succeeded, its success came from the import of its message or from the moving quality of some particular story it had to tell' (*105,* p. 9). Medieval religious drama 'existed for itself and for the discharge of a religious purpose and not as an early stage of secular drama' (*105,* pp. 6–7). Craig's static views attested to the accepted infallibility and impregnability of

84

the nineteenth-century understanding of medieval theatre during the first half of the twentieth century.

But with the close of World War II, a new critical attitude began to appear. Harold C. Gardiner's *Mysteries' End* (1946 [*104*]) may be reckoned the first serious questioning of the critical tradition. Gardiner maintained that the cycles were not secularised but remained under the control of the Catholic Church; the cycles came to an end, 'not from an internal decay, but from an external force, the hostility of the Reformation' (*104*, p. xii). Rejecting by implication the evolutionary conception of the cycles' formation, Gardiner dissolved the distinction between medieval and Tudor or Elizabethan, showing that the young Shakespeare might well have attended a performance of a mystery cycle, which was still at that time a lively event. The suppression of the cycles was further confirmed by F. M. Salter's *Mediaeval Drama in Chester* (1955 [*186*]), which argued for a later date than commonly accepted for the Chester cycle.

With the exception of Gardiner and Salter, studies of the medieval theatre had remained, as Wickham then noted, essentially moribund: 'It would seem as if, apart from minor shifts of emphasis and factual corrections, the past fifty years had failed to provide us with any new knowledge adequate to resolve the many age-old conundrums that have baffled students for so long' (*107*, p. 118). And Wickham himself in *Early English Stages* (1959 [*107*]) launched the first major assault on the accepted history of medieval drama. Gardiner's theory of the demise of the cycles, Wickham realised, must colour any assessment of the plays and their staging:

The idea, however, that possibly the plays did not die a natural death, but were deliberately extirpated, must cause us to think again. Nor is this idea just a casual hypothesis. It corresponds altogether too accurately with the mysterious disappearance of all but a fraction of the many texts known to have existed, and also with the long-established knowledge that other artistic manifestations of Catholic doctrine – statues, frescoes, stained glass – were defaced, despoiled or removed at precisely this time. (*107*, p. 113)

To answer the questions by the need 'to think again', Wickham studied all available evidence, insisting on seeing the plays not as literary texts but as texts in performance; his observations demanded an entirely new understanding of medieval staging.

Two years after the publication of *Early English Stages*, two more books followed Wickham's counsel 'to think again'. Arnold Williams' *The Drama of Medieval England* (*108*), an introduction addressed to the general reader, devoted an entire chapter to 'The Literary Art of the Cycles', exploring the sources, the humour, the folk traditions and the versification of the cycle plays. Eleanor Prosser's *Drama and Religion in the English Mystery Plays* (*149*), an analysis of the theme of repentance and salvation in selected mystery plays, further challenged nineteenth-century critical positions: 'For the moment we must forget about sources and places and dates and try to picture the plays as they were actually produced for an audience of average

David Staines

intelligence and honest faith' (p. 15). Like *Early English Stages*, the books by Williams and Prosser were summarily and rudely dismissed by Craig.[24] What shocked him and traditional scholars of medieval theatre and what was causing new interest in their field were the stagings of cycle plays in the 1950s, beginning with E. Martin Browne's staging of the York cycle in 1951. All subsequent critics and scholars would acknowledge and profit from performances they witnessed. The new assault on nineteenth-century attitudes developed, to a large degree, from the impact made by modern stagings of the cycle plays.

In *Christian Rite and Christian Drama in the Middle Ages* (1965 [46]), O. B. Hardison Jr launched a second major assault. While Wickham had concentrated on details of performance, Hardison returned to the liturgical drama, proving that the evolutionary approach reorganised the chronology of the plays to fit a theory. Although his major concern was the liturgical drama, he argued convincingly that the mystery cycles were not the final product of the liturgical plays but had their own separate existence: 'the evidence favors the idea that the movement from isolated play to cycle was brought about by a new way of regarding the subject matter rather than by a gradual, unconscious process of aggregation' (p. 286). At last the cycles had been cut free from their supposed roots in liturgical drama.

In *The Play Called Corpus Christi* (1966 [151]), V. A. Kolve focussed on the mystery cycles in a third major assault: 'Many of the questions I raise are here being considered for the first time. Others are not new, but the customary answers have seemed to me unsatisfactory' (p. 1).[25] Prosser had hinted at the possibility of studying the cycle as a unique entity: 'The cycles are not compiled by a loose following of chronology, from Creation to Judgment. Episodes have been carefully selected to fulfill a strictly theological theme: man's fallen nature and the way of his Salvation' (*149*, p. 23). Her book, however, examined episodes common to the cycles rather than any individual cycle. Kolve turned to the cycles themselves, their common features and their differences. The cycles came into being, he argued, not through evolutionary expansions, but through principles of selection. Kolve showed that a protocycle, 'the essential structure gradually achieved by the various cycles in probably various ways' (*151*, p. 51), included plays on the Fall of Lucifer, the Creation and Fall of Man, Cain and Abel, Noah's Flood, Abraham and Isaac, the Nativity sequence, the Raising of Lazarus, the Passion and Resurrection sequence and Doomsday. Its centre was the life of Christ. The Old Testament stories have figural significance.[26] And the cycle found its final shape in Creation and Doomsday, the beginning and the end of historical time: 'The shape of the drama is a linear progression, a sequence of pageant wagons or self-contained episodes on a stationary stage, but the metaphysic of its structure is centrifugal' (*151*, p. 119).

Kolve came to his comprehensive approach to cyclic form through a study of late-medieval works of religious meditation and instruction. Although the latter had often been posited as sources for some of the cycles, he rejected

86

this assumption: 'The relationship I postulate between the drama and these vernacular works is one not of parentage but of cousinship' (*151*, p. 2). The mystery cycles become, then, analogues to the encyclopaedic vernacular works of devotion. David Mills suggested that this consideration of the religious writings be supplemented by similar attention to Old English poetry, which often treats many of the same biblical episodes: 'This long interaction of liturgy, scripture and poetic tradition had already made certain episodes more familiar to writers and their audience and made them obvious candidates in a sequence of Biblical subjects for vernacular treatment' (*115*, p. 53).

Like Wickham and Hardison, Kolve challenged tradition, advocating careful attention to the individual cycle as an embracing and coherent form. He pointed out the necessity of studying a cyclic episode in comparison not only to its treatment in each cycle, but also, and crucially, to other episodes of the same cycle. Most importantly, he presented a theory of the unified form of the cycle. And once the form is acknowledged, various kinds of criticism become possible which assume an overall form, underlying themes and some form of controlling intelligence, all of these working contextually.

Wickham demanded a reappraisal of early English stage history, Hardison a new understanding of liturgical drama and Kolve a new literary approach to the mystery cycles. The groundwork for the serious study of medieval English drama had been laid.

In the two decades since the publication of Kolve's book, studies of the cycles have become so numerous, research in the field so variegated, that simple categorisation becomes almost impossible. Nevertheless, two main literary approaches to the cycles can be discerned: the thematic study of the individual cycle, which is usually indebted to Kolve's pioneering work, and the comparative analysis of the same episode in all the cycles.

Thematic criticism has focussed most often on the N-Town cycle. Long before Kolve's book appeared, Timothy Fry had argued that the entire cycle was designed around a particular Patristic theory of the Redemption known as the abuse-of-power theory. When Adam and Eve fell, according to this theory,

Satan was permitted to inflict death on them and all mankind and hold them captive in hell. Christ born of the Immaculate Virgin Mary, was not subject to that law of death. Satan, however, was deceived by the human nature of Christ, and, in bringing about His death, abused his power, and lost the souls in hell. (*178*, p. 529)

The cycle's Marian plays are crucial to this thematic approach because 'the virgin was married so that the devil could not suspect anything out of the ordinary in the birth of the Divine Person, Christ, from a virgin' (*178*, p. 536). Claude Gauvin's *Un Cycle du théâtre religieux anglais au moyen âge* (1973 [*181*]), the first book on the cycle, acknowledged Kolve's influence and reiterated the abuse-of-power theme as controlling the cycle's action.

The abuse-of-power theme has not been unreservedly accepted as the

David Staines

structural centre of the N-Town cycle. Kathleen M. Ashley sees learning and wisdom as the controlling theme: 'Christ is the personification of Wisdom in this cycle, and all human knowledge must be measured against that divine standard' (*183*, p. 123). David Mills finds 'an overall thematic concern' in 'the grace of God available to penitent Man. Set against this is a stern justice evoked as a second divine attribute which is to be tempered until Doomsday by the primary attribute of love' (*127*, p. 197). While detailing the cycle's use of figural interpretation and the typological design that results from it, Martin Stevens expands and develops Ashley's theme of learning and wisdom and relates the theme to the nature of faith (*155*, pp. 181–257).

Such an array of themes illustrates the complexity and the dangers of thematic criticism. A theme often determines the manner in which an episode is treated, and becomes, therefore, a structural principle. Yet the thematic critic must always acknowledge the initial problem of a cycle's composite authorship, even where a single intelligence seems responsible, as for example for the final compilation of the N-Town manuscript. Thematic critics need to realise that a medieval cycle rarely has one dominant theme that controls the entire cycle. Repentance, redemption and grace, such are essential dimensions of salvation history, which is the central story of the mystery cycles. A cycle may well give evidence of individual themes that control some or much of the dramatic action. To posit a single exclusive theme may reduce the cycle to variations on the theme, however, and the thematic critic too often explores only a few plays that seem to illustrate the chosen theme.

The comparative analysis of cycle plays has a longer tradition than the thematic approach, for the latter presupposes an underlying unity to the cycle where the former compares various treatments of the same cyclic episode with little attention to an individual cycle. Rosemary Woolf's *The English Mystery Plays* (1972 [*153*]), the most comprehensive example of the comparative approach, offered perceptive and suggestive interpretations of all the plays of the cycles. Yet as literate as her readings are, Woolf revealed the innate drawback to this approach. The cycle itself disappeared within the fragmented divisions created by the separate plays. A cycle's individuality could not be appreciated but only the diversity of presentations possible for any one biblical incident.

The comparative approach should serve as the perfect and necessary complement to the thematic approach. To acknowledge and to appreciate the varied treatments of individual episodes underlines differences among the cycles and also restrains rash attempts to discover a cycle's dominating theme. The thematic and the comparative approaches need to operate together, the comparative preventing the thematic from becoming reductionist, the thematic preventing the comparative from being fragmentising.

Where Kolve turned to vernacular religious writings as analogues to the cycles, Woolf turned to medieval art to supplement her reading. The relationship between drama and art, she suggested, is also one of cousinship rather than parentage. Woolf was not original in her use of medieval art to illuminate her understanding of the drama. Early students of medieval art had observed the parallels in iconographic presentation between the visual arts and drama.[27] Some critics argued that many graphic depictions were based on the cycle plays.[28]

Clifford Davidson set out to correct the hypothesis that much visual art was indebted to the cycles. Visual artists and dramatists, he observed, were portraying the same biblical history, often working from the same common fund of knowledge and information. Although causal connections are usually difficult, perhaps even unimportant, to verify, the visual arts are an important supplement to any appreciation of the cycles, for they, like the vernacular religious writings, are part of the cultural fabric of the later Middle Ages. Davidson's *Drama and Art: An Introduction to the Use of Evidence from the Visual Arts for the Study of Early Drama* (1977 [*123*]), the first volume in a series designed to catalogue medieval art relevant to the drama, and his own reading of the York cycle, *From Creation to Doom* (1984 [*129*]), reveal the shared background of knowledge and beliefs that stands behind the visual arts and the drama. And the sequential patterns in illuminated manuscripts, roof bosses, stained glass and other forms of medieval art offer further analogues to the cyclic structure of the drama.[29]

Earlier than the thematic and comparative approaches is the critical investigation of the plays' versification. Nineteenth-century criticism examined versification carefully, indeed laboriously, to determine possible authorship of the cycles or levels of authorship, implying that the more complex a play's verse, the later the date of composition of that play in its cycle. Such examinations rarely studied the beauty or the effectiveness of the poetry because the poetry was, by definition, inferior verse, and subsequent criticism continued to assume that the cycle plays, which are, after all, verse dramas, contained in most cases only bad verse.

Richard J. Collier's *Poetry and Drama in the York Corpus Christi Play* (1977 [*160*]) reopens the study of versification in the York cycle and underlines the need for further exploration of language in all the cycles. Establishing poetry as a crucial element of the cycle, Collier divides the language into three predominant but not mutually exclusive voices: the homiletic, the lyric and the narrative. The fusion of formality and naturalness in the poetry is, according to Collier, the mark of the cycle as a whole. His unfounded contention that the medieval playwright would have thought of himself as a poet, not as a dramatist, does not detract from the importance of his study as a corrective to earlier attitudes to the poetry of the cycles.

Patterns of versification have led editors and critics to ascribe individual plays to the same writer, for the question of authorship, the most complex question in medieval drama criticism, admits of no easy solution, and versification seemed to many students of the drama a possible avenue to authorial identity. Such designations as 'author', 'dramatist', 'playwright', 'adaptor', 'compiler', 'reviser' and 'play-doctor' appear with frequency but

David Staines

not clarity in current studies, and emphasise the fact that the plays were communal works that may have undergone a series of revisions. The manuscripts of the cycles offer no evidence about authorial identity, and historical documents shed no light in this area. Yet the need to create authors was and is powerful.

Eight plays in the York Passion sequence have been identified as the work of one man, the so-called 'York Realist', on the basis of their alliterative verse and their detailed realism. Just as traditional assumptions about versification in the cycles are being re-examined, so too must conclusions about authorship that are based on versification.[30]

The Towneley cycle provides the most cogent example of the quest for authorship. The cycle contains six plays that have been identified as the work of one author, the so-called Wakefield Master, on the basis of their nine-line alliterative stanza and their colloquial idiom. (The same stanza, it should be noted, is also used in parts of seven other plays in the cycle.) In addition to their superb verse and its natural, often racy language, the six plays also display 'a lively use of gesture and action, an outspoken criticism of contemporary abuses, a bold rehandling of secular material for comic purposes, and an unusual skill in characterization' (*166*, p. xx).

Because of the identification of the so-called Wakefield Master, much of the criticism of the Towneley cycle has restricted itself to the plays ascribed to him. For example, Hans-Jürgen Diller argues that the six plays consciously make characters subservient to plot. The author's 'mastery of character-drawing is in fact inseparable from his skill in plot-construction. As a comic playwright he is not so much interested in the conflicts and passions of the individual as in the enrichment of the action by individual characteristics' (*168*, p. 287). The author's skill in versification makes Martin Stevens consider language 'a major thematic concern in the cycle ... The essential premise of the Towneley cycle as a whole about language is that simplicity and artlessness mark the speech of the virtuous' (*171*, pp. 101–2). Though purportedly studying the cycle as a whole, John Gardner's *The Construction of the Wakefield Cycle* (1974 [*169*]) focusses primarily on the plays of the so-called Wakefield Master. Gardner facilely divides the plays into good plays, that is those whose versification is effective and therefore the probable work of the Master, and dull plays which show no trace of the Master's work. And when Jeffrey Helterman explores in detail *Symbolic Action in the Plays of the Wakefield Master* (1981 [*172*]), he accepts without question the identity of the Wakefield Master.

There is no denying the dramatic power of the verse of many plays in the Towneley cycle, which does contain more humour and more racy dialogue than the other cycles. Yet the time is opportune for a reassessment here too of the question of authorship. The supposed identity of the Wakefield Master was originally based on a study of versification, and later criticism did not carefully examine or challenge the conclusions reached by such studies. The desire to posit an author to these anonymous plays is powerful, natural and also dangerous. Perhaps there was a master dramatist in or around Wakefield. Or perhaps, as John Gardner suggests, there was a playwrighting school (*169*, p. 138). In any case, the question of authorship remains the most irresolvable question in medieval drama criticism.

As nineteenth-century critical assumptions about medieval drama are questioned and, in many cases, reformulated, the need for proper scholarly texts confronts the critics. The Chester cycle, a sequence that lacks a definite form, provides a model for the kind of scholarship the other cycles await. Once considered the oldest cycle, the Chester is now known to be the latest of the extant cycles. Surviving in full in five manuscripts, none of them compiled before 1591, the term 'Chester cycle' is, therefore, 'a convenient abstraction; there is no reconstructable definitive form of the cycle, but a text that perhaps from the outset incorporated a number of different possibilities and that in any case was subject to frequent revision' (*200*, p. 67).

In 1955 Salter's *Mediaeval Drama in Chester* (*186*) challenged the traditional dating as well as the theory that the cycle originated as a translation and adaptation of a French cycle from the fourteenth century. The editorial studies of Robert M. Lumiansky and David Mills (*188–90, 196, 200–4* and see chapter 4, pp. 75–8, this volume), the important research of Lawrence M. Clopper (*141, 187, 192, 194*), Sally-Beth MacLean's catalogue of Chester's medieval art (*198*) and the complete concordance to the plays (*197*) provide the ideal background, which no other cycle has so fully received, for interpretative studies of the plays.

Exemplary in its use of the comparative approach to complement a careful thematic reading, Peter W. Travis' *Dramatic Design in the Chester Cycle* (1982 [*199*]), the first and only book-length study of the cycle, places the plays in their historical and cultural context. The scriptural allegiance and conservative aesthetics of the plays represent a deliberate return to ancient authorities – artistic, scriptural and theological: 'Chester's dramatic style, homiletic strategies, and conservative theology are not only all inter-dependent phenomena but are all part of a deliberate "archaizing" spirit which informs the entire cycle' (p. 171). Alone of all the cycles, the Chester realised, according to Travis, the potential for incorporating the essential articles of faith from the Creed into the very design and texture of the plays.

Dramatic Design in the Chester Cycle offers a careful reading of the cycle that would have been impossible without the historical and editorial investigations that preceded it. At the same time, however, the book tends to overlook the dramatic dimensions of its subject, becoming a forceful reminder of the perennial problem of drama criticism, the seemingly inevitable divorce between literary appreciation and theatrical observation. Travis, for example, applauds the Wrights' play of the Nativity: 'the pageant's structural unity, its patterning of various discrete illuminations, serves as the foundation for its major strategic design – to effect in the audience a renewed recognition that Christ is born for the salvation of all' (p. 116). Stanley J. Kahrl's stage-oriented *Traditions of Medieval English*

David Staines

Drama (1974 [*119*]), however, finds nothing to applaud in the play: 'the play-wright constructing the Chester Wrights' play has no sense of form. There is no stage in the author's mind for which he is writing ... we cannot even reconstruct the staging of this play with any certainty, for the playwright had no very clear understanding of what constituted drama' (pp. 57–8). The union of the dramaturgic and the literary is the goal of all drama criticism. To combine literary appreciation with analysis of the dramatic dimensions of the plays is to create that ideal form of criticism which the mystery cycles await.

To the nineteenth century, the cycle, a romance or a play cycle, was a late-medieval form that lacked design and unity. Tennyson's observation about Malory – 'there are very fine things in it, but all strung together without Art' – epitomises the century's attitude toward the cycle.[31]

Recent studies have begun to see the cycle as a unified art. Larry D. Benson has related Malory to the Arthurian prose cycles as they developed in the thirteenth and fourteenth centuries:

These cyclic romances – and almost all Arthurian prose romances are cyclic – are not distinct and independent tales in the manner of earlier verse romances; each is part of a larger and coherent 'history' that comprehends all stories of Arthur and his knights. The thirteenth-century cyclic romances are apparently a by-product of the general thirteenth-century tendency toward the organization of all knowledge, history, and stories into *summae*, *encyclopediae*, universal chronicles, and vast cycles of the tales of Charlemagne and his peers or of Arthur and his knights.[32]

Like the earlier romance cycles, the mystery cycles are universal chronicles, indeed the most universal, choosing as their subject the history of the world from Creation to Doomsday. The nineteenth century wisely sensed a similarity between cyclic romances and drama sequences, yet failed to perceive their similar form of unity. Modern criticism has challenged and rejected the assumption of disunity and is now examining the nature of cyclic creation.

When Kolve argued that the mystery cycle had its own unity, he referred to Aristotle: 'without the dramatists' needing to know Aristotle, something like Aristotle's "beginning, middle, and end" may be claimed for these cycles' (*151*, p. 58). The three advents of God, when He made man, when He became man and when He shall come to judge man, became, for Kolve, the beginning, the middle and the end of the cycle. As alluring as such unity may be, the cycle, by its very nature, has no defined middle, but only a fixed beginning and end, with intervening scenes or episodes forming a set of variables that give the art its unique degree of elasticity.

The romance cycles had many ways of informing the reader of their unity:

If the reader was to accept a romance as an integral part of the true history of the Arthurian court, he had to be shown the many ways in which each individual romance was related to the whole cycle, and the writers of the prose romances showed such relationships by establishing networks of references to other parts of the cycle and by frequent statements of exactly how the episodes in the particular branch were related to events in the rest of the cycle.[33]

The English mystery cycles

Through their biblical episodes, the mystery cycles have the advantage of typology, which provided 'networks of references' from Old Testament plays to New Testament plays. The themes that many critics have discovered in individual cycles reveal further forms of unity. The need to combine literary interpretation and theatrical observation becomes crucial here, for a final device for unity is the theatre itself: character groupings, placement of stage properties and scenic arrangements both on scaffolds and on wagons. A complete exploration of stage presentation will reveal that such theatrical patterns are visual equivalents of the 'frequent statements' and linking *explicits* in the romance cycles.

More than a collection or series of plays, the English mystery cycle is a dramatic sequence with its own artistic rules and demands, a sequence from a particular beginning to a particular end and, in that movement, which includes a selection of interdependent plays, is a unity created by thematic emphases that are underscored by visual theatrical patterns. A structural and contemporary analogue to the mystery cycle is not only the romance cycle, but also what is perhaps the most famous poetic cycle of the Middle Ages, Chaucer's *Canterbury Tales*. Beginning with the Knight's ordered tale of bygone days of chivalry and ending with the Parson's preparation for spiritual fulfilment, *The Canterbury Tales* has no Aristotelian middle, and its very form is one of elasticity, variability and almost endless amplification. Chaucer's most famous pilgrim, the widow from suburban Bath, frequented the mystery cycles, and the Miller, another pilgrim equally familiar with the plays, told of a carpenter and a clerk who have knowledge and experience of the Noah and the Herod plays.

Like *The Canterbury Tales*, the English mystery cycle is more than a frame around a collection of scenes; it is a distinctly late-medieval art that embraces a sequence of plays that are related both to their common subject, Christ, and to one another. The artistry of the cycle does not lie in the plot, which is well known both to the dramatists and their audience. What is fluid and variable in the cycle is the treatment of the biblical events and the selection of stories that clarify and develop the cycle's thematic emphases. The interrelatedness of the parts is the originality and the accomplishment of the dramatists, for the patterns that inform the cycle and its component parts offer the only unity possible in this art.

As nineteenth-century assumptions about cycles give way to contemporary appreciation of their form, the need to define an aesthetics becomes evident, an aesthetics not of medieval drama, for such a term is too encompassing to embrace a single aesthetics, but of the English mystery cycles.

The N-Town, York, Towneley and Chester cycles are community theatre, the responsibility of the craft and religious guilds that formed much of their audience. They are theatre of the people and for the people. 'It is clear, as a means of rehearsing this essential story, that the cycles addressed themselves above all to the unlettered and the un-Latined', Kolve noted (*151*, p. 3). Their audience, therefore, influences the treatment of the plays. Travis

David Staines

describes the Chester audience: 'To be a viewer of the Chester Passion was to be a participant in a painful yet purgative celebration, as the Savior through the ritual strategies of the dramatic performance is reunited once again with the community of his faithful' (*199*, p. 191). And Travis is the first critic to underline the importance of the audience:

In analyzing Chester's design of salvation history, I have chosen to include the viewers' involvement as part of that design. Likewise, I find it unavoidable to include the viewers within the cycle's design of the education of the Christian Everyman ... As the spirit of Everyman advances from Creation to Doomsday, the viewers reexperience the major events of history, they relearn the fundamental tenets of Christian belief, and they are reminded of the primary importance of their own daily acts of corporal mercy. (*199*, p. 251)

'Never was suspension of disbelief invited', Kolve declared in regard to the mystery cycles. The aim of the plays, he continued, 'was to celebrate and elucidate, never, not even temporarily, to deceive' (*151*, pp. 27, 32). Here is a point of departure for the development of an aesthetics of the mystery cycles, for the focus of Kolve's reflections is not the play but the audience, who are also the participants and the creators of their own theatrical experience.

Studies of the English mystery cycles began when the nineteenth century found them the distant and dull background to the glories of Shakespeare and the Elizabethan theatre. Now, with our new knowledge of some of the history of the cycles, we can begin to investigate and appreciate them, not as the remote past of the Elizabethans, but as vital and complex drama worthy of attention in its own right.

All surviving texts of the mystery cycles are Tudor documents. When the Chester cycle was produced for the last time in 1575, the Middle Ages was still a presence. The English mystery cycles emphasise the impossibility of distinguishing between the Middle Ages and the Renaissance, between medieval and Tudor, on the stages of the towns and cities of England.

Only three decades ago, scholars began to challenge critical assumptions about the mystery cycles that had persisted for more than a century; the cycles themselves, it should always be remembered, survived for nearly three centuries. 'A critic entering the field of medieval drama', David Mills observes, 'is uneasily aware of the absence even of agreed terminology, the considerable variety of critical attitude and the rapidly changing state of scholarship' (*127*, p. 83). The definitive history of early English drama and, in particular, of the mystery cycles is still to be written.

NOTES

1 The N-Town cycle, also known as *Ludus Coventriae* and as the Hegge plays, takes its title from the phrase 'N-Town', which appears in the banns to the cycle; 'N' stands for *nomen* (name), meaning that the bann-criers would insert the appropriate name of a town. The cycle may have been performed at Lincoln; see

179. For the most recent edition of the cycle, see *177*; for a complete description of the surviving manuscript, see *182*. Stanley J. Kahrl observes: 'The cycle itself is a composite, and contains plays written for station-to-station staging, left pretty much as they were handed down from the past, as well as a group of plays on the life of the Virgin which were for the most part written for the wagon stages, but apparently adapted to production in a single location as part of a place-and-scaffold production' (*119*, p. 59).

2 The first edition of the cycle was Lucy Toulmin Smith, ed., *The York Plays* (London: Oxford University Press, 1885). For the most recent edition, see *163*.

3 For the most recent edition of the cycle, see *165*. For the relationship between the Towneley and York cycles, see M. C. Lyle, *The Original Identity of the York and Towneley Cycles* (Minneapolis, MN: University of Minnesota Press, 1919).

4 For the most recent edition of the cycle, see *190* and *203*. For the dating of the cycle, see the chapter 'The Texts of the Chester Cycle' in *200*, pp. 3–86.

5 *A History of English Dramatic Literature*, 3 vols. (London: Macmillan, 1875), vol. I, p. 30.

6 The seminar was given by John Leyerle, hence 'Poculi Ludique Societas' whose initials come from *Professor Leyerle's Seminar*. Nine years later, I offered a similar course at Harvard University, where the seminar members staged the 'Cain and Abel', 'Noah' and 'Abraham and Isaac' plays from the Towneley cycle; two years later, the seminar staged the Buffeting, Crucifixion and Resurrection plays from the same cycle. The Poculi Ludique Societas productions are in Middle English; the Harvard productions used original verse translations.

7 J. Raine and J. Gordon, eds., *The Towneley Mysteries* (London: Surtees Society, 1836). The introduction, unsigned, is variously assigned to James Raine, the secretary of the Surtees Society, and to J. Hunter.

8 James Orchard Halliwell, ed., *Ludus Coventriae* (London: The Shakespeare Society, 1841).

9 Thomas Wright, ed., *The Chester Plays* (London: The Shakespeare Society, 1841–7).

10 William Marriott, ed., *A Collection of English Miracle Plays or Mysteries* (Basel: Schweighauser, 1838), p. v.

11 Thomas Wright, 'On the History of the Drama in the Middle Ages', *Essays on Archaeological Subjects*, 2 vols. (London: J. R. Smith, 1861), vol. I, p. 174.

12 Henry Morley, *English Writers*, 2 vols. (London: Chapman and Hall, 1867), vol. II, p. 349.

13 Ward, *A History of English Dramatic Literature*, vol. I, p. 34.

14 John Payne Collier, *The History of English Dramatic Poetry to the Time of Shakespeare*, 3 vols. (London: Bell, 1879), vol. II, p. 65.

15 F. J. Furnivall, ed., *The Digby Mysteries* (London: The New Shakespeare Society, 1882), p. vii.

16 Marius Sepet, 'Les Prophètes du Christ: Etude sur les origines du théâtre au moyen âge', *Bibliothèque de l'Ecole des Chartes* 28, series 6, number 3 (1867): 2. This and four subsequent articles in the same journal under the same general title were published as a book with the same title (Paris: Didier, 1878). For an analysis of Sepet's theories of the origin of medieval drama, see *35*.

17 Marius Sepet, *Le Drame chrétien au moyen âge* (Paris: Didier, 1878), p. 49.

18 'Abraham and Isaac, a Mystery Play; from a Private Manuscript of the 15th Century', *Anglia* 7 (1884): 317–18. In the same year, 'cycle' was also employed in relation to the groups of mystery plays by John Addington Symonds, *Shakespere's Predecessors in the English Drama* (London: Smith, Elder, 1884). No earlier Shakespearean scholar used the term, and Symonds' employment of

it reflected his familiarity with contemporary French criticism of medieval drama.

19 *The York Plays*, pp. lxiv–lxviii.

20 Hermann Deimling, ed., *The Chester Plays*, vol. i, EETS Extra Series 62 (London: Oxford University Press, 1892); Osborn Waterhouse, ed., *The Non-Cycle Mystery Plays*, EETS Extra Series 104 (London: Oxford University Press, 1909).

21 For a brief bibliographical account of the development of medieval drama, see *121*. For a complete analysis of the evolutionary approach to the development of drama, see *46*, pp. 1–34.

22 *A History of English Dramatic Literature*, 2nd edn, 3 vols. (London: Macmillan, 1899), vol. i, pp. 63–4.

23 Alfred W. Pollard, ed., *English Miracle Plays, Moralities and Interludes* (Oxford: Clarendon Press, 1895), pp. xxix–xxx.

24 For Craig's reviews, see *Speculum* 34 (1959): 702–5; 36 (1961): 695–8; 37 (1962): 295–8.

25 Jerome Taylor (*150*) had argued two years earlier for an effective and unified dramatic structure to the mystery cycles.

26 For the importance of typology to the cycles, see *106* and *152*. For the view that typology is not exclusive enough to function as a principle of selection in the Old Testament plays, see *194*.

27 The pioneering work was Emile Mâle, *L'Art religieux du XIIIᵉ siècle en France* (Paris: A. Colin, 1898).

28 For example, W. L. Hildeburgh, 'English Alabaster Carvings as Records of the Medieval Religious Drama', *Archaeologia* 93 (1949): 51–101, and also *110*.

29 For a fine introduction to the subject, see *109*, and also *184*.

30 In a detailed analysis of the eight plays, J. W. Robinson begins: 'I should add that it is only partly for the sake of convenience that I write of the art of the hypothetical "York Realist", rather than of "eight York Passion plays that technically resemble each other"; the particular excellence of these plays excites a corollary interest in the purposiveness of their composer' (*156*, p. 241). There is a critically unfounded jump from 'eight York Passion plays that technically resemble each other' to the 'York Realist'.

31 Hallam, Lord Tennyson, *Alfred Lord Tennyson: A Memoir*, 2 vols. (London: Macmillan, 1897), vol. i, p. 194.

32 Larry D. Benson, *Malory's Morte Darthur* (Cambridge, MA: Harvard University Press, 1976), p. 5.

33 *Ibid.*, p. 12.

6

Castles in the air: the morality plays

DAVID BEVINGTON

In order to discuss trends and new developments in the study of morality drama during the last twenty-five years or so, we need first to say a word as to what scholarship had achieved by 1965. Robert Potter has aptly summarised the earlier history of attitudes toward the morality in his chapter on 'Rediscovering the Evidence: 1660–1914' in his book, *The English Morality Play* (1975 [225]), and I need not retrace his steps in detail. The story is largely one of neo-classical preconceptions against a drama so distinctively non-classical in form and substance, of haphazard collection of materials by antiquarians (Robert Dodsley's *Old English Plays*, 1744,[1] being compiled chiefly from the Harleian collection that Dodsley had recently acquired and thus happened to have at hand), of Romantic apathy towards an anonymous drama so theologically plodding and lacking in individuality of self-expression and of Protestant Victorian distaste for a drama that was so egregiously Catholic and so irredeemably bawdy or scatological. Important discoveries were made, to be sure, including the recovery of *Everyman* and the Macro manuscript, but virtually in despite of scholarly antipathy towards the material under consideration. Morality plays were curiosities to be catalogued and collected like specimens (as suggested by John Matthews Manly's title, *Specimens of the Pre-Shaksperean Drama*, 1897[2]). The plays' main interest was in their very distant foreshadowing of the greatness to come in Elizabethan drama, a greatness that indeed was attributed chiefly to classical models rather than to native ones. Performance was unknown. The staging of *Everyman* in 1901 by William Poel's Elizabethan Stage Society was a remarkable occasion, even something of a freak, though the surprising success it achieved with reviewers indicated better things to come.

Well into the twentieth century, morality drama was condescended to by scholars trained in the Whig-Liberal and Protestant tradition of regarding medieval culture exclusive of Chaucer as priest-ridden and naive, the product of the 'Dark Ages'. E. N. S. Thompson's 'The English Moral Plays' (1910)[3] studied the drama seriously in the context of medieval sermons, but was published in an obscure series and remained largely unnoticed. Works by Catholic scholars like Sister Mary Philippa Coogan (1947)[4] tended also to be buried in little-known publications and to be suspected of special pleading, though to a more sympathetic reader her view of *Mankind* as a product of medieval Catholic culture, fully embracing both the secular and the spiritual,

David Bevington

Carnival and Lent, offered a liberated way of seeing what was at work in the play. Source studies dominated this era of historical criticism. The ideology of Darwinian evolution employed the humble and vulgar artefacts of late-medieval culture as a way of understanding some roots of Elizabethan drama. Dating, auspices and staging information were always safe subjects for scholarly investigation, in any case, and so information accumulated.

Not until the late 1950s and the 1960s did morality drama begin to gain a respectful hearing as dramatic art. Encouraged by O. B. Hardison's lucid critique of the Darwinian and anti-Catholic assumptions lying behind the study of liturgical and Latin drama, *Christian Rite and Christian Drama in the Middle Ages* (1965 [46]), and by Madeleine Doran's sympathetic view of a coherent form to be found in the best of native literary production,[5] scholars began to look at the morality in its own terms. Bernard Spivack's *Shakespeare and the Allegory of Evil* (1958)[6] was to be sure a historical study, searching in morality drama for the dramatic precursor of Vice figures in Shakespeare such as Richard III, Falstaff, Don John, Iago and Edmund, and relying on a vocabulary of development of types, but his approach had the advantage of regarding the Vice as a central figure, and his readings brought to life a number of plays that had previously shown all the signs of rigor mortis. Two studies of Skelton, Arthur Heiserman's *Skelton and Satire* (1961 [243]) and William O. Harris' *Skelton's Magnyfycence and the Cardinal Virtue Tradition* (1965 [248]), combined historical scholarship in medieval traditions of *speculum principis*, the seven Cardinal Virtues and Ciceronian ethics with a new sensitivity to the formal characteristics of texts. The result took issue with the more narrowly drawn historical scholarship of Robert L. Ramsay's EETS edition of *Magnyfycence* (in its time – 1906 – a very substantial contribution to learning),[7] to argue that *Magnyfycence* was not simply a topical polemic of the moment against Cardinal Wolsey but a serious play about statecraft in the tradition of moral struggle as defined by the morality play.

Glynne Wickham's *Early English Stages 1300 to 1660*, volume 1 (*107*), though not chiefly concerned with morality drama, gave a stirring analysis of theatrical aspects of street pageantry, royal entries and other ceremonial events from which important implications could be derived about the staging of morality drama in the round. Richard Southern's *The Medieval Theatre in the Round* (1959 [*122*]) propounded a theory about the staging of *The Castle of Perseverance* that remains controversial today, but which had the salubrious effect of imagining the play in a live, presentational theatre with the audience intimately involved in the action. Southern's book prompted in turn a serious look at the nature of the morality play before 1500 by Arnold Williams (1963 [*215*]); Williams found *The Castle of Perseverance* to be 'an epitome of a great deal of the artistic and intellectual achievement of the middle ages' in its schematic organisation, its symbolic costuming, its stage literalisation of metaphor – all more meaningful to Williams than the inert values conveyed by the literary term 'allegory'.

Castles in the air: the morality plays

Douglas Cole offered a plausible discussion of Marlowe's debt to morality tradition in his *Suffering and Evil in the Plays of Christopher Marlowe* (1962 [267]). My own *From 'Mankind' to Marlowe* (214) had the good fortune to come along at a time (1962) when it too could argue the inventiveness and cohesion of the morality play; here the emphasis was on ways in which an antithetical and alternating dramatic structure of comic and serious action arose in part out of the casting demands of the troupes that itinerantly performed the plays. T. W. Craik's *The Tudor Interlude* (242) appeared in 1958, with its lively theatrical analysis of costuming, properties and other aspects of staging in many plays that had never been dealt with closely before in these terms. Overall, the most significant achievement of these years was the establishment of the morality drama as inherently worthy of further study. Thus matters stood in 1965, give or take a dissertation or two.

To see what has happened since, I should like to focus on what seem to me a few of the most significant achievements, rather than attempt to survey all. A good place to begin is with Robert Potter's *The English Morality Play* (1975 [225]), since it is one book in the last twenty years that deals most wholly with morality drama and since it throws down a number of gauntlets. Several worthy assumptions underlie Potter's work: that morality drama is presentational in its staging, that it is of a piece with other genres of medieval drama, that it is best understood in the context of continental morality drama rather than as part of an isolated English experience, that as a quintessentially medieval form it expresses a universal Christian story of temptation, fall, penitence and redemption and that its ritual origins are best comprehended in anthropological terms as a way of teaching humanity to cope with critical rites of passage from birth into life and thence into death.

These assumptions, and the seriousness with which Potter confronts morality drama, are symptomatic of the new scholarship of the 1960s and 1970s. So too is the strong sense of break with the inadequacies of the past. The morality play is not the lifeless abstraction, writes Potter, to which it was reduced by too much historical pedantry. Its characters are parts for actors, and on the presentational stage they come to life. William Poel's success with *Everyman* in 1901 coincided, but not coincidentally, with the reintroduction of a kind of staging that had originally given the play and others like it such vitality. Played outdoors by Poel's company, in a monastic setting, involving the audience in the experience, *Everyman* called attention to its own theatricality and exploited the resources of a multi-level stage not unlike the *sedes* and *platea* arena so often used in medieval times. Nor, insists Potter, is the morality play the lifeless derivative of Prudentius' *Psychomachia*, that distant fourth-century poem touted by historical scholars. Instead, says Potter, the morality play grew out of sermons and penitential literature in the late Middle Ages. It arose in the midst of other forms of religious drama, such as the Corpus Christi plays, and remained more like those other forms than different from them, focussing on the central experience of fall and penitence. It absorbed materials from folk drama, from Pater Noster plays designed as *remedia* for sin, from traditions of the seven Deadly Sins and Cardinal Virtues and from allegorical works like *Piers Plowman*.

Potter is too dismissive of the Psychomachia tradition of combat between virtues and vices; I see no reason why one cannot regard such combat as complementary to the portrayal of fall and penance, rather than excluded by it, and the combat is certainly there in a play like *The Castle of Perseverance*. Still, Potter's emphasis on the centrality of penance is effective in describing not only early morality plays but also their polemical successors during the Renaissance and Reformation. Potter is right to stress the importance of penance to the King in *Magnyfycence*, in Bale's *King Johan* and later indeed in Shakespeare's *1 Henry IV* and *King Lear*. No less commendable is his call for more work on continental morality drama, although in his own book (designedly focussed on English morality drama) the continental materials are confined chiefly to one chapter on the subject where their pertinence to developments in England is not always easy to determine.

At any rate, Potter's gracefully written book is full of new challenges and serves here as a convenient point of departure for further analysis of recent developments. Following his arguments, I should like to concentrate on a few problems, as follows: (1) staging, (2) morality drama in relation to later Elizabethan drama and (3) English morality drama in relation to other contexts, such as continental drama, anthropology and iconography.

In matters of staging, the morality play confronts us with a variety and uncertainty that calls into question the very concept of a single entity called 'the morality play'. Probably it is better to assume, with Potter, that morality drama is of a piece with medieval drama generally and shares its diversity of staging methods. Certainly morality drama before 1500 shows this diversity, so much so that one must wonder how the itinerant moral drama of the sixteenth century evolved its staging methods out of a play like *The Castle of Perseverance* – if in fact it did so.

The Castle of Perseverance is at the centre of an important debate about medieval staging in the round (see also chapter 8, pp. 135–7). How are we to interpret its famous staging diagram? Richard Southern argued in 1957 (*122*) that the 'ditch' called for in the diagram is to be constructed around the whole playing arena, to provide a barrier for entrance, to supply seating along its banked inner walls for the spectators and to support the scaffolds of God, World, Flesh, Devil and Covetousness – all but the last of these located on the four primary points of the compass, with Covetousness relegated to one of the interstices since he is not of the same rank as God and the Devil. Southern's playing area is roughly fifty feet across, with the castle of Perseverance in the centre and raised on supports to aid the sightlines. Ushers, the 'stytelerys' mentioned in the diagram, control the spectators sitting or standing on the level ground below the banked seats, in order to facilitate the many processions of this play from scaffold to scaffold and to provide room for the action immediately around the castle. Southern argues so cogently that many of his conclusions still command assent, and even his controversial ideas remain the focus of meaningful debate. His was a visionary book, well timed to meet a new interest in presentational staging in the round for other medieval drama and for more modern plays as well.

From the first, however, Southern's ditch presented serious problems. R. P. Ryan, in a review (1958),[8] calculated that some 20,000 cubic feet of earth would have to be moved and 150,000 gallons of water provided to fill the ditch. Why not employ guards, and the strong barring all about also mentioned in the diagram, to keep out non-paying guests? Mark Eccles, in his EETS edition of *The Macro Plays* (*217*), was similarly sceptical. Natalie Schmitt has provided the fullest reply (*114*) in her re-examination of the evidence for a medieval theatre in the round. Her proposal is that the ditch is a castle moat surrounding the castle in the centre of the acting arena. She agrees with Southern that the audience is on all sides of the circular arena, keeping free the 'midst of the place', and that the *sedes* are raised scaffolds on all four sides (along with Covetousness' *sedes* at an irregular point on the circle), but contends that the famous drawing is a set design more than a realistic scale drawing of a theatre. Schmitt's thesis eliminates the large cost of constructing a mammoth earthwork – all the more daunting in view of the play's banns that posit performance in a variety of locations. She draws usefully on medieval allegories of castles, especially Bishop Grosseteste's *Le Chasteau d'Amour* (*c.* 1230), in which the castle symbolises the protection offered by the Virgin, or *The Castle of Love*, with its four colours of red, blue, green and white suggestive of the coloured mantles for the four daughters of God in *The Castle of Perseverance*. Such allegorical castles often feature a moat, one that has the allegorical significance of cleansing. To cross over water when entering the castle of the Virgin or of the soul is to experience a cleansing transformation. The *Castle* design thus offers a symbolic world in which every physical aspect of staging has a counterpart in the allegorical conflict of good and evil for the soul of mankind.

The special strength of Schmitt's argument is that it answers Southern in the pragmatic terms of staging requirements. Schmitt is not an iconographical student, though she has consulted pictures of medieval allegorical castles, but a theatre historian interested (as is Southern) in blocking, sightlines and properties. In her theatre, the symbolic actions of *The Castle of Perseverance* can easily be adapted to performance on a village green, and make rich capital out of the play's theatrical environment. The battle between the Virtues and Vices, expressed in taunts hurled across a symbolic moat and then in physical action on the green, is a lively one. The water becomes central, first when Chastity quenches the 'fowle hete' of Lechery by throwing her in the moat (ll. 2302, 2390, in *19*) and then when Sloth attempts to divert the waters from the ditch with his spade. The water is Mary's grace; Sloth represents spiritual dryness, and is comically foiled in his assault. Mankind's departure from the castle seems to take account of his crossing the ditch, and his corpse may later be thrown into it by World's Boy as a final dismal token of his fallen spiritual fortunes.

David Bevington

Schmitt's theory is impressive in terms of the practicalities of dialogue and stage directions, but her concluding argument meets with less success when she attempts to throw doubt on the whole hypothesis of medieval theatres in the round. Her argument is well taken that huge earthworks would often have been impractical for the putting on of touring plays, but even she does not attempt to deny, as Neville Denny (206) and Richard Hosley (253) have argued, that rounds like those in Cornwall were occasionally used for performance. The Fouquet miniature painting *Le Martyre de Sainte Apolline*, other pictorial evidence presented by Hosley and still more witnesses are too clear for us to doubt that staging in the round was known. Still, Schmitt is generally on the right track to stress the comparative rarity of monumental earthworks and the likelihood instead of flexible acting conditions.

The critical issue of flexibility is at stake in a consideration of Merle Fifield's 1967 *The Castle in the Circle* (216). Fifield begins with a useful essay on the kinds of street pageants analysed by Wickham (107), showing not only the ubiquitousness of staging in the round on such occasions but the frequent utilisation of symbolic towers. Tower stages in the Great Conduit in Cheapside greeted Richard II during his coronation progress of 1377 and again in 1392. They turned up in the lavish reception for Catherine of Aragon in 1501. Spectators on such occasions not only surrounded the procession passing through the streets but were close to the scaffolds and to any dramatic action taking place on the open area lying before the scaffolds. Pictorial evidence from the period, assiduously collected by Fifield (218, 224) is not lacking in similar towers and surrounding crowds, although the pertinence of this material to the theatre is often open to question. When Fifield attempts to demonstrate the employment of what she calls a *Castle* stage in a preponderance of morality plays before 1500, in any case, she ends up demonstrating the reverse, that is, a marked difference from play to play. Only by excessive ingenuity can one hypothesise a *Castle* stage for *Mankind*, with four separate mansions assigned to Mercy, Mankind, Myscheff and New-Guyse, Now-a-days and Nought, a *platea*, and an audience on the *platea* among the mansions. *Everyman* could no doubt 'effectively utilize the central tower, a mansion, and the open *platea*' (216, p. 39), but the text offers no positive evidence of the sort demonstrated in *The Castle of Perseverance* by Southern and Schmitt. *Wisdom* is so markedly different in its staging requirements that even Fifield is obliged to treat it as anomalous, bolstering her argument with allegations that the play is theologically anomalous as well.

I do think the *Castle* stage or something like it was in use for plays other than *The Castle of Perseverance*, especially in the Lincoln–Cambridgeshire–Norfolk–East Midlands area, and especially when we look beyond the few surviving early moralities to other genres, to the Digby *Mary Magdalene* with its allegorical figures placed alongside historical ones, or the N-Town cycle's Passion sequence. To make such a connection across genres is to

Castles in the air: the morality plays

stress once again the variety of medieval drama, for the similarities of staging transcend generic boundaries and indeed reveal how evanescent those boundaries can be. Staging considerations before 1500 do not encourage the view of a monolithic generic identity for moral drama.

Revivals of morality drama in the 1970s and 1980s, though few in number, add to our impression of versatility and range. The Toronto production of *The Castle of Perseverance* (1979) was the first Toronto staging of a major work in the round, though the university's medieval acting company, Poculi Ludique Societas (PLS), had of course experimented with presentational staging of *Mankind* and other moral plays on a smaller scale. (*The Castle* had earlier been staged by Philip Cook, in the cloister of Abingdon Priory in 1974 and then indoors at the University of Manchester in 1981, and other settings have been attempted elsewhere; see Proudfoot, *236*.) The *Castle* set at Toronto featured a castle on stilts, and showed that it was not only possible but theatrically attractive to play around, under and through this commanding structure. A symbolic moat surrounded the castle, as in Schmitt's reconstruction. Audiences seated on bleachers discovered that action located on a scaffold across the playing area could seem quite distant and at times inaudible. Strongly compensating for this attenuating effect of distance was the symbolic logic of the set as a whole, the visible presence of God's scaffold and the Devil's dungeon throughout, impressive ceremonial processions across the playing area, the assembling of brightly costumed actors for a battle and the stylised contrasts of the Virtues and the Vices as they contended for Mankind's soul at the centre of the cosmic arena. The event took five hours of playing time. Similar visual juxtapositions have since been employed at Toronto in other performances in the round, as in the N-Town Passion sequence (1983), thereby demonstrating once again the ability of medieval staging techniques to cross generic boundaries.

A performance of *Wisdom* at Trinity College, Connecticut, in 1984, directed by Milla Riggio and played in conjunction with a conference on various aspects of the play, effectively illustrated a very different kind of staging. The play was located indoors, in a college hall, and was surrounded with a series of ceremonial occasions. Costumed actors in procession filed into the hall, after having performed a fealty ceremony for King Edward IV and his queen in the nearby Trinity Chapel, thereby recreating a hypothetically possible circumstance of original production – an abbot's banquet masque presented to the king on the occasion of his visit to Bury St Edmunds in 1474. (Gail Gibson [*239*] argues that such a visit could indeed have taken place, but in 1469 rather than 1474.) A medieval banquet before the play added to the sense of festive occasion. Spectators were arrayed along both sides of the hall, with the king and his royal party on the dais at the lower end of the hall. A small stage with rising steps stood at the opposite end, near the entrance doors. Ceremonial action, such as the exchanges between Wisdom and Anima, occurred usually on this stage, whereas the livelier action of the three Mights took to the floor among the spectators. The scenes of tempta-

David Bevington

tion and fall are not raucous and bawdy in this play, as they are in *Mankind*, but in the Trinity production they were absorbing and colourful, with an appropriate emphasis on masking and dancing. Indeed, the whole production made the point that a theologically serious play, written under religious auspices and perhaps for a distinguished courtly audience along with its clerical spectators and other guests, might well have taken its theatrical style from the courtly masque. Considerable attention was paid to symbolic meanings of costume, grouping of actors and gesture. The papers of the conference, edited by Riggio and published by the AMS Press in 1986 (*103*), amplify the sense of cohesiveness in this play when it is viewed as both a philosophical work and an effective piece of theatre. And the point was made that performance is an invaluable form of research and criticism. (At least one other such learned conference on medieval drama attached to a performance, that of the Benediktbeuren Passion Play at Indiana University in 1982, is worth noting here even though not related to morality drama, for it too illustrated the very real benefits of bringing together scholarly investigation and performance.)

The bulk of morality drama was written neither for performance by large casts on multiple scaffolds in the round, nor for the studiously clerical auspices of *Wisdom*, but for itinerant troupes of 'four men and a boy' and for the varied conditions they must have met in churches, guildhalls and the great halls of the aristocracy. Recent performances of *Mankind* and similar plays by the PLS and other groups at Kalamazoo and Toronto (see for example David Parry and Kathy Pearl's PLS performance text of *Nice Wanton* [*260*], and the stage history in Ian Lancashire's edition of *Two Tudor Interludes* [*262*]) have made clear the debt of these lively plays to folk drama, to improvisational theatre with a minimum of heavy properties and to presentational staging in the midst of spectators. T. W. Craik (*242*), Richard Southern (*268, 273*) and Richard Hosley (*253*), along with Glynne Wickham (*107*) and Walter Hodges,[9] have made extraordinary contributions towards our understanding of how these plays were mounted, costumed and acted. The Tudor morality emerges from such study as a primary workshop in which sixteenth-century dramatists learned the trade that was to produce such excellence by the end of the century. Nothing could more effectively discredit the previous neglect and condescension with which this drama had been treated than a living demonstration of its vibrant theatricality.

I wish to enter only one major caveat as a corrective and basis for further analysis. The critics cited here are virtually unanimous in regarding the Tudor morality as an entity, a coherent body of drama normally acted in Tudor halls for patrician audiences (albeit with servants present). Disclaimers are offered, to be sure, but these critics still agree in the main with Craik's pronouncement that 'indoor performance was, I think, the kind of performance for which most Tudor interludes were designed' (*242*, p. 9). Craik's very choice of the term 'interlude' for his title tends to impose on a heterogeneous drama an assumed set of common aims and methods. Southern's deft recon-

Castles in the air: the morality plays

structions of performances for plays like *Nature* and *Fulgens and Lucrece* (both by Henry Medwall; see Alan Nelson's edition [*263*]) help us visualise what the action would be like in front of a hall screen featuring two doors, with spectators lining the two sides of the hall and sitting on the dais opposite the screen. Southern is quite rightly interested in the evidence as to how actors go out of the 'place' of acting, or enter a doorway crowded with attendants who must be pushed aside. He examines references to performance 'this night', to the hall itself and its occupants. In later Tudor plays he looks for evidence of a 'travers' or curtained recess into which noble figures in the play can retire from view without leaving the acting arena, of a 'stage' raised on the floor of the hall and of action 'above'. Wickham provides illustrations of the way stage 'houses' were constructed for courtly entertainments. Outdoor dramatic occasions are examined as well, but the repeated implication is of an unbroken tradition linking indoor courtly entertainments (especially morality drama) with the late-sixteenth-century Elizabethan stage. Southern is explicit on the visual link. Performance on a raised stage in front of a hall screen, with its two or more doors and a musicians' gallery above, resembles not coincidentally the sketch of the Swan Theatre (*c.* 1596) by Johannes de Witt, he insists; one is the prototype of the other. Hosley bolsters the case with further arguments. The workshop in which sixteenth-century drama grew to maturity, it turns out, was indoors and patrician; though morality drama had a popular function as well, its staging methods were devised primarily for performance in front of the hall screen.

Before this unitary view of Tudor morality drama hardens into an orthodoxy (unless it has already done so), let me review some obverse considerations. The casting evidence I surveyed in *From 'Mankind' to Marlowe* (*214*) argues for itinerant drama of a popular sort, one that brought to a whole nation entertaining performances dealing with issues of broad social, religious and educational concern. The actors played under varying conditions, often indeed at court or in noble households, though the vagaries of surviving texts may accentuate this aspect of their activities. Certainly when they took their plays into a great hall, the actors made use of the screen and hall floor. Even so, as I have previously argued (*255*), there is a vital difference between a performance of *Horestes* (1567) and *Gorboduc* in such a venue. The former, with its popular use of alarums, sieges, hangings and the like, anticipates the kind of theatrical gymnastics we find in Shakespeare's *Henry VI* plays. The play deals with serious political issues suitable for courtly presentation, but it is also fully adapted to touring performance with scaling operations devised for a booth stage set up in a guildhall, an inn-yard or wherever. (For a contrary argument in favour of courtly auspices, see Marie Axton's edition of *Three Tudor Classical Interludes* [*265*].) *Gorboduc*, on the other hand, studiously avoids stage violence and pyrotechnics as courtly drama of the period usually does, and could have been staged only at the Inns of Court for a Christmas revels at considerable expense. Performance was not repeated, since it depended for its political effect on the presence of Queen Elizabeth, to whom advice on the question of the succession was being gratuitously offered. Interaction between courtly and popular drama was of course an essential feature of sixteenth-century English drama, fortunately for both, but the ignoring of the distinction in an appraisal of the evolution of staging techniques is too likely to produce the distortion we also see in recent attempts to turn most of Shakespeare's later plays into entertainments for the court of King James (as, for example, in Henry Paul's *The Royal Play of 'Macbeth'*, 1950).

Another orthodoxy needs to be examined, and that is the assumption that the morality play deserves the place accorded it in standard literary histories as a major link between medieval and High Renaissance drama. John Wasson has urged forcefully, and indeed with a calculated intemperance, that the morality play ought to be dethroned. To begin with, records of performance so carefully gleaned by Wasson and other members of the REED (Records of Early English Drama) team are revelatory. Drama performed in the late Middle Ages was far more apt to be folk drama, saints' lives and non-cycle drama than anything else; even the cycle plays that figure so prominently in our view of medieval drama represent only a small fraction (16 percent) of performance records, while the morality comes in even below that. In Lincolnshire, Norfolk and Suffolk, the presumed home of early moralities like *The Castle of Perseverance*, the record on morality performance is silent. Saints' lives continued well on into the sixteenth century; folk drama continued later still. Professional acting companies are found in the fourteenth and fifteenth as well as the sixteenth century, well before they are acknowledged to have existed in most literary histories, usually composed of two, three or four members until the early 1570s. (See also Bevington [*276*], and Kahrl [*119*], on the extent of professionalism in late-medieval drama.) The actors performed mainly in churches and guildhalls. References to inn-yards are scattered, though inn-yards probably became more necessary in the later sixteenth century as actors were increasingly banned from churches and guildhalls. Even so, performances in churches continued well on into the Reformation, despite prohibitions. Large properties were minimal, and only rarely does one hear of actors erecting a special stage. Actors ordinarily performed before the choirscreen in church or on the bare floor of the guildhall. Indoor performance allowed them to control payments, but they did at times also play in churchyards, hall gardens, marketplaces, castle yards and the like. Morality drama, Wasson believes, was largely a product of the universities and secular schools. The preserved texts distort the historical reality (Wasson, *280* and *131*).

Wasson's case is deliberately overstated, and the force of his argument against morality influence on High Renaissance drama needs to be qualified by definition of terms. To say that the word 'morality', or words like it, occur rarely in the records is not to say that the plays we know, and others like them, were left unperformed; even Wasson does not go that far. Alexandra Johnston (240) hypothesises that the ephemeral nature of morality drama, its continually adapting itself to the controversial issues of the moment, may explain why it was so seldom put down in the records. In any case, plays with pronounced morality elements in them, even if they might not be labelled 'moralities', certainly played an important role in the development of sixteenth-century genres and staging methods. No doubt some extant moralities of the sixteenth century are academic or cloistered in their auspices (see *From 'Mankind' to Marlowe* [214], p. 67), but it is equally certain that plays with morality elements were professionally acted. Wasson's argument that the casting charts in these plays were intended for schoolboy performance doesn't make sense; with schoolboys one wants to employ as many young actors as possible, and in fact schoolboys' plays reveal precisely this characteristic in their lack of doubling. If we change the wording from 'morality play' to 'Tudor drama', we can then surely hope that the extant texts give us some real indication of what was actually being performed in England, and then we must take cognizance of the presence in so many of these plays of morality elements – of the omnipresent Vice, to name but one such. I cannot see that Wasson has cut the ground out from under Spivack's argument in favour of the influence of the Vice on later Elizabethan drama.

Some quibbling about the term 'morality' may be at stake here. Nevertheless, Wasson's scepticism is invaluable in urging us to reassess the centrality of whatever it is we are talking about. When he urges that the saint play is of more significance to the English history play than is the morality, or that Renaissance comedy owes much to folk drama and medieval secular comedy that need not have been filtered through the morality, or that tragedy may have enjoyed a dramatic tradition of its own in the late Middle Ages (though here he is less convincing, and ought to take another look at the arguments of Happé [247] and Margeson [270] in favour of morality influence on English tragedy), Wasson poses an iconoclastic challenge to those who continue to urge the influence of moral drama on the work of Shakespeare and his contemporaries. It is to this question of the legacy of moral drama that I turn next.

The search for a moral legacy in Renaissance drama is today's quest for the Northwest Passage or a pot of gold at the end of the rainbow. Many are convinced it is there, but establishing the definite link proves difficult. Potter (225) proposes the terms of the search when he lists some otherwise puzzling elements of Shakespeare's plays that may have their 'original rationale' in stock episodes of the morality play:

The moral prologue which outlines the whole of the play's action in advance (e.g. the prologues to *Romeo and Juliet* and *Pericles*).
The instruction of the hero by good counsel (e.g. Gaunt to Richard II, Polonius to Laertes).
The conspiracy of vice, disguising itself as virtue (e.g. Richard III and Buckingham, the Witches in *Macbeth*).

David Bevington

The initiation of the naive hero into experience (e.g. Brutus in *Julius Caesar*, Troilus in *Troilus and Cressida*).
Virtue unjustly cast out (e.g. Adam in *As You Like It*, the Soothsayer in *Julius Caesar*).
The delinquent hero's recognition of his state of sin (e.g. Antony in Egypt, Clarence's dream in *Richard III*).
The providential intervention of God's mercy (e.g. the rebirth of Hermione in *The Winter's Tale*, Portia in *The Merchant of Venice*).
The formal confession and repentance of the hero (e.g. Kate's recantation in *The Taming of the Shrew*, Richard II in the tower [*sic*]).
The unmasking and punishment of disguised vice (e.g. Malvolio in *Twelfth Night*, Iago's unmasking by Emilia).
The moralizing epilogue, implicating the audience (e.g. Feste in *Twelfth Night*, Prospero in *The Tempest*). (p. 124)

This list runs the gamut from particulars that do seem to have historical links in morality drama (especially Richard III and the Vice) to more general situations with other plausible sources, such as providential intervention (as in saints' plays) or the formal confession and repentance of the hero (as in many a religiously inspired fictional narrative, or indeed in the Bible and liturgy). Similarly, Potter's account of morality-play elements in *Volpone* is on relatively strong grounds when he discusses Volpone as a Vice figure, much as Alan Dessen (*244*) argues for the influence of the 'estates' morality play of the early Elizabethan period in *Volpone*'s exposure of avarice and corruption among various social classes and professions, but Potter is less convincing in his analysis of the play's move towards justice through a comparison with *The Castle of Perseverance*. Like Merle Fifield (*216*) and Edmund Creeth (*277*; see below), Potter begins to build *Castles* in the air.

Edgar Schell (*222*, *237*) conveniently focusses the discussion onto one important metaphor, that of life as a pilgrimage. Certainly one could not ask for a more central image to serve as the action of a drama. Schell's contention of its centrality to morality drama is neither more nor less true than Potter's contention that moral drama centres around the action of fall and penance, or Spivack's thesis (see note 6) that morality drama is about the Psychomachia battle between virtue and vice with Mankind as the disputed prize. All are ways of describing the story, so central to the culture of the period, of humanity's expulsion from Eden and eventual salvation.

The allegorical pilgrimage has many medieval antecedents, of course, in Guillaume de Deguileville, in John Lydgate, in Saint Bernard and others. They share 'a common sense of the significant form of Christian life' (*237*, p. 24). Schell argues that the plays he chooses to analyse – *The Castle of Perseverance*, *The Marriage of Wit and Science*, *Woodstock*, *Volpone* and *King Lear* – are all 'shaped with reference to that action'. The model is plainly suited to *The Castle of Perseverance*, designed as it is to represent the whole life of man from his birth until the day of his judgement before God's throne. Schell's focus does well with *The Castle* in the theatre; the play's many journeys, its playing area with the castle at the centre, provide 'a theatrical equivalent of the moral landscapes found in the literary pilgrimages and allows for similar metaphors of action' (*237*, p. 43). The *platea* is a neutral ground, a place of moral change. Mankind's journey encompasses all the major stages of life's pilgrimage found in the non-dramatic allegories. In *The Marriage of Wit and Science* we see a journey no less clearly, this time metaphorically applied to the hero's quest for learning. Much of the play can be accounted for in terms of the romance of knight-errantry, but pilgrimage is a revealing and pertinent metaphor as well.

To see Richard II in *Woodstock* as an example of the king as pilgrim and to press an analogy with *The Pride of Life*, however, is to raise the troublesome issue argued by Wasson in his sceptical view of the Elizabethan history play's presumed debt to the moral drama. Is the connection tangible? On Schell's side of the argument, Skelton's *Magnyfycence* and Bale's *King Johan*, among other plays, do put kings on stage amidst moral abstractions and subject those kings to the tribulations afflicting many a mortal on life's pilgrimage. Still, *Woodstock* is so manifestly peopled with figures from history and concerned with issues of political confrontation that Schell is repeatedly obliged to concede that we are not talking about a morality play. *Woodstock*'s indebtedness, he argues, is more broadly a matter of thought, the logic of action, the construction of characters and 'the conception of the relationship between the way in which a king is related to the political community in a history play and the way in which Mankind is related to the theatrical "country" he inhabits in a morality play' (*237*, pp. 83–4). *Woodstock* 'follows the model of the morality drama in its larger movements, reshaping the facts of history to embody political responsibility in Richard's uncles and vanity in Bushy, Bagot, and Greene in order to illustrate the essential form of Richard's career' (p. 105). The dramatist 'thinks like a morality playwright' in reshaping history's pattern to one of 'everyman's moral pilgrimage' (p. 111). The reading illuminates the play, but as historical argument it leaves unanswered the question as to whether the author found the pervasive metaphor of pilgrimage in morality drama or in other places. *Volpone*'s revelling in disguise can similarly look to other precedents, and in *King Lear* Schell must argue that the author mounts a radical attack on the very morality form he inherited. Schell's argument thus resembles Maynard Mack's reading of *King Lear* as anti-romance (*269*), creating expectations of comfort that are then disastrously undercut. Shakespeare's play, says Schell, is almost Shavian in the way it 'turns a familiar dramatic form against itself and the assumptions it embodies' (*237*, p. 194). Schell's reading of *Lear* is enlightening, but the question persists: did Shakespeare need to go specifically to the morality drama for the idea of life as a pilgrimage, and would his audience have recognised an allusion to this particular dramatic genre in order to understand that the form was being undercut? What I am arguing is perhaps analogous to Frederick Crews' recent attack on psychological and Marxist criticism;[10] the undoubted fact that such analysis can produce new insights into literary texts, says Crews, does not in itself prove that psycho-

David Bevington

analysis and Marxism are scientifically valid as disciplines. (To this the
literary critic can, of course, say, 'So what?' and proceed heuristically on his
way.)

Edmund Creeth, in his *Mankynde in Shakespeare* (277), explores a more
daring, and hence more unlikely, 'hitherto undiscovered kinship' (p. 4)
between Elizabethan and morality drama by limiting himself to the legacy of
the oldest and most universal of the moral plays, *The Castle of Perseverance*,
The Pride of Life and *Wisdom*. Dismissing sixteenth-century morality plays
(unfairly, I think) as too apt to settle for a simple moral lesson, Creeth sees
the pre-1500 drama as the most serious of the genre and hence the most
deserving to be linked with Shakespeare. Creeth goes in quite an opposite
direction, then, from Alan Dessen, who takes the more historically plausible
line that moral drama of the 1560s, 1570s and 1580s was part of the theatrical
world in which Marlowe and Shakespeare grew up.

Creeth's schematic design encourages him to link *The Castle of Perseverance* with *Macbeth*, *Wisdom* with *Othello* and *The Pride of Life* with *King
Lear*, calling the later plays 'tragic avatars' of the earlier works in that they
'shape themselves according to one of the two designs for Mankynde's
experience, the temptation plot and the coming of death', thereby moving
towards 'tragic recognition on the part of each protagonist of the folly of his
chosen way of life' (p. 6). The employment of a Hindu metaphor of reincar-
nation may suggest something about the historical imprecision of this idea
and a reliance instead on an article of faith. Indeed, Creeth appeals metaphorically to 'a new calculus, a new instrument and language' in order to
compare works 'that employ radically different modes of imitating human
life' (p. 5). Creeth will have nothing to do with traditional historical scholarship and its concern with evidence about sources. He thus stands at an
opposite extreme to J. M. R. Margeson, for example, whose carefully argued
The Origins of English Tragedy (270) sees the morality play's protean ability
to adjust to social and political change as its greatest contribution to High
Renaissance drama; or my own *Tudor Drama and Politics* (249); or Werner
Habicht (246) and John Velz and Carl Daw (250), whose judicious studies of
the so-called 'Wit Interludes' and their part in the formulation of pre-
Shakespearean romantic comedy are models of plausible and original his-
torical scholarship. Yet, for all his intolerance of historical scholarship,
Creeth insists that Shakespeare knew the archetypes with which this book
deals 'in some version'.

The result of Creeth's juxtaposing Shakespeare with the fifteenth century
is at least new and unexpected. To view *Macbeth* as an avatar of *The Castle of
Perseverance* is to concentrate on the presumed similarity between Mankind's bitter realisation of the emptiness of his worldly career and Macbeth's
discovery that the future belongs to Banquo rather than to him. With
obstinate courage, Creeth refuses to pursue the easier path of Willard
Farnham[11] and others in looking more generally at *Macbeth* as 'a morality
play written in terms of Jacobean tragedy'; but courage is not all that is

required, and Creeth would have done better to heed the advice of Calpurnia to her husband, 'Alas, my lord, your wisdom is consumed in confidence.' Similarly, one can't help admiring the perversity of tracing *Othello*'s presumed morality roots not to the Vice, as in Spivack's study of Iago, but to *Wisdom*, a play that is unusual among moralities for its omission of the Vice. Here Desdemona becomes Othello's 'soul's joy', that is, Christ; their marriage is the marriage of Mankind and Christ, flawed by man's fallen nature. Parallels of course abound, since both plays draw on the same universal story of temptation and fall, but the predictable ease of the analogy, and the irresistible impulse towards allegorisation of Shakespeare's characters, illustrate well the dangers of such comparison. As Fluellen says, when driven to justify his comparison of King Henry V to Alexander the Great, both were born on rivers, 'and there is salmons in both' (4.7.30–1). I will leave it to the reader of this chapter to figure out the resemblance of *King Lear* and *The Pride of Life*. Hint: there is a king in both. Creeth insists, nonetheless, on a 'historical relationship' between the two enabling us to appreciate *King Lear* 'with fresh eyes, our critical faculties alerted and guided in a new way' (277, p. 112).

Alan Dessen's work, already cited approvingly, offers a more viable approach to the problem. He confronts directly the issue of objective evidence for a connection between Shakespeare and what Dessen calls 'the late moral plays' (282), and indeed he provides us a host of allusions to moral drama in works of the High Renaissance. Here is a pertinent answer to Wasson: in the 1580s and afterwards, something called 'a Moral' is described again and again in revels accounts and the like. Bolstered then by objective evidence that Elizabethan dramatists were aware of the moral play, Dessen concentrates on the 'morals' most probably known to Shakespeare and his contemporaries, those of the 1560s and afterward.

Dessen characterises in particular a 'dual phase' of action in the late moral plays that pits a Vice figure against a virtuous protagonist and gives to their encounter a social and public relevance. His application of the pattern works best with *Richard III*, by illuminating the balanced and antithetical engagement between Richard and Richmond with which the play ends, though even here one must ask whether Shakespeare is not also importantly indebted to Edward Hall's *Union of the Two Noble and Illustre Families of Lancaster and York*, in which the providential interpretation of Nemesis presumably owes more to popular theology and Tudor propaganda than to the moral drama. The advantage of Dessen's scheme of dual protagonists in *1 Henry IV* is that it accounts for Hotspur's role in a way that John Dover Wilson's study of Falstaff and the Vice (1943)[12] does not; Hotspur and Hal are engaged in a Psychomachia conflict that also forms the centre of late moral plays like *Enough Is as Good as a Feast*, where the battle is between Worldly Man and Heavenly Man. Again we must remember that Shakespeare was reading Samuel Daniel's *Civil Wars* for his view of Hal and Hotspur in conflict, and there is no proof that Daniel cared much about morality drama. *2 Henry IV*, like the 'estates' morality, features a two-phased structure through which we comprehend the divisions of a diseased and disordered kingdom. These three history plays do, moreover, make specific mention of the Vice. Dessen confesses to being on shakier ground with his analysis of conversion in *All's Well That Ends Well* (conversion can be widely found in medieval and Renaissance literature) or the use of characters like Lepidus and Pompey in *Antony and Cleopatra* to act out (in morality-play style, argues Dessen) significant facets of Antony's tragic career.

Dessen's candour and relentless sleuthing after historical evidence give us the clearest picture yet, perhaps, of the occasionally real uses and the no less real limits of the argument for moral legacy in Renaissance drama. He himself has provided a lucid review article on the subject (279), and in his other writings (245, 252, 275) repeatedly urges a visual linking between certain conventional gestures on the morality stage and their counterparts in later Elizabethan drama. Sometimes Dessen's visual analogues turn on a speculative and even circular reconstruction of staging, but the attention to theatrical matters is surely a way of finding what is most specifically stage-worthy in the legacy of the moral play.

Huston Diehl's approach (29) to the legacy of moral drama is both theatrical and iconographic. Through her comparative methodology, Diehl offers a compelling thesis of the way dramatic images were transformed by the Reformation. Protestant iconoclasm in northern Europe increasingly forbade the presentation of the Deity onstage, as part of a more comprehensive ban in all the visual arts. Drama's solution was that of her sister arts, Diehl claims: images considered idolatrous gave way to allegorical depictions that 'put us in remembrance' of divine truth. 'These images are not repressed by the Reformers; instead, they are transformed and reinterpreted according to the tenets of the new Protestant faith' (p. 179). In the visual arts, as for example in Hans Mielich's painting of the Regensburg Town Council, the traditional scene of the Last Judgement is replaced by a scene of a human court of justice, while on the wall of the assembly room we can make out a depiction of the actual Last Judgement. An implicit analogy is drawn between earthly and divine justice, allowing for similarity and profound difference. St Jerome, in Jan Massys' painting of 1535, sits at his desk and meditates on an illustration of the Last Judgement in his Bible. The inset scene makes its point while satisfying Protestant concerns that the visual object should not be confused with the divine object it signifies; 'sign and thing remain clearly separate'. In the moral drama, a similar transformation is achieved by replacing scenes of Last Judgement with the kinds of judgement so common at the end of late moralities, such as that visited upon Moros in *The Longer Thou Livest the More Fool Thou Art*. The agent of divine vengeance in this case is called God's Judgement; the scene is allegorised and no longer potentially idolatrous. The properties of judgement are present – the sword of justice, the cup of wine – but they too are transformed by the allegorical nature of the treatment. (Murray Roston pursues a related argument in his *Biblical Drama in England* [*113*], describing how Protestant artists of the period exchanged the typological readings of pre-humanist art for a new way of relating biblical story to contemporary life, one in which the stories of Susannah, Esther, Daniel and so on illustrate the nature of justice in this world.)

Diehl finds a similarly redirected portrayal of justice in the endings of such High Renaissance plays as Marston's *The Malcontent*, Shakespeare's *Measure for Measure* and Webster's *The Devil's Law Case*. The results here are not as convincing as Diehl's thesis of transformation in the morality play, since one wonders again if non-dramatic sources may not have provided a model for judging in a play like *Measure for Measure* and since the morality-play model tends to reduce the complexity of Shakespearean drama, but Diehl's method does usefully call attention to the symbolic nature of stage properties and gestures like kneeling and falling down. *The Atheist's Tragedy* yields arresting images of judgement in Diehl's interpretation – the graveyard, skull, ghosts, falling axe, various features of a trial – although Diehl's search for conventions in visual signs on stage may tend to overlook the reflexive and even campy way in which this Jacobean play ironises its source materials (*264*). Diehl does of course recognise the presence of irony; indeed, the title of one of her best essays is 'Inversion, Parody, and Irony: The Visual Rhetoric of Renaissance English Tragedy' (*266*). Noting many ways in which Tudor moralities use symbolic properties, gestures and costuming to establish a 'visual rhetoric' of signs expressive of moral conflict, Diehl then moves forward into mimetic Renaissance drama where this visual rhetoric 'becomes assimilated into a more representative, more sophisticated drama. Iconic, visual detail becomes increasingly implicit, subtle, and submerged in the realistic action of the mature tragedies, but the visual conventions themselves do not really change very much' (p. 200). Wrestling matches, purses of gold, decks of cards are the details out of which this visual rhetoric is constructed.

Her thesis sometimes leads Diehl to overstate her case. Is the sword of Tybalt in *Romeo and Juliet*, for example, really a symbol of wrath as explicitly developed in the morality play? Are the icons Diehl describes in 'The Iconography of Violence in English Renaissance Tragedy' (*261*) really traceable in the ways she specifies, as for example from Hieronimo's flinging away his dagger and halter in *The Spanish Tragedy* to a similar gesture in *The Tide Tarrieth No Man*? Still, the merging of iconography with stagecraft, and the analysis of Renaissance iconoclasm in terms of the semiotic language of signs, are so potentially fruitful that the subject deserves further investigation. Diehl offers a visual way of comprehending what is both mimetic and symbolic in Elizabethan stage action.

These reflections on iconographical method introduce my last topic, that of contexts for morality drama. Potter (*225*) has challenged us to do more with continental moralities, and some efforts have been made along this line,

David Bevington

such as Peter Houle's publication of the English morality fragment called *Somebody and Others* along with portions of the French morality, *La Vérité cachée*, from which it was translated as a Reformation tract (228). Merle Fifield's attempt to describe 'The Community of Morality Plays' (226), on the other hand, leaves unanswered the question of influences across national boundaries and finds only broad terms like 'dialogue' and 'debate' under which to attempt a synthesis of 'the' morality play. Her claim that the composition of morality plays 'was an international movement' rests on a contention that all such plays exhibit a rhetorical structure in five actions, from exposition to intrigue to denouement. Aristotle, anyone? Much surely remains to be done in this field.

The anthropological method of Victor Turner (*The Ritual Process*, 1969) and others, briefly noted by Potter, remains largely unexplored. Analysis of the visual language of stage gesture in drama, which can profitably be studied in the context of Turner's 'liminal' phase in rites of passage, has been attempted of late in Shakespeare studies but almost not at all in the drama of his contemporaries, let alone his Tudor and medieval predecessors. Icono-graphical research is more evident, as in Gail Gibson's provocative essay on *Wisdom* and the artistic traditions of Bury St Edmunds (239); archival evidence of dramatic performance at Bury is 'as fragmented and as tantalizing as the rubble of the abbey itself', Gibson freely admits, though she goes on to make a plausible case for monastic auspices in a play about the temptation of abandoning the contemplative life. Her rigorous work calls on not only the discipline of the art historian but also that of the archivist and social historian.

Political and social history as a context continues to bear fruitful results, as in Joanne Kantrowitz's study of Lindsay's *Ane Satyre of the Thrie Estaitis* (257, 258) and in Milla Riggio's 'The Allegory of Feudal Acquisition in *The Castle of Perseverance*' (231a), tracing the emergence of topical satire back to this early play in its association of economic and social abuse with feudal patronage. Audience-response criticism finds a practitioner in Robert C. Jones (256), who describes ways in which morality dramatists worked to resolve the conflicts audiences were bound to feel between the theatrical attractiveness of the Vice and his morally reprehensible ideas.

Increasingly, new contributions to the understanding of the morality are going to require interdisciplinary skill. It is noteworthy that a number of recent contributions to the study of medieval drama are collaborative efforts stressing in their very titles the value of comparative method. Clifford Davidson and others have edited *The Drama of the Middle Ages: Comparative and Critical Essays* (5), drawing materials chiefly from the pages of *Comparative Drama* and including a wide-ranging essay by Natalie Schmitt on 'The Idea of a Person in Medieval Morality Plays' (233) that argues for the mimetic in place of the allegorical. Jerome Taylor and Alan Nelson's valuable *Medieval English Drama: Essays Critical and Contextual* (100) contains a fine essay by V. A. Kolve on '*Everyman* and the Parable of the Talents'

(*220*), explaining the play's emphasis on 'reckoning' and 'account' in terms of the biblical parable, and another by David Leigh on 'The Doomsday Mystery Play: An Eschatological Morality' that usefully breaks down generic barriers between the mystery cycles' last scene of judgement and treatments of that theme in morality drama. The collection edited by Paula Neuss, *Aspects of Early English Drama* (*101*), pays particular attention to modern productions of medieval drama: 'The Virtue of Perseverance' by Richard Proudfoot has a useful recent stage history of *The Castle of Perseverance* (though most of the essay is old stuff); Tony Davenport examines the symbolic meaning of clothing in his study of 'Lusty fresche galaunts' (wherein most of the dramatic associations of extravagant costume are negative); and Robert Potter explores the ways in which, through costuming and other stage presentation, late-medieval English drama (including the morality) presents the issue of justice.

Milla Riggio's *The 'Wisdom' Symposium* (*103*), growing out of her 1984 production and conference at Trinity College in Hartford, Connecticut, includes the iconographical research of Gail Gibson, already discussed; Riggio's introductory essay on 'The Staging of *Wisdom*' describing the rationale of the production; an essay on 'Stage Picture in *Wisdom*' in which I argue that the play's dramaturgical method is to find visual embodiments for the oxymoronic metaphors of black and white, foul and fair, set forth in Walter Hilton's *Scale of Perfection*; an argument by Donald Baker that *Wisdom* is 'professional' in the sense of being theatrically successful, despite what scholars have said about its 'aureate' Latin and its staginess; and a study of the external evidence on performance at Bury or any other place (mostly negative) by Alexandra Johnston (*240*). *Homo, Memento Finis* (*29*), a study of the iconography of just judgement in medieval art and drama, is, whatever else its merits, collaborative and comparative in method; Pamela Sheingorn, an art historian, contributed materially to all the chapters of the book and collaborated with me on a study of visual signs in the judgement pageants of the Corpus Christi cycles. Throughout, the book attempts to locate the interconnection of spoken and visual language in the theatre, and my own essay on stage pictures in *The Castle of Perseverance* is particularly concerned with ways in which the visual arts of the period can help define a visual vocabulary for the dramatist in matters of costuming, antitheses of male and female, stage properties, gestures and vertical movement.

This interest in comparative studies is encouraging, but I feel I must end on a note of exhortation still. Are medieval drama studies – indeed, medieval studies as a whole – in danger of becoming too intellectually and academically conservative? Are we, as a group, turning our backs on the challenges of post-structuralism, semiotics, anthropology, Marxism, feminism and the like? We see lots of activity in the medieval area, but I for one find the atmosphere at the annual International Congress on Medieval Studies at Western Michigan University, Kalamazoo, one of seeking safe haven from the insanities of theory-driven criticism. I can sympathise with this impulse,

David Bevington

but when I raised this issue at a Kalamazoo medieval drama session in May of 1985 I was greeted with such a unanimous chorus of objections that I ended by ironically congratulating the assembled group for having been goaded into such a harmonious and even complacent sense of mutual accomplishment. Clifford Davidson's assurances that I was asking for trouble, and that he (as editor of *Comparative Drama*) gets plenty of deconstructive readings of medieval drama – all of them bad – could prove either his point that the deconstructive analyses written so far are mostly nonsense, or my suspicion that Davidson is inclined to view any such undertaking as unproductive by definition. Or both. I don't know the answer, certainly, and I imagine I am indeed asking for something I wouldn't want to read. But I do find myself asking, where are the new historicist types when it comes to early Tudor drama? Isn't this material in the late Middle Ages and early Renaissance suitable for Marxist interpretation? Aren't there feminist issues to be explored? Without being intellectual groupies, can we find ways of staying in touch with what is happening in current criticism? I would prefer to stay in touch, and would be grateful to anyone who can show how this is to be done.

NOTES

1 Robert Dodsley, ed., *A Select Collection of Old English Plays* (London, 1744; 4th edn by W. Carew Hazlitt, London: Reeves and Turner, 1874–6).
2 John Matthews Manly, ed., *Specimens of the Pre-Shaksperean Drama*, 2 vols. (Boston and New York: Ginn and Co., 1897–8; repr. New York: Dover, 1967).
3 E. N. S. Thompson, 'The English Moral Plays', *Transactions of the Connecticut Academy of Arts and Sciences* 14 (1910): 291–414.
4 Sister Mary Philippa Coogan, *An Interpretation of the Moral Play, Mankind* (Washington, DC: Catholic University of America Press, 1947).
5 Madeleine Doran, *Endeavors of Art* (Madison, WI: University of Wisconsin Press, 1954).
6 Bernard Spivack, *Shakespeare and the Allegory of Evil* (New York: Columbia University Press, 1958).
7 Robert L. Ramsay, ed., *Magnyfycence*, EETS Extra Series 98 (London: Oxford University Press, 1906).
8 R. P. Ryan, review of Richard Southern, *The Medieval Theatre in the Round*, *Quarterly Journal of Speech* 44 (1958): 444–6.
9 C. Walter Hodges, *The Globe Restored* (London: Benn, 1953; New York: Coward-McCann, 1968).
10 Frederick Crews, *Out of my System: Psychoanalysis, Ideology, and Critical Method* (Oxford: Oxford University Press, 1975).
11 Willard Farnham, *The Medieval Heritage of Elizabethan Tragedy* (Berkeley: University of California Press, 1936).
12 John Dover Wilson, *The Fortunes of Falstaff* (Cambridge: Cambridge University Press, 1943).

7

'All the world was a stage': Records of Early English Drama

ALEXANDRA F. JOHNSTON

Over the past two decades, an increasing number of scholars have turned their attention to the surviving external evidence of dramatic activity in Great Britain in the late Middle Ages and early Renaissance. Earlier scholars led the way. J. O. Halliwell-Phillipps, in the nineteenth century, toured the provincial towns in search of Shakespeare.[1] J. Tucker Murray, less particular in his search, gathered evidence of the Elizabethan and later Stuart dramatic companies. Local antiquarians, such as the three generations of the Raine family in York, toiled over editions and collections of local records published by antiquarian societies. E. K. Chambers used many of these works to compile his still important general studies of early English theatre.

The year 1955 is a seminal year in the study of early drama, for in that year two very different books appeared. The one, *English Religious Drama of the Middle Ages*, by Hardin Craig (*105*), was the culmination of a lifetime of study and marked the end of the old-style scholarship that tended to generalise, homogenise and patronise the religious drama of the late Middle Ages. The other, *Mediaeval Drama in Chester*, by F. M. Salter (*186*), was also written by a man at the end of a long and distinguished career. Salter presented his material first as one of the prestigious series of lectures, the Alexander Lectures, at the University of Toronto. He re-examined the surviving external evidence concerning the formation of the Chester cycle, exploding most of the existing theories and going on to proclaim boldly not the theological significance of the play but its commercial importance to the city that sponsored it.

In the twenty years following 1955, younger scholars coming fresh to the plays and excited by their dramatic power, began to turn, as Salter had, to the surviving evidence. Giles Dawson went to Kent. Stanley J. Kahrl turned his attention to Lincolnshire. Lawrence M. Clopper followed Salter to Chester while R. W. Ingram returned to his native Coventry. David Galloway, too, returned to work in Norwich where he had grown up. He was joined in East Anglia by John Wasson who turned his attention to the county records of Norfolk and Suffolk. John Coldewey undertook research in Essex for his doctoral dissertation under the direction of Donald Baker, while JoAnna Dutka used external evidence extensively in her dissertation on music in the cycle plays written under the direction of John Leyerle, later published in the 'Early Drama, Art and Music' (EDAM) series (*125*). Meanwhile, Arthur

Cawley of Leeds had suggested that J. J. Anderson investigate Newcastle and had set a young Australian research student, Margaret Dorrell (now Margaret Rogerson), to work in York. It was there that I met her when I went to York myself in pursuit of some answers to the tantalising questions raised by the York cycle.

Meanwhile, Ian Lancashire, another student of John Leyerle, had begun the same search on a different level. He began to assemble a supplement to Stratman's *Bibliography of Medieval Drama*,[2] but once he moved into the publications of local antiquarians and record societies, it was clear that what he was collecting went far beyond a mere supplement. The first collected result of his work has been published as *Dramatic Texts and Records of Britain: A Chronological Topography (130)*.

The work of Dawson, Kahrl and Wasson was accepted for publication by the Malone Society. However, the collections being gathered by Ingram, Galloway, Clopper, Anderson and Rogerson and myself were far too large to be brought out by Malone. And so, in 1974, two decades after Salter had delivered his lectures on the Chester cycle at the University of Toronto, the first steps were taken, again at Toronto, to co-ordinate the work of all the scholars in the field of records research and to find a publisher for the material. During the next winter an agreement was reached with the University of Toronto Press and in February 1975 Records of Early English Drama[3] was founded in Toronto. Over the last fifteen years REED has brought together the talent and energy of over fifty scholars who have systematically pursued what one reviewer has called their 'remorseless way into the record offices' of Britain.[4] Although we have made some quite startling single discoveries such as the description of the 1433 Judgement wagon in York (*142*, I, 55–6), the impact of the project is not and will not be the result of such discoveries, but rather the accumulation, from all over the kingdom, of small details of performance practice. A single payment to a player is not revolutionary. What is revolutionary is the pattern that is emerging – a pattern that is profoundly altering our understanding of early drama in England. We now know, for example, that the genre of Corpus Christi play did not exist. What did exist was a form of episodic drama telling the story of salvation history. Such episodic drama was not played exclusively on Corpus Christi day but frequently at Whitsun. Conversely, such folk drama as Robin Hood plays was often performed on Corpus Christi. Any interpretations of the biblical drama based on the office of Corpus Christi, therefore, are inappropriate. We have also learned that the long episodic drama was more the exception than the rule. Evidence for dramatic activity abounds from all over the country, but it also represents smaller, less ambitious productions presented by towns or parishes or by the astonishing number of travelling players that toured the countryside from the mid-fifteenth century onward. It is also clear that the distinction between 'medieval drama' and 'Renaissance drama' can no longer be clearly drawn. The biblical cycles of Coventry, Chester and York were suppressed between 1575 and 1580. They were being performed in all their 'medieval' glory after the opening of the professional theatre in London. What we have long thought of as medieval morality forms co-existed with the school plays of the mid-sixteenth century with no apparent sense of incongruity. Through a study of the drama of English society we are documenting a social continuity from the late fourteenth century to the Civil War in the seventeenth century spanning that 'lost' period of English literature, the fifteenth century.

Evidence for dramatic activity has been found in an astonishing variety of documents. Equally astonishing are the number and variety of playing places, most frequently space designed for other purposes adapted to the use of the players. Far from being a minor literary genre, early English drama was a major vehicle for the expression of social and cultural values. Despite the fact that we have few surviving texts compared to the richness of European drama, we are now beginning to understand, through the external evidence, the significance of the lost body of literature that they represent. By focussing first on the variety of documentary evidence and then on the diversity of playing places, I hope to illustrate, in this chapter, some measure of this significance.

I

In the first decade of the twelfth century, the house of the sacrist of St Alban's, Dunstable burned to the ground (130, p. 125). In 1200, a miracle was performed in Beverley Minster by a man later to be called St John of Beverley (130, p. 82). In 1300, the prioress of Clerkenwell brought a suit for property damages against some citizens of London before the king (130, p. 112). In 1345, the servants of the lord bishop of Carlisle and Sir Peter de Tilliol were cited before a royal commission in Carlisle for brawling in public (148, pp. 63–4). In 1498, a riot broke out in the parish of Walsall in Staffordshire that resulted in an appeal to the high court of justice.[5] In 1525, the Lady Hungerford and her husband, Sir Richard Sacheverell, moved into the College of Newarke, Leicester.[6] In 1536, Sir Humphrey Ferrers of Tamworth, Staffordshire had his shins broken by a chain (130, p. 271). And in 1582, a murder was committed in Norwich (147, pp. 70–6).

Each of these events, separated by almost five hundred years, contains a record of dramatic performance. The sacrist of St Alban's was storing costumes in the house that burned. Two boys were, according to legend, so anxious to see a saint play performed in Beverley Minster that they fell to the floor of the nave from a great height only to be revived by the saint. The prioress of Clerkenwell felt her landscaping had been trampled by citizens flocking to see the plays performed by the clerks, and the occasion of the brawl in Carlisle was another performance by clerks of 'quendam ludum' in the market place. The riot in Walsall occurred during a Robin Hood play. Lady Hungerford, her husband 'and other of their friends' caused such a disturbance in Leicester that an inquiry was undertaken by Bishop Longland.

Alexandra F. Johnston

The thirteenth question put to each witness sought information about whether bear-baitings, Maygames or common spectacles (which had been prohibited within the College of Newarke) had taken place there while Lady Hungerford and her party were in residence. The replies elicited several responses that Maygames, Robin Hood and St George came into the college 'wheyer lady hungerford be here or not' and another that the parishioners of St Margaret's came with twelve pageants to play for Lady Hungerford because she rewarded them well. It was a pageant devil in chains that broke Sir Humphrey Ferrers' shins and the murder in Norwich involved three of the most famous Elizabethan players, John Bentley, John Singer and Richard Tarlton.

The documents containing these records are equally various. Four are in the Public Record Office in London. The affray at Carlisle is in the series of Parliamentary and Council Proceedings, the one at Walsall and the unfortunate laceration of Sir Humphrey's shins are in the records of the Court of Star Chamber and the one at Norwich is in the series of Controlment Rolls. Two others, the fire at Dunstable and the prioress' complaint about her property, are in documents belonging to two religious houses. The extraordinary story of Lady Hungerford is in the Visitation Book of Bishop Longland in the Lincolnshire Record Office.

Each of these records provides insights into the nature of the performance of medieval and Tudor drama. We learn of costumes from Dunstable and Tamworth; the size and behaviour of the audience from Beverley, Carlisle, Clerkenwell and Norwich; the nature of local drama from Walsall and Leicester; the importance of patronage from Leicester; and many details about the activities of the touring companies and their playing places from Norwich. And yet the references to drama are entirely incidental to the purposes of each document. Two, Dunstable and Clerkenwell, are primarily concerned with the loss or preservation of property. The reference to the play in Beverley is part of a miraculous legend told to honour St John. Bishop Longland had the unhappy task of attempting to impose civil harmony in the face of an imperious and unruly lady of the realm, Sir Humphrey was seeking redress for personal damages and the three riots were what we would call today 'police matters'. Records of early English drama, then, can turn up almost anywhere where the activities of human communities – lay or religious – are documented.

The most informative documents concerning drama come from the records of the towns and parishes that themselves sponsored dramatic activity. The episodic biblical plays performed in York, Chester, Coventry, Newcastle and Beverley, although the full texts of only two sequences survive, are well attested to in the guild and town records. Ordinance and council minute books show in sometimes exhaustive detail how the plays were a strong binding force in the social and commercial fabric of each town. Guild and civic accounts tell us how much money was spent on dramatic activity. The rich Coventry accounts, for example, provide such details as the

price of making three worlds to be burned at the end of the cycle and the cost
for hiring a man to 'Sett the worlds on fyre' (*145*, pp. 217, 230 and *passim*).
We learn the price of renting angel wings in York (*142*, p. 95) and for
painting Beelzebub's club in Newcastle (*146*, p. 56). On a larger scale we
learn how much the corporations of these towns were prepared to spend
annually on these lavish shows. The plays were, after all, in the Anglo-
Norman words of a 1399 York ordinance, 'mayntenez & sustenez par les
Comunes & Artificers demesme la Citee en honour & reuerence nostreseig-
nour Iesu Crist & honour & profitt de mesme la Citee...' (*142*, p. 11). The
profit for each of these cities was, of course, commercial as well as spiritual.
The days of the plays were great fair days bringing visitors from every
stratum of society into town to see the show and buy the wares of the crafts
while, at the same time, enjoying the craft play. The records of these
northern towns demonstrate how completely playmaking was integrated
into the social and commercial life of the city. The interrelationships among
the various craft guilds in York, for example, were defined through the
payment of money to support the pageants. The York Corpus Christi play
was not just an annual dramatic presentation, it was the vehicle for the
expression of *communitas*.[7]

Parish drama, though not as fully documented as civic drama, seems to
have been equally integrated into its communal setting. The types of drama
ranged from apparently lavish plays as in Chelmsford, Essex[8] to simple
Maygames. Most of the evidence for this drama survives in churchwardens'
accounts and the motivation seems to have been more directly to make a
profit. The corporate towns were large social organisms with many individual cells uniting to produce the play. The communal act of playmaking
was as important as the financial profit. In smaller units, like the parishes,
however, drama was only one aspect of the communal life of the people.
Their corporate expression of unity was made in the liturgy itself. But
playmaking was an important adjunct to parish life since it generated the
funds to fix the roof or repair the porch or re-lead the window of an ancient
and decaying parish church.

Towards the end of the reign of Elizabeth, general prohibitions against all
local drama were issued by the civil and ecclesiastical authorities. Although
these were not universally enforced, mimetic activity became increasingly the
subject of litigation. Most frequently the actions were taken by the ecclesiastical courts as bishops' visitations uncovered the continuing existence of
unlawful parish practices. Short notices of these cases appear in Act Books
but longer, more detailed, accounts can be found in Books of Presentiments
either for the bishop's court or the archdeacon's court. At the parish level,
the activities being suppressed are often related to the increasingly enforced
sabbatarian rules invoked against country folk engaged in dancing, music or
folk customs during service time. One of my favourite ecclesiastical court
records, however, is not associated with breaking the sabbath. The churchwarden of the parish of Didcot in Berkshire was cited in 1580 for having

Alexandra F. Johnston

made off with the Communion linen. He spoke up vigorously in his own defence, protesting that the clothes were not missing through his negligence but that 'They were fett owte of his howse by the morrice Dancers in his absence.'⁹

Civil courts during the same period were moving against the great biblical drama. The Council of the North, working with the Archbishop of York, confiscated the playbooks of the city of York (*142*, p. 390) and perhaps the most famous direct suppression of biblical drama came from the Council and its Ecclesiastical Commission of the North in a letter from their secretary, Matthew Hutton, to the bailiff burgesses of Wakefield prohibiting a performance 'in Whitsonweke next or theraboutes' of a biblical play that may have survived to us as the Towneley cycle.¹⁰

Eight years earlier, Hutton had written to the city council of York advising them not to perform the Creed play stating that 'now in this happy time of the gospell, I knowe the learned will mislike it and how the state will beare with it I know not' (*142*, p. 325). For Hutton and his masters, the performance of Catholic drama came close to treason. On the other hand, in 1551, in Bishopstroke in Hampshire, one Henry Brabon had accused a servant 'as a heretic and a knave' for taking part in John Bale's Protestant 'comedie', *The Three Laws* (*130*, p. 85). His accusation also extended to Bale himself. Bale, the best-known writer of polemical Protestant drama, is an example of how some reformed clergy, rather than seeking to suppress drama, used it for their own propaganda. An important part of the history of Tudor drama is the widespread use of plays to promote the godly intent of one side or another in the complex web of religious and political controversy. Bale was one of the central figures in the struggle of the mid-century. His company acted for Thomas Cromwell in 1538 (*130*, p. 104). In 1553, during his time in Kilkenny, Ireland, Bale continued to produce his anti-Catholic drama (*130*, p. 329). Similar activity was being undertaken by other writers such as Thomas Kirkmayer in Cambridge in the 1540s (*130*, p. 97) and Lewis and William Wager in the 1550s in London (*130*, p. 98). Bale returned to London in 1560 and accused some conservative (and so Catholic) Kentish men 'of mocking Protestant preachers with May games' (*130*, p. 105).

Another incident in Essex points up the close relationship between playmaking, religion and libellous attacks. A churchwarden named Bushe from the parish of Hornchurch was presented to the archdeacon's court because he 'did bring into the churche certeyn play*ers* the which did playe and declare certayn things against the ministers'.¹¹ What was said against the ministers is unfortunately not recorded, but it may have been similar to the Maygame mocking to which Bale objected. Earlier, Stephen Gardiner, Bishop of London, 'forbad the players of london ... to play any mo playes of Christe·/ but of robin hode and litle Johan / and of the Parlament of brydes and such other trifles' (*130*, p. 205). But, as Bale noted, even these 'trifles' could be used for political purposes. Perhaps equally important, they could be used to distract the common people from such godly pastimes as preaching. In a

122

sermon preached before Edward VI, Bishop Latimer confessed that he had
once been unable to muster a congregation because all the inhabitants of the
town were engaged in celebrating 'Robin Hoodes day'. He rather ruefully
remarked 'I thought my rochet would have been regarded, but it would not
serve; it was faine to give place to Robin Hoodes men.'[12]

In 1549, the City of London appealed to Richard Rich, then Lord Chan-
cellor, for help in banning 'all comen interludes & pleys' in the City and
suburbs (130, p. 208). Later that year the London council introduced a form
of censorship presumably to screen out papist tracts. In the first year of
Elizabeth's reign, St Olave's Church in Silver Street, London, staged a play
'of a godly matter' on 29 July. However, on 5 September, action was taken
against a group of players proposing to perform a 'lewde' play called *Sak full
of Newes* (130, p. 216). The texts of very few of these plays have survived.
Among those that do is *The Most Virtuous and Godly Susanna*, thought to
have been performed around 1562 (130, p. 28). Though firmly Protestant in
its theology, this play is a lively example of the late morality genre with a
ranting devil providing the impetus through the Vice figure, Ill Report, for
the lust of the elders.

Evidence for drama is also found in court records unconnected with
religious issues. References to drama appear very early in cases involving
slander and libel. For example, in 1352 an attempt was made to stop a play in
Exeter considered to be insulting to the leather-dressers (148a, p. 11). Late in
Elizabeth's reign, Henry, Earl of Lincoln brought a libel suit 'against Sir
Edward Dymock and others, for contriving and acting a stage play on a
Sabbath day upon a Maypole green near Sir Edward Dymock's house,
containing scurrilous and slanderous matter against the ... Earl by name'.[13]
It was considered that to act out a libel was to publish it. The incident is part
of a long-standing quarrel between Lincoln and Dymock. A more general
libel against the upper class was prosecuted in the Star Chamber in 1621 as a
result of a 'stage plaie at Kendale Castle' where 'manie Lordes of the
Mannors of the said Countie' were represented as being in Hell for their
unfair treatment of their tenants (148, p. 188). This representation of the
perceived enemies as damned souls in Hell as late as 1621 may reflect the very
late survival of the Kendal biblical play (148, pp. 18 and 180). An equally
lively, if more homely, use of slander was heard before the Bishop of
Salisbury in 1614. Alice Musitian of Salisbury went to the trouble of erecting
a scaffold or stage in her back yard, charging people a small admission fee and
proceeding to present a dramatisation of the adulterous affair of one of her
neighbours. We are even told the roles of the actors in this little domestic
farce. Her neighbour retaliated by suing her for slander before the bishop.[14]

Even from this random and, indeed, arbitrary selection of the records it is
clear that evidence for dramatic performance is found everywhere. Furthermore, the references are so casual as to emphasise the normative nature of the
activity. It seems that to engage in mimetic imitation in the period was as
common as engaging in trade.

Alexandra F. Johnston

11

Similarly, drama was to be found physically almost anywhere, both inside and out, in a very great variety of forms. Although some Roman amphitheatres have survived from antiquity in Britain such as those at St Alban's, Hertfordshire (*130*, pp. 257–8) or Yeaverton in Northumberland (*130*, p. 292), there is no evidence that they were used as theatres during the late Middle Ages and Renaissance. There are, however, some references to permanent playing places, such as 'La Batailplace' outside Lincoln, that may have been used for plays as well as games and preaching (*130*, p. 168). Many permanent playing places seem to have been rounds. These were most common in Cornwall, where some can still be seen, but there are also references to rounds in East Anglia from King's Lynn in Norfolk[15] and Walsham-le-Willows in Suffolk where the round is described as having a stage in the middle (*130*, p. 278).

Producers also used permanent features of the local landscape whose original purpose had not been theatrical. For example, a ruined castle was pressed into service in Truro, Cornwall (*130*, p. 277). More interesting is the recent discovery by REED's Shropshire editor, J. A. B. Somerset, of a local quarry being used as a playing place.[16] The quarry is described by Thomas Churchyard as having the features of a classical theatre[17] but was clearly the happy discovery of local playmakers seeking good acoustics and sightlines.

Other locations could be considered almost as permanent. Churchyards provided the sites for drama for centuries, and it was churchyards as well as churches that were targetted by the Puritan bishops in their visitations in the early seventeenth century. Ecclesiastical concern over the use of churchyards as playing sites is of long standing. The Register of Bishop John Grandisson, Bishop of Exeter, records a monition against one Robert Lucy in the year 1339 because he 'notoriously maintains a balcony or canopy erected and constructed upon posts fixed in ground known to be sacred and dedicated within the boundary of the churchyard of our aforementioned church of Exeter'. It was alleged that under this balcony 'Occurs a gathering of rogues, actors, whores, and other vile persons ... putting on stage-plays...' (*148a*, p. 320). Although such a permanent structure is unusual, when parish drama was performed outdoors it was almost exclusively performed in churchyards all over the kingdom. Evidence is also accumulating that these open spaces next to churches were sometimes used by professional companies. The Queen's Players played in 'the Colledge Churche yarde' in Gloucester in 1589–90 and received the handsome payment of thirty shillings from the corporation for their performance (*148*, p. 311).

Less popular, despite the long-standing assumptions of scholars of Elizabethan drama, were inns or inn-yards. The assumption that inns were common playing places has been based on such misanthropic city ordinances as the one passed by the Chester city council in 1614. In it they ban all stage plays as encouraging the disturbance of the peace. They report they have also been informed 'that mens servantes and apprentices neglectinge their Masters busines doe Resorte to Innehowses to behold such Plaies...' (*141*, p. 293). REED has uncovered very few other references to playing in inns or inn-yards in the provinces. The earliest reference I know to be among the REED evidence is the story of the affray at Norwich involving the murder in 1582 (see above). There are no references to inns and inn-yards at all in Devon although the editor, John Wasson, himself an Elizabethan drama scholar, was expecting to find some. Two other isolated references are quite late. One mentions the Angel in Coventry in 1600 (*145*, p. 356) and the other the Crown in Cheltenham (*148*, p. 288). It is important to note that, except for the Norwich affray, all these references to inns, and those listed by Glynne Wickham for the London area (*111*, pp. 186–96), do not specify the yard of the inn. The many references to players performing in what seem to be relatively modest houses of the middle-class town councillors (see below) suggests that most, if not all, the inn references are not references to inn-yards as playing places but interior inn rooms. Further evidence to suggest that performances in inns might be quite modest in size comes from the work of Peter Clark, who has found evidence of players resorting to the even smaller ale-houses in the seventeenth century.[18]

Open fields and gardens seem to have been frequently used for plays. The parishes of Maldon and Chelmsford in Essex set up the lavish stages for their substantial performances of religious drama in the 1560s in the open fields.[19] Plays are recorded several times at the end of the fifteenth century in Coventry in a space known as Little Park (*145*, pp. 74 and 100). Many ceremonial masques and compliments to royalty took place in unspecified open spaces such as the gardens of Sudeley in Gloucestershire (*148*, p. 288) or those of Bisham in Berkshire and Caversham across the river in Oxfordshire.[20] The open space in front of the house sometimes itself became the 'set' for a complimentary welcome as when Elizabeth visited the Cecil family at Theobalds.[21] Thomas Churchyard and his troupe of young players seem to have made plans to waylay the Queen from behind bushes during the famous visit to Norwich in 1578 (*144*, p. 276).

Finally, and perhaps the most familiar outdoor spaces of all for early drama, are the streets of the English towns. The streets of London, York, Chester, Coventry, Newcastle, Beverley and many other towns saw plays enacted against the backdrop of their own familiar city. I have argued elsewhere that the custom of performing salvation history in the city streets had a profound impact on the audiences who gathered to participate in a communal mimetic action.[22] This widespread custom of transforming the world of everyday life into the mythic world of sacred story is an aspect of all early drama that should not be overlooked as we seek to interpret the surviving texts.

Equally interesting evidence is being amassed by REED editors concerning the size and variety of interior playing spaces. In 1612, the Lady Elizabeth's Players presented their license to play to a somewhat reluctant

Alexandra F. Johnston

city council in York. By the license they were given leave to play 'in all moote halls skoolehowses [and] towne halls' (*142*, p. 538). There is little evidence, so far, for the use of schoolhouses by travelling companies but abundant evidence for the use of almost any other meeting space. For example, after the dissolution of the Blackfriars' house in 1538, the city of Norwich acquired the property. The nave of the Blackfriars' church has been used ever since as a form of civic centre (*144*, p. xxx). In the mid-sixteenth century it was called the common hall or new hall and repeatedly used for play performances (*144*, pp. 20–1 and *passim*). Its dimensions are 125 feet by 70 feet. Another interior playing space in Norwich was the Assembly Chamber in the Guildhall which measures only 36 feet by 30 feet (*144*, p. lxxxiv). The size of the Assembly Chamber in the Guildhall in Leicester is similar. It seems that many of the professional troupes from London staged their mandatory performances before the mayors and councils in these rooms and similar rooms all over the kingdom. When we realise that the audience would consist of at least thirteen men (the mayor and twelve aldermen) seated around a solid table in sturdy Elizabethan chairs, there is little room left for a large playing area. This fact alone should prompt some rethinking of the nature and possible variety of the repertoire of the touring companies.

Larger civic halls were also used by travelling players. These range from the guildhalls of Exeter from 1431 (*148a*, p. 92), Barnstaple, Devon and Kendal from 1592 (*148a*, p. 46; *148*, p. 174) to the common halls of York from 1527 (*142*, p. 243) and Chester from the early seventeenth century (*141*, p. 292), to the halls of religious fraternities such as St Anthony's Hall in York (*142*, p. 449) and the Boothall in Gloucester that housed the Woolmarket (*148*, pp. 423–4).

The great halls of the Oxford and Cambridge colleges and such schools as Eton were constantly used for plays performed by the students during this period. Christmas time was the favourite time for playmaking at Eton where dozens of candles were regularly provided to light the hall for the performances.[23] Many of the university halls survive almost unaltered today. A revealing feature of some of these halls is the position of the fireplace in the sixteenth century. In the hall of Queen's College, Cambridge, the fireplace was in the centre of the room. Interludes that include characters drawing close to the fire may well have been played 'in the round' in such halls rather than in the formation more normally assumed for them of a stage built across the end of the hall opposite the dais where the fellows dined. A document survives from Queen's, Cambridge from the early seventeenth century which gives detailed instructions for the building of seating against the walls of the hall.[24] The research undertaken by REED has identified many playing places that still stand. The next step will be for other researchers to investigate the history of each building to determine the size and nature of each hall in our period.

It is a commonplace of early drama scholarship to recognise the churches themselves as venues for dramatic performance. In any single location, the church, be it a tiny structure, a handsome wool-town parish church or a cathedral, was the gathering place of the community. The size of the available space generally reflected the size of the community. The most common dramatic presentation inside the church was drama connected with the liturgy. The chapter of York Minster had a device to bring the star of the Nativity down the great length of the cathedral (*142*, p. 1). In Sherbourne, Dorset, a play was performed on Corpus Christi day inside the church from 1543 to 1572 using scaffolds that appear to be like modern risers constructed before the two low altars (*130*, p. 262). Many other religious plays are recorded as taking place inside the churches. What is less well known, however, is that secular plays were played in churches as late as the early seventeenth century. In 1600–1, the parish of Tewkesbury sponsored three stage plays in the nave of the old abbey (by then the parish church) in order to make money (*148*, p. 340). The town of Barnstaple paid for a play in the parish church in 1548–9 (*148a*, p. 40) while the Dartmouth town government did the same in 1552–3 and 1567–8 (*148a*, pp. 64, 66). Other evidence from Dartmouth names Leicester's Men as the troupe playing in the church (*148a*, p. 67) and Warwick's Men played in the church in Tavistock in the 1570s (*148a*, p. 279). Even these limited references underline the fundamental inadequacy of earlier theories of the 'secularisation' of vernacular drama moving in inevitable progression from church to churchyard to market place to inn-yard to professional playhouse.

Finally, there is abundant evidence that private houses of every size were venues for plays. There is frequent reference, as already noted, to the mandatory performance by travelling companies for the mayor and council taking place in the mayor's house. Most mayors were middle-class business-men and, from the evidence that survives of the houses of such men, their homes were substantial but not commodious town houses. In 1559–60 the then mayor of Plymouth requested that the performance be put on in the vicarage, although the chamber paid for it (*148a*, p. 234). In 1587–8 in Kendal there was a play 'at mr wilsons' (*148*, p. 173) and two years later the Kendal chamberlains record a payment to one John Coller 'for his lofte for ye playe' (*148*, p. 173). In 1595 Lord Willoughbie's players performed in an unspeci-fied private house in York (*142*, pp. 464–5). Also in York from 1576 on, there are records of payments made from the privy purse account of the chamberlains of York Minster for performances by such travelling com-panies as 'Essex Men' and 'Lord Stafford's Men' for the entertainment of the Dean and Chapter (*142*, pp. 382 and *passim*). Similar privy purse payments can be found in other accounts of religious officials such as Prior More of Worcester who was a lavish patron of drama in the mid-century.[25] Some, at least, of the performances paid for by More took place in the priory. Larger houses and castles such as Kendal Castle where the slanderous performance of 1621 took place (see above) were, of course, widely used for dramatic presentations. Quite lavish entertainments also took place in the homes of the lesser gentry. The famous funeral portrait of Sir Henry Unton depicts

Alexandra F. Johnston

just such an entertainment performed apparently for a family party waited on by only two servants.[26] Just as the size of exterior space varied enormously, so the size and shape of interior space must have presented constant challenges to the adaptability of the players. Virtually any type of space could be and was used for dramatic activity.

Dramatic activity was all-pervasive in English society before the Civil War. The world of the Church from the great cathedrals to tiny parish churches, the world of the merchant towns, the world of the gentry and royal court drew both life and a sense of unity from plays commonly performed and commonly enjoyed. There was no area of life that was untouched by performance traditions and no place in town or countryside where playmaking was an unexpected happening. As the research of Records of Early English Drama continues, it is becoming clearer and clearer that the establishment of the professional theatres in London in the late sixteenth century not only heralded the beginning of the period of the greatest dramatic literature in English, it also began the process of the decline into decadence and decay of that literature. The establishment of the theatres coincided with the actions to suppress community drama. For a while the playwrights and players in the professional theatre could draw on the vital traditions of the past and rely on an audience who had themselves taken part in dramatic activity. But gradually the transitional generation died and with it died the memory of community drama. The taste of the court came to dominate the theatre during the reign of James I until, in the reign of his son, the nature of the genre had changed utterly. And then the theatres closed and a generation passed when no Englishmen were trained in the complex techniques of dramatic production. The new drama introduced to England from the French court at the Restoration owed nothing to the centuries of native English tradition. Only in this generation have we begun to come closer to an understanding and appreciation of the vitality, variety and all-pervasiveness of that tradition.

NOTES

1 Halliwell-Phillipps collected his evidence in scrapbooks now mainly deposited in the Folger Library in Washington, DC. The evidence has been indexed by J. A. B. Somerset (*143*) and can be obtained through Records of Early English Drama.

2 Carl Stratman, *Bibliography of Medieval Drama*, 2nd edn, 2 vols. (New York: Frederick Ungar, 1972).

3 The first ten years of Records of Early English Drama were made possible through two large grants from the Canadian government (first through the Canada Council and then through the Social Sciences and Humanities Research Council of Canada), several smaller grants from the American government (through the National Endowment for the Humanities) and the University of Toronto (through its many constituent parts). In 1986, the Connaught Fund of the University of Toronto became the major source of REED support. Research has been undertaken in over forty areas of Great Britain. Eight collections have now been published with many others close to completion. This paper is based on

both the published and unpublished work of REED editors. I am particularly
grateful to Dr Theodore De Welles, the senior REED bibliographer, for his help.
4 William Tydeman, in a review of *Records of Early English Drama: Norwich
1540–1642 (147), Theatre Research International* 2 (1986): 156.
5 F. W. Harlwood, *Staffordshire Customs, Superstitions and Folklore* (London:
Scolar Press, 1974), pp. 37–9. See also research in progress by J. A. B. Somerset.
6 Lincolnshire County Archives, Lincoln MS vj 8. Bishop Longland's Visitation of
Newarke College, Leicester 1525. From research in progress by Alice Hamilton.
7 I have discussed this aspect of the York play at greater length in 'Cycle Drama in
the Sixteenth Century: Texts and Contexts', a paper delivered at the thirteenth
ACTA Conference at the State University of New York at Binghamton, April
1986 (now published as 'Cycle Drama in the Sixteenth Century', in *Early Drama
to Sixteen Hundred, ACTA*, 13 [1987]: 1–15).
8 John Coldewey, 'Early Essex Drama: A History of its Rise and Fall', unpublished
Ph.D. dissertation, University of Colorado, 1972; see especially pp. 289–327.
9 Berkshire Record Office, D/A2/C.16, fo. 89, from my own research in progress.
10 A. C. Cawley, ed., *The Wakefield Pageants in the Towneley Cycle* (Manchester:
University of Manchester Press, 1958), p. 390.
11 Coldewey, 'Early Essex Drama', pp. 156–7.
12 Quoted in Thomas Wainwright, *The Bridport Records and Ancient Manuscripts*
(compiled from *Bridport News*, mainly 1898), p. 44.
13 N. J. O'Conor, *Godes Peace and the Queenes* (London: Oxford University Press,
1934), p. 108.
14 Wiltshire Record Office, D1/42/29. The case is recorded 2 December 1614. I am
particularly grateful to Dr T. De Welles for this reference.
15 Richard Beadle, 'The East Anglian "Game-place": a Possibility for Further
Research', *REED Newsletter*, 1978:1, pp. 2–4.
16 J. A. B. Somerset, 'Local Drama and Playing Places at Shrewsbury: New Findings
from Borough Records', in *132*, pp. 1–32.
17 Thomas Churchyard, *The Worthiness of Wales* (1587), sig. L. Cited in Somerset,
'Local Drama', p. 28.
18 Peter Clark, *The English Alehouse: A Social History 1200–1830* (London: Long-
mans, 1983), pp. 151–7.
19 Coldewey, 'Early Essex Drama', pp. 268 and 289–327.
20 John Nichols, ed., *The Progresses and Public Processions of Queen Elizabeth*,
vol.. III (London: J. Nichols and Son, 1823), pp. 130–6, and *The Progresses,
Processions, and Magnificent Festivities of King James I*, vol. II (London: J. B.
Nichols, 1828), pp. 630–9.
21 Edward McGee, 'Entertainments at Theobalds: The Audience and the Artistic
Design', from a paper read to the Renaissance Society of Canada, Winnipeg, May
1986.
21 See above, note 7.
23 A regular payment for candles for plays appears after 1552 in the Eton Accounts,
see Eton College Audit Book III, pp. 145 and *passim*.
24 Queen's College, Cambridge, MS 75, pp. 378–81. This document is part of Alan
H. Nelson, ed., *Records of Early English Drama: Cambridge*, 2 vols. (Toronto:
University of Toronto Press, 1989), vol. I, pp. 688–93.
25 E. S. Fegan, ed., *The Journal of Prior William More*, Worcester Historical Society
(1914).
26 The painting is now in the National Portrait Gallery, London. The most easily
accessible reproduction is on the cover of volume III of the *Revels History of
English Drama* (London: Methuen, 1975).

8

The staging of medieval English plays

STANLEY J. KAHRL

In 1959 appeared a radically different account of the beginnings of the English theatre from that proposed just four years before by Hardin Craig in *English Religious Drama of the Middle Ages* (*105*).[1] Craig began his own review of the first volume of Glynne Wickham's *Early English Stages 1300–1660* (*107*) with magisterial disdain: 'It is unfortunate for scholarship when young scholars under stress of what they think of as new conceptual plans throw out areas of accepted knowledge.' What had Wickham thrown out? That which Craig called 'one of the best established of all important beliefs', the 'abundantly documented *belief*' (italics mine) in the 'incremental growth of the religious drama from the liturgy itself and the manner of the spread of liturgical plays by imitation and casual new creation'.[2] Once Wickham had spent the necessary two or three years learning about liturgy, Craig was sure he would grow up and acknowledge as well the certainty of this belief.

Craig was right to sense danger from this quarter. For one thing, he had been found out. When Wickham asserted that in this 'most recent, authoritative, history of English medieval drama' Hardin Craig had 'given yet a further blessing, with only minor alterations and caveats, to the standard assumptions about the origins, nature and development of the Miracle Cycles that stem from the late Sir Edmund Chambers' *The Medieval Stage*', he was absolutely correct. To Wickham, it seemed, 'the past fifty years had failed to provide us with any new knowledge adequate to resolve the many age-old conundrums that have baffled students for so long' (*107*, p. 118). Indeed this was the case. Craig's major research activities in the field of medieval drama apparently had ceased around 1914.[3]

To develop answers to those still-puzzling conundrums, Wickham undertook a new kind of research. Instead of going once again to the texts of the plays, all of which had been known for decades, and attempting yet again to sort them out in some kind of developmental order, Wickham decided 'to use the practical conditions of stage performance as a starting point and to work from there towards the text' (*107*, p. 118). The search for evidence of these practical conditions led Wickham to study records detailing the staging of tournaments, to search out chronicles describing how street pageants were prepared for royal entries and to pore over manuscript descriptions of theatrical entertainments at royal feasts. The degree to which this kind of evidence was new can be determined by glancing over the series of endnotes that conclude *Early English Stages*. There one finds reference after reference to manuscripts, mostly to be found in the British Library, many unnoticed before Wickham brought them to light.

But for Craig, all this was a side-show. 'The author', he averred (throughout the review, Craig never referred to Wickham by name) was guilty of using faulty methodology, that is, he failed dismally to preserve generic distinctions: 'The author regards all the spectacular arts as drama and confuses his readers by the continual use of such words as "stage" and "theater" and "auditorium" for every sort of ornament or *mise-en-scène*.' Why was this so serious a matter? Because 'It is universally held and is as true as any obvious definition can be that the criteria at the basis of drama are event, impersonation, and dialogue.'[4] Spectacle, as any follower of Aristotle knows, is the least important aspect of a play, that which fades quickest and that which the literary critic studies little if at all. Wickham, by lumping spectacle with 'drama', had thus vitiated his entire effort. Craig advised 'the author' to follow his enthusiasm for spectacular theatrical effects, but to leave the study of drama to those qualified to undertake such study.

The conflict between Craig and Wickham arises wherever and whenever plays are performed. Between those who present the play – and this group includes the writer(s) as a member or members of the team of presenters – and those who study texts there is a great gulf fixed. Craig, for example, attended the performance of the York cycle which E. Martin Browne directed in York as a part of the Festival of Britain in 1951, undoubtedly the single most influential event in the modern rediscovery of the power of medieval drama. Craig, however, was not impressed. To him,

Modern histrionic and theatrical techniques simply did not seem appropriate. The performance was right enough, no doubt, but it was not the York plays. As for mock holiness, in places almost as artificial as *Murder in the Cathedral*, it seemed a poor exchange for the simple piety of medieval people. There is no harm in going through what are thought to be medieval motions, but in fact *medieval religious plays seem to be lost in the tide of time* [italics mine].[5]

Wickham also attended that performance of the York cycle (*107*, p. xxvi; *271*, p. 6). He also attended the performances of the Chester cycle at Chester and was fortunate enough to direct the N-Town Passion and Nativity plays in Tewkesbury Abbey. From that experience he drew the by-now-obvious conclusion that 'The fact that the audiences, and the critics who speak for them, appear to support these revivals enthusiastically contrasts so sharply with the words "primitive", "naive", "crude" and other such patronizing epithets of traditional critical evaluation, that modern minds are now keenly awake to the idea that they may have been misinformed' (*107*, p. 114). The two men saw the same event and drew diametrically opposite conclusions from that experience.

For Craig, and others like him, a medieval play text provides an opportunity to perform mental operations utilising esoteric knowledge and

Stanley J. Kahrl

obscure terms in order to construct a theoretical abstract construct. The existence of this construct then becomes, as we have seen, a matter of belief. The mental construct has no necessary connection with any real world, past or present. Any real-time approximation of the construct is thus doomed to failure, just as any approximation of any other Platonic reality will only be a pale shadow of the reality it seeks to imitate. Only those initiated into the mysteries of the belief system can know the reality. Whether the belief system is actually worth knowing, of course, is immaterial. Craig's scorn for the amateur actors who presented the crude medieval texts he studied, with their 'simple piety', is apparent on every page he wrote. It appears most forcefully in his rejection of Arnold Williams' (to him) foolish attempt to get at the undying power of medieval drama in his book *The Drama of Medieval England (108)*.[6] Nor, during the fifties, was such scorn exhibited only in the writings of Hardin Craig. Rereading Wickham's great study again for the first time in many years, one is struck by the often shrill quality of his prose, the repeated insistence that the medieval theatre was serious business, managed by respectable people who knew what they were doing. From today's vantage point, at a time when the British National Theatre performs *The Mysteries* to packed houses, and on national British television, it is hard to recall how lonely Wickham must originally have felt.

For Wickham was a prophet. As he himself has acknowledged, he was a disciple of Gordon Craig, a man who believed 'that no text in the theatre can ever be more than shorthand notes for actors' (*107*, p. xxvi). For Glynne Wickham, and for many of those who have followed his lead in the study of medieval English drama, the play is indeed the thing, but only in performance. Let us first, then, review what conclusions Wickham himself drew concerning the nature and qualities of medieval English drama, using as his approach a scholarly study of medieval documents illuminating the practical conditions of the stage, and then suggest some of the modifications to his proposals that have followed from experience gained through modern productions which have sought, as much as possible, to re-create the original conditions of performance. To be sure, such performances are always a kind of laboratory experiment, in which the laboratory setting can never re-create exactly the original conditions of production. But just as Shakespeareans have learned much about the imaginative power of Shakespeare's plays from modern performances on thrust stages unencumbered by the scenery so popular in Victorian England, so medievalists have come to understand better the theatrical dynamics of medieval play texts when they have been performed with knowledge and respect for the original conditions of performance. Conclusions drawn from modern performances as to original dramatic effects must be used with caution, but they are not, therefore, less valuable than scholarly ratiocination about isolated but verifiable facts of performance. The two activities must complement one another at every step of our journey towards understanding of the staging of medieval English drama.

First and foremost, then, Wickham rediscovered a world of marvellous

The staging of medieval English plays

theatrical images. Ben Jonson's disdain for cloud machines and 'creaking thrones' is not shared by Wickham. With the essential eye of wonder he recalls for us colourful, elaborate theatrical structures upon which costumed characters declaim elaborate verse, descend on cloud machines, to present gifts of great value to watching monarchs, meanwhile showering the onlookers with comfits, or gold-covered candy. It is a world of allegorically costumed mistresses presiding over the combat of warriors who are, themselves, playing parts. And finally, it is a world of gorgeous ships rolling into great halls where they are then boarded by costumed warriors, who are repelled in turn by those already inside the ships. It is also a world of elaborate stage discoveries, managed by stage designers familiar with a whole bag of tricks, armed with winches, windlasses, gears and pulleys of all sorts. All the structures described were, of course, gaily painted in bold primary colors, covered with gold and silver foil; all were simply magnificent. Wickham had the sense to do some comparative analysis of the sums spent, a notoriously difficult thing to do, but the way had already been shown by F. M. Salter, in his seminal chapter on 'A Day's Labor' in *Mediaeval Drama in Chester* (*186*). From such analysis he made it abundantly clear that the structures he was re-creating were elaborate, expensive and visually impressive. Equivalents were to be found in the drama of France, where performances like that of the *Mystère des Trois Doms* showed just how elaborately theatrical a medieval play could become. Once having read *Early English Stages*, one ever afterwards had to imagine the structures employed in a medieval play in a totally new light.

Problems arose, however, when Wickham came to imagine the moving theatrical spaces of the streets, that is, the pageant wagons of medieval England. Wickham had offered a most important distinction in his study of theatrical structures, proposing that we think either of indoor or outdoor theatres. Each has its own strengths and liabilities, none of either having to do with the old distinction between 'religious' or 'secular' drama. However, when he came to reflect on how the rather special, and unusual, form of outdoor theatre known as the pageant wagon came to be used, Wickham's world of elaborate theatrical images undid him. Having filled the pageant cart(s) with the machinery found in other structures, he found too little acting space for his actors, and thus was forced to propose a second wagon, empty, which accompanied the elaborate structure through the streets and offered a thrust stage similar to that found in the Globe Theatre that C. Walter Hodges had recently rebuilt along similar lines to those Wickham was proposing for medieval theatre.[7] Evidence for the second wagon was slim; if one was not persuaded that the second wagon existed, one was left with a wagon full of scenery, and little acting space. And there the matter was left for some years.

One final word is in order on Wickham's rejection of 'belief' in the theory that 'incremental growth of the religious drama from the liturgy itself' led to a secular form enshrining the 'simple piety' of theatrical amateurs. Wickham concluded that the spectacular stage structures he had virtually rediscovered were characteristic of late-medieval culture, which had little to do with the forms of art produced in early-medieval Europe. The early liturgical plays possessed characteristics akin to Romanesque art, whereas the later drama was most like the art of the Gothic cathedrals. Furthermore, whereas the Latin liturgical plays focussed on the events surrounding the Resurrection, the central event in all Christian history, and then on the Nativity that made the Resurrection possible, the later vernacular drama, usually associated with the feast of Corpus Christi, focussed instead on the institution of the Eucharist and on the brutal facts of the Crucifixion which followed. As Wickham put it,

the liturgical drama of the churches is most unlikely to have developed *into* the secularized drama of the streets ... A much more likely conjecture would appear to me to be that original plays of the Fall, Crucifixion and Judgement were presented out of doors during the thirteenth century at the insistence of friars or like-minded priests and clerks, who were determined to bring the relevance of Christ's sacrifice to bewildered mankind in the market place: and that these new plays attracted to themselves such other dramatic narrative as had been formulated within the worship of the Church...   (*107*, p. 316)[8]

Two important studies which appeared in the next decade did much to show how prescient was this suggestion. Following O. B. Hardison Jr's collection of essays on *Christian Rite and Christian Drama in the Middle Ages* (*46*), in which Hardison demonstrated the fallacious biological metaphor that underlay Chambers' and Young's hypothetical history of the origins of early English drama, V. A. Kolve went on to show, in *The Play Called Corpus Christi* (*151*), that the Corpus Christi plays were indeed a new form, invented for a new occasion. Kolve, furthermore, advanced considerable persuasive historical evidence demonstrating that the Latin liturgical plays never 'developed' or 'budded out' into anything new because as particular enhancements of the liturgy they fulfilled the function for which they had been invented, and remained a part of the liturgy as long as that liturgy was performed (*151*, pp. 39–44). By 1974, when my *Traditions of Medieval English Drama* (*119*) appeared, what had been a suggestion by Wickham could be considered as the proper account of events. The importance of this change of focus cannot be overemphasised. Freed from the old biological metaphor, scholars were now able to concentrate on late-medieval English drama as a thing important in and of itself. It could be studied as part of a particular world with a specific culture, one which provided the controlling influence that gave the vernacular English drama flourishing in the fifteenth and sixteenth centuries its particular shape. Part of that shape was the stage or stages upon which the plays were performed.

Although those studying the original conditions for staging medieval English plays often drew their inspiration from a modern performance such as that at York, none of the initial modern re-creations were at all faithful even to Chambers' concept of the original staging conditions. E. Martin

Browne completely abandoned performance on pageant wagons when he re-created the York plays. His choice of staging – a wide, shallow acting area set up against a ruined wall of St Mary's Abbey, in which limited structures were arranged along a flat, two-dimensional space – was copied, for example, by Margaret Birkett in her production of the *Ludus Coventriae* staged before St Wulfram's Church, in Grantham, Lincolnshire, in 1966.[9] Copied, too, was Browne's staging of the Crucifixion. At York Browne arranged a façade of flags around the prostrate figure of Christ and the tormenters, who then, silently, screened discreetly from the audience, attached the actor to the Cross, raised them both and then, after the Cross had been set in its base, turned and faced the audience as the flags were lowered. The striking text of the York 'Crucifixion' was not used. When asked why she, who had shown considerable imagination in her staging of the torture scenes, had retreated from performing the ultimate horror, Margaret Birkett defended this staging by saying that 'a modern audience could not take anything so cruel on stage'. Shades of Samuel Johnson's response to the death of Cordelia! It was not, in fact, until 1969, with Neville Denny's production of the Cornish cycle according to principles developed from historical research, that the Crucifixion was staged with anything like the power that lies so obviously in the original text.

It was not particularly surprising that a performance of the Cornish cycle should have appeared at that moment in history. One of the landmark studies of the fifties had been Richard Southern's *The Medieval Theatre in the Round* (*122*). Southern's interest was that of a designer of scenery, 'someone', as he said in his original preface, 'concerned with the ways which the theatre offers of shaping a show, and of putting that show over to an audience so as to make it most kindling, most illuminating and most vivid to them, and most direct in what it has to say' (*122*, p. xii). Southern had begun a project of surveying scenery design in the contemporary theatre, and had been driven ever further back in time as he became increasingly aware of 'the amazing influence the playhouse has on the scene' (*122*, p. xiv). He also had come to see that earlier stages, especially those before the advent of movable scenery, had operated in a manner very different from that of the contemporary theatre – except for Brecht, to whom, and to whose company, *The Medieval Theatre in the Round* was not surprisingly dedicated. Southern shared his discovery of *The Open Stage* of the Elizabethans with the Drama Department of the University of Bristol in 1953 as a set of four lectures,[10] and then went on to discover where that openness had originated. Having been brought up to think of 'medieval theatre in Britain [as] chiefly pictured as a system practiced by amateur players, in which they employed a succession of wagons pulled about the streets of a city', he was understandably excited to discover 'a more consciously theatrical tradition', that of the 'epic play', *The Castle of Perseverance* (*122*, p. xvi). (The term 'epic', of course, derives from Brecht's usage.)

The Medieval Theatre in the Round was a landmark in drama scholarship because it studied a play in a theatre (see also chapter 6, pp. 100–2). Wickham had sought out stages, but the only text he mentioned was a dreary mumming by Lydgate. Salter had much new to say about Chester, but nothing to say about the Chester cycle. But Southern had a text to explicate, in highly visual theatrical terms. This was the more surprising if one had read the *Castle* before reading Southern. Seen without Southern's eye, the play appears merely 'talky' to most readers at first glance. Southern, however, saw that the speeches, often four stanzas long, were designed to be delivered to the four points of the compass within the circular theatre pictured in a diagram preceding the play's text. Southern reconstructed a theatre based on that diagram, placed a set of booth stages on the rim of a raised earthen bank, peopled it with actors in colourful costumes and a lively, involved audience, and then brought the play to life.

The immediate effect of Southern's theatrical reading of *The Castle of Perseverance* was to stimulate interest in similar texts.[11] Martial Rose in particular saw interesting parallels between the N-Town Passion sequence and the theatrical world Southern drew for the *Castle*. He came to believe as well that the final revision of the Wakefield cycle was written for the same theatrical space, following his experimental productions of portions of that cycle at Bretton Hall College at Wolley Hall, Wakefield, in 1954 and 1958. He included these ideas in the introduction to his full translation of the Wakefield cycle, which he began for his own production in 1958, expanded for the famous production of Colin Ellis and Sally Miles at the Mermaid Theatre, London in 1961 and published in 1962 (*167*, Introduction, pp. 17–48). Rose's translation of the Wakefield cycle provided a teaching text of a full cycle at a crucial moment in the modern revival of interest in medieval drama, and his translation of the N-Town Passion sequence made Margaret Birkett's production at Grantham possible. It is, I believe, the one used at Lincoln several times since. These are just a few of the immediate results of Southern's vivid picture of how the medieval place-and-scaffold theatre worked in practice.

The most controversial of Southern's suggestions was the proposal that the ditch mentioned in the diagram had to be tied to a bank, however. The theatre Southern called for seemed to require an immense effort in digging out a great trench, the dirt being transferred to create a large bank upon which the booth stages were arranged. The purpose of Southern's ditch was to keep out non-paying customers. The cogency of Southern's practical argument sent scholars like Richard Hosley off scouring the countryside of Britain for round earthworks that might have been used as medieval theatres, the sensible thought being that once that much earth had been moved, it stayed put. (Who would want to put it back?) The result should still be visible. Though little physical evidence of such theatres could be turned up in the most probable area of production of the *Castle*, East Anglia, the search did draw scholars' attention to the Cornish rounds. From today's vantage point, as a result of the work of people like Natalie Crohn Schmitt,[12] we can see that Southern's most valuable contribution was not his imagined theatre but rather his conclusion that the *platea* or 'place', mentioned so often in the *Castle*, was not, as Chambers suggested, the forestage, but rather the open square of any village or town in Europe, the space on ground level where the audience stood, and where much of the action, particularly the most vigorous action (such as the siege of the Castle itself) took place. His other major contribution was his demonstration of the fluidity of the action of the *Castle*, his sense that the play worked as much by processions from one raised stage to another as by any other single kind of stage action.

The Cornish rounds, known locally as *plan-an-gwarry*, were there, however, and a seventeenth-century historian spoke of plays performed within them.[13] In addition, there were plays, particularly a full cycle play, in Cornish, which included diagrams similar to that in the text of the *Castle* illustrating how the booth stages were to be arranged around the edge of the circle. Edwin Norris had published a translation of the Cornish cycle years before so that it was possible to see how some of the concepts Southern had developed applied to the Cornish cycle as well. Though the Cornish diagrams located nothing like the castle in the centre of the circle, Neville Denny, for example, saw that the play texts called for central structures towards which action flowed and ebbed from the circle of surrounding structures. Denny concluded that a single dominating structure would be inappropriate for the staging of this cycle. For one thing, he claimed that the sight lines would be impaired by such staging. Secondly, because the structures called for are not one single castle, but a succession of buildings, interruption of the action to introduce new stage structures would, in his view, severely distort the flow of the play's action. Instead Denny proposed a set of three focal points, which 'could be used alternately ... as principal foci of action. Both the few scenic units required and the principal dramatic localities could usefully be located in these areas', Denny claimed, 'and the position always so manipulated as to leave one focal point free, for scene-shifting etc., while the audience's attention is concentrated on another, leaving the powerful – indeed the dominant – stage-position of in-the-round theatre, the centre, always free for its proper exploitation in the overall *mise-en-scène* (3, pp. 131–2).

In the event the Cornish round proved as flexible and effective an acting area as Denny had believed it would be.[14] Though the circle's diameter was over 100 feet, and the walls of the circle low, offering apparently little reflective surface for the sound, in performance the actors could be heard in almost every part of the central acting area. Crowds of actors formed and dissolved, the action shifted rapidly from one area of interest to another and then back, 'cutting', as Denny himself saw, from one focal point to another much in the manner of a modern cinema camera. One may argue that this effect was created by Denny's direction of the play. He it was who wanted 'the audience's eyes' to be 'darting everywhere, like spectators' at an ice-hockey match. In theatrical terms, the effect is electric and unique', he argued (3, p. 139). And so it was.

Stanley J. Kahrl

Details of the production showed the effects of scholarly research as well. Costuming, for example, was closer to the costumes seen in late-medieval European manuscript illustrations of biblical scenes than had been true in many previous productions. The serpent in the garden appeared as an attractive long-haired blonde female, her serpentine tail created by a body stocking. No slinking male Satan effected Adam's fall. Instead he fell to the wiles of two women. A classic example of medieval misogyny was given effective modern life. Hellmouth was spectacular, as were the costumes of the devils. Eruptions from the source of Evil were accompanied by smoke and din. At the conclusion of every Old Testament play, from the death of Abel on, those who died before the Incarnation were carried off to Hell. After the shock came the recognition. Of course! For the Harrowing of Hell to be necessary, this had to have been happening. A theological concept as old as the Nicene Creed became real in theatrical terms with Abel's exit through the Hellmouth of Perran Round.

Because dominant productions of medieval drama during the fifties and sixties were staged primarily in the British Isles, Arnold Williams recognised that one person could not begin to see them all. He thus scheduled an informal discussion for the 1961 Modern Language Association meeting, using the 'seminar' format, where those who had attended modern perform-ances of medieval drama could compare notes and share what they had learned.[15] The idea was so popular that the seminar became a permanent fixture of the MLA meeting. Reports presented on research in progress conveyed an infectious sense of excitement. Because Williams himself wel-comed new ideas, younger scholars found a place to speak in a supportive atmosphere. The existence of such colloquia, where both reports and informed discussion are rapidly published in the year following the event, does more to stimulate the development of a field, particularly if younger scholars are encouraged to participate, than any other form of research communication. Periodic reviews of the sort this volume represents then can assess what has been accomplished over a longer period of time, and make the lasting results known to a larger audience.[16]

One young scholar who had a particularly strong impact on the study of the staging of medieval English drama was Alan Nelson. At the MLA meeting held in December 1969, Nelson presented a paper entitled 'Prin-ciples of Processional Staging: York Cycle' (*157*). There he argued, on the basis of mathematical analysis of the evidence, that it was impossible to perform the plays in the York cycle in one day, on pageant wagons. The paper was controversial. Arthur Cawley, who attended that meeting, was one of those rejecting Nelson's hypothesis. Upon his return to England the following year, he encouraged Margaret Rogerson to review the archival evidence pertaining to the staging of medieval plays in York. Alexandra Johnston, who also rejected Nelson's thesis, independently undertook the same mission. Happily the two young women worked out a *modus vivendi*, and the search of the York records began.

Nelson understood that those who disagreed with him did so on the basis of evidence in local records which seemed to contradict the results of mathematical analysis. He therefore extended his argument using records which had either been published only in obscure local histories, or not at all, in *The Medieval English Stage: Corpus Christi Pageants and Plays (154)*. It is a flawed book. Written in haste, it presents many points to which one might, and to which reviewers did, object.[17] His solution to the problem of the excessive length of the surviving York plays – that they were never performed in public, the pageant carts only appearing as do the floats in the annual Tournament of Roses parade in California, as tableaux in a procession, the plays themselves being presented after the Corpus Christi procession had ended, in a private chamber – appealed to very few (*154*, pp. 65–81). His extension of his idea to places like Lincoln persuaded no better.[18] The book's importance cannot be overemphasised, however. Incorporating as it does a set of radically altered descriptions of how religious plays were performed during the late Middle Ages in the cities of England, *The Medieval English Stage* forced everyone to rethink the relationship that existed between the plays and the procession.[19] One could no longer speak blithely of the civic religious plays originating from the procession which was the only invariable element in the new feast of Corpus Christi without facing the fact that processions are time-consuming events involving many people. Plays, too, take time. And both occupy real space. If one wished to argue against Nelson, one was forced to find a time and a place for both plays and procession. To do so required much greater knowledge of the local conditions of performance than one could possibly obtain from the pages of *The Medieval English Stage*.

Wickham had seen that Chambers' sources were partial. Others too were learning how very limited were the sources of Chambers' knowledge. Though he quoted from a wide range of local histories, those histories were biassed and unscholarly. Quaint entries were plucked out of full accounts, the routine and mundane being of little interest. Nelson had at least looked at originals unknown to Chambers. But to argue with him one needed to know the local histories and manuscript records from which he drew his evidence as well as or better than he did himself. Furthermore, since his method of citation was sketchy, it was often hard to locate the context of problematic evidence even if one knew the records well. Everyone in the field needed better access to more complete sets of local records.

The problem lay, of course, in the means of publication. The local records of Lincolnshire, modelled on the work of Giles Dawson for Kent (*138*), was to have been published by the Malone Society in 1969, but did not appear until 1974 (*139*). It was thus not available, for example, to Nelson. But it, and Dawson's volume, were a start. Others had also been at work on similar research projects – David Galloway in Norwich, Reg Ingram in Coventry, Larry Clopper in Chester and of course Alexandra Johnston and Margaret Rogerson in York. Presented with this gathering body of archive material,

Stanley J. Kahrl

Richard Proudfoot chose not to divert the Malone Society from its major task, publishing accurately printed black-letter copies of early dramatic texts. The 'Collections' had always been something of a sideline, though extremely valuable, and had, perforce, concentrated on dramatic records illustrating staging conditions for the Renaissance stage. Hence the starting date of 1450 for Dawson's volume. Yet for the study of the conditions of production of medieval drama to continue, such research had to have an outlet. Thus it was that in 1974, shortly after the appearance of Nelson's book, a committee formed the Records of Early English Drama to publish early English dramatic records. The formation of REED thus grew directly out of research focussed primarily on the conditions of performance for early English drama, research that can fairly be said to have taken a new beginning with the publication of the first volume of *Early English Stages*.

The REED organisation was not solely concerned to publish early records, however. Since the project was supported by public funds provided by both the Canadian and the United States governments, communication of the research findings to an audience of the general public was required. Logically the best method of communication was the performance of plays. Productions such as Neville Denny's performance of the Cornish cycle, conceived as laboratory experiments where one could test theories hitherto refined only by logical argument, were seen as a necessary complement to the scholarly editions of early dramatic records. The productions sponsored jointly by REED and the Poculi Ludique Societas have thus become an important additional way to understand the staging of medieval English drama.

The most important discovery turned up by Johnston and Rogerson in their search through the York records was an indenture describing properties for the York Mercers' pageant of the Last Judgement.[20] This discovery, and Arthur Cawley's continuing interest in proving that the York cycle was indeed performed 'processionally', that is, on movable wagons, at a series of stations, undoubtedly led to the decision taken in 1974–5 (one notes again the proximity of this event to the publication of *The Medieval English Stage*) to perform the York cycle in its entirety, on wagons, at three separate stations, on the streets of Leeds. The production, directed by Jane Oakeshott, thus broke completely with the by then 'received tradition' of performing that cycle continuously on a single-stage set. Though only thirty-six pageants were produced on simply furnished farm wagons, the production demonstrated that processional staging could be far more effective than had been supposed. The relative success of this production encouraged the REED Executive Committee to sponsor as their first major production a similar event.[21]

Despite the terrible rains that drove much of the production indoors, this experimental production was also a success. The impact of that performance is preserved, not only in the reports delivered to the MLA seminar, published in *RORD* for 1977, but also in papers delivered at a meeting held on 7 April

1979, at the University of Lancaster discussing current research on 'the Pageant Waggon', published in the first volume of *Medieval English Theatre*. What essential conclusions can we draw from that experience? First, while it may still interest some to speculate on whether medieval pageant wagons did or did not have the six wheels that Rogers' description of the Chester wagon stage implies, that issue is really a dead letter.[22] Four-wheeled wagons are and have been ubiquitous for centuries. Their operation it is that we need to understand.[23] Secondly, the range of effects that one could achieve in what was still a rather small (12 feet by 6 feet) acting area was found to be larger than expected because the acting area was quickly found to be far larger than the wagon stage alone. As David Parry explained in the meeting at Lancaster, 'the standard 12' by 6' deck ... is remarkably large once you come to play on it. And when the street is used as well, the possibilities really are endless.'[24] Ladders or steps made descents to the surrounding 'place' easy from stages that were never over four feet in height. As the audience in Toronto formed a dense circle around a popular play like 'The Harrowing of Hell', one saw immediately how well the wagon stages would have functioned in the narrow streets of York, where the most that any station could accommodate might be 700 or 800 people. Gail Gibson has expressed how great an impact a pageant-wagon play could have on a member of the audience:

The most gifted acting I saw was in the Cornell *Christ Led Up to Calvary* where, without a single false note, the boasts and jests of the Roman soldiers sprawled about a stump in the foreground playing area conveyed just that complex mixture of unawareness and cruelty which gives the York *tortores* their horrible fascination. A tragic chorus of Jesus' followers dressed in muted gray garments, offered a counter-point to the cruel actions of the soldiers with their moving plaints; their gestures were choreographed with the precision of a dance, their voices a haunting music. And there were audible gasps at the end of the play when the gaunt, bearded Jesus, about to be dragged away in chains, approached within arm's reach of the spectators and, for one, painfully long minute, wordlessly searched the faces in the audience with an expression at once dazed and reproachful. It was for me the single most extraordinary moment of the entire Toronto production.[25]

Above all the experiment at Toronto demonstrated that people who presented plays in the Middle Ages knew what they were doing. They developed particular conventions of staging because those conventions were effective. To reach and experience directly the full power of such plays we must understand fully the staging conventions for which the texts were written. Every play text is written with a particular theatre in mind. One need not necessarily re-create, with pedantic exactitude, the precise space Ibsen, Shakespeare or Wycherley had in their heads as they peopled their mental stages to produce their plays today. Nevertheless, the more one understands the original conventions, and how they worked, the more effective will be the adaptation.

Knowledge of such conventions is not yet widely shared by modern directors of medieval plays.[26] Yet we should not be surprised at this. Neville

Denny's production of the Cornish cycle only took place a little over fifteen years ago. Until 1975 the dynamics of wagon stages were imperfectly understood. Not until the performances of the Chester cycle at Toronto, Leeds and Chester in 1983 were wagon sets dragged along anything like medieval streets in the fair atmosphere which originally prevailed. Even within the scholarly community the practical experience gained through the use of practicable stages constructed on the basis of scholarly research is not always trusted.[27] Yet direct hands-on knowledge gained from working with wagons has transformed many scholars' ideas of how wagon stages work. Their proper theatrical use demands awareness of their strengths and limitations, however. As David Mills said in summing up his experience of the Toronto performance of the Chester cycle, 'Finally, a producer needs to "think waggon" to give the action visual focus. For me the most effective productions concentrated the action on the waggon and the area immediately in front of it.'[28]

Following the performance of the York cycle, the Poculi Ludique Societas and the Graduate Centre for the Study of Drama at the University of Toronto and REED chose in 1979 to present *The Castle of Perseverance* to learn more about the dynamics of the place-and-scaffold theatre. In performance *The Castle of Perseverance* proved quite as theatrically exciting as Southern had argued it would be. Richly costumed forces of evil first identified themselves on their scaffold stages and then dominated the circular space within which Mankind played out his life. The visual contrast between the defenceless, naked (i.e., body-stockinged) figure of Mankind – forced to choose between the moral imperatives of the Good Angel and the blandishments of the Bad – and the regally proud Seven Deadly Sins made Mankind's decision to choose World's clothing as inevitable as Original Sin. Yet the solid castle was always there, and ultimately became the appropriate place of defence when Mankind chose to leave the life of sin. Here above all one was reminded that to read a play properly one must always recall that there are long moments when, in performance, there are few lines but much action. 'The large cast allowed a mighty and picturesque assault on the castle in the middle section of the play. World led his retinue to war on his horse, the Devil directed his cohorts from a chariot, and Flesh proceeded in a sedan chair. These villains stormed the castle in turn with every conceivable medieval weapon', in stylised combat that was both believable and exciting:

Finally Sloth dug into the moat [which had been placed in the centre of the acting area, not outside the audience] to allow the water from it to drain and the vices ran from the playing area carrying the blue-cloth water overhead. They returned with ladders to scale the castle walls, but at the moment of their apparent victory, they were repelled by the virtues who cast down upon them roses symbolizing Christ's passion. This great battle made a marvelously theatrical center for the play and it also made clear that Mankind is faithfully and powerfully protected by the virtues and that he departs from grace altogether of his own accord.[29]

This battle also made clear that the ditch/barrier of the original drawing could function effectively as a portion of the *mise-en-scène*, as opposed to the exterior location proposed by Southern. And, as Natalie Crohn Schmitt also noted, the large number of actors required to stage so impressive a performance was not assembled by any touring company thus far identified in the dramatic records of medieval England.[30]

Those attending this splendid performance saw, then, a demonstration of how medieval theatre-in-the-round works at its best.[31] To see the play, however, they sat on most modern pipe-rack bleacher seats whose overpowering visual presence dominated the scene and removed the audience from the action. Kathy Pearl, assistant director for the *Castle* production, chose therefore to dispense entirely with pre-arranged seating in the subsequent performance of the N-Town Passion, billed as 'The Toronto Passion'. The initial audience response was one of confusion, described well in Meg Twycross' account of the production.[32] By intermission on the first day instructions to the audience were clearly needed. However once people learned to find a spot they liked and then to settle there, seeking other vantage points only occasionally, the result was one of the most moving performances of the Passion ever experienced. As Theresa Coletti and Kathleen Ashley reported,

The Toronto Passion emphatically conveyed the idea that Christ's sacrifice took place in this world, in our midst, for the acting space and the audience space were virtually coterminous. There were no seats: the audience had a choice of sitting on the grass in the middle of the action or of moving around as the action shifted. Staging the play in and around the audience quite literally transformed the spectators into active participants in the Passion story. The development of that story within human time, the narrative and dynamic element, emerged in this production as vividly as it does in the visual arts ... [A]s is the case with many late medieval representations of the Passion that require of the viewer a sequential 'reading' of their content, the play could only be experienced as a series of discrete actions that added up to the whole greater than the sum of its parts. There was no 'perfect' position, no 'eye of God' from which all events and relationships could be seen in proper perspective; one could only have a human and limited perspective. The resulting multiplicity of actions and experiences might have fragmented the drama. Instead, it produced a dynamic and organic whole that enveloped the entire Victoria College quadrangle – stages, grass, actors and audience – in the highly charged iconographic world of the Passion.[33]

As Jesus' beaten figure staggered past, nearly collapsing under the weight of the Cross, down the lane that had quietly opened through the audience that formed the outside of the circle, the feeling that one was present at Calvary was overpowering.[34]

The experimental productions thus far described have all been cases where the conclusions drawn from contemporary research into the conditions of production for pageant-wagon stages, or place-and-scaffold theatres, were used to stage texts of plays clearly written for one or the other theatrical environment. But what theatrical space did the writer of 'The Second Shepherds Play' imagine as he created his masterpiece? As already noted, Martial Rose had concluded as early as 1961 that the plays in the Towneley manuscript were written for place-and-scaffold theatre (*167*, pp. 30, 32). To test Rose's theory, therefore, Garrett Epp was asked to produce the plays in the Towneley manuscript in the round, using the courtyard of Victoria College which had served so well as a setting of place-and-scaffold theatre for the 'Toronto Passion'. The production, though instructive, was only a qualified success, however. Visual unity was achieved through Epp's central control over the decor of the various stages. David Mills' highly evocative description of what it felt like to be a member of the audience conveys well the sense of how the staging worked: 'In a cycle whose dramatic modes twist and change abruptly, the audience itself is to be moved and turned physically, never allowed to rest *but always required to react* [italics mine].'[35] However, as Martin Stevens concluded, 'the action almost never requires more than one stage ... in fact, the stage design at Victoria College may well have been the cause rather than the effect of the interesting simultaneous staging we so often saw in the performance.'[36] If there was a procession, it was a single procession, from a distant spot to the point of focus of the play. The 'First Shepherds Play' began on the hill and moved to the manger. But again, had the manger been located on a wagon stage, the entire action of the first half of the play could have taken place on the place before the wagon set. In fact, every play added by the Wakefield Master can be played on a single stage. If we assume that his work represents the last best thoughts on how the cycle should be written, then it seems that the dominant theatrical space in the minds of the cycle's writers was the theatre of origin of so many of the cycle's scenes, the pageant-wagon stage of York. Yet the play worked well as theatre in the round. Something is there in the text, the kind of evidence that Rose responded to when he began to work out the structures called for, that suggests the presence of a set of structures whose functions are repeated from play to play.[37] One can build such structures for the occasion, or one can haul them through town in a procession, and then, having circled a square, use the wagons as structures in a place-and-scaffold theatre. This seems the most satisfactory resolution to the puzzling nature of this still-to-be-fully-understood cycle. Without productions that try out medieval modes of staging with integrity and skill, such conclusions are impossible to verify by anything other than logic.[38]

Medieval drama is a vibrant, fascinating area of study in which much that was 'known' twenty-five years ago no longer seems true. Fortunately for those beginning a study of this field, fixed points exist. William Tydeman's out-standing description of *The Theatre in the Middle Ages* (25), though drawing much of its evidence from continental sources, is nevertheless the place to start. Utilising the distinctions proposed originally by Wickham, that is, the division of the subject according to the nature of the spaces utilised for the plays themselves, in other words, 'Indoor Theatre', 'Street Theatre', and 'Open-air Theatre', Tydeman draws on every scrap of published research available, as well as his own practical theatrical experience, to present a clear, reasonable account of the theatrical conditions governing the performance of medieval plays.[39] But to William Tydeman we owe even more! Though for individual scholars knowledge of medieval staging can seem to be a sufficient end in itself, for ordinary students of drama such knowledge is only a means to an end. That end, finally, is an increased ability to read or to perform medieval dramatic texts. Since the appearance of my *Traditions of Medieval English Drama* (*119*), few major studies have appeared which use a solid knowledge of medieval staging practices to develop theatrically oriented readings of medieval plays.[40] It is a pleasure to conclude this review, therefore, by stating that Tydeman's *English Medieval Theatre 1400–1500* (*135*) provides readings of key texts illustrating performance practices as they may have existed in medieval England. The stages illustrated are the booth stage, for which *Mankind* is the text; the Croxton *Play of the Sacrament*, as illustration of a play utilising multiple structures; a new reading of *The Castle of Perseverance* within a simpler theatre-in-the-round; processional staging as it might have occurred in York; and finally great-hall theatre, as exemplified in the play *Fulgens and Lucrece*. Because Tydeman has set his plays in hypothesised medieval locations, this study contains much more speculation than does *The Theatre in the Middle Ages*. With individual decisions individual scholars then will quibble. For example, to those who believe with Wickham that inn-yards were seldom if ever used for the performance of the plays of strolling players (*111*, pp. 187–96), staging *Mankind* in an inn-yard will seem a mistake. The actual staging proposed, however, is so close to that developed for the Poculi Ludique Societas production of *Mankind* by David Parry, and performed widely both in North America and in Great Britain, that those teaching the play will find this chapter invaluable.

A definitive account of the staging of drama in medieval England does not now exist. As Wickham cautions, in lamenting the fact that the increased flow of information from such sources as the volumes of REED

does not help the historian to provide a short and concise account of how [civic religious drama] was organized, financed and stage-managed ... Students must accept the fact that while it may be possible to define in some detail and with some claim to accuracy what occurred in one city or in a particular group of smaller townships and country parishes, the information supplied by the one may very well appear to contradict that supplied by the other. (*17*, p. 69)

Yet we are certainly much further ahead than we were twenty-five years ago in our understanding of medieval English staging practices. I have concentrated in this chapter upon our gradually expanding understanding of the two dominant modes of staging that are peculiarly medieval, both lost with the appearance of the wooden theatres in Elizabethan London. I have not discussed either 'indoor theatres', or the booth stage for a simple reason. Anyone who has acted on a pageant-wagon stage knows as much as he or she needs to know about the use of a booth stage. Structures indoors function as they do in the open, except that the space available outdoors will certainly be larger, and the effects therefore potentially grander. Where no structures are

Stanley J. Kahrl

used, as in *Fulgens and Lucrece*, the actors function exactly as they do in the place that fronts the structures we have been examining. *Mankind* is still an outstanding example of what I have called 'the Anyplace Play'. It has been performed with equal effect in a hall and on a green. The only space it does not easily inhabit is a post-Renaissance theatre. But Parry's actors learned to perform that play as much from their experience on the pageant wagons of the York cycle and the spaces before them as from any other source.[41] William Tydeman's *English Medieval Theatre 1400–1500 (135)* shows just how far we have come, and how much we now can state with confidence about the staging of plays in medieval England.

Editor's note: Stanley J. Kahrl, Professor of English at Ohio State University, died on 3 December 1989. We will long remember him as a distinguished scholar and a generous colleague.

NOTES

1 Arnold Williams concluded his review of Craig's book by saying that although there were a number of 'controversial positions' with which he would disagree (as indeed there were!), nevertheless *English Religious Drama* 'will be the natural point of departure from which new students and critics will enlarge and refine our understanding of this most characteristic contribution of the Middle Ages, the drama' (*Speculum* 31 [1956]: 351).
2 *Speculum* 34 (1959): 702.
3 When I wrote to him in 1965 for any help he might offer before undertaking a new review of the evidence for the performance of plays in medieval Lincoln, he wrote in answer that he had not consulted the records 'since the war', and thus did not know how well catalogued the archives now were in Lincoln. It turned out that the war to which he was referring was the Great War!
4 *Speculum* 34 (1959): 704.
5 *Speculum* 36 (1961): 696; review of *108*.
6 *Ibid.*
7 For the full discussion of this idea, see *107*, pp. 169–74; for Hodges' landmark study, see *The Globe Restored: A Study of the Elizabethan Theatre* (London: Ernest Benn, 1953).
8 In place of the old theory of origins, Wickham offered the following 'presumptive chronology' (*107*, p. 317):
   (i) Dramas of the period 975 A.D. – 1220/25 were conceived and written exclusively in Latin.
   (ii) Plays of the Fall, Crucifixion, Antichrist and Judgement written between 1225 and 1350 were conceived alternatively in Latin or the vernacular, with a marked tendency to prefer the vernacular after 1300.
   (iii)Old, liturgical dramas of the Nativity and Resurrection were either adapted or translated into the vernacular after 1300.
   (iv)A full vernacular cycle was a possibility at any time after 1350.
9 For a list of twentieth-century revivals of medieval plays, see *17*, pp. 221–6, covering productions through 1973. For a more complete study of this subject, see *136*.
10 (London: Faber & Faber, 1953).

11 See, for example, Kenneth Cameron and Stanley J. Kahrl, 'The N-Town Plays at Lincoln', *Theatre Notebook* 20 (1965–6): 61–72; 'Staging the N-Town Cycle', *Theatre Notebook* 21 (1967): 122–38, 152–65.

12 See *114*. For a defence of Southern's views, responding to Schmitt, see *223*, pp. 124–32. Schmitt's revision has gained wide acceptance, however. For a return to Wickham's old interest, the tournaments, and the application of tournament settings to the *Castle*, see *241*.

13 Neville Denny (*3*, p. 130, n. 3) quotes John Scawen's statement to this effect.

14 Though no conclusive evidence has yet been found to prove that the three surviving Cornish plays were actually performed in the circular *plan-an-gwarry*, Evelyn Newlyn, editing the surviving Cornish records for a forthcoming volume in the REED series, is convinced, on the basis of her examination of the additional inferential evidence she has located, that the Cornish rounds were used to perform the surviving play texts.

15 At the 1964 meeting of the MLA, Samuel Schoenbaum, sponsor of another annually occurring seminar, 'Research Opportunities in Renaissance Drama', whose proceedings he then would publish and distribute free, suggested enlarging the *RORD*. The 'Medieval Supplement' thereafter became a permanent feature.

16 Testimony to the value of the MLA seminar came in an unexpected form several years later. Responding to populist pressures, the Modern Language Association eliminated many long-running scholarly seminars from the program to provide space for seminars on new topics, often of a trendy nature. One of the seminars eliminated was the seminar on medieval drama. Those who had found the seminar on medieval drama too valuable to lose, acting under the inspiration and determined leadership of David Bevington, formed the Medieval and Renaissance Drama Society, whose purposes include scheduling meetings at the MLA. For a prior example of such a conference, see *The Drama of Medieval Europe* (*22*).

17 For representative reviews, see Arnold Williams, *Speculum* 52 (1977): 414–15; Alexandra Johnston, *University of Toronto Quarterly* 44 (1975): 238–48.

18 Stanley J. Kahrl, *CD* 8 (1974–5): '...I find it impossible to conceive of a town which did have mobile stages, requiring considerable expense to construct and maintain, a town which furthermore had a civic play of the type for which such stages were developed, abandoning those stages in the cathedral grounds to troop into a private home where only the canons of the cathedral and their friends were to see the play' (pp. 388–9).

19 See *154*, pp. 42–7, for discussion of processions at York; pp. 88–91 at Beverley; 105–13 at Lincoln. Discussions of other processions in other towns follow.

20 For their own description of this finding, see Alexandra F. Johnston and Margaret Rogerson, 'The Doomsday Pageant of the York Mercers, 1433', *LSE* n.s. 5 (1971): 29–34, and 'The York Mercers and their Pageant of Doomsday, 1433–1526', *LSE* n.s. 6 (1972): 10–35.

21 See 'The York Cycle at Toronto: October 1 and 2, 1977', *RORD* 20 (1977): 107, 114. For strictures on the cramped quality of such stages, see *119*, pp. 39–40.

22 For a review of the discussion see John Marshall, 'The Chester Pageant Carriage', *Medieval English Theatre* 1 (1979): 49–55.

23 'Development of the York Mercers' Pageant Waggon', *Medieval English Theatre* 1 (1979): 5–18.

24 'The York Mystery Cycle at Toronto, 1977', *Medieval English Theatre* 1 (1979): 19–31, p. 19.

25 'The York Cycle at Toronto: October 1 and 2, 1977', *RORD* 20 (1977): 116.

26 For a thoughtful critique of the faults of Bill Bryden's production, see Darryll

Grantley, 'The National Theatre's Production of *The Mysteries*: Some Observations', *Theatre Notebook* 40 (1986): 70–3.

27 See the discussion of 'ij shorte rolls of tre', *Medieval English Theatre* 1 (1979): 17. For an alternate interpretation which also makes theatrical sense, see *161*, pp. 77–8.

28 'The Chester Cycle of Mystery Plays, PLS, Toronto; 21st–23rd May, 1983', *Medieval English Theatre* 5 (1983): 51.

29 'The Castle of Perseverance: August 4–6, 1979, University of Toronto', *RORD* 22 (1979): 144.

30 *Ibid.*

31 For a description of a contrasting performance, where the staging was altered to suit interior circumstances inimical to fully circular staging, see David Mills' 'The Castle of Perseverance at Manchester: 29th April–2nd May, 1981' in *Medieval English Theatre* 3 (1981): 55–6.

32 'The Toronto Passion Play; Toronto, 1st–3rd August, 1981: Poculi Ludique Societas', *Medieval English Theatre* 3 (1981): 123.

33 The full flavour of the production, as well as an understanding of the iconographic principles developed from extensive study of medieval iconography by the dramaturge, Ted De Welles, to give the production visual unity, is well conveyed by Coletti and Ashley's review. See *RORD* 24 (1981): 181–7. For a contrasting view, see Meg Twycross' review, cited in note 32, above.

34 For perceptive comments on the role of the audience in modern productions of medieval plays, see *126*, pp. 98–[101].

35 'The Towneley Cycle of Toronto: The Audience as Actor, May, 1985: Poculi Ludique Societas', *Medieval English Theatre* 7 (1985): 52.

36 'Processus Torontoniensis: A Performance of the Wakefield Cycle', *RORD* 28 (1985): 193.

37 After working closely with the text in performance, Epp has concluded that 'I really do not think [that the Towneley play] is a cycle.' While some plays required only a single stage structure, others, particularly the 'Conspiracy', demand more. The recurrent hill also seems to demand more than one structure. For Epp the solution is to view the Towneley manuscript as a partly revised text, in which such inconsistencies are unresolved (personal correspondence, 10 July 1986).

38 For an extensive collection of texts illustrating the theatrical practice throughout Europe, see *28*.

39 Glynne Wickham's own text on the same subject (*17*), though full of valuable individual insights, spends too much time discussing the old arguments over origins, and is too loosely organised to serve as a good introduction to the subject.

40 A notable exception is W. A. Davenport's *Fifteenth-Century English Drama* (*232*). Though Davenport's subtitle indicates properly his major focus, 'The Early Moral Plays and their Literary Relations', a major strength of the book is the fact that Davenport's reading of individual scenes is always tied to a sure sense of theatrical reality.

41 A videotape version of the PLS performance can be obtained as part of the series 'Early English Drama', produced by Stanley J. Kahrl with the assistance of a grant from the National Endowment for the Humanities, from station WOSU, Ohio State University, Columbus, Ohio 43210. The entire series is keyed to texts found in the anthology most often used in North America, *Medieval Drama*, edited by David Bevington (*19*). Slides and videotapes for all the major PLS productions mentioned in this chapter are also obtainable from the Poculi Ludique Societas c/o REED, 150 Charles St. West, Toronto, Ontario (M5S 1K9), Canada.

PART III
Continental drama

9

France

ALAN E. KNIGHT

The study of medieval French theatre has always lagged far behind that of the English theatre of the same period. This seems particularly ironic in view of the fact that surviving play texts and records of performance are far more numerous in France than in England. Yet the reasons for the disparity are not hard to find. After Francis I had created a taste for the works of the Italian Renaissance, the stars of the Pléiade set out to recast French language and literature in an antique mold. By the next century the royal court had established a hegemony of arts and letters, which the Sun King used to reflect his own absolute rule. Ever since that time the undisputed brilliance of the classical French theatre has eclipsed the unique qualities of all preceding drama. Perhaps the crucial difference between France and England in regard to the development of the theatre is that the French playwrights of the sixteenth century attempted to make a complete break with their medieval antecedents, while their English counterparts did not. Consequently, France produced no Shakespeare, whose works would one day prod scholars into a search for medieval roots, which in turn would reveal a new world of stagecraft, fascinating in its own right. Racine has no medieval roots, and thus, like his royal patron, remains an absolute in French cultural thought. The break with the theatrical tradition of the Middle Ages was so complete by the seventeenth century that Boileau could claim: 'Chez nos devots Ayeux le Theatre abhorré / Fut long-temps dans la France un plaisir ignoré.'[1]

This total ignorance of the medieval theatre was but little relieved in the eighteenth century by the studies of a pair of antiquarians, the Frères Parfaict, who compiled a lengthy history of the French theatre that included copious quotations from the medieval play manuscripts that they found in libraries.[2] Even the Romantic rediscovery of the Middle Ages failed to fire the enthusiasm of researchers for the theatre, despite the publication of several anthologies of early plays. Instead, the epic and the romance captured the imagination of both scholars and the reading public. It was only slightly more than a century ago that Louis Petit de Julleville made the first systematic study of the medieval French theatre.[3] During the second half of the nineteenth century a number of important editions of medieval plays was made by such scholars as Emile Picot, James de Rothschild and Anatole de Montaiglon. Regrettably, this flurry of excitement for the early theatre was to be short-lived, possibly because the researchers ultimately found nothing in it to match their classical poetic ideals. Petit de Julleville himself deemed the religious theatre of the Middle Ages to have been a failure: 'L'idée était grandiose, l'œuvre fut manquée';[4] and he saw the comic theatre as scarcely more successful: 'l'œuvre comique du moyen âge est imparfaite et grossière'.[5] The first half of our own century was therefore not distinguished for its studies of the medieval theatre, despite the valuable contributions of such scholars as Gustave Cohen, Emmanuel Philipot, Eugénie Droz and Grace Frank. The second half of the century, however, has seen a strong renewal of interest in the medieval theatre of France. Indeed, the appearance in 1954 of Grace Frank's widely read study, *The Medieval French Drama* (283), seems in retrospect to have signalled a new attitude toward the medieval French theatre and a new enthusiasm for studies in this long-neglected area. Frank's admiration of the plays as works of art and her sensitivity to their social context are characteristics of a new respect for the genre that has continued to develop. Today there are more people engaged in medieval French theatre studies than at any other time in the past. It is highly appropriate, therefore, that we take stock of what has been accomplished in these years of growth. It is especially important to assess the directions that our studies have taken and to identify the areas of research that should be dealt with in the future.

In this chapter I have divided the field of medieval French theatre into two historical periods. The first treats the vernacular drama from its earliest appearance in the late eleventh century to the end of the thirteenth century. Though the number of plays surviving from this period is not great, their high quality has given rise to numerous studies and editions. The second period begins around 1300 and goes to the middle of the sixteenth century, at which time the medieval genres began to give way, sometimes by decree, to the new dramatic styles of the Renaissance. There is a generic unity to this period that is most clearly represented by the origin, development and ultimate demise of the Passion play. Because of this and because of the great quantity of surviving texts, the plays of the late period can most easily be grouped by genre. We shall begin, however, by reviewing some of the recent studies that treat the medieval theatre in a more general sense.

Several bibliographical works are now available to aid the researcher in medieval French theatre. Carl Stratman's *Bibliography of Medieval Drama*, which originally appeared in 1954, was revised in 1972,[6] but even the new edition is by this time somewhat dated. More recent and much more complete for the area covered is the second edition of Halina Lewicka's *Bibliographie du théâtre profane* (295). Two very helpful bibliographical essays have been written by Graham Runnalls and Alan Hindley. The former reviews recent studies of religious drama (292), and the latter does the same for comic drama (93).

Very little of a purely theoretical nature has been written about medieval French theatre, though much of the more general theory of medieval litera-ture can be fruitfully applied to theatre studies. It is fitting, therefore, to begin our survey with reference to Rainer Warning's caveat about the alterity of medieval drama (26). Not only in the liturgical drama, but also in the late Passion plays, he sees a 'cultic seriousness' suggesting that 'fiction and reality had not yet separated ... This unity of play and reality is no longer accessible to our experience. We can only struggle to reconstruct it' (p. 290). It is the effort to reconstruct the medieval theatrical experience that is at the heart of our endeavour, and it is precisely this effort that seems to have motivated some of the recent general works on medieval French drama.

Two important books on staging have given us striking new insights into what spectators actually saw when they went to a play and how they saw it. Henri Rey-Flaud in *Le Cercle magique* (*13*) argues that virtually all the 'grands mystères' of the late Middle Ages were staged in theatres in the round. He takes as his point of departure Jean Fouquet's fifteenth-century painting of a performance of the *Martyre de sainte Apolline*, which is depicted in such a theatre, and supports his contention with numerous quotations from play texts and records of production. He does not claim that 'la solution du rond soit la solution exclusive pour les organisateurs médié-vaux' (p. 55) – plays were staged in halls, for example, where such a con-figuration would not be practical – but he believes that most theatres were constructed in the round. Rey-Flaud contends, moreover, that a single artifact has prevented historians from seeing this truth. It is Hubert Cail-leau's painting of a linear stage, which is found in both manuscript copies of the *Mystère de la Passion* played at Valenciennes in 1547. Because Cailleau illustrated the two texts thirty years after the performance, Rey-Flaud insists that his paintings of the stage cannot be taken to represent the theatre as it actually existed. Indeed, the costumes and the architectural details found in these and the other paintings of the two manuscripts are the same as those that Cailleau used to illustrate earlier non-dramatic manuscripts. Rey-Flaud believes that his illustrations for the Valenciennes play give us 'une somme de ses aspirations personnelles au terme de son évolution artistique' (p. 218), but not a picture of how the play was staged. Elie Konigson's *L'Espace théâtral médiéval* (*21*) is a more theoretical study that deals with medieval concepts of urban space and how they influenced the various configurations of theatrical space. Konigson describes five basic configurations of space for theatrical events. First and perhaps oldest is the use of the principal public square, where the stage settings are placed on the ground and where there is no clear distinction between actors and spectators. Second is the central raised platform, usually rectangular in shape, with seating constructed for the spectators on the two long sides. The third type of theatre is a transformation of the first two: a frontal or linear 'stage', where the settings may be either on the ground or on a raised platform, but where the audience is placed only in front of the stage. The fourth configuration is that of the theatre in the round as illustrated in Fouquet's miniature. Finally, the city streets become linear theatres in royal entries and other processional observances.

Because Konigson's study had already been completed when Rey-Flaud's work appeared in print, the former could respond only by a long footnote to his introduction. There Konigson limits himself to pointing out an inconsistency in Rey-Flaud's argument about the Valenciennes play, without addressing the serious questions that the argument raises. He offers his own book as a sufficient response, 'parfaitement fondée sur les documents' (p. 10), to Rey-Flaud's tendency to interpret all documents in a manner consistent with *his* thesis. Despite a few contradictions, however, both works are largely complementary and both have greatly advanced our knowledge of medieval staging. Nevertheless, one may regret that the disparities in the two critics' approach to the subject have not evoked a clarifying debate in the years since, because the study of medieval staging still bristles with unsolved problems. These are attributable in part to the continuing difficulty of understanding certain technical terms in descriptions of stages, despite Rey-Flaud's helpful discussion of them in *Le Cercle magique*. The difficulty becomes all the more apparent when one reads the English translations of certain documents related to theatre in the collection *The Staging of Religious Drama in Europe* (*28*). To take but one example, the translator of the French section, attempting to adapt words to different contexts, translates the staging term *parc* variously as 'auditorium' (p. 63), 'audience' (p. 91), 'playing area' (p. 97) and 'enclosure' (p. 193). Clearly the word had more than one meaning in relation to dramatic spectacles, but it is often difficult for us to know with precision what was meant in a particular case. An important contribution of a more limited scope is Graham Runnalls' clear demonstration that the term *mansion*, commonly used by modern historians and critics to designate staging elements, had no status whatsoever as a technical term (*297*).

The comic theatre has been the object of two general studies in recent years. Jean-Claude Aubailly (*288*) sees the comic plays of the thirteenth century as being too localised to represent the beginnings of a truly popular comic theatre. He therefore seeks the origins of the late-medieval flourishing of comic genres in the revelry of holiday celebrations and in the mocking spirit of the *sociétés joyeuses* that existed in most cities and towns. He sees the late-medieval farces and *sotties* as developing directly from the comic monologues that became a favourite holiday entertainment in the fourteenth century. Though Aubailly's evolutionary theory may be controversial, the notion that the comic theatre is firmly anchored in urban soil is not. Konrad Schoell (*290*) also stresses the urban origins of the comic theatre and analyses the social conditions that fostered the rise of the farce in the fifteenth century. He sees this as connected with the revival of the towns after the Hundred Years' War. Jean-Charles Payen (*299*) also considers the town to be the birthplace of dramatic genres. In another approach to the social context of the theatre (*294*), I have tried to show that the cities of northern France used playing troupes as ambassadors of goodwill among themselves. Richard Axton (*18*) takes a broader view of the origins of medieval drama by attempting to reconstruct three separate traditions of secular drama – mimicry, combat, the dancing-game – that parallel the ecclesiastical tradition. He feels that the clerical bias of surviving texts has obscured the important influence that the first three traditions had on the development of the early drama throughout Europe. He cites evidence that mimicry and dancing were significant elements of medieval French culture, though the combat seems to have been more a Germanic tradition.

Petit de Julleville firmly believed that 'les distinctions de genres littéraires étaient vagues au moyen âge'.[7] Neither he nor his contemporaries realised that the vagueness resulted from the practice of assigning medieval plays to generic categories, such as serious and comic or religious and profane, that they do not fit. Clearly such categories were derived from the familiar classical (and modern) distinction between tragedy and comedy, not from the less familiar categories of medieval thought. For over a century now, the notion that medieval playwrights were ignorant of genre distinctions has been a commonplace of French theatre criticism. If, however, one grants that all understanding of verbal meaning is genre-bound,[8] then it becomes apparent that much misunderstanding can result from imposing alien generic notions on medieval plays. In *Aspects of Genre* (298) I propose a basic generic distinction between the plays that represent the world as it was perceived historically and the plays that represent an imagined or fictional universe. The historical genres include biblical plays, miracle plays, saints' lives and plays based on profane history. The fictional genres include morality plays and farces. Within the fictional category I propose a further generic distinction based on the differences between the world depicted in the morality play (an ordered world ruled by reason) and that depicted in the farce (a chaotic world ruled by folly). The primary action in a farce is trickery; the farce world, therefore, is 'an ethical jungle in which only the shrewd and the wily are fit for survival. It is a world of retributive justice with no possibility of appeal because there is no higher law or higher power' (p. 53). The primary action in a morality play is moral choice based on reason; and though we find some of the same kinds of folly as in the farce, 'there is always a higher power to punish the wicked and reward the good' (p. 54). These distinctions are derived from the plays themselves and are corroborated by other evidence of medieval thought patterns.

From the two centuries that comprise the early period of medieval French theatre, there survive only nine plays in the vernacular, one of which is a fragment. Two are written partly in Latin, and two others may have been written as dialogues not intended for stage presentation. One might suppose that so limited a corpus of plays from the High Middle Ages would be well exploited by now. Such is not the case, however. Three plays – *Le Jeu d'Adam*, *Le Jeu de Saint Nicolas* and *Le Jeu de la feuillée* – have received virtually all the critical attention, including multiple editions. It is true that all three are attractive, well-written plays that reward researchers' efforts; but it may also be true that they simply conform more closely to our preconceived notions of what a medieval play should be. In that case we may be missing meanings that were apparent to medieval spectators because we do not fully

Alan E. Knight

understand the whole context of medieval dramatic production. The plays that are less rewarding from a literary point of view may indeed be more important historically than the ones that have received the most attention. The *Seinte Resureccion*, for example, a fragment of less than 400 lines, has been compared unfavourably with the *Jeu d'Adam*, its contemporary. Anne Amari Perry (*330*), however, rejects this comparison, arguing that the two plays represent different dramatic traditions and are therefore not comparable. The *Jeu d'Adam*, with its responses sung in Latin, is related to the stylised liturgical drama, while the *Seinte Resureccion* is the earliest example of the historical realism characteristic of the later Passion plays. Perry shows how the author has developed a logical plot and life-like characters, who are 'ignorant of the fact that they are participating in an event of central importance' (p. 43). The playwright's aim, she believes, was to create suspense in a well-known story by delaying the characters' recognition of the sublime truth of the event.

Among the recent editions of the *Jeu d'Adam*, three are worthy of note. Leif Sletsjöe (*304*) published a photographic reproduction of the manuscript along with a diplomatic transcription of the French parts of the text. The earlier edition by Paul Aebischer (*302*) should be mentioned because of the influence it has had on subsequent studies of the play. In the manuscript the play is immediately followed by *Les Quinze signes du Jugement*. Aebischer believes that this narrative piece was recited at the end of the play to bring the action to a clear conclusion. Because of the tripartite nature of the play – 'Adam and Eve', 'Cain and Abel', 'Procession of Prophets' – there has been much discussion about its unity. In her analysis of the themes and structure of the *Jeu d'Adam* (*307*), Lynette Muir finds unity on three levels: feudal, theological and formal. Tony Hunt (*308*) adduces evidence from the theological and exegetical traditions to argue for a typological unity in the play. Neither Muir nor Hunt finds the *Quinze signes* necessary for the completion of the play. Similarly, M. F. Vaughan, whose study concentrates on the somewhat neglected 'Procession of Prophets' (*311*), finds the play essentially complete as it stands. Taking a slightly different point of view, Jean-Charles Payen (*306*) considers the work to be an extended *Ordo Prophetarum* in which the first two prophecies, those of Adam and Abel, have been developed to the point of forming semi-independent plays. Maurice Accarie (*310*), on the other hand, sees a tripartite structure in each of the first two parts, but which appears in the third part only if the text of the *Quinze signes* is included. The most recent and most complete edition of the *Jeu d'Adam* is that of Willem Noomen (*305*). Its completeness is attributable not to the *Quinze signes*, which is omitted, but to the inclusion of the complete text of all the Latin responses. For the first time we can see how much of the play is in Latin and how closely related to the liturgy it is. In a seminal study of the play (*303*) Noomen demonstrates that the work is related to the liturgy of Septuagesima, and he provides convincing evidence that it was played inside the church, not outside, as has always been presumed. Steven Justice (*313*),

however, takes the opposite view in comparing the play to the ritual of penitential excommunication, which took place before the doors of the church on
Ash Wednesday. Relating the play to contemporary society, Per Nykrog
(*309*) sees it as a warning against the temptations to create a courtly society and
to delve into pagan philosophies. Jean-Pierre Bordier (*312*), on the other
hand, whose elegant thematic analysis adds much to our understanding of the
play, sees in it an effort to reconcile Christianity and lay culture, an enterprise
that was taken over by Arthurian literature after Robert de Boron.

Jean Bodel's *Jeu de saint Nicolas* is a miracle play written in the city of
Arras in the year 1200. Its combination of high seriousness and comic tavern
scenes has given rise to a vigorous debate as to whether it is a comic or a
religious play. Gustave Cohen once went to the extreme of dividing his
discussion of the play between the two volumes of his *Théâtre en France au
Moyen Age*.[9] This is one more example of forcing medieval plays into alien
generic categories. Albert Henry's excellent edition of the play (*314*) has
made possible a number of interpretative studies. Still, one of the continuing
debates concerns the authenticity of the Prologue. Henry, on the basis of
contradictions between prologue and text, rejects its authenticity, but Tony
Hunt (*315*) attempts to explain the contradictions. Henri Rey-Flaud (*296*)
makes a lengthy analysis of the play and its staging in an effort to demonstrate that dramaturgical principles remained the same throughout the
Middle Ages. One might object that his argument is circular, since he 'stages'
the *Jeu de saint Nicolas* on the basis of Jean Fouquet's fifteenth-century
painting of a scene in performance from the *Martyre de sainte Apolline*.
Moreover, his method of presentation, without notes or documentation,
renders the book of little use to scholars who might wish to pursue interesting references or quotations.

The play from the early period that has received the most critical attention
is the *Jeu de la feuillée* by Adam de la Halle. It is a brilliant, enigmatic and
very funny play that can be both frustrating and disconcerting for the
modern reader. On the surface it appears to be a satirical revue without plot,
yet this apparent lack of structure has challenged virtually every critic to find
an underlying unity. To add to the play's difficulty, the principal characters
are real people, citizens of Arras, who play themselves. Adam is the protagonist, if such a word is appropriate for his role. Ever since Alfred Adler's
ground-breaking study of 1956 (*320*), in which he asserts that the play's
coherence derives from Adam's personal conflict, an intense debate has raged
over whether the work is a psychodrama or merely a satirical revue. Two
new editions have appeared in recent years: one by Otto Gsell (*321*), with a
German translation; the other by Jean Dufournet (*326*), with a modern
French translation. Normand Cartier (*322*) analyses the play in terms of the
opposition between enchantment and disenchantment, an image taken from
the opening lines, and finds a unity deriving from Adam's personal situation.
Claude Mauron (*324*) makes a psychocritical analysis of the comic techniques utilised by Adam and finds an underlying affective unity. Dufournet's

Alan E. Knight

two books on the *Jeu de la feuillée* (*325*, *327*) provide detailed studies of the author, the city of Arras and the play itself. He believes that the difficulty we have in understanding the play comes from the fact that it comprises several levels of meaning: one addressed to the public at large, the second to the author's intimate friends and the third expressing his deepest feelings and anxieties (*327*, p. 15). In a later study (*328*) Dufournet suggests what is essentially a fourth level of meaning: that the play presents the general problem of the poet and his function in society. Michel Rousse views the *Jeu de la feuillée* in terms of its relation to folk culture (*329*). He believes it to have been performed at the annual convocation of the 'Confrérie des jongleurs et bourgeois' of Arras, which took place on the Thursday after Trinity Sunday, the day that would come to be called Corpus Christi. He connects many aspects of the play with the traditional folk customs of May, one of which was the setting up of a leafy bower or *feuillée* for the Queen of May and her court. In the play it is the fairies who occupy the bower.

The other plays from the early period have received very little attention in comparison with the three preceding plays. There are, however, two new editions among them, which should encourage further study. The *Sponsus*, a late-eleventh-century dramatisation of the parable of the wise and foolish virgins, was newly edited in 1965 (*300*). Still, it was almost twenty years before a significant new study appeared (*301*); Tony Hunt convinces us that the play must be understood in the context of the medieval exegesis of the parable, which was established by Augustine and Gregory, and which was still prevalent at the time of the play. *Courtois d'Arras*, a dramatisation of the parable of the prodigal son, has been edited anew by Giuseppe Macrì (*317*), who based his work in part on the textual study of Knud Togeby (*316*). Though a new edition of *Le Garçon et l'Aveugle* is needed, Jean Dufournet's recent translation (*331*) has drawn attention to this early farce. Accompanying the translation are studies of the play and of the medieval attitude toward the blind, as well as a number of medieval texts relating to blindness. Rutebeuf's *Le Miracle de Théophile* has recently been studied by Stéphane Gompertz (*318*) and Emanuel Mickel (*319*). Finally, Adam de la Halle's other play, *Le Jeu de Robin et Marion*, a dramatic *pastourelle* or shepherds play, which is interspersed with songs and dances, is beginning to receive some of the attention it deserves. Dufournet (*327*) suggests that it was written before *Le Jeu de la feuillée*, not after as has always been assumed, though the evidence for this is somewhat thin. While Charles Mazouer (*323*) finds artless characters in a play little related to courtly convention, Kevin Brownlee (in a paper delivered in 1986 at the 21st International Congress on Medieval Studies at Kalamazoo) convincingly demonstrates that the shepherds and their relationships are images of courtly society.

In the late Middle Ages the theatre in France, as elsewhere in Europe, experienced an unprecedented flourishing. This corresponded to a general theatricalisation of public ceremonies and official observances, particularly in the fifteenth century. At that time the number of plays written seems to have increased exponentially, and playwrights were continually testing the limits of dramatic works by increasing their length and complexity. It is likely that most of these works have been forever lost. Still, what remains in the French area amounts to a staggering number of plays that have hardly begun to be studied and understood. Graham Runnalls once calculated that the corpus of medieval French religious drama alone comprises '150 plays totalling almost one million lines' (292, p. 84). Since he wrote that, however, a collection of 72 previously unknown processional plays has been discovered, as we shall see (p. 166, below). In addition, some 150 farces and some 70 morality plays are extant. I would estimate that less than half the total volume of surviving French plays is available to scholars in modern editions. Even so, many of these editions are old and faulty, and some were printed in so few copies that they are almost as rare as the originals. Obviously, one of the most urgent needs of medieval French theatre studies is new editions, particularly of plays that still languish untouched on library shelves. It is encouraging to note that in recent years there has been a modest increase in the number of new editions appearing.

There were two kinds of history play in the late Middle Ages: those that dramatised universal history from Creation to Doomsday (both biblical and extra-biblical events perceived as having significance for people as a group), and those that dramatised personal or individual histories (both lives of the saints and significant events, such as miracles, in the lives of others). Among the history plays the most numerous by far are the biblical plays. Among these the most important are the Passion plays, so called even though most of them treat the whole life of Jesus and contain a few prefigural scenes from the Old Testament as well. The earliest of these plays, from the beginning of the fourteenth century, is the *Passion du Palatinus*. Jean-Pierre Bordier (*338*) has made a major contribution to our understanding of this neglected, but very important, play. He points out that the playwright continually stresses the kingly nature of Jesus as opposed to his other attributes. He also shows how the play's christology implies 'une ecclésiologie de l'autorité' and suggests that all Passion plays 'témoignent d'une lecture de l'Ecriture dans un contexte culturel' (p. 432). Given the need for new editions, it is regrettable that one play, *La Passion Nostre Seigneur* from a manuscript in the Bibliothèque Sainte-Geneviève, was recently edited twice (*339, 340*). Apparently neither editor knew the other was working on the play. The *Passion de Semur*, an unusual play that deserves much more study, has been newly edited by Peter Durbin and Lynette Muir (*344*). Not long before, however, the old edition of that play had been reprinted.[10] A reprint that fills a real gap is that of *La Passion d'Arras*,[11] a play usually attributed to Eustache Marcadé.

These four early Passion plays, which are listed in chronological order, represent significant stages in a developing genre. One notes not only increasing length (from 2,000 to 25,000 lines), but also changing concepts of the nature of the Passion play. Marcadé, for example, was the first to frame

Alan E. Knight

the life of Jesus with the 'Procès de Paradis', an allegorical debate between Justice and Mercy that ends with the decision to provide a saviour for mankind. The availability of these four plays makes it possible to study the antecedents of the two great Passion plays of the fifteenth century, those of Arnoul Gréban and Jean Michel. We are indebted to Omer Jodogne for superb editions of these two plays (*332* and *333*), each of which is over 30,000 lines in length. Since their appearance, scholars have begun to turn their attention to these fascinating works, and we are beginning to see studies that, in essence, teach us how to read them. One such study is Dominique Gangler-Mundwiler's analysis of the Hell scenes or *diableries* in the Passion plays (*342*). Rejecting the received notion that such scenes were added to the plays merely to please the crowd, she examines the relationship of the devils to the principal action in all the plays, and shows how Gréban fully integrated their machinations into his drama. Claude Thiry (*346*) also examines all the Passion plays from the point of view of a single element – in this case the characterisation of Procula, the wife of Pilate. His analysis leads to a re-examination of current ideas on the relationships among the plays. Maurice Accarie's brilliant study of Jean Michel's Passion play (*343*) has revealed new and unsuspected meanings in that work. Where others had seen a less than satisfactory reworking of Gréban's play, Accarie finds a new conception of the genre. He shows how Michel shifts the emphasis from the story of Redemption to the human characters involved in that story. This infuses the play with a moral dimension and an individualism unknown to his predecessors.

The Passion plays of Gréban and Michel were so well known that for almost a century other playwrights adapted them for production in their own towns. One such adaptation of Gréban is the recently edited *Passion de Troyes* (*350*), a three-day play that was staged several times in that city in the late fifteenth century. Of its 23,000 lines, some 6,000 are original. In addition, the play is unusual in having numerous stage directions. Several fragments of Passion plays, both early and late, have recently been published. Graham Runnalls found and edited a 237-line fragment preserved at the University of Leiden (*348*). The *Leiden Fragment* is of particular significance because of its provenance and its early date. Copied in the first half of the fourteenth century, its language points to a late-thirteenth-century original from Normandy. If this is the case, the fragment not only comes from one of the earliest French Passion plays, but also indicates that there was theatrical activity in Normandy much earlier than previously suspected. A late-fifteenth-century fragment from a manuscript at Harvard was edited and translated by John Elliott and Graham Runnalls under the title of *The Baptism and Temptation of Christ* (*341*). Later Runnalls was able to connect the Harvard manuscript with two fragments in the Bibliothèque Nationale, which he edited as *La Passion d'Auvergne* (*345*). As a result, we now have three days (the first, third and fifth) of a Passion play written for the city of Montferrand in Auvergne. Alessandro Vitale-Brovarone has just edited a unique Provençal text that is somewhat fragmentary because of the damage it sustained in a fire (349). It is a director's notebook with instructions for staging a Passion play. The publication of this work significantly increases our knowledge not only of the little-known theatre in medieval Provence, but also of staging techniques in general.

There are, of course, other Passion plays that have never been edited, perhaps because their length is daunting. There is, for example, Jean Michel's *Resurrection* with its invaluable stage directions (20,000 lines). There are two sixteenth-century Passion plays from the city of Valenciennes, one to be played in twenty days (40,000 lines) and one to be played in twenty-five days (50,000 lines). Elie Konigson (335) made a detailed analysis of the production of the latter play based on the numerous documents that have survived. His book also reproduces the miniatures that precede each of the days.

In addition to the Passion plays, there were many other biblical plays that dramatised the history of the world both before and after the life of Jesus. Among these were a number of plays depicting episodes from the Old Testament. In the mid-fifteenth century an anonymous compiler gathered many of these plays into a single work called *Le Mystère du Vieux Testament*. Though the complete text was edited in the nineteenth century,[12] it has received very little critical attention. Barbara Craig re-edited the first three episodes of the work (334) and later included a fourth episode in an edition of three plays dealing with the story of Abraham and Isaac (347). Since the other two Abraham and Isaac plays are from the sixteenth century, Craig is able to show how the same story was transformed to appeal to different audiences at different times. An independent version of *La Pacience de Job* was edited by Albert Meiller (337). The history of the world after the life of Jesus is most prominently represented by *Le Mystère des Actes des Apôtres*, attributed to Simon and Arnoul Gréban. It is a play of great length (62,000 lines) and of many lively scenes, from which we could learn much about play writing and production in the late Middle Ages. Despite this, the play has never been edited, and no significant study of it has appeared since 1929.[13] The popular legend surrounding the destruction of Jerusalem was dramatised in several versions known as *La Vengeance de Nostre Seigneur* (22,000 lines). Again, there is no edition, and virtually no critical attention has been paid to this work.[14] Finally, Moshé Lazar has edited *Le Jugement Dernier* (336), a Provençal play from the fifteenth century. His production of the play at the University of Kansas in 1970 was, for those who saw it, both a delight and a revelation of how directly the medieval theatre could speak to a modern audience.

Two of the surviving mystery plays are unusual in that they deal with non-biblical history. One is Jacques Milet's *Histoire de la destruction de Troye la grant*. Despite its length (30,000 lines), it circulated in many copies in the Middle Ages, of which thirteen manuscripts and twelve printed editions survive. Though it was edited in the nineteenth century,[15] no work has been done on it until recently. Marc-René Jung (see 387) is currently preparing a new edition. The other non-biblical history play is the *Mystère du siège d'Orléans*. It is unusual in that it dramatises a local event from the very recent past as opposed to the distant events of sacred history. It too was edited in the nineteenth century,[16] but has been virtually ignored since.

Among the history plays treating individuals, the most important group is the fourteenth-century collection of forty miracle plays called the *Miracles de Nostre Dame*. They were written for production at the annual assembly of the Paris goldsmiths' guild, with a new play being staged each year. Though a few scholars have all along been attracted to these fascinating works, it is Graham Runnalls who has taught us most in his recent studies of them. He has been able to date the manuscript (*351*) and to date the plays more precisely than previous scholars (*353*). In addition, he has studied the Paris goldsmiths' guild and the dramatic activities of guilds in general (*352*). Despite Runnalls' work and that of a few others in recent years, the level of scholarly activity surrounding the *Miracles de Nostre Dame* remains disappointingly low. Still, one is somewhat encouraged by the fact that two later miracle plays have recently appeared in modern editions (*354* and *355*).

Even more encouraging is the number of saint plays that have been made available in recent editions. Among the earliest of such plays are the *Geu saint Denis* (*358*) from the Bibliothèque Sainte-Geneviève manuscript and a cycle of martyrs (*359*) from the same source. The enormously important *Mystère de saint Martin* by Andrieu de La Vigne has finally received a modern edition (*361*). One regrets that La Vigne's short farce and morality play from the same manuscript were not included, though the latter has now been edited separately (*371*). The recently edited *Vie de Marie Magdaleine* (*364*) is a play from Lyons that dramatises the saint's conversion of the city of Marseilles. We also now have editions of *Le Mystère de saint Sébastien* (*356*) and *Le Mystère du roy Advenir* (*357*). The latter is a dramatisation of the legend of Barlaam and Josaphat made by Jean du Prier for the court of René, duke of Anjou. René was much enamoured of the theatre, and his influence on the dramatic practices of his day remains to be studied. Among the critical works dealing with saint plays is the detailed analysis by Elizabeth Schulze-Busacker of the fourteenth-century Provençal *Jeu de sainte Agnès* (*363*). She shows how the playwright enhances the dramatic qualities of this highly original play with complex systems of metrics and music. A significant trend in this area is the study of saint plays in relation to the guilds that were responsible for many of them. Both Runnalls (*360*) and Lalou (*362*) have made studies of this kind. Lynette Muir's essay, 'The Saint Play in Medieval France' (in *8*, pp. 123–80), provides a much-needed overview of this field. Muir includes the miracle play in her survey and makes many helpful comparisons with plays and practices in other European countries. She also draws up a descriptive list of some 120 surviving saint and miracle plays in French. Finally, the two valuable books of Jacques Chocheyras inform us of the persistence of medieval religious theatre, both biblical and saint plays, in two provinces of France, Savoie (*286*) and Dauphiné (*289*). He finds that in both places medieval plays continued to be performed into the seventeenth and eighteenth centuries. He also links the productions to sieges of the plague, suggesting that they were the result of vows made during an attack. One hopes that this kind of study will ultimately be made for other provinces.

The explicit function of medieval morality plays was to teach, though they often entertained in the process; the function of medieval farces was to amuse, though there was usually a lesson implicit in the joke. The morality play created a world in which the protagonist had to use his reason to choose between right and wrong; the farce presented a world of trickery, bereft of reason, in which the survival of the cleverest was the only law. The plays of both genres are based on invented plots rather than history. Because farce techniques seem to be a universal attribute of world theatre, the farces have been among the most appreciated, and therefore most studied, plays of the medieval French theatre. By contrast, the morality plays, probably because of their didacticism and their allegorical mode of presentation, have been among the most misunderstood and most scorned of medieval French plays. It is only within the last fifteen years that scholars have begun to turn their attention to these neglected works.

Most of the farces and some of the short morality plays have survived in four large collections (one manuscript, designated La Vallière, and three printed volumes, designated British Museum, Trepperel and Florence). Two of these were edited in the nineteenth century[17] and a third in 1949.[18] The fourth has been only partially edited.[19] Though most of the farces have long been available to scholars, none of the editions except that of the Trepperel collection is close to satisfactory. An attempt to remedy this situation was made by publishing facsimile editions of three of the collections (284, 285, 287). This can be considered a temporary measure at best, since some of the reproductions, particularly those of the manuscript, are quite difficult to read. Still more recently, Slatkine published three volumes of facsimile editions of morality plays, most of which exist in unique copies in the Bibliothèque Nationale (369). Again, the solution to the problem of lack of editions is not entirely satisfactory, since the quality of reproduction is such that one is discouraged from spending much time reading the texts.

Happily there have been several critical editions of morality plays in the recent past. Werner Helmich has edited the *Moralité de Pauvre Peuple* (366) and Jonathan Beck has given us an edition of one of the earliest surviving morality plays, *Le Concil de Basle* (367). The latter is accompanied by a penetrating study of the political background of the play and of the play's relationship to the conciliarist movement of the early fifteenth century. Beck has also edited six polemical morality plays from the La Vallière manuscript and has studied their role in the reform movement in Normandy (373). He sees the theatre of the sixteenth century as a mass medium parallel to the pulpit both in the spread of the new Lutheranism and in the Catholic defence against it. The plays all come from Rouen; five of them are from the

Alan E. Knight

Protestant point of view and one from the Catholic. Also from the sixteenth century is the morality of *L'Enfant prodigue*, now available in an excellent edition by Giuseppe Macrì (*370*). Werner Helmich has made an important study of allegory in the late-medieval French theatre, dealing mainly with morality plays (*291*). In addition to providing analyses of many of these plays, he views them against the background of Christian allegorisation in general. I have examined the role of some of the morality plays in the education of upper-class youth in the early sixteenth century (*372*). Peter Houle tries to reconstruct the staging of the longest of these plays from the stage directions found in the text (*368*). Not all of the morality plays are in dead earnest. One of the most delightful is a whimsical piece called *La Condamnation de Banquet*, whose author tries to convince his audience (members of the royal court) of the dangers of overindulgence. Max Parfondry has contributed to our understanding of both the play and its author, Nicole de La Chesnaye (*365*).

Though the farce had attracted some degree of critical attention all along, Barbara Bowen's study of its essential characteristics (*375*) marked the beginning of a resurgence of interest in that genre. One of the most devoted students of the farce was Halina Lewicka who studied all its aspects – history, structure, dramatic techniques, language and so on. Some of the best of her articles were revised for publication in a single volume (*379*). Her study of the language of the comic theatre (*374*), though never completed, will remain a valuable research tool for many years. Today the *doyen* of French farce studies is Michel Rousse, whose eight-volume dissertation on the genre is probably too long to be published in its entirety. An indication of its quality, however, may be found in Rousse's study of stage space in the farce (*383*). More recently Bernadette Rey-Flaud completed a lengthy study of the farce (*385*), in which she examines its origins, its originality and its structure. André Tissier has undertaken the project of providing new and completely annotated editions of thirty-six of the best farces. The first three volumes have already appeared (*386*) and three more are anticipated.

The undisputed masterpiece of the farce genre has long been *Maître Pierre Pathelin*, a play of uncommon subtlety in which the fundamental axiom of the farce world, 'à trompeur, trompeur et demi', is exemplified twice over. There has been no shortage of editions, translations and adaptations of this play. What is significant, however, is Jean-Claude Aubailly's edition (*381*) of a version of the play that was previously thought to be both late and faulty because of a number of omissions in the text. Aubailly deduces from the watermarks in the manuscript, however, that this is quite possibly the earliest extant version, and that the passages thought to have been omitted are in reality additions to the later texts. Michel Rousse, in an important study of *Pathelin* (*378*), rejects the critical tradition dedicated to identifying the author and locale of the play, as if it were a realistic *farce à clef*, and instead attempts to place it in the theatrical tradition of the time. Donald Maddox has given us an extended study of the figures of deceit in *Pathelin* (*384*). He

164

examines, among other aspects, the rhetorical and legal contexts of the play and, in one especially penetrating chapter, shows how Pathelin's 'death scene' is a parody of a popular *Ars moriendi* of the time.

One of the sub-genres of the farce is the *sottie* or fools' play. It is populated with *sots* or fools of all stripes and uses the mask of folly to disguise its sharp satirical thrusts at social abuses. In its day the *sottie* spared no class or estate and was particularly hostile to the new values that were being imposed by wealthy patrician merchants newly entrenched in urban centres of power. Moreover, the fool's disguise was not limited to costume and make-up, but extended to the very fabric of his language. The verbal folly of these plays is so pervasive that it ultimately raises questions about the ability of language to communicate. Words become counterfeit coins spent by clowns in a grotesque parody of the economic evils of the day. The use of such techniques in the late-medieval theatre has given rise to a comparison with the twentieth-century theatre of the absurd (*377*). Because the humour is topical, however, and the attacks disguised, the *sotties* are very difficult plays to understand. It is perhaps this very difficulty that has stimulated a number of recent studies in this area. Jean-Claude Aubailly (*380*) provides us with a thorough analysis of the genre, which he sees as a kind of 'théâtre de combat'. He not only examines the characters and the staging, but also relates the *mise en scène* to the satiric purpose of the plays. He points out that the *sotties* portray a world in which the old values have been distorted and in which the quest for money has become the dominant behaviour. Heather Arden (*382*) examines the objects of satire in the *sotties*, which she finds to be the *haute bourgeoisie*, the nobility, the higher clergy, women and even the peasants. In addition, she deals with the theme of appearance and reality that is inherent in the very concept of satire by fools. Arden and Aubailly not only teach us a great deal about the plays themselves, but also show us clearly how they functioned in late-medieval society.

Related to the full-fledged stage play, and very popular in late-medieval France, was the dramatic monologue. Indeed, the monologues may well be considered one-character plays. A masterpiece such as *Le Franc Archier de Bagnolet* (*376*) has all the characteristics of a play: impersonation, costume, gesture, conflict and action. The result in this case is a one-man farce, but other monologues can be considered to be *sotties* or morality plays. A large sub-set of dramatic monologues is comprised of parodic sermons called *sermons joyeux*. There has been a recent increase of interest in these works, aided by Jelle Koopmans' excellent edition of four representative sermons (*388*). Indeed, Koopmans' editorial work teaches us how to read these long-neglected, but very amusing pieces.[20]

In addition to published research, other significant events have taken place in the field of medieval French drama. In 1974 a conference was held at Leeds, England, for the purpose of bringing together people interested in the study of medieval theatre. Three years later in Alençon, France, a formal society was founded, known as the Société Internationale pour l'Etude du

Alan E. Knight

Théâtre Médiéval (SITM). The society promotes the study of all areas of medieval drama. For several years the *Section Française* of the SITM published a journal called *Tréteaux*, which contained articles relating to medieval French theatre. So far there have been six meetings of the society with an increasing number of participants at each meeting. The latest colloquium was at Lancaster, England, in July 1989. The acts of four of the colloquia have thus far been published.[21]

Current research in the field involves a wide variety of projects: editorial, interpretative and sociological. One of the editing projects derives from a recent major discovery of texts. In 1983 I learned of the existence of a collection of medieval French plays in the Herzog August Bibliothek in Wolfenbüttel, West Germany. When I visited the German library that summer, I found a late-fifteenth-century illuminated manuscript containing seventy-two previously unknown plays from the city of Lille in northern France. The plays range in length from 200 to 1,900 lines, making over 40,000 lines in all. Each play is preceded in the manuscript by a painting that illustrates its central theme. Sixty-five of the plays are dramatisations of biblical events, while the remainder are based on Roman history and Christian legend. The majority of the biblical plays are drawn from the Old Testament and depict such figures as Abraham, Joseph, David, Ruth, Esther and Susannah. The New Testament plays are drawn from the Gospels and the Acts of the Apostles, but they include none of the dramatised events of the Passion. The plays were performed at the 'Grande Procession de Lille', an annual religious and civic observance for which the city was renowned for over 500 years. Like the cycle plays in England, they were mounted on *charettes* or pageant wagons. They were staged by various rhetorical societies and neighbourhood associations of the city and were produced under the aegis of the Bishop of Fools. The Lille plays are unique in that they are the first examples to be found of processional pageant plays from France. We have long known from contemporary records that such plays were performed, but it was generally believed that all of them had been lost. This discovery increases by half the number of titles of religious plays in French surviving from the Middle Ages. Because of the importance of the collection, and with the help of a grant from the National Endowment for the Humanities, a US federal agency, I have undertaken a critical edition of the Lille plays.

Graham Runnalls is currently working on what he calls a typology of theatre manuscripts. All who have worked with these manuscripts have noted different kinds, ranging from acting roles to directors' copies to illuminated presentation copies. Runnalls is making a systematic study of the different types in order to learn what the physical manuscripts can tell us about the plays they contain. Having been one of the most active editors in the field, Runnalls will continue in that endeavour. Jean-Pierre Bordier is completing a study of the representation of humanity in the French Passion plays. Both Jean Dufournet and Michel Rousse are currently working on

France

Maître Pierre Pathelin. Jean-Marie Privat is preparing a study of the *sotties* from a socio-critical point of view. He is particularly interested in the ethno-historical background of medieval popular theatre. Jelle Koopmans is preparing further editions of *sermons joyeux.*

Looking to the more distant future, the most urgent need of medieval French theatre studies is editions of plays that are presently not available to scholars or students of the field. Only after they have become available can interpretative work come close to its goal of achieving a full understanding of medieval theatre. At the same time, however, we need to think more about methodologies for dealing with the vast amount of material that will eventually be at our disposal. We also need to establish a theoretical context for dealing with these plays that are so disparate and so distant. At the present time many studies of limited aspects of medieval theatre seem to fit no coherent pattern. Despite the fact that in the past fifteen years we have had several excellent studies of staging, we still need far more work in that difficult, but crucial, area. In medieval theatre especially, understanding the plays is inseparably linked to understanding their staging. In addition to visualising the spectacle, we need to study acting styles to the extent that they are accessible to us. Was there, for example, a change in the way actors performed in the sixteenth century that made the plays risible to some and dangerous to others? Or was there a change in the way the spectators perceived the plays? In either case we need to study more closely the reception of the plays by their audiences and the effects the plays had on the society that created them. Ultimately, scholars in the French area will have to set up a program for systematically exploiting the municipal and departmental archives of France for references to all dramatic activities in the Middle Ages. The experience of the REED project for the English theatre could be used as a starting point for such a project.

In summary, the past twenty-five years have seen a remarkable resurgence of interest in medieval French theatre studies. The interest seems to have developed first outside of France, particularly in English-speaking countries, but now is beginning to be felt in France itself. There are today many young scholars in both Europe and America who are working in this field. Much needs to be done, but the future of research in medieval French drama is bright.

NOTES

1 Nicolas Boileau-Despréaux, *L'Art poétique*, Bibliothèque de la Pléiade (Paris: Gallimard, 1966), p. 171.
2 François and Claude Parfaict, *Histoire du théâtre françois*, 15 vols. (1735–49; Geneva: Slatkine Reprints, 1967).
3 Louis Petit de Julleville, *Les Mystères*, 2 vols. (Paris: Hachette, 1880); *Répertoire du théâtre comique en France au Moyen Age* (Paris: Cerf, 1886).
4 *Les Mystères*, vol. 1, p. 6.
5 *La Comédie et les moeurs en France au Moyen Age* (Paris: Cerf, 1886), p. 4.

Alan E. Knight

6 Carl J. Stratman, *Bibliography of Medieval Drama*, 2nd edn (New York: Ungar, 1972).
7 *Les Mystères*, vol. II, p. 93.
8 E. D. Hirsch, *Validity in Interpretation* (New Haven: Yale University Press, 1967), p. 76.
9 Vol. I, *Le Théâtre religieux*, pp. 34–6; vol. II, *Le Théâtre profane*, pp. 15–16 (Paris: Rieder, 1928–31).
10 Emile Roy, *Le Mystère de la Passion en France du XIVe au XVIe siècle* (1903; Geneva: Slatkine Reprints, 1974).
11 Jules-Marie Richard, ed., *Le Mystère de la Passion: Texte du manuscrit 697 de la Bibliothèque d'Arras* (1891; Geneva: Slatkine Reprints, 1976).
12 James de Rothschild, ed., *Le Mistere du Vieil Testament*, 6 vols. (Paris: Firmin Didot, 1878–91).
13 Raymond Lebègue, *Le Mystère des Actes des Apôtres: Contribution à l'étude de l'humanisme et du protestantisme français au XVIe siècle* (Paris: Champion, 1929).
14 The following study appeared after the above had been written: Stephen K. Wright, *The Vengeance of Our Lord: Medieval Dramatizations of the Destruction of Jerusalem* (Toronto: Pontifical Institute of Mediaeval Studies, 1989).
15 E. Stengel, ed., *L'Istoire de la destruction de Troye la grant*, by Jacques Milet (Marburg and Leipzig, 1883).
16 François Guessard and Eugène de Certain, eds., *Le Mystère du siège d'Orléans* (Paris: Imprimerie Impériale, 1862).
17 A. Leroux de Lincy and Francisque Michel, eds., *Recueil de farces, moralités et sermons joyeux*, 4 vols. (Paris: Techener, 1837); Viollet le Duc, gen. ed., *Ancien théâtre français*, vols. I–III, ed. Anatole de Montaiglon (Paris: P. Jannet, 1854).
18 Gustave Cohen, ed., *Recueil de farces françaises inédites du XVe siècle* (Cambridge, MA: The Medieval Academy of America, 1949).
19 Eugénie Droz, ed., *Le Recueil Trepperel: les sotties* (Paris: Droz, 1935); Eugénie Droz and Halina Lewicka, eds., *Le Recueil Trepperel: les farces* (Geneva: Droz, 1961).
20 Koopmans' edition of the remainder of the corpus has now appeared: *Recueil de sermons joyeux* (Geneva: Droz, 1988).
21 See items 4, 6 and 22 of the bibliography. The Perpignan acts have just appeared, see the Recent works section of the bibliography.

10

Italy: liturgy and christocentric spirituality

SANDRO STICCA

Although historians of dramatic literature have not accorded to the theatre of medieval Italy a status equal to that assigned to the medieval drama of England, France and Germany, dramatic activity in Italy between the tenth and the fifteenth centuries parallels in length and complexity the development of medieval drama in the various countries of western Europe. The systematic research undertaken, in recent years, into the theatrical history of medieval Italy has raised serious questions about the validity of traditional assumptions and prompted a re-evaluation of its dramatic production, from the liturgical drama to its indigenous vernacular dramatic forms: the *lauda* and the *sacra rappresentazione*.

Liturgical drama in Italy is copiously represented by texts dating from the tenth to the fifteenth centuries. The twelfth-century Montecassino Latin drama is the oldest known Passion play and the fourteenth-century Cividale *Planctus Mariae* ranks among the most remarkable monuments of liturgical drama in Europe. Diffusion is attested by texts originating from Benedictine monasteries, cathedral schools and liturgical centres such as Montecassino, Ivrea, Nanantola, Cremona, Aquileia, Cividale, Parma, Sutri, Padua, Bari, Barletta, Sulmona, Venice, Vercelli and from other locations in Abruzzi and Sicily.

But it is the *lauda*, a poetico-musical composition originating in liturgical psalmodic singing, that must be looked upon as the matrix of Italian vernacular theatre. Widely disseminated in Italy from the thirteenth to the fifteenth centuries, the *lauda*, in its earliest form, was lyrical in character, reflecting the spirit of the liturgical *laudes* (songs of praise) which were chanted in the office of Matins, in the *Alleluia* and in the 'troped' *Gloria*.[1]

Composed mainly as a ballad, the *laude* (or *laudi*) soon came to be associated with the devotional practices of groups of lay people, confraternities of *laudesi* (singers of *laude*) – formed in the early thirteenth century in cities like Florence, Siena and Bologna – who sang *laude* in praise of the Virgin Mary and Christ's suffering. The earliest attested company of *laudesi* was the 'Compagnia dei Laudesi della Beata Vergine Maria' of Florence which by the year 1183 was associated with the parish of Santa Reparata. Companies of *laudesi* soon formed throughout Umbria and Tuscany, fostered by the spiritual reform inspired by St Francis of Assisi and by a vast devotional movement following the religious revival of 1223, the so-called 'year of the Alleluia'.

That year, in an atmosphere of chiliastic fears, collective visionary expectations and religious exaltation, masses of people, led by Dominican and Franciscan friars, marched in great processions through the cities and countryside of Italy, appealing for peace and harmony amidst political strife. They sang early forms of *laude* in honour of the Holy Trinity and the Virgin Mary, distinguished by the repetition of the refrain 'Alleluia'.[2] An understanding of the metrics and the literary style of the *laudesi's* early compositions can be gained by looking at one of their oldest poems, a monorhymed *lauda* in honour of the Virgin, written before the year 1254 and beginning: 'Rayna potentissima, sovra el cel siti esaltata, / sovra la vita anzelica vu siti santificata...'

While the beginnings of the *lauda* are associated with Florence, its birthplace, and its early phase with the religious activities of the *laudesi*, the full flourishing and dissemination of the *lauda* is tied to the *flagellanti* movement that began in Perugia in the year 1260 when the hermit Raniero Fasani founded a lay confraternity of *Disciplinati* (disciplinants).[3] The reform movement of the *flagellanti* (flagellants) arose in the wake of the Messianic and millenaristic preaching of Joachim of Flora who prophesied a new age.[4] The year 1260, which according to Joachim's theology of history was to mark the beginning of the age of the Spirit, also witnessed the rise of itinerant flagellants.

Inspired by Fasani and his followers, the flagellant movement spread from Perugia throughout Umbria, then to most of Italy and later to countries such as France, Germany and Poland. Chroniclers such as Salimbene and the anonymous Paduan of S. Giustina relate how processions of men and women, clergy and laity, marched through the cities of Italy publicly scourging themselves while singing both penitential songs – 'cantio poenitentium lugubris', 'cantu lamentabili' – and hymns in praise of the Virgin and the Passion of Christ.[5]

It was in the period of stability that followed the turbulent movement of 1260 that fundamental changes occurred both in the nature of the *lauda* and in the organisation of the confraternities. Companies of *laudesi* joined confraternities of *Disciplinati* in leaving the streets to seek permanent residence in urban churches.[6] Numerous companies of *laudesi* even changed their name to *Disciplinati*. At the same time, the popular singing of the *lauda* became a devotional practice and the Dominican and Franciscan orders, in attending to the spiritual needs of the *Disciplinati*, integrated their devotional rites into the official liturgical calendar of the Church.

This period of tranquillity, moreover, provided the confraternities with the opportunity to codify their statutes and rituals, to record traditional, orally transmitted *laude* and to produce new ones. These collections of *laude*, called *laudari*, are remarkable documents that shed information not only on the growth of the confraternities and *laude* but also on the development of Italian vernacular theatre. Indeed, an imposing number of over two hundred *laudari* originating from Cortona, Perugia, Fabriano, Gubbio,

Italy

Arezzo, L'Aquila, Orvieto and Rome, show the popularity of the confraternities and the wide dissemination of the *lauda*. Particularly interesting is the *Ordo* governing the confraternities' performance of the *devozione* in their *Oratori*, for it often provides information on the *lauda*'s passage from lyrical to dramatic form that occurred before the middle of the fourteenth century (*412*). It is within the perspectives offered by Franciscan spirituality, by the confraternal movements of the *laudesi* and *Disciplinati* and the lyrical impulses of the early *laude* that we shall take a closer look at the drama of medieval Italy.

Rigorous criticism of medieval drama ought to be anchored to a specific approach, a semiotics or epistemology of theatre study, for analysis entails discussion of the rapport between dramatic texts and theatrical performance. This issue has been discussed, in the past decade and a half, in a series of interdisciplinary studies that appeared in several volumes of *Biblioteca Teatrale*. Janssen, for instance, has argued that the written text together with the performance constitute the real object of a critical analysis (*400*); Ruffini, on the other hand, has pointed out that very often the text alone survives: 'the literary text finds itself chosen, against its will, as the only significant component of the spectacle' (*398*, p. 2). According to Zampino, since the text constitutes the only invariable as against the variables represented by the different performances, the theatre historian should concentrate on the text itself and the cultural milieu that produced it (*399*).

This particular critical perspective resembles the approach outlined a few years ago by Walter Binni for whom 'historical consciousness and artistic perception' constitute indispensable tools for interpreting personalities and works in literary history.[7] Binni's 'coscienza storica e senso dell'arte' appear to be sound guidelines for the study of the Italian medieval theatre, with the possible exception of liturgical drama which has not transmitted to us a clear understanding of its cultic and ritual stylisation, its mimetic and emotional content, that iconic ensemble of musical expression and hieratic gesture which still remains, as Jonsson aptly puts it, 'quelque chose de totalement insaisissable'.[8] Indeed, notwithstanding scholarly inquiry devoted to it in the last thirty years, the liturgical drama of western Europe remains elusive to us on the question of the relationship between ritual and drama on the one hand and dialogue and music on the other (*100*, pp. 55–63, and *54*, pp. 291–2).

By and large, the texts that have survived attest only to what was said on the stage and may summarily relate what took place on that stage. Although, as Jodogne observes, 'le texte est loin d'être toute l'oeuvre dramatique' (in *2*, p. 20), it is the destiny of every theatrical performance to die in the very hour in which it lives. It is the text, then, whether accompanied by stage directions or not, that most often constitutes the only document available for study. In reporting on the research done, I will be guided by two special concerns: liturgy and christocentric spirituality. They mark the origin and development of the two most representative Italian forms: the liturgical drama and the *lauda*.

171

Sandro Sticca

In the history of medieval dramaturgy, the Italian theatre occupies a distinguished position because of early and copious records and eyewitness accounts of performances. It is ironic, therefore, that nineteenth-century literary historians should have bemoaned the paucity of theatrical documentation. As late as 1955, for instance, Brugnoli could state: 'studies on the origins of the theater are extremely scanty in Italy'.[9] The vitality of religious drama is, however, attested not only by the large number of liturgical texts – dating from the tenth to the fifteenth centuries – but by a wealth of early documents concerning performances at single locations.[10] In addition, we have an eyewitness account of performances, at Florence, of an Annunciation and an Ascension play that took place on 25 March and 14 May 1439 (436) – considered by Nagler 'a source without parallel in the history of medieval theatre' (24, p. 25). Another source is Vasari's description of stage machinery, the *ingegni* invented by Filippo Brunelleschi (1377–1446) and again by Francesco d'Angelo (1441–81, called 'il Cecca'), for the performances of *sacre rappresentazioni* in Florence which were witnessed by Vasari himself.[11]

This rich tradition notwithstanding, early historians of the Italian liturgical drama were excessively deferential to France. This can be seen as late as 1954 when Gustave Cohen, the dean of French theatre historians, having been invited by the *Rivista di Studi Teatrali* to expound on the liturgical drama, apprised his Italian readers that it was fortunate that some enterprising 'pieux liturgistes français' invented liturgical drama.[12] Two decades earlier, in one of the rare histories of the Italian theatre in English, Joseph Kennard had stated, similarly, that 'in the earliest period, the Italian sacred drama was less fully developed than that in other parts of Europe' (389, I, p. 19).

This view goes back to De Bartholomaeis who asserted in 1889 that the fourteenth-century Passion fragment *Officium Quarti Militis* from Sulmona was a French text and that it was to France that belonged the distinction of having introduced the liturgical drama to Italy.[13] Two years later appeared, in a second and definitive edition, D'Ancona's monumental *Origini del teatro italiano* (see n. 10). Here the distinguished critic refers with deference to the seminal works of Magnin, Du Meril and Petit de Julleville and concedes that in medieval religious drama the primacy belonged to France.[14] Although D'Ancona wrote the first comprehensive study of the Italian medieval theatre – the liturgical drama, the *lauda drammatica* and the *sacra rappresentazione* – his treatment of the liturgical drama turned out to be a discussion of the French tradition. The oldest Italian records known to him dated from not earlier than the thirteenth century.[15]

Some thirty-three years were to elapse before the appearance of De Bartholomaeis' *Origini della poesia drammatica italiana* which made available new texts, both Latin and Italian. De Bartholomaeis' great merit is to have provided the first detailed assessment of the Italian liturgical drama,[16] thus laying the foundation for the work of Liuzzi, De Vito and D'Amico. Liuzzi was mainly concerned with illustrating how the music of liturgical drama sustains the dramatic expression phrase by phrase.[17] De Vito dealt primarily with questions of origins, coming to the conclusion, after comparing Byzantine, French and Roman liturgical ceremonies, that 'the source from which the liturgical drama springs is the Roman liturgy'.[18] Although D'Amico was the first scholar in Italy to teach a course (in 1935) on the history of the theatre, his book (11) touches only briefly on the liturgical drama. It is rather a comprehensive survey of dramatic art from its Greek and Roman forms to medieval European theatre.

It was left to Mario Apollonio to provide impetus to the study of the liturgical drama in Italy by moving from traditional historical considerations to an analysis of the character of the Roman liturgy and of the creative modalities at the beginning of liturgical drama (391). Three years earlier had appeared Paolo Toschi's famous work, *Origini del teatro italiano* (390); an indefatigable student of medieval Italian dramaturgy,[19] questioning and transcending D'Ancona's evolutionary concept, Toschi widened the horizon by adopting the critical methodology employed by Robert Stumpfl in his *Kultspiele der Germanen als Ursprung des mittelalterlichen Dramas*[20] and hence considered not just the text, but other theatrical elements such as dance, music, mask, processions, the *maggio* and the *cortei*. Toschi's volume, by virtue of its historical scope and the breadth of material examined, is well deserving of Bronzini's assessment of it as a 'monumentale edificio'.[21] Departing from the traditional view and influenced by the work of La Piana,[22] Toschi postulated a first birth, 'prima nascita', of the medieval religious drama at Byzantium out of the liturgical rites of the Eastern Church and a second birth, 'seconda nascita', at Rome out of the liturgical ceremonies of Holy Week (390, pp. 644–63). In the 1960s, general and undifferentiated discussions of the Italian liturgical drama appeared in such comprehensive histories of the theatre as Ghilardi's (392) and Pandolfi's.[23]

The most systematic research on the origin of the liturgical drama was undertaken in the 1970s by Johann Drumbl with a series of learned essays (48, 49, 52) culminating, in 1981, with a full volume on the subject (53). Drumbl argues that the *Quem quaeritis* arose as an independent composition and not as a trope, that sacred drama emerging from the liturgy was drama at its very birth (48, p. 36). He contends, in fact, that Church drama was born not as an amplification of the liturgy but in opposition to it, as a distinctive 'cerimonia elitaria': medieval theatre arose as a cultural fact and as an element extraneous to the cult (53, pp. 364–5). Drumbl's thesis runs counter to the traditional stream of Italian scholarship typified by the work of Franceschini, who looked upon the tenth-century *Quem quaeritis* trope as the beginning[24] and Avalle (80) who in 1984 sustained its Benedictine origin.

Research on the Italian liturgical drama has not been conducted in Italy alone nor has it been limited to the *Quem quaeritis*. In 1970, in the light of Inguanez's discovery of a twelfth-century liturgical Passion play at Montecassino (67), I published the first comprehensive study of the Latin Passion play in its European context (69). I showed that while the story of Christ's

Sandro Sticca

Passion became increasingly popular, beginning in the tenth century, as one of the sacred mysteries, new forces that allowed a more eloquent and humane visualisation of Christ's anguish first appeared in the eleventh and twelfth centuries: in liturgy, a concentration on christocentric piety; in art, a more humanistic treatment of Christ; and in literature, a consideration of the scenes of the Passion as dramatic and human episodes. In 1977, the Monte-cassino *Passion* was the subject of a critical reading by Robert Edwards (70) who tried to show the connection between doctrine and aesthetics. Follow-ing an essay on the theatrogenetic elements of the Christian liturgy (59), I turned to an historical analysis of the Italian *Quem quaeritis* which appeared in 1980 as a contribution in the only book-length study in English, since 1932, dedicated to Italian medieval and Renaissance theatre (401). After work on the *planctus Mariae* by Ermini, focussing on its lyrical voice,[25] by Wechssler,[26] Young (31, vol. 1), Lipphardt[27] and Grano, who studied its use in the liturgical drama (73), and by Smoldon, who was concerned with its dramatic effectiveness within the liturgical and musical framework that sustains it (93), I published in 1984 the first comprehensive study of the 'Lament of the Virgin' in medieval drama (74). After examining the begin-nings of the motif in the Eastern Patristic tradition and suggesting that it came to the Western Church through the mystic spirituality of Anselm and Bernard, I traced the incorporation and growth of the *planctus* in drama throughout Europe.

Drumbl's research on the *Quem quaeritis* provided the stimulus for an ambitious investigation into the dramatic nature of the medieval liturgy in the form of a 1976 conference sponsored by the Centro Studi sul Teatro Medioevale e Rinascimentale of Viterbo, newly founded by Federico Doglio of Rome (62). Described as an attempt to shed light on the dramatic rebirth that took place from the tenth to the twelfth centuries within the confines of the Latin liturgy, the symposium brought together scholars from several European countries who dealt with the theatrogenetic aspects of the liturgy: the *Adoratio Crucis*, the *Depositio*, the rites of Holy Week, the liturgical chant, the *Quem quaeritis* trope, the Good Friday liturgy in the Iberian peninsula, the origin of the *Improperia* in the Western Church's Holy Week liturgy, relations between the Roman liturgy and Franco-German culture, and so on.

Moving to the secular theatre, the Centro, in the following year, organised a *Convegno* on 'Il contributo dei giullari alla drammaturgia italiana delle origini',[28] designed to explore the contribution of the mimes and *jongleurs*, the *giullari*. Studies of the *giullari* – heirs to a millenary histrionic tradition – are limited by the scarcity of documentation and marked by the anathemas frequently pronounced by the Church against *mimi* and *histriones*. For these reasons, little of their *teatralità laica* has been transmitted to us – in the main, evidence from sculpture and paintings.

In 1978 the Centro continued its investigation of secular dramatic activity with a conference on the classical heritage: *L'eredità classica nel Medioevo: il linguaggio comico.*[29] Orlandi (pp. 19–42) dealt with two ninth-century re-elaborations of the fourth-century *Cena Cypriani*, the second of which, a rendition in verse, appears to have been destined for representation at the Lateran in the Rome of Pope John VIII. I discussed both the influence of classical drama on Hrotswitha of Gandersheim and of the medieval histrionic tradition on the *Mystère d'Adam* (pp. 43–62). Dafydd Evans (pp. 209–33) and Jean-Charles Payen (pp. 235–53) offered an analysis of the theatrical aspects of some Old French comedies. The majority of the *congressisti*, however, like Ferruccio Bertini (pp. 63–80), considered the question of the genre to which twelfth-century *comoediae elegiacae* – Latin poems written in elegiac verse, partly in narrative and partly in dialogue form – belong, whether they are comedies or elegies, whether they contain dramatic elements and whether they were intended to be staged. Bertini is the editor of a five-volume critical corpus of the *comoediae* giving for each text an ample historical, philological and literary introduction.[30] As to the question of staged performance, it appears that these *comoediae*, compositions halfway between drama and narrative poetry, with the possible exception of the *Babio*, were destined for dramatic or mimed reading. The existence of a secular dramatic tradition based on the medieval understanding of comedy and on the performance of the *mimi* has also been the subject of several individual studies, such as those of Franceschini on the *Babio*, of Padoan on the meaning of theatre in the Middle Ages and later of Doglio on the various forms of pre-humanistic dramaturgy.[31]

It was also Doglio who in 1982, in his *Teatro in Europa: Storia e documenti*,[32] offered the most comprehensive history of European theatre from the end of the Roman Empire to the humanistic theatre of the Trecento and Quattrocento. Enriched by text selections and documents, the volume – the first of a survey leading up to modern times – is made up of three major divisions: *L'eredità del teatro antico*, *Lo spettacolo medievale*, *Il teatro umanistico*.

In 1981 the Centro continued its examination of secular theatre by having its sixth *Convegno* investigate the ancient and medieval roots of popular spectacles (402). Departing from the historical, philological and literary approach that had characterised previous conferences, scholars speaking at *Rappresentazioni archaiche della tradizione popolare* drew on other disciplines, such as anthropology, sociology, ethnomusicology and the rich patrimony of popular culture and oral tradition. The conference was distinguished by papers on specific aspects, regional and national, of popular and folkloric spectacles in Italy and France. Giovanni Bronzini (402, pp. 43–79) held that, at the creative level, the two cardinal ways of representing reality were the allegorical and the carnivalesque. The allegorical view, corresponding to the spiritual, was governed by the Church; the carnivalesque approach, which reflects the corporeal, was used by both *giullari* and preachers to teach and to delight. Gabriella Pittaluga (402, pp. 145–96) suggested that the theatrical value of the medieval liturgy is to be found not so much in the codified ritual, its processions and gestures, but in the presence and participation of the people. Roberto Cipriani (402, pp. 253–315) described one of the most peculiar and archaic manifestations of Italian popular drama: the four processions held annually at Cerignola, in Puglia, on Holy Thursday and Good Friday. They are marked by the presence of a 'Cristo rosso' (a Christ in a red robe) – usually portrayed by a confraternity member – who, wearing a crown of thorns and carrying a heavy Cross, personifies Christ on the way to Golgotha.

While the first five *Convegni* of the Centro were concerned with the study of sacred or secular drama and the sixth with the survival of archaic forms in popular tradition, the seventh conference (1982) fostered interdisciplinary and diachronic research – literary, iconographical and musical – on 'convivial' performances, public and private, the popularity of which is attested from classical antiquity to the Renaissance: *Spettacoli conviviali dall'antichità alle corti italiane del 1400*.[33] Mario Bonaria (pp. 119–47) explored literary and epigraphic evidence on the role played by music in convivial banquets from the second century BC to the High Middle Ages. Maria De Marco (pp. 149–69) documented the uninterrupted presence of the convivial mime from the fourth to the tenth centuries. Raoul Manselli (pp. 219–41) noted that although entertainment had been part of banquet ritual for centuries, it was only after 1100 that spectacle and theatre became attached to the convivial banquet at the courts of France, Germany and, later, Italy.

In 1983, on the eighth year of its founding, the Viterbo Centro hosted the fourth colloquium of the Société Internationale pour l'Étude du Théâtre Médiéval (6), devoted to three themes: 'Processo in Paradiso e in Inferno', 'Dramma biblico' and 'Tecnologia dell'Allestimento scenico'. Of the forty-seven papers read, only three, Anna Cornagliotti's (6, pp. 35–44), Adriano Magli's (6, pp. 215–33) and Doglio's (6, pp. 275–95), dealt with the Italian drama. While the first two will be considered below in my discussion of the *lauda*, Doglio's interesting paper centred on a subject rarely treated in Italian colloquia, the *Officium Stellae*, notwithstanding the fact that numerous texts have survived and that confraternities of the Magi are known to have been very active in the presentation of religious and secular pageantry.[34]

Before I turn to a discussion of the *lauda*, mention ought to be made of the valuable Italian contributions to the critical literature on the tenth-century German nun Hrotswitha of Gandersheim who modelled her texts on the Roman playwright Terence. Although the Benedictine canoness received critical attention in Italy as early as 1869,[35] modern research began in 1938 with Franceschini who maintained that her 'dramas' were intended for recitation or reading,[36] and with D'Amico who posited that they were meant to be staged (*11*, p. 186). While scholars like Brugnoli agree with D'Amico,[37] others feel that Hrotswitha's dramatic dialogues exhibit only a general sense of theatricality (*392*, p. 112). A new critical direction has been taken by Vinay who argues that Hrotswitha's genius is fundamentally lyrical, not dramatic, and that her work cannot be considered theatre.[38] More recently,

Bertini and I have thrown new light on Hrotswitha's writings through formalistic approaches designed to explore allegorical, exegetical and symbolical structures of signification distinguishing each of her 'plays'.[39]

Ever since Ernesto Monaci's publication of a partial corpus of Umbrian *laude* in 1872 and 1875,[40] Italian scholarship on the subject has been devoted primarily to three basic historical problems: determining chronological priority between the Perugia and the Assisi *laude*, assessing the connection between the liturgical drama and the *lauda* and identifying the moment when the *lauda* passed from the lyrical to the dramatic stage. The question of priority has been hard to answer. For while the centres of production and dissemination of the *lauda* were in Umbria, Abruzzi and Tuscany,[41] its origin is tied to the spiritual currents emanating from thirteenth-century Umbria, especially those connected with the Dominicans in Perugia and the Franciscans in Assisi. Although the *lauda* is associated with the *Disciplinati*'s penitential movement started in 1260 by friar Raniero Fasani of Perugia,[42] recent studies have cast doubt on Perugia's claim to be 'the oldest workshop of laude' (*413*, p. 485) and given precedence to the thirteenth-century *laudario* collection of Cortona (*411*, p. 660, and *421*, I, p. vii). Of significant interest among the Perugian *laudari* is the *laudario* of the confraternity of St Andrew. The *terminus ad quem* for this collection of 122 dramatic and lyrical *laude* of varying length has been set by Kathleen Falvey at about 1333. Falvey began a provocative reading of this *laudario* with essays on the plays of the Passion (*440*), the Deposition (*441*) and the Last Judgement (*442*). She has also provided us with an interesting study of the Italian saint play, concentrating on its beginning in Perugia around 1330 against the background of hagiographical cults and the performance of vernacular poetic narratives known as the *cantari* (*444*).

As to Assisi, although the primacy of its *laudari* was maintained early on by Galli,[43] it was left up to Baldelli (*406*) and, especially, Fortini (*407*), in well-documented studies, to establish Assisi and the Franciscan movement as home ground of the *lauda*. The Franciscan influence on Italian theatre – occasionally noted[44] – was the subject of a 1982 conference at San Miniato. Its papers, published in 1984 (*404*), constitute the first attempt at a more comprehensive assessment of the rapport between Franciscan spirituality and the new Italian theatre. More specifically, the essays illustrate the influence exerted by the Franciscans, during the second half of the thirteenth century, on the lay movements of *flagellanti*, *battuti* and *penitenti umbri* as they began to dramatise subjects up to then found only in Church plays of Benedictine provenance. Doglio explains the stimulus provided by St Francis' peculiar kind of preaching, by the *Meditationes Vitae Christi* and by the Franciscan 'sermone semidrammatico' to play productions of the various confraternities (*404*, pp. 9–12). Carlo Paolazzi (pp. 71–120) and Manselli (pp. 121–35) are concerned with the contribution of St Francis' theme of 'lode' and 'cantico' to the vernacular literature of the *laudesi* and with the preaching and dramatic interests of the Franciscan movement. Attilio Langeli

Sandro Sticca

(pp. 41–58) traces the cultural and linguistic roots of Franciscan popularity and Alfonso Pompei (pp. 21–40) the social and cultural impact of the Franciscan movement. The remaining essays deal with particular aspects of Franciscan influence, such as the presence of St Francis in the *laude* and the *sacra rappresentazione* (pp. 135–47) and theatrical techniques and modalities – *inventio, dispositio, elocutio, actio* and *memoria* – in the sermons of St Bernardine of Siena (pp. 177–94).

The second problem, the relationship between the *lauda* and the liturgy, has drawn general attention ever since in 1872 Monaci postulated a direct link between the *lauda* and liturgical drama[45] and D'Ancona asserted in 1875 that the *lauda* arose as an independent dramatic form.[46] In modern times, the view that liturgical drama and the *lauda* are connected, advocated recently by Toschi and Baldelli, has become majority opinion. Paolo Toschi pointed out that when the *Disciplinati* came on the scene in 1260, Italian religious poetry was already affiliated with liturgical drama (*390*, p. 677).[47] The lyrical *laude* were in essence versions of the liturgical *laudes*, he notes, and the *lauda*'s oldest antecedent is the vernacular *planctus Mariae* found in the twelfth-century Montecassino *Passion* (*390*, pp. 674–6).[48] Widening the historical and geographical horizon, Ignazio Baldelli proposed a link between the Benedictines of Montecassino and the Franciscans of Umbria who had close rapport with the *Spirituali marchigiani* (*406*, p. 410, and *419*).[49]

Thus while most critics tie the *lauda* to liturgical drama (*413*, p. 487, and *416*, p. xl),[50] a few, such as Apollonio (in *408*, p. 409) and Faccioli (*397*, pp. xviii–xix), regard it as the product of a coalescence of the penitential and flagellant movement with Latin Church plays. A recently discovered fourteenth-century *laudario* from Arezzo, for instance, belonging to the confraternity of St Anthony, offers texts connected with a Latin Office (*424*, pp. 158–60). Another small group look upon the *lauda* as the last step in the process of 'farcitura', initiated mostly in Benedictine monasteries, whereby passages in 'volgare' were inserted into Latin texts.[51] The prominent example would again be the vernacular *planctus Mariae* closing the Montecassino *Passion* (*69*, pp. 62–3).[52]

The third historical problem, the transformation of the lyrical to the dramatic *lauda*, has been debated ever since De Bartholomaeis stated that this occurred when monologues were assigned to particular characters, initially Christ and the Virgin.[53] The question received wide critical attention with the publication of papers from three major conferences on the historical and religious context of the *laude* in 1962 (*408*), 1972 (*415*) and 1981 (*420*). The papers of the 1960 conference, held in Perugia on the occasion of the seventh centenary of the foundation of the flagellant movement, represent a monumental contribution to the study of the confraternities and the Umbrian *lauda*. The volume offers not only articles on the history of individual confraternities and on the *lauda* (music, metrical form, iconography, pre-history), but also makes available unpublished documents. The topic of the dramatic *lauda* is addressed by Apollonio and Angela Terruggia.

Apollonio (*408*, pp. 409–13) argues that the lyrical *lauda* became dramatic by investing liturgical plays with the new confraternal spirit of the *laudesi*, especially their concern with the Passion of Christ and the compassion of the Virgin. Rather than speaking of derivation of the *lauda drammatica* from liturgical drama, one ought to speak of the acquisition on the part of the former of the theatrical modes of the latter. Terruggia, on the other hand, contends (*408*, pp. 458–9) that so long as the custom prevailed among the *Disciplinati* of scourging themselves in the streets, so too prevailed the singing of narrative *laude*. The dramatic *laude*, which were sung during the *devozione* in the *Oratorio*, became true dramatic representations when they were performed for the people, first in church and then outside. Terruggia assigns the 'representation' of narrative *laude* to the early fourteenth century and the creation of dramatic and theatrical *laude* to about the middle of that century.

Similar to Apollonio, Raffaello Morghen asserts that the early *laude*, sung during processions, became drama when the suffering of Christ and of the *mater dolorosa* assumed central importance in the confraternal *devozione* (*415*, p. 323).[54] Morghen's essay appears in *Risultati e prospettive della ricerca sul Movimento dei Disciplinati* (*415*), a conference held in Perugia some ten years later to ensure the continuity of the project and to report on ongoing research. Its papers deal with topics such as the topography and dissemination of the confraternities, their statutes and registers, their economic and financial life, the iconography of the *Disciplinati* and the literary documents owned by the Perugia Centro.

The question of the transition of the *lauda* from lyrical to dramatic form was also discussed in two studies published in 1981 in the papers of the fifth conference of the Viterbo Centro: *Le laudi drammatiche umbre delle origini* (*420*). Maggiani finds the impetus for dramatising the *lauda* to lie in the shift from personal liturgical *devotio* to liturgical *partecipatio* of the *Disciplinati* in their *Oratorio* as expression of the *communitas* (420, pp. 65–79). Magli and Anna Marina Storoni, on the other hand, following Konigson (*21*), ascribe the rise of the dramatic *lauda* to its movement from the restricted space of churches to the theatrical expanse represented by city streets, thus changing the concept of space and time (420, pp. 201–15). Also of value are Pietro Scarpellini's essay on the iconography of the *lauda* (420, pp. 165–85) and Enrico Menestò's fine analysis of the dramatic *laude* of Jacopone da Todi in whom Benedictine and Franciscan culture were joined (420, pp. 105–40). As to the thirty-two *laude*, out of a corpus of ninety-two, which show dramatic form, Menestò deems them representative of Jacopone's particular kind of theatrical sense which he calls 'drammaticità spirituale' – spiritual theatricality (420, p. 140). Its most sublime manifestation is the *Donna de Paradiso*, Jacopone's masterpiece, considered by Menestò (420, p. 135) and by Toschi (*428*, p. 38) 'the most ancient and finest example of the Umbrian lauda and the archetype of the new Italian theater'.[55] A close reading of the dramatic structure of this *lauda* is given by Bertelli who points out that the tragedy centres on the Mother's grief and the expressive encounter between human and divine.[56] The idea of finding the dramatic potential of Jacopone's *laude* and of the *lauda* in general in their internal structure is supported by Moleta and Musarra in two fine essays (*432* and *425*).

During the past thirty years Jacopone has been the object of keen scholarly attention,[57] culminating in 1953[58] and in 1974 (*431*) with the most important editions of his *laude* since the *editio princeps* of 1490. To these must be added Bettarini's superb edition of the *laudario* of the flagellants of the Holy Cross of Urbino (*429*) in which she traces the influence of Jacopone, and Mazza's edition of the fourteenth-century *laudario Jacoponico* of the Biblioteca Civica 'Angelo Maj' of Bergamo (*426*). A comprehensive study of Jacopone's *laudario* was undertaken at a conference held at Todi in 1980 on the occasion of the 750th anniversary of his birth (*435*). The papers presented place into true perspective the singularity and complexity of Jacopone da Todi. Ovidio Capitani notes his existential anguish and his will to action (*435*, pp. 11–30). Scarpellini underlines the visual and figurative elements that distinguish his *laude* (*435*, pp. 65–84), while Moleta and Menestò deal with the sense of time in Jacopone (*435*, pp. 93–128) and the philosophical and theological roots of his 'contemptus mundi' (*435*, pp. 129–53). Also illuminating are Franco Mancini's study of traditional and innovative themes in the *lauda Donna de Paradiso* (*435*, pp. 155–76) and Silvestro Nessi's excursus on Iacoponic criticism of the last one hundred years (*435*, pp. 37–64). Of the two editions mentioned above, Mancini's (*431*) is the more valuable. It not only addresses the problem of the *laude*'s authenticity but that of Jacopone's language: Mancini frees it from the traditional association with *rozzezza* (coarseness) by illustrating its refined Tuscan and archaic tone.

The *lauda*, in general, and the confraternities have been the subject of productive investigations. Pericoli studied the confraternity of S. Maria Maggiore in Todi (*409*) and sought to establish Todi as the birthplace of Jacopone's dramatic *lauda* (*405*, pp. 133–41). Magli considered the function of the devils in the *lauda drammatica* (in 6, pp. 215–33).[59] Marinelli brought out an annotated bibliography of 5,692 items on the artistic, religious and literary activities of the Perugian confraternities up to the year 1860.[60] Lazzarini examined the fifteenth-century *laudario* of the Confraternity of St Francis of Orvieto and the theatrical activities of the town's five confraternities, and D'Accone and Weissman have provided information on the numerous confraternities of *laudesi* and *Disciplinati* that flourished in Florence from the beginning of the thirteenth century.[61] In addition, we have Gasca Queirazza's study of northern *laude* and *laudari* (*417*); Falvey's selected bibliography of the Italian vernacular religious drama of the fourteenth to sixteenth centuries (*403*); Varanini, Banfi and Ceruti Burgio's edition and study of the Cortona *laude* (*421*) plus Varanini's essay on the *lauda* of the Trecento (*414*); Toscani's edition of the sixteen Tuscan *laude* contained in the fifteenth-century codex *Vaticano Chigiano*;[62] and Faccioli's edition of several *laude* (*397*, pp. 48–128).[63] A valuable contribution to the study of various aspects – liturgical, musical and lyrical – of late-thirteenth- and early-fourteenth-century *laude* is offered by Cyrilla Barr in her recently published volume on the monophonic *lauda* (see the 'Recent works' section of the bibliography).

The edition by Varanini, Banfi and Ceruti Burgio (*421*) is an ambitious project designed to make available the vast corpus of *laude cortonesi* from the thirteenth to the fifteenth century. The first three volumes published (a final volume is in preparation) are enriched by an ample philological and exegetical commentary. The aim of the project is to establish, by analysing their internal structure, the historical and individual make-up of each of the *laudari*. Varanini, Banfi and Ceruti Burgio give us also an exegetical and linguistic examination of the texts themselves and their relation to medieval hymns and the hagiographic and scriptural tradition. We also owe Varanini the edition of thirty-five thirteenth-century *laude*, which includes not only texts from such eminent *laudari* as the Cortona and the Jacoponic ones but also fragments from Vicenza, Verona, Urbino and the Abruzzi and Lombardy regions (*416*). Finally, worthy of note are the fourteenth-century *Passione* by Cicerchia (*418*) – a Passion poem that exerted influence on some *laude* of the *Disciplinati* of Siena – and Cornagliotti's illustrated edition – with contemporary scenes of the Passion – of *La Passione di Revello* (*439*), written in Piedmont about 1482 under French influence.[64] The rich critical apparatus of this edition closes with a bibliography of 592 entries.

Scholarship on religious drama in Italy has concentrated on the origin and growth of the *lauda*. We have relatively few studies concerned with the other form of religious theatre, the *sacra rappresentazione*.[65] This is a dramatic spectacle that began in the second half of the Trecento and flourished throughout the Quattrocento until it degenerated, toward the end, into sentimental and spiritual tableaux.[66] Although the old theory positing a direct descent of the *sacra rappresentazione* from the *lauda* and the *devozione* has been challenged,[67] it is not always possible to draw a clear line between *lauda drammatica* and *sacra rappresentazione*.[68] Their coexistence is often attested. While a general literary affinity can be established between these two play types, in its themes and theatrical form the *sacra rappresentazione* is clearly different from the *lauda drammatica*.

Generally written in *ottava rima*, the salient features of the *sacra rappresentazione* are a preference for subjects taken from the Old Testament and from saint legends rather than from the New Testament, the inclusion, in the same play, of the Passion chant and the Easter chant, thus introducing polyphony, and, above all, an overriding concern for theatrical effects. By adapting to its needs the grandiose and spectacular pageantry that often accompanied the civic feasts and processions of the time,[69] the *sacra rappresentazione* became, in Faccioli's words, 'an autonomous and accomplished form of spectacle' (*397*, p. xxvii). Indeed, Molinari goes so far as to regard the *sacra rappresentazione* as nothing other than 'one of the numerous festive spectacles of the Florence of the Quattrocento'.[70]

Sandro Sticca

It is in the city of Orvieto that the term *ripresentationi* – rather than the traditional *laudi* – was first used in connection with the earliest known texts of *sacra rappresentazioni* (about thirty-seven) from a *laudario* compiled in the year 1405 by a certain Tramo di Leonardo, a *Disciplinato* of the confraternity of St Francis.[71] Five of these are of Perugian origin. Of great interest is that these *sacra rappresentazioni* from Orvieto offer stage directions in Italian rather than in Latin and dramatise unusual subjects: *La creazione del Mondo* (*The Creation of the World*), *Rappresentazione d'Ognissanti* (*All Saints Play*), *L'esaltazione della Croce* (*The Exaltation of the Cross*) plus various saint legends.

The most productive centre of *sacre rappresentazioni* in the Quattrocento remained Florence. Here the plays came into contact with both the mundane and spectacular pageantry linked with civic feasts and the theatrical innovations of the so-called 'ingegni', invented by people such as Brunelleschi and il Cecca.[72] An impression of the elaborate staging given *sacre rappresentazioni* at Florence in the Quattrocento can be gathered from an account of the Russian bishop Souzdal (*436*)[73] who visited the city in 1439 during the feast of the Annunciation. Such was the intrusion of the spectacular and visual that by the end of the Quattrocento the Florentine pageants for the feast of San Giovanni had been 'transformed from a series of pious *rappresentazioni*' into spectacles celebrating the splendour and authority of the Medicis.[74] The most famous of Florentine playwrights was Feo Belcari (1410–84), composer of such plays as the *Rappresentazione del Giudicio finale*, *L'Assunzione* and *L'Annunciazione*. His most renowned work is the *Rappresentazione di Abramo e Isacco*, first staged in 1449, which has been wrongly regarded as the prototype of the Florentine religious theatre. Of signal importance, in this context, is the recent publication by Newbigin of a corpus of thirteen *sacre rappresentazioni* that can be dated before 1485, the year of the first datable printing of a *sacra rappresentazione*, Belcari's *Rappresentazione di Abramo e Isacco*. Newbigin's work (*438a*) is the best study on the *sacra rappresentazione* in recent times. Moreover, six of the thirteen *sacre rappresentazioni* she edits had never been published, while the others were available only in early printed editions. For the Florentine *sacra rappresentazione*, mention should be made of other playwrights such as Bernardo and Antonia Pulci, Castellano Castellani and Antonio Araldo. Of truly ample proportions is the *Passione di Cristo*, a *sacra rappresentazione* composed in 1545 by the Franciscan Stefano Quinzani. Discovered in 1930 in the library of the Convent of St Francis in Milan, this *sacra rappresentazione* boasts more than 111 characters while depicting, in three acts, the events of Christ's Passion from the raising of Lazarus to the Crucifixion and burial.[75]

Important for its age and diversity is the dramatic activity of the Abruzzi region, which has left us the greatest wealth of theatrical documents, coming from such places as L'Aquila, Chieti, Sulmona, Penne, Capestrano and Città Sant'Angelo and consisting of *laudi*, *devozioni*, *sacre rappresentazioni* and *Passioni* (*391*, pp. 197–212).[76] The most significant production of *sacre rappresentazioni* took place in L'Aquila where the *Disciplinati* formed their earliest confraternity, the 'Confraternita di Santa Maria della Pietà', in the year 1264.[77] The vitality of the *sacra rappresentazione* in L'Aquila is reflected primarily in the *laudario* of St Thomas compiled by the confraternity of St Thomas Aquinas in the second half of the fifteenth century. One of the most remarkable monuments of Italian religious theatre, this *laudario*, which has not yet received full critical attention, is characterised by the use of the Passion chant: endecasyllabic sestets at times interspersed with endecasyllabic quatrains. The most notable *sacra rappresentazione* in this *laudario* is the *Legenda de Sancto Tomascio* (Legend of St Thomas), a three-day spectacle marked by the appearance of numerous historical and legendary figures. It is regrettable that the vast corpus of medieval plays from Abruzzi made available by De Bartholomaeis in 1924[78] still awaits systematic linguistic and literary analysis.

Tied to the dramatic *laudi* of Umbria and Abruzzi, from which it derives, was the religious theatre at Rome, especially the one connected with the confraternity of the *Gonfalone* which, in 1486, began producing *sacre rappresentazioni*: Passion plays every Good Friday at the Colosseum and plays of the Resurrection either at St John Lateran or in St Peter's Basilica (*390*, pp. 697–98).[79] These plays, their lines spoken, but interspersed with musical *intermezzi*, were a mixture of the sacred and the popular. The sacred texts often paled before the majesty of the ancient edifices in which they were performed. It is no wonder that, in 1539, Pope Paul III put a stop to the spectacles.

While the research done has significantly increased our understanding of the origins and development of Italian medieval religious drama, liturgical and vernacular, the area of its *mise-en-scène*, drama as theatre, needs further study. Early works on staging such as Garrone's *L'apparato scenico del dramma sacro in Italia*,[80] examining the function of church and altar in liturgical drama, and the public square and *il monte* in the dramatic *lauda*, has never been superseded. Studies such as Bigongiari's[81] do not bear on the Italian medieval religious drama and even the works of Fagiolo (*396*), Dorigo and Molinari offer only general and undifferentiated comments on the staging of Italian plays.[82] It is only in such formal studies as Molinari's and Newbigin's on the *sacra rappresentazione*,[83] Ricci's on the Italian *teatri* (*395*, pp. 61–6), Battisti's on 'theatrical gesture',[84] Cattaneo's on the relationship between church space and liturgical practices (*37*), Pittaluga's on the 'teatralità popolare' (in *402*, pp. 145–95), Doglio's on the transition from medieval scenography to humanistic spectacle[85] and Cardini's on the 'spettacolo medievale'[86] that one finds some groundwork towards a comprehensive investigation of the Italian religious stage. Luigi Allegri's recently published volume (1988; see the 'Recent works' section of the bibliography), entirely dedicated to an analysis of the theatrical elements of medieval dramaturgy, constitutes an auspicious beginning. What is presently needed is a closer study of all extant *laudari* in order to ascertain, by examining the stage

Sandro Sticca

directions implicit and explicit, not only the performance modes peculiar to each *laudario*, but also the degree of theatrical realisation that characterise the various *laudari*. Such a systematic investigation, together with information culled from art and architecture, combined with research on the *mise-en-scène* of the liturgical drama, would lead us towards a comprehensive reconstruction of the medieval Italian stage.

Although scholarship on the Italian medieval drama entered a dormant period at the beginning of this century, recent research has brought new life to a tradition that, by virtue of the diversity of its dramatic forms and the wealth of texts preserved, stands out as one of the most vibrant periods of Italian literature and Western drama.

NOTES

1 Adalberto Di Rosa, 'Le laude nella cultura medioevale', in *Dal Medioevo al Petrarca, Miscellanea di Studi in Onore di Vittore Branca*, vol. 1 (Florence: Leo S. Olschki Editore, 1983), pp. 449–50.
2 Vincenzo De Bartholomaeis, *Origini della poesia drammatica italiana* (Turin: Società Editrice Internazionale, 1924; second edn, 1952); see also 407, pp. 9–11, and Elise Murray Cambon, *The Italian and Latin Lauda of the Fifteenth Century* (unpublished dissertation, Tulane University, 1975), p. 20.
3 See especially Meersseman, in *408*, pp. 47–9, and Ardu, also in *408*, pp. 368–70. On the flagellant movement, see also John Henderson, 'The Flagellant Movement and Flagellant Confraternities in Central Italy, 1260–1400', *Studies in Church History* 15 (1978): 147–60.
4 See Morghen, in *408*, p. 30, and also Manselli, in *408*, pp. 99–108.
5 Meersseman, in *408*, p. 51; see also his 'I Disciplinati nel Duecento', in his *Ordo Fraternitatis, Confraternite e pietà dei laici nel medioevo*, vol. 1 (Rome: Herder Editrice e Libreria, 1977), pp. 458–9 and 504–5.
6 Meersseman, in *408*, pp. 58–61.
7 Walter Binni, 'Poetica, critica e storia letteraria', *La Rassegna della letteratura italiana* 64 (1960): 33.
8 Ritva Jonsson, 'Quels sont les rapports entre Amalaire de Metz et les tropes liturgiques?', in *Culto cristiano. Politica imperiale carolingia, Convegni del Centro di Studi sulla Spiritualità Medievale, Todi, 9–12 ottobre 1977* (Todi: Accademia Tudertina, 1978), p. 171.
9 Giorgio Brugnoli, 'Intorno alle origini del teatro moderno', *Cultura neolatina* 15 (1955): 150.
10 De Bartholomaeis, *Origini della poesia drammatica*, pp. 112–41. On the subject, see also Alessandro D'Ancona, *Origini del teatro italiano*, vol. 1 (Turin: Ermanno Loerscher, 1891), pp. 87–105.
11 On Brunelleschi's stage machinery and the *sacre rappresentazioni*, see Carlo L. Ragghianti, ed., *Le Vite di Giorgio Vasari* (Milan: Rizzoli Editore, 1945), vol. 1, pp. 627 and 820. See also *437*.
12 Gustave Cohen, 'Le Drame liturgique en France (X^e–XIIe siècles)', *Rivista di Studi Teatrali* 11–12 (1954): 31.
13 Vincenzo De Bartholomaeis, 'Ricerche Abruzzesi', *Bullettino dell'Istituto Storico Abruzzese* 8 (1889): 169. On this *Officium*, see 71.
14 D'Ancona, *Origini*, vol. 1, p. 7.
15 *Ibid.*, p. 87.

16 De Bartholomaeis, *Origini*, chapter II, part III, pp. 112–50.
17 Ferdinando Liuzzi, 'L'espressione musicale nel dramma liturgico', *Studi Medievali* 2 (1929): 74–109.
18 Maria Sofia De Vito, *L'origine del dramma liturgico* (Milan: Società Anonima Editrice Dante Alighieri, 1939), p. 175.
19 See also his *L'antico dramma sacro italiano*, 2 vols. (Florence: Libreria Editrice Fiorentina, 1925–6) and *Dal dramma liturgico alla rappresentazione sacra* (Florence: G. C. Sansoni, 1940), reprinted with additional studies as *L'antico teatro religioso italiano* (Matera: Montemurro, 1960).
20 Berlin: Junker and Dünnhaupt, 1936.
21 Giovanni Bronzini, 'Le origini del teatro italiano', *Cultura Neolatina* 16 (1956): 238.
22 Giorgio La Piana, *Le Rappresentazioni sacre nella letteratura Bizantina dalle origini al secolo IX* (Grottaferrata: Tip. Italo-Orientale 'S. Nilo', 1912) and 'The Byzantine Theater', *Speculum* 11 (1936): 171–211.
23 Vito Pandolfi, *Storia universale del teatro drammatico*, 2 vols. (Turin: Unione Tipografico-Editrice Torinese, 1964), vol. I, pp. 429–63.
24 Ezio Franceschini, 'Il teatro post-carolingio', in *I problemi comuni dell'Europa post-carolingia* (Spoleto: Arti Grafiche Panetto e Petrelli, 1955), vol. II, p. 209.
25 Filippo Ermini, *Lo Stabat Mater e i Pianti della Vergine nella lirica del Medio Evo* (Rome: Scuola Tipografica Salesiana, 1899).
26 Eduard Wechssler, *Die romanischen Marienklagen* (Halle: M. Niemeyer, 1893).
27 Walther Lipphardt, 'Marienklagen und Liturgie', *Jahrbuch für Liturgiewissenschaft* 12 (1932): 198–205.
28 *Atti del II° Convegno di Studio, Viterbo, 17–19 giugno 1977* (Viterbo: Bulzoni Editore, 1978).
29 *Atti del III° Convegno di Studio, Viterbo, 26, 27, 28 maggio 1978* (Viterbo: Agnesotti Editore, 1979).
30 Ferruccio Bertini, ed., *Commedie latine del XII e XIII secolo*, 5 vols. (Genoa: Istituto di Filologia Classica e Medievale, 1976–86).
31 Ezio Franceschini, *Teatro latino medievale* (Milan: Nuova Accademia Editrice, 1960), pp. 91–3; Giorgio Padoan, 'Il senso del etatro nei secoli senza teatro', in *Concetto, storia, miti e immagini del Medio Evo*, ed. Vittore Branca (Florence: Sansoni, 1973), pp. 325–38; Federico Doglio, 'La drammaturgia protoumanistica e Rosvita', *Schede Medievali* 1 (1981): 1–27.
32 Vol. I (Milan: Garzanti, 1982).
33 *Atti del VII° Convegno di Studio, Viterbo, 27–30 maggio 1982* (Viterbo: Agnesotti Editore, 1983).
34 A notable exception to the dearth of research on the subject is the work of Musumarra (*438*). An illuminating essay on the confraternities of the Magi is provided by Rab Hatfield in 'The Compagnia de' Magi', *Journal of the Warburg and Courtauld Institutes* 33 (1970): 107–61.
35 Paolo Emiliani-Giudici, *Storia del teatro in Italia* (Florence: Successori Le Monnier, 1869), pp. 135–42.
36 Ezio Franceschini, 'Per una revisione del teatro latino di Rosvita', *Rivista Italiana del Dramma* 1 (1938): 308; see also his 'Il teatro post-carolingio', p. 37, and his *Teatro latino medievale*, pp. 57–8.
37 Giorgio Brugnoli, 'Note di filologia medioevale. Teatro latino medioevale', *Rivista di Cultura Classica e Medioevale* 3 (1961): 116.
38 Gustavo Vinay, 'Umanità di Rosvita', *Convivium* 17 (1948): 563–75, and 'Rosvita: una canonichessa ancora da scoprire?', in his *Alto medioevo latino* (Naples: Guida Editore, 1978), pp. 483–554.

39 Sandro Sticca, 'Hrotswitha's *Dulcitius* and Christian Symbolism', *Mediaeval Studies* 32 (1970): 108–27; 'Hrotswitha's *Abraham* and Exegetical Tradition', in *Saggi critici di filologia classica in onore di Vittorio D'Agostino* (Turin: Baccola & Grilli, 1971), pp. 359–85; 'Sacred Drama and Comic Realism in the Plays of Hrotswitha of Gandersheim' (in 6, pp. 141–62); 'Sacred Drama and Tragic Realism in Hrotswitha's *Paphnutius*' (in 7, pp. 12–44); and 'The Hagiographical and Monastic Context of Hrotswitha's Plays', in *Hrotsvit of Gandersheim, Rara Avis in Saxonia?*, ed. Katharina M. Wilson (Ann Arbor: Marc Publishing Co., 1987), pp. 1–34. See also Ferruccio Bertini, *Il 'teatro' di Rosvita* (Genoa: Casa Editrice Tilgher, 1979), 'Simbologia e struttura drammatica nel *Gallicanus* e nel *Pafnutius*' (in 7, pp. 45–59) and *Rosvita. Dialoghi Drammatici* (Milan: Garzanti, 1986).

40 Ernesto Monaci, 'Appunti per la storia del teatro italiano. Uffizj drammatici dei Disciplinati dell'Umbria', *Rivista di Filologia Romanza* 1 (1872), 235–71; 2 (1875): 29–42.

41 Achille Tartaro, *La letteratura civile e religiosa del Trecento* (Bari: Laterza, 1981), p. 132.

42 Meersseman, *Ordo Fraternitatis*, vol. 1, pp. 462–4; see also the chapters by Ardu, Meersseman and Morghen respectively in *408*, pp. 368–70, pp. 47–9 and pp. 32–9. A fine analysis of the origin and development of the *lauda* can be found in Elisabeth Diderichs' *Die Anfänge der mehrstimmigen Lauda* (Tutzing: Hans Schneider, 1986), pp. 11–40.

43 Giuseppe Galli, 'I Disciplinati dell'Umbria del 1260 e le loro *Laudi*', *Giornale Storico della Letteratura Italiana*, Supplement 7–9 (1904–6): 69–70.

44 See Sticca, *14*, and Fernando Ghilardi, 'Le origini del teatro italiano e San Francesco', *L'Italia francescana* 30 (1955): 341–51; 31 (1956): 81–7. See also Erich Auerbach, *Mimesis* (New York: Doubleday Anchor Books, 1957), pp. 148–51; and David L. Jeffrey, 'Franciscan Spirituality and the Rise of English Drama', *Mosaic* 8 (1975): 25–34, and 'St. Francis and Medieval Theatre', *Franciscan Studies* 43 (1983): 321–46.

45 Monaci, 'Appunti' (1872), pp. 252–3.

46 Alessandro D'Ancona, 'Due antiche *devozioni* italiane', *Rivista di Filologia Romanza* 2 (1875): 10.

47 On this point, see also Doglio (*422*, pp. 276–7). On the liturgical tradition of the *lauda*, see Di Rosa's essay in *Dal Medioevo al Petrarca*, especially pp. 449–50.

48 See also his *L'antico teatro religioso italiano*, pp. 47–9.

49 See also his 'L'uso del volgare nel Ducato di Spoleto', in the *Atti del 9° Congresso Internazionale di Studi sull'Alto Medioevo, Spoleto, 27 settembre – 2 ottobre 1982* (Spoleto: Presso la Sede del Centro, 1983), especially pp. 678–82.

50 See also Siro A. Cimenz, 'La poesia religiosa Umbra del Duecento', in *L'Umbria nella storia, nella letteratura, nell'arte* (Bologna: N. Zanichelli, 1954), pp. 184–5.

51 See Luigi Cellucci, 'Il latino di fronte al volgare in Italia nei secoli XIII e XIV', *Cultura Neolatina* 1 (1941): 23–4; Angelo Monteverdi, 'Lingue volgari e impulsi religiosi', *Cultura Neolatina* 6–7 (1946–7): 11–13; and Doglio, *Teatro in Europa*, vol. 1, pp. 233–4.

52 See also Ghilardi, 'Le origini del teatro', p. 345; Ruggero Ruggeri, *Romanità e cristianesimo nell'Europa medievale* (Rome: Edizioni Studium, 1975), pp. 212–13.

53 De Bartholomaeis, *Origini della poesia drammatica*, pp. 212–13.

54 See also Angela Terruggia, 'Lo sviluppo del dramma sacro visto attraverso i codici di Assisi', in the *Atti del Centro Studi Origini del Teatro Italiano*, taken from the *Annuario XI*, Accademia Etrusca di Cortona (Cortona: Tipografia Commerciale,

1960), pp. 181–4. On the importance in the *laude* of Christ's *Passio* and Mary's *Lamentatio*, see Mancini (in *420*), pp. 141–64.

55 George Peck (*434*, p. 132) refers to the *lauda Donna de Paradiso* as 'Jacopone's only dramatic poem ... a giant step toward the evolution of the sacred drama of the later Middle Ages in Italy'.

56 Italo Bertelli, *Impeto mistico e rappresentazione realistica nella poesia di Iacopone. Appunti sulla lauda 'Donna de Paradiso'* (Milan: Bignami, 1981).

57 See *405*, *413* (pp. 493–541), *420* (pp. 105–40), *410*, *427*, *428*, *430*, *433*, *434* and *435*.

58 Franca Ageno, ed., *Iacopone da Todi, Laudi, Trattato e Detti* (Florence: Le Monnier, 1953).

59 On this subject, see also Lazar (*394*).

60 Olga Marinelli, *Le confraternite di Perugia dalle origini al secolo XIX. Bibliografia delle opere a stampa* (Perugia: Edizione Grafica, 1965).

61 Andrea Lazzarini, 'Il codice Vitt. Em. 528 e il teatro musicale del Trecento', *Archivio Storico Italiano* 113 (1955): 482–521; Frank A. D'Accone, 'Le Compagnie dei *Laudesi* in Firenze durante l'*Ars Nova*', in *L'Ars Nova del Trecento* (Certaldo: Centro Studi sull'Ars Nova Italiana del Trecento, 1970), pp. 253–80; Ronald F. E. Weissman, 'From Traitor to Brother: Social Organization and Ritual Action in Florentine Confraternities, 1250–1494', in his *Ritual Brotherhood in Renaissance Florence* (New York: Academic Press, 1982), pp. 43–105. On the Florentine theatre see also Richard C. Trexler, 'Florentine Theater, 1280–1500. A Checklist of Performances and Institutions', in Robert J. Rodini, ed., *Medieval and Renaissance Theater and Spectacle*, special issue of *Forum Italicum*, 14 (1980), pp. 454–75.

62 Bernard Toscani, ed., *Le laude dei Bianchi* (Florence: Libraria Editrice Fiorentina, 1979).

63 Some remarks on the *lauda* are also found in David Jeffrey's *The Early English Lyric and Franciscan Spirituality* (Lincoln: The University of Nebraska Press, 1975), pp. 118–54 *passim*, and in Patrick S. Diehl's *The Medieval European Religious Lyric* (Berkeley: University of California Press, 1985), pp. 46–8 and 60–1.

64 D'Amico (*11*, p. 227) considers the *Passione di Revello* the only example of an Italian 'mystery cycle'. Other examples of Italian Passion plays under French influence are the Franco-Venetian *Passion* of Niccolò da Verona, written around 1350, and the one contained in the Marciano VI manuscript, composed about 1371 (see, respectively, Franca Di Ninni, 'La "Passion" di Niccolò da Verona fra traduzione e tradizione', *Studi Francesi* 1 (1970): 18–39, 108–18, 208–31 and A. Boucherie, 'La Passion du Christ, poème écrit en dialecte franco-vénitien du XIVe siècle', *Revue des langues romanes* 1 (1970): 407–23).

65 Besides the early work of Alessandro D'Ancona (his edition of the *Sacre rappresentazioni dei secoli XIV, XV e XVI*, 3 vols., Florence: Le Monnier, 1872) and Vincenzo De Bartholomaeis (who edited *Laude drammatiche e rappresentazioni sacre*, 3 vols., Florence: Le Monnier, 1943), the following studies exist: M. Bonfantini, ed., *Le sacre rappresentazioni italiane* (Milan: Bompiani, 1942); Cesare Molinari, *Spettacoli fiorentini del Quattrocento* (Venice: Neri Pozza, 1961); L. Banfi, ed., *Sacre rappresentazioni del Quattrocento* (Turin: UTET, 1963); G. Ponte, ed., *Sacre rappresentazioni fiorentine del Quattrocento* (Milan: Marzorati, 1974) and Musumarra (*438*).

66 Douglas Radcliff-Umstead, 'Florentine Sacred Drama in the Late Renaissance', *Italian Culture* 4 (1985): 43; Vittorio Rossi, *Il Quattrocento* in *Storia Letteraria d'Italia*, vol. v (Milan: Vallardi, 1949), p. 306.

67 Walter Tortoreto, *Genesi di una sacra rappresentazione abruzzese* (L'Aquila: DASP, 1983), p. 9.

Sandro Sticca

68 Mario Bonfantini, 'Sacra rappresentazione', *Enciclopedia dello Spettacolo*, vol. VIII (Rome: Editrice Le Maschere, 1961), p. 1370; Faccioli, *397*, p. xxv.

69 See Ghilardi (*392*, p. 132), D'Amico (*11*, pp. 227–31), Apollonio (*391*, vol. I, p. 196) and Philippe Van Thieghem, *Histoire du théâtre italien* (Paris: Presses Universitaires de France, 1965), pp. 10–11.

70 Molinari, *Spettacoli fiorentini*, p. 12.

71 Rossi, *Il Quattrocento*, p. 292; De Bartholomaeis, *Origini della poesia drammatica italiana*, pp. 255–73; Bonfantini, 'Sacra Rappresentazione', p. 1370.

72 See Mario Fabbri, Elvira Garbero Zorzi and Anna Maria Petrioli Tofani, eds., *Il luogo teatrale a Firenze* (Milan: Electa Editrice, 1975), pp. 13–15, and Achille Tartaro, *Il primo Quattrocento toscano* (Bari: Laterza, 1981), p. 110.

73 Also Fabbri *et al.*, *Il luogo teatrale*, pp. 13–14. On Florentine theatre for the period 1280–1500, see Richard Trexler in *401*, pp. 454–73.

74 Nerida Newbigin, ed., *Nuovo corpus di sacre rappresentazioni fiorentine del Quattrocento* (Bologna: Commissione per i Testi di Lingua, 1983), p. L.

75 *Passione di Cristo. Sacra Rappresentazione*, ed. Carlo Varischi (Milan: Edizioni Centro Studi Cappuccini Lombardi, 1976).

76 De Bartholomaeis, *Origini della poesia drammatica*, pp. 289–351; Bonfantini, 'Sacra Rappresentazione', p. 1373.

77 Tortoreto, *Genesi di una sacra rappresentazione abruzzese*, p. 49; De Bartholomaeis, *Origini della poesia drammatica*, p. 290.

78 Vincenzo De Bartholomaeis, *Il teatro abruzzese nel Medio Evo* (Bologna: Arnaldo Forni Editore, 1924; repr. 1979).

79 Bonfantini, 'Sacra Rappresentazione', p. 1373; D'Amico, p. 227; Doglio, *Teatro in Europa*, vol. I, pp. 459–60; see also the pioneering work of Marco Vattaso, *Per la storia del dramma sacro in Italia* (Rome: Tipografia Vaticana, 1903), pp. 72–4.

80 Turin: Tipografia Vincenzo Bona, 1935.

81 Dino Bigongiari, 'Were There Theaters in the Twelfth and Thirteenth Centuries?', *Romanic Review* 37 (1946): 201–24.

82 Carlo Alberto Dorigo, *Studi di storia del teatro* (Malta: University's Italian and Modern Languages Department, 1968); Cesare Molinari, *Theatre Through the Ages*, trans. Colin Hamer (New York: McGraw-Hill, 1975).

83 Molinari, *Spettacoli fiorentini*; Newbigin, *Nuovo corpus*.

84 Eugenio Battisti, 'A caccia del gesto teatrale', in *Il teatro italiano del Rinascimento*, ed. Maristella de Panizza Lorch (Milan: Edizioni di Comunità, 1980), pp. 403–23.

85 Doglio, *Teatro in Europa*, vol. I, pp. 492–534.

86 Franco Cardini, 'Lo spettacolo medievale come fonte storico-antropologica', *Schede Medievali* 6–7 (1984): 19–24.

Spain: Catalan and Castilian drama

RONALD E. SURTZ

Modern Spain is divided linguistically between two Romance languages: Castilian and Catalan. (The linguistic enclaves now known as the Basque Country and Galicia acquired literary importance only in the last century and are not relevant to our present concerns.) The union of the royal houses of Castile and Aragon brought about by the marriage of Isabella of Castile and Ferdinand of Aragon in the late fifteenth century joined in confederation two regions that differed as much in cultural and historical development as they did in language. More intimately engaged in the Reconquest against the Moors, Castile had long remained a frontier society of warriors and settlers whose economy was based on sheep-farming. In contrast, the Catalan-speaking Crown of Aragon (a federation of Aragon, Catalonia and Valencia) developed a mercantile society with a powerful bourgeoisie and a Mediter-ranean empire.

Despite the geographic proximity of Castile and Catalonia, drama devel-oped independently and at different paces in the two regions. Catalonia had profound cultural ties to southern France, and the development of its dramatic tradition paralleled that of northern Europe. From the eleventh century on, the cathedrals of Catalonia were important centres for drama that was distinguished for both its variety and its innovative character. Castile, on the other hand, appears to have had but isolated instances of dramatic activity until the latter half of the fifteenth century, when drama began to flourish. As if to compensate for the relative scarcity of theatre in medieval Castile, Golden Age Spain's cult of the medieval manifested itself in the spectacular *autos sacramentales*. The *autos* reach their artistic apogee in the seventeenth century, but remain essentially 'medieval' in their use of pageant wagons and simultaneous staging.

CATALAN DRAMA

The Catalan theatre is of potential interest to students of other literatures for two reasons. First, it appears that the Catalan dramatic tradition was inno-vative in its precocious and sometimes unique treatment of several themes. A fourteenth-century play from Santa Maria de l'Estany is the only surviving Latin liturgical drama to dramatise the Assumption. The twelfth-century Vich Easter play is apparently the first to include the merchant scene. A

late-fourteenth-century play from Tarragona appears to be the earliest vernacular Assumption drama. Second, the Catalan tradition is noteworthy for
its conservatism and longevity. Sixteenth-century religious plays were still
largely sung in the manner of the Latin liturgical drama. The practice of
performing Easter plays survived well into the nineteenth century. Finally,
the Elche Assumption play, which is still performed today, maintains more
or less intact its medieval theatrical practices.

Surveys and general studies

The current state of research on the medieval Catalan vernacular theatre is
most cogently examined in two articles by Pere Bohigas. The first, 'Lo que
hoy sabemos del antiguo teatro catalán' (454), surveys the extant texts and
explores the survival of the medieval theatre in the sixteenth to nineteenth
centuries. The second, 'Més notes sobre textos de teatre català medieval'
(458), discusses linguistic aspects of the extant plays and their relevance to
questions of dating.

Bohigas' articles may be complemented with three studies which, while
focussing on the survival of the medieval Catalan theatre in later centuries,
contain data on earlier periods as well. Massot i Muntaner (446) studies
ecclesiastical prohibitions and other evidence for the performance of plays in
Mallorca and the mainland. In an appendix he includes a number of previously unknown texts of the prophecy of the Sibyl as well as a fragment of
the *Fet de la Sibilla i l'enperador*, a dramatisation in the vernacular of the
legend of the Araceli. Romeu i Figueras (447) surveys the extant Catalan
Passion plays, which range from the thirteenth to the eighteenth centuries.
Llompart (457) studies the evolution of the paraliturgical ceremony of the
Deposition from its origins in the vernacular in the late fourteenth century
through the change to Latin at the end of the seventeenth century to its
modern form as a pantomime without spoken text.

The corresponding chapters in Riquer's *Història de la literatura catalana*
(460) constitute a general overview of the vernacular Catalan theatre. In the
first volume of the *Història del teatro en España* edited by Díez Borque (461)
I provide a brief introduction to the medieval Catalan theatre. Shergold
(450) discusses the staging of vernacular plays. Fuster (456) considers the
medieval and Renaissance Valencian theatre from the viewpoint of the effects
of the irruption of Castilian into sixteenth-century Valencia and the conco-
mitant displacement of Catalan as a literary language. If the popular Corpus
Christi *autos* continued to be written and performed almost exclusively in
Catalan, the cultural Castilianisation of the upper classes ensured that Castilian would become the language of court plays and of those performed by
travelling theatrical troupes.

Donovan's 1958 monograph (445) is still the indispensable point of departure for the study of the medieval Catalan liturgical drama. Concentrating on
Vich, the Seo de Urgel, Gerona, Mallorca and Valencia, Donovan surveys the

extant manuscript sources and transcribes the pertinent texts. The dramatisation of the hymn, *Victimae Paschalis Laudes*, on Easter Tuesday morning during Mass in the fourteenth and fifteenth centuries in the cathedral of Palma de Mallorca provides a notable example of the often innovative character of the liturgical drama in medieval Catalonia. After the Epistle, a priest impersonating Mary Magdalene entered, began to sing the *Victimae*, and was answered by the choir. At the verse 'Dic nobis, Maria', Mary Magdalene got up on a small stool, and in the dramatic dialogue that followed she responded to the questions of twelve priests and at the appropriate moment displayed certain emblems of the Passion to the congregation. This dramatic dialogue was sung in Catalan, and Donovan (*445*, p. 132) comments on the striking use of the vernacular during Mass itself. At some point in her song, the Magdalene must have mentioned resurrected corpses, for a number of altar boys would roll out from under the altar as if rising from the dead. The play ended with the spectacular appearance of an angel, who entered dramatically from the darkness of the gallery above the chapel of St Gabriel, his wings glowing with lighted candles.

In his 'Two Celebrated Centers of Medieval Liturgical Drama: Fleury and Ripoll' (*33*) Donovan turns once again to the Vich Easter play. Previously (*445*), in seeking the causes for the relative scarcity of liturgical drama in medieval Castile, he had suggested that whenever religious plays began to be introduced on a large scale, they were already in the vernacular. His 1970 study (*33*) provides additional support for the hypothesis of the early composition of vernacular plays in the peninsula. Commenting upon the uniqueness of the merchant scene in the twelfth-century Vich Easter play and upon early sculptured representations of the scene, Donovan suggests that both the Latin liturgical play and the sculptures could have been inspired by analogous episodes in Easter plays that were already being written and performed in the vernacular.

The scrutiny of archival sources, mostly account books, from the fourteenth to the nineteenth centuries, has helped to shed light on dramatic activity in Barcelona (Llompart [*449*]), Gerona (Vila and Bruget [*463*]), Lérida (Rubio García [*455*]), Mallorca (Llompart [*449, 452* and *459*]), Tarragona (Tomás Avila [*448*]), Villarreal (Doñate Sebastiá [*451*]) and Saragossa (Llompart [*452*]). Such sources provide detailed information on Christmas, Easter and Corpus Christi festivities. Typical of the many research problems posed by this body of data is the phenomenon of the participation of Jews in the representation of the Passion on Good Friday at Villarreal in 1376, 1380, 1413 and 1418 (Doñate Sebastiá [*451*] and Romano [*453*]). The Jews were habitually rewarded with wine for their performance, and expense accounts for 1376 indicate that they wore masks, but it is not known exactly what role they played.

Assumption plays

The medieval and Renaissance Catalan Assumption plays (Tarragona [fourteenth century], Valencia [fifteenth century], Elche [probably second half of the fifteenth century]), stand apart from other vernacular plays because of the pervasive presence of music in their performance. If vernacular plays normally make but incidental use of song, the pre-eminent role of music in the Catalan Assumption plays underscores their kinship with the Latin liturgical drama. The Elche play even today is entirely sung without any recited passages, while the Valencia and Tarragona plays alternated recitation and singing. Stage directions in both plays indicate that the sung passages are to be accommodated to pre-existing melodies; the melodies are liturgical hymns in the case of the Tarragona play and secular songs in the Valencia play. The Tarragona Assumption play makes artistic use of said melodies to characterise its protagonists and antagonists. The latter (the Jews and devils) never sing; they only recite. Furthermore, recurring melodies are used to link one scene to a later one. The melody of the hymn *Veni Creator* is used in the scene in which the Virgin expresses her desire to die so that she can be reunited with her Son. The same music reappears when the angels announce the Virgin's imminent death, when Christ descends to receive His mother's soul, and when Christ descends once again to return the Virgin's soul to her body. The same melody thus links the episode in which the Virgin longs for death to the scene in which that desire is fulfilled. Furthermore, the repetition of the hymn tune in Christ's two descents reinforces the theological point of the Virgin's Assumption in both body and soul.

All three Assumption plays are ultimately based on the apocryphal Gospels via Voragine's *Golden Legend*, but each play highlights different themes or episodes of that traditional material. The Tarragona play emphasises the episode in which the Jews conspire to steal and then burn the Virgin's body. There is also a parallel comic episode in which devils meet in Hell to decide which of them shall seize the Virgin. Eventually the devil Mascarón undertakes the task, only to be driven away from the Virgin's house by Christ Himself, who strikes the unfortunate devil with the Cross. Soberanas i Lleó is preparing a critical edition of the Tarragona Assumption play.

The fifteenth-century Valencia play contains a scene in which St Michael returns the soul to the body of the Virgin, who is then resurrected. This resurrection episode accentuates one of the distinguishing features of the play, namely, its highlighting of the parallel between the death, 'resurrection' and Assumption of the Virgin and the death, Resurrection and Ascension of Christ. Sanchis Guarner's study and re-edition (*464*) of the play corrects the obvious errors in Ruiz de Lahory's 1903 palaeographic transcription. Although the original manuscript contained only the role of the Virgin Mary, it is nonetheless possible to get a reasonably good idea of what the play was like because the codex included detailed stage directions and indicated the first lines of the other characters.

The *Misteri d'Elx*, which is still performed today, conserves its essentially medieval staging practices, but despite its inherent interest, the play has not received the scholarly attention it deserves. Albet and Alier (*465*), the authors of a critical bibliography of the *Misteri*, frankly admit that the majority of their numerous entries are of dubious value to the modern scholar. Lázaro Carreter's 'Sobre el *Misteri* de Elche' (*466*) surveys the play's sources and analogues, observing that the work abandons fidelity to sacred history and legend for the notion of theatre as spectacle. Calling attention to the fact that the earliest surviving manuscript dates from the seventeenth century, Lázaro Carreter cautions that the extant texts, while possibly derived from a medieval archetype, are nonetheless a product of the seventeenth century.

The Folger Shakespeare Library has produced a film of the Elche play. Jesús-Francesc Massip has published a critical edition (*469*) of the 1709 *Consueta* (*ordinarium* or ceremonial) of the *Misteri*. His introduction discusses the play's dating (probably to the second half of the fifteenth century), authorship, versification, manuscripts and previous editions. In a separate volume María Carmen Gómez i Muntané has edited the music to which the play is sung, supplying critical notes and a brief introduction. The third volume contains a facsimile edition of the manuscript.

Two recent studies consider the entire corpus of Catalan Assumption drama. Focussing on the questions of staging and the handling of source materials, Romeu i Figueras (*468*) attempts to delineate the salient traits that give each play its particular physiognomy. His study also discusses a late-fifteenth-century Assumption play from Lérida, whose text is no longer extant, but which can be reconstructed from the cathedral account books. Massip's book (*467*) on the Assumption plays foregrounds the notion of medieval drama as spectacle, emphasising the staging of the plays and their symbolic use of space. In a trope from the monastery of Santa Maria de l'Estany, the choir symbolises the Earth and the altar represents Paradise. It appears that the Tarragona play was originally conceived for performance inside the cathedral. From the late fourteenth century on, however, it was staged in a public square in a place-and-scaffold setting that ranged from Hell in the west to Earth in the middle to Heaven in the east. The audience was located to the north and south. The Valencia and Elche plays were performed inside a church and used both horizontal and vertical staging, corresponding to the spaces of Earth and Heaven respectively. Machines were used to raise and lower images representing the soul of the Virgin, the Virgin herself, Christ and an angel.

Non-Assumption plays

An important collection of Catalan plays is the so-called Llabrés manuscript (MS 1139 of the Biblioteca de Catalunya), which contains the texts of forty-nine works performed in the churches of Mallorca in the sixteenth century. Although a few individual plays had been made available in less than satisfactory editions, it was not until 1957, when Romeu i Figueras published his *Teatre hagiogràfic* in three volumes (*470*), that a representative selection of the Mallorcan texts could be studied seriously in reliable editions. Romeu edits eight Mallorcan saint plays (about St Francis, St George [two], St Christopher [two], Sts Crispin and Crispinian, St Peter and St Paul) to which he adds farced Epistles of St Stephen and St John the Evangelist, a Boy Bishop sermon, the Valencian St Christopher play and two incomplete plays from the town of Sant Joan de les Abadesses (St Agatha and St Eudaldus). His introduction discusses each individual play, addressing questions of sources, style, versification, language, staging and use of music.

Romeu set the pattern for the publication of the sixteenth-century Catalan drama in volumes that group the plays by theme. His edition of the hagiographic plays was followed by Huerta i Viñas' *Teatre bíblic: Antic Testament* (*472*), which brings together the seven extant Old Testament plays: the Valencian *Misteri d'Adam i Eva* performed during the Corpus Christi procession and six plays performed in the cathedral of Mallorca (on the Sacrifice of Isaac, Joseph and his Brothers, Tobias, Judith, King Ahasuerus and Susannah). The editor provides a substantial introductory essay in which each work is analysed individually. Of particular interest is the fact that while all the plays alternate recited and sung sections, the proportion of sung texts is particularly high in the Mallorcan plays, which for the most part appropriate the melodies of liturgical chants.

Huerta i Viñas, in collaboration with Cenoz i del Aguila, has in press a volume of *Teatre de Nadal* which contains these extant Catalan Christmas plays: two Sibyl plays, a shepherds play, the Valencian Herod play and seven Mallorcan texts (four shepherds plays, a prophets play and two Three Kings plays). Cenoz and Huerta i Viñas also plan to edit the series of New Testament plays. They have already published (*477*) the Mallorcan play based on the story of the Prodigal Son and a Resurrection of Lazarus play, also from the Llabrés manuscript.

Cornagliotti (*474*) has published a reliable edition of the fourteenth-century Catalan Easter play from Vich. The text is neither a translation nor an adaptation of the Latin liturgical play performed at Vich in the twelfth century; it is an independent dramatisation of sacred history that freely re-creates the biblical narrative while exploiting the expressive possibilities of the vernacular.

In 1915 Agustí Duran i Sanpere published part of a Passion cycle that had been performed at Cervera in the period 1534–45. The fragment corresponded to the Good Friday and Holy Saturday performances: the Passion properly speaking, the Descent into Hell, the laments of St John and Mary Magdalene and the Descent from the Cross. Duran i Sanpere later discovered the texts of two other plays from the same cycle (the Entry into Jerusalem and the Trial of Christ) performed on Palm Sunday. Before his death in 1975 Duran i Sanpere prepared for publication the newly discovered parts and a more careful edition of the rest of the cycle; unfortunately, the revised text could not be found among the papers he left behind. For that reason, Eulàlia Duran's recent edition (*476*) of the extant parts of the cycle is based on her father's 1915 transcriptions and on the original manuscripts. She also includes an introductory essay that her father had written in which he discusses the play's dating, authorship and sources.

In 1957–8 Romeu i Figueras published his study and edition of the *Representació de la Mort* (*471*), a dramatised dance of death from Mallorca. In a more recent study Romeu (*473*) attributes the play to Francesc d'Olesa (c. 1485–1550). Massot i Muntaner (*475*) seconds his predecessor's attribution and provides textual notes and emendations to Romeu's edition.

Massot i Muntaner's *Teatre medieval i del Renaixement* (*462*) is a convenient anthology of texts, some of them in modernised versions and with regularised orthography. The volume contains a Christmas play (*Consueta per la nit de Nadal*), sections of the Cervera Passion play, a hagiographic play (*Consueta del misteri de la gloriosa Santa Agata*), a dramatised dance of death (the *Representació de la Mort* attributed to Francesc d'Olesa), the 1639 text of the *Misteri d'Elx*, Timoneda's *L'Església militant* and Fernández de Heredia's *La vesita*. There is a brief introduction for each text, but no notes or glossary.

Final considerations

The most urgent task for students of the Catalan theatre, but one whose completion is relatively certain, is the publication of the remaining unedited plays. To be sure, substantive introductory studies have accompanied the works published to date. But when the entire corpus of extant plays is available, scholars will be better able to essay new critical approaches and to undertake comparative studies that will result in a more nuanced evaluation of the Catalan theatre's place in the history of the European drama.

CASTILIAN DRAMA

The origins question

While the medieval Catalan theatre can boast of a continuous tradition from the Middle Ages through the eighteenth and nineteenth centuries even to the present, critics were hard-pressed to explain the apparent lacuna in the Castilian theatre between the twelfth-century *Auto de los Reyes Magos* and Gómez Manrique (c. 1412–1490). One solution was to assume that Castile must have had a flourishing dramatic tradition analogous to that of France, Italy and England, a tradition whose textual evidence had been all but lost. Or, faced with this dearth of texts, critics chose to consider as theatre anything that could remotely be considered 'dramatic' (the *Danza de la muerte*, dialogue poems etc.). The recognition of Castile's cultural differentiation from the rest of Europe has made it unnecessary and even unwise to postulate a medieval dramatic tradition paralleling that of the rest of Europe. A more critical and discriminating concept of what constitutes theatre as well as the discovery of new texts and documentary evidence of the performance

Ronald E. Surtz

of plays have given us a better idea of the extent to which theatre was present in medieval Castile.

Donovan's study (*445*) of the liturgical drama in Spain documents conclusively the limited penetration of Latin plays in medieval Castile. His examination of more than 315 manuscripts and early printed books of the kind that in other countries would typically contain liturgical plays revealed only a handful of texts. Moreover, the majority of those texts turned out to be isolated borrowings from abroad or belonging to the sixteenth century. Donovan attributes this scarcity of plays to several factors. First, the Mozarabic rite, which was unacquainted with the practice of composing tropes and apparently with the liturgical drama as well, was used in Castile until the eleventh century. Second, when the Roman-French rite was introduced into Castile, the reforming monks to whom the task was entrusted were either Cluniacs or influenced by Cluniac ideas. Yet no evidence of liturgical drama has been found at Cluny. Donovan suggests a third reason, namely, that the change in rite coincided with the rise of vernacular literature and that plays were already being composed in Castilian. (Nonetheless, in other countries vernacular plays did not drive out Latin plays: the two traditions coexisted.)

Without doubt in reaction to the school of thought that would postulate a lost dramatic tradition, López Morales (*480*) denies the existence of a Castilian theatre before Gómez Manrique. Such a 'doubting Thomas' approach to the lack of texts reflects a narrow concept of theatre as text in opposition to theatre as performance. López Morales draws heavily on Donovan's study of the liturgical drama in medieval Spain to support his hypothesis. To be sure, the relatively few texts that Donovan discovered seemed adequate proof of the extremely limited penetration of Latin liturgical drama in medieval Castile. But López Morales' use of Donovan's study is selective: he rejects Donovan's hypothesis that the Latin liturgical drama did not flourish because theatre was already being composed and performed in the vernacular. It is precisely this intransigence on the part of López Morales which has been considered the major flaw in an otherwise illuminating and pioneering study.

In *The Birth of a Theater* (*486*) I argue that even if theatre was at best a sporadic phenomenon in late-medieval Castile, playwrights of the generation of Encina (1468–1529/30) and Fernández (1474–1542) had at their disposal two important models of theatre: the sacred drama of the Mass and the court entertainment. In response to Donovan's conclusions regarding the scarcity of Latin liturgical plays in medieval Castile, García de la Concha (*489*) has argued that certain local liturgical practices are actually dramatisations of the liturgy and as such bespeak a more widespread diffusion of liturgical drama in Castile than the sporadic cases cited by Donovan. Of significance for the study of the traditions upon which Encina and Fernández drew is García de la Concha's conclusion that the early-sixteenth-century playwrights incorporated elements of such liturgical practices into their Passion plays.

The discovery of previously unknown dramatic texts has helped to illuminate the question of the origins of the Castilian theatre. López Yepes (*510*) has published what he calls a *Representación de las sibilas (Ordo Sibillarum)* from a late-fourteenth- or early-fifteenth-century manuscript found in the cathedral of Córdoba. The brief text (twenty-eight lines) consists of the prophecies of ten Sibyls, in Castilian or Latin or a mixture of both. López Yepes views the text as a calque of the *Ordo Prophetarum* with Sibyls replacing the traditional prophets. He also relates the playlet to the ceremony performed at Christmastime in many peninsular churches in which a single personified Sibyl sang verses that combined the prophecy of Christ's birth with that of the Last Judgement. More recently, however, Feliciano Delgado ('Las profecías de sibilas en el ms. 80 de la Catedral de Córdoba y los orígenes del teatro nacional', *Revista de Filología Española* 67 [1987]: 77–87) has argued that the text in question is not a play but a scholastic exercise penned by a student at Salamanca, who attempts to translate the sibylline prophecies from a book by Philippus de Barberiis that was published in 1481.

Torroja Menéndez and Rivas Palá (*511*) have investigated the cathedral account books from fifteenth-century Toledo and revealed a previously unsuspected tradition of dramatic activity. The most elaborate spectacles were reserved for Corpus Christi, which was celebrated with a procession as early as 1418. Accounts for the year 1465 speak of some sort of representation, and by 1476 plays were being performed on pageant wagons as part of the procession. The plays were non-cyclic and were based on a wide variety of themes: Adam and Eve, the Last Judgement, the Sacrifice of Abraham, the Assumption, St George and so on. The Toledo account books are to date the most significant source for the study of late-medieval Castilian stagecraft. Some plays used several carts to represent different settings. Special machines were employed to stage the Ascension or the apparition of an angel. The account books also give a good idea of the variety of costumes used in the performances. The angels wore white albs and wigs made of dyed hemp. St John the Baptist had a long tunic to which had been sewn sixty cow's tails. The devils were dressed in animal hides. The principal roles were acted by clerics or cantors associated with the cathedral, but minor roles were taken by laymen, such as the *espartero* (basket-maker or mat-maker) who played an executioner in the play based on the beheading of St John the Baptist.

Unfortunately, of the thirty-three different Corpus Christi plays performed in the period 1493–1510, no texts have been preserved, with the exception of the outline for a play based on the legend of St Sylvester and Constantine the Great. The lack of texts for the Corpus plays has been somewhat offset by the discovery of a Passion play attributed to Alonso del Campo, who was responsible for the Corpus festivities in the period 1481–99. Although the text is incomplete and but a rough draft, it does convey a good notion of what the finished play might have been like, with its juxtaposition of mimetic representation and lyrical lamentation. Of interest for the study of the relation between drama and religious poetry in the

Ronald E. Surtz

fifteenth century is the fact that nearly a quarter of the verses in Alonso del Campo's Passion play are borrowed from Diego de San Pedro's narrative poem, the *Pasión trobada*.

Similar investigations of archival materials from fifteenth-century Murcia (Rubio García [492]), Málaga (del Pino [482]) and Asturias (Menéndez Peláez [487], and García Valdés [491]) reveal a parallel situation, at least as regards the Corpus Christi festivities. Thus, we now know that the Corpus was celebrated with the performance of plays in Murcia since at least 1470, and in Málaga and Oviedo since 1498. (Málaga had only been reconquered from the Moors in 1487; the earliest extant account books from Oviedo come from 1498.) While such documentary evidence is often scanty or discontinuous, the development of the Corpus Christi festivities in other cities appears to have paralleled the case of Toledo: in the second half of the fifteenth century, both the procession and the plays become more and more elaborate. Thus, while our knowledge of drama in Castile before the sixteenth century is still incomplete, it is now evident that the new departure in the Castilian drama evinced by the court theatre of Encina and Fernández did not arise from a void, but rather against the background of a flourishing dramatic tradition, at least as regards the Corpus Christi plays.

Surveys and general studies

Students and specialists alike will have to await the publication of Charlotte Stern's *Taking Possession of the Stage: Church Drama in Medieval Castile* for an up-to-date monograph on the medieval Castilian theatre. Meanwhile, Làzaro Carreter's preliminary study to the third edition (497) of his anthology of medieval Castilian plays in modernised versions remains a useful introduction to the subject. Shergold (450) provides the most comprehensive study to date of Spanish stagecraft. In the collective *Historia del teatro en España*, edited by Díez Borque (490), I attempt to view the Spanish theatre as more than a collection of written texts and discuss such aspects of performance as authors, actors, acting style, staging and spectators. My study (494) of the place of the theatre in sixteenth-century notions of play as *eutrapelia* (virtuous recreation) provides a theoretical framework that is applicable to the late-medieval religious theatre.

Anthologies

A series of anthologies brings together a number of medieval and Renaissance plays in modern editions. I have edited (499), with slightly modernised orthography, six medieval texts: *Auto de los Reyes Magos*, Gómez Manrique's *Representación del Nasçimiento de Nuestro Señor* and *Lamentaciones*, Alonso del Campo's *Auto de la Pasión*, the *Auto de la huida a Egipto* and the *Diálogo del Viejo, el Amor y la hermosa*. The volume contains an introductory study, bibliography, glossary and brief textual and lexical notes. Lázaro

Spain

Carreter's collection of modernised versions (497) of medieval dramatic texts includes the *Representación de los Reyes Magos*, four works by Gómez Manrique (*Representación del Naçimiento de Nuestro Señor, Llanto por Nuestro Señor* and two mummings), Cota's *Diálogo entre el Amor y un Viejo*, Francisco de Madrid's *Egloga*, two *cancionero* dialogue poems and the *Auto de acusación contra el género humano* from the *Códice de autos viejos*. The substantial introduction addresses, among other questions, the problem of theatre in medieval Castile.

Sixteenth-century Christmas and Easter plays, each with its own brief presentation, are conveniently brought together in Moll's *Dramas litúrgicos del siglo XVI: Navidad y Pascua* (496). There is a glossary, but no notes. The volume contains Pero López Ranjel's *Farsa*, Pedro Suárez de Robles' *Danza del Santísimo Nacimiento*, Jaime Torres' *Lucha alegórica para la noche de la Natividad*, Pedro Altamirando's *La aparición que Nuestro Señor Jesucristo hizo a los dos discípulos, que iban a Emaús* and three plays from the *Códice de autos viejos* (*Auto de la huida a Egipto, Auto del descendimiento de la cruz* and *Auto de la Resurrección de Cristo*). The two-volume collection of *Autos, comedias y farsas de la Biblioteca Nacional* edited by García Morales (495) provides facsimile editions of twenty-seven rare plays. Finally, Arias' edition of *Autos sacramentales* (498) offers ten works from the sixteenth century: the *Farsa sacramental* of López de Yanguas, the anonymous *Farsa sacramental de 1521*, the *Farsa de la iglesia* of Sánchez de Badajoz, four anonymous plays (*Auto sacramental de los amores del alma con el príncipe de la luz, Farsa sacramental de la residencia del hombre, Aucto de los hierros de Adán* and *Farsa del sacramento del entendimiento niño*) and three plays by Timoneda (*Aucto de la oveja perdida, Aucto de la fuente de los siete sacramentos* and *Aucto de la fee*). Each text is annotated, but some are taken from previous editions that do not measure up to modern standards of textual criticism.

Poetry and theatre in the fifteenth century

In a series of articles Stern explores specific points of contact between poetry and drama. In 'Fray Iñigo de Mendoza and Medieval Dramatic Ritual' (478) she studies the influence of the *Vita Christi*'s pastoral episode on similar scenes in the early theatre, while in 'The *Coplas de Mingo Revulgo* and the Early Spanish Drama' (484) she turns her attention to the tradition of pastoral allegory. Finally, her 'The Genesis of the Spanish Pastoral: From Lyric to Drama' (485) shows how certain early plays are essentially an elaboration of pastoral lyrics.

A typical case of the close relationship between debate or dialogue poetry and the theatre is Rodrigo Cota's *Diálogo entre el Amor y un Viejo*, critically edited by Aragone (507). Aragone's introduction calls attention to the debate's dramatic features and hypothesises that it was intended for performance. In an appendix Aragone edits an anonymous reworking of Cota's dialogue, which was copied down under the heading 'Interlocutores senex et

Ronald E. Surtz

amor mulierque pulchra forma'. Now generally known by the Castilian title, *Diálogo del Viejo, el Amor y la hermosa*, the text was in all probability intended for performance.

Theatre and folklore

Studies of the relationship between drama and folklore have gone beyond the search for parallels and analogues to stress the vital links between the early theatre and ritual. Such an approach is a valuable antidote to the tendency to conceive of the theatre in terms of Aristotelean criteria or nineteenth-century realism, for if we are to appreciate duly the medieval drama, we must do so in terms of its own aesthetic basis. Charlotte Stern's studies are particularly illuminating in this respect because of their insistence on the alterity of the medieval theatre. Stern touches this question briefly in her 'Fray Iñigo de Mendoza and Medieval Dramatic Ritual' (*478*) and 'Some New Thoughts on the Early Spanish Drama' (*479*), and then develops it most cogently in 'The Early Spanish Drama: From Medieval Ritual to Renaissance Art' (*481*), which significantly focusses on the transition from ritual modes of theatre to the Renaissance notion of drama as illusion.

Inquisition and theatre

An unexpected factor to be considered in studying the development of the Spanish drama is the role played by the Inquisition. It is generally agreed that the inquisitorial indexes had a negative effect on the development of the sixteenth-century Castilian theatre. Nonetheless, the intervention of the Inquisition also had a positive consequence, at least as far as literary history is concerned, for inquisitorial records often provide documentary evidence of theatrical practices or preserve texts that might otherwise have been lost. Flecniakoska's study (*483*) of inquisitorial archives supplies additional proof of widespread theatrical activity in rural sixteenth-century Castile as well as information on the nature of such performances. The parts were written out separately to make acting copies for each individual player. The actors were all amateurs, and men played the female roles. The authors were similarly amateurs: the town surgeon composed a play performed at Orihuela in 1558 in which the Virtues battled the Vices. There was doubling of the roles, and the actors charged admission.

The 'Auto de los Reyes Magos'

The twelfth-century Epiphany play, the *Auto de los Reyes Magos*, has finally begun to be appreciated for its high literary merits. The play is notable for its independence from the liturgical tradition and is unique in its dramatic use of scepticism (the Kings' gifts are offered as a test of Christ's identity). Menéndez Pidal's pioneering edition has been reprinted in Volume XII of his

Spain

collected works (502). Stebbins (504) offers his own edition of the Castilian text with facing English translation, textual notes and glossary. As the original manuscript does not indicate the distribution of dialogue among the various speakers, Senabre (503) proposes a new division of the text based on the criterion of a greater consistency in the characterisation of the Three Kings.

Studies of the *Auto* were for a long time limited to questions of vocabulary, versification and sources, but then in 1955 Wardropper (500) published his brief but perceptive appreciation of the text as a piece of literature. Hook and Deyermond (505) question the prevailing view that the *Auto* is incomplete, arguing that the play's abrupt ending is artistically satisfying. They also discuss the *Auto*'s use of figural interpretation, disagreeing on some points with Foster's 1967 study (501). Lapesa's latest essay (506) reviews the varying opinions regarding the nationality of the play's author. Lapesa reiterates his thesis that the author, most probably from Gascony, was one of the many French clerics who monopolised the ecclesiastical posts of twelfth-century Toledo.

Late fifteenth-century drama

López Estrada has published a critical edition of Gómez Manrique's Christmas play, the *Representación del Naçimiento de Nuestro Señor* (514). The work is noteworthy for its juxtaposition of the Nativity and the Passion: angels present the instruments of the Passion to the Child Jesus. López Estrada bases his edition on two manuscript collections of Gómez Manrique's poetic works and makes a series of pertinent observations on the ways in which the scribal conventions of *cancionero* poetry are applied to the copying of a play. In a complementary article López Estrada (515) analyses the play as theatre, addressing such matters as the stage directions, actors, audience and place of performance. Special emphasis is given to the author's innovative treatment of the Nativity theme. Sieber (508) discusses the play's symmetries and contrasts from both a structural and a thematic viewpoint. While occasionally forced, his study is nonetheless one of the first to consider the play from an aesthetic perspective. Zimic (512) studies both the *Representación* and Manrique's *Lamentaciones fechas para Semana Santa* (a *planctus Mariae* in which St John is also present). If his interpretation of the Christmas play as a vision sent to St Joseph is unconvincing, his comments on the dramatic quality of what is possibly an Easter play help support his thesis that the text was intended for performance.

Amícola (509) has re-edited the anonymous *Auto de la huida a Egipto*, a play notable for its juxtaposition of the themes of the Flight into Egypt with the penitence of John the Baptist in the wilderness. The non-biblical character known only as the Pilgrim links the two plots and serves as the dramatic double of the spectators. In his introduction Amícola rejects the attribution to Gómez Manrique and observes that the notable differences between the

Ronald E. Surtz

Auto and the plays of Encina and his followers suggest the coexistence of two parallel dramatic traditions in late-medieval Castile. I come to a similar conclusion in my study of plays closely associated with convents of Franciscan nuns (*493*), among which plays are both Gómez Manrique's Nativity play and the *Auto de la huida a Egipto*. Blecua's edition (*513*) of the *Egloga* (1495?) of Francisco de Madrid corrects numerous errors in previous transcriptions. The play is a pastoral allegory that attempts to justify Ferdinand the Catholic's intervention in the Italian wars. Blecua's critical introduction goes beyond the study of the play's historical background to consider its literary antecedents and the ways in which motifs of varied provenance are combined to form a sort of anti-war play.

The popular religious theatre of the sixteenth century

The late-fifteenth- and early-sixteenth-century court theatre of Juan del Encina, Lucas Fernández, Gil Vicente (who wrote in both Portuguese and Castilian for the Portuguese royal court) and Bartolomé de Torres Naharro signifies a new departure in the development of the Castilian drama. But the popular religious theatre of the Middle Ages does not die out with the advent of the new forms. Oleza Simó (*488*) views the sixteenth-century Spanish drama in terms of a dialectic among three different dramatic practices: a popular theatre, originally grounded in religious drama, but which eventually gives rise to the first professional theatrical troupes; a court theatre written for a social elite and reflecting its values; and a learned theatre composed by Spain's intellectual minority. The popular religious drama flourishes in the sixteenth century (most notably in the little-studied *Códice de autos viejos*) and undergoes a final transformation in the seventeenth century in the artistically elaborate *autos sacramentales*.

Several studies consider the popular religious theatre of the sixteenth century in connection with the development of the *auto sacramental*. Wardropper (*521*) provides a historical survey of the evolution of the Corpus Christi play. Flecniakoska (*516*) discusses the staging of the *autos*, their debt to religious poetry and to the Jesuit theatre, their structure, principal themes and use of allegory. His observations are grounded in an extensive corpus of texts that includes many manuscript plays. Both Gewecke (*526*) and Fothergill-Payne (*529*) attempt to analyse and categorise systematically that same group of texts. Gewecke is especially useful on the ways in which the *autos* use biblical and Patristic texts. Fothergill-Payne sees the Battle and the Quest as the two basic patterns that underlie the *autos sacramentales*. Finally, Arias (*533*) provides in English an overview of the Corpus Christi plays from the early sixteenth century to the post-Calderón epoch.

González Ollé (*522*) has re-edited the anonymous *Farsa sacramental* of 1521, supplying textual and critical notes and an introduction which situates the play in the context of the development of the *auto sacramental*. In this Corpus Christi play Faith explains to three shepherds the meaning of the

Eucharist. I have published Juan Pastor's *Aucto nuevo del santo Nacimiento de Christo Nuestro Señor* of 1528 from the 1603 imprint (*535*). Pastor dramatises episodes of the Nativity that Encina and Fernández would narrate, with the result that the sacred event becomes the core of the play, and the antics of the rustics remain a subplot until the final scene (the Adoration of the Shepherds) in which both plots converge.

The extant plays of Fernán López de Yanguas, published separately by various scholars at the beginning of this century, are now conveniently brought together in González Ollé's careful edition (*520*). The works include a Christmas play (*Egloga de la Natividad*), a morality play that turns into an Assumption play (*Farsa del mundo y moral*), a festival piece (*Farsa de la Concordia*) celebrating the Peace of Cambray (1529) and fragments of a Corpus Christi play (*Farsa sacramental*). In his introduction González Ollé discusses each individual work as well as more general problems of language, style and so forth.

The *Recopilación en metro* (1554) of Diego Sánchez de Badajoz contains twenty-seven plays based on a wide variety of themes (the Old Testament, the New Testament, hagiographic narratives etc.). The *Recopilación* has finally been carefully edited by a team of scholars under the direction of Weber de Kurlat (*523*). Unfortunately, her otherwise exemplary edition contains notes relating only to textual questions and is thus of limited value in solving the multiple linguistic problems presented by Sánchez de Badajoz. That shortcoming is partially remedied by Díez Borque's edition (*531*) of five plays (*Farsa theologal, Farsa de la Natividad, Farsa de Salomón, Farsa del colmenero* and *Farsa militar*) and Pérez Priego's edition (*539*) of seven plays (*Farsa theologal, Farsa racional del Libre Alvedrío, Farsa de Ysaac, Farsa del molinero, Farsa de Abraham, Farsa de la muerte* and *Farsa del juego de cañas*). Both volumes have substantial introductions and copious annotations. Pérez Priego's book (*536*) on the theatre of Diego Sánchez de Badajoz emphasises the ways in which the playwright's essentially didactic orientation is balanced with festive laughter. Although he stresses the doctrinal content of the plays, Pérez Priego also considers such questions as their structure, characters and staging.

Sebastián de Horozco was active in the mid-sixteenth century as the author of four dramatic works: a play on the parable of the Labourers in the Vineyard, a comic skit composed for performance in a convent on the feast of St John the Evangelist, a play on the curing of the blind man (John 9) and an incomplete version of the story of Ruth and Naomi. The plays have received three modern editions. Weiner edits Horozco's entire *Cancionero* (*528*), thereby presenting the plays in the context in which they have been preserved. The editor's brief introduction discusses Horozco's misogynist stance and the probable *converso* status of his family. According to Weiner, the plays present a positive image of the *cristiano nuevo* and constitute a plea for tolerance. The textual notes are adequate. Mazur's edition of the plays (*530*) reproduces the orthography of the extant manuscript and contains an

Ronald E. Surtz

introduction in which he discusses characterisation, versification and language, but his remarks on the plays amount to little more than plot summaries. Finally, González Ollé's 1979 edition (*532*) comments at length on the plays with regard to their versification and re-creation of source materials. Vitse's review article (*534*) on this edition attempts to situate Horozco's theatre in the context of the contemporary debate on mendicancy and social welfare.

The so-called *Códice de autos viejos* (Biblioteca Nacional, Madrid, MS 14711) contains ninety-six texts (Old Testament, New Testament, hagiographic, Corpus Christi and Marian plays) in Castilian, which are usually ascribed to the period 1550–75. Although the plays in the collection are discussed by Flecniakoska (*516*) and Fothergill-Payne (*529*), they have otherwise received scant critical attention. Flecniakoska (*517*) analyses the disguises and dramatic function of the devil, while Rodríguez-Puértolas (*524*) discusses topical allusions and the ways in which certain plays reflect the social preoccupations of sixteenth-century Spain. Ferrer Valls (*538*) addresses briefly the problems posed by the manuscript and then discusses in some detail the only play in the collection whose author is mentioned, the *Auto de Caín y Abel* of Jaime Ferruz (1503/4–1594). Ferrer Valls sees Ferruz, a humanist and a participant in the discussions of the Council of Trent, as attempting to create a new kind of learned theatre that would serve to disseminate Counter-Reformation doctrine. This handful of studies scarcely begins to address the cultural, historical and linguistic problems presented by the *Códice de autos viejos*. Highly desirable is the publication of Mercedes de los Reyes Peña's doctoral dissertation ('El *Códice de Autos Viejos*: un estudio de historia literaria', University of Seville, 1983), in which she provides a study and re-edition of the entire manuscript.

My 1982 study (*537*) demonstrates the relationship between a sixteenth-century Castilian Assumption play from the Franciscan convent of Santa María de la Cruz and a sermon delivered by the Castilian mystic, Mother Juana de la Cruz (1481–1534), during one of her trances. The play is unusual because it juxtaposes the theme of the Fall of Lucifer with the Assumption in order to demonstrate the Immaculate Conception of the Virgin. I have published both the corresponding fragment of the sermon and a more accurate transcription of the play than has been previously available. The sermon, which appears in a manuscript dated 1509, provides both a *terminus a quo* for the composition of the play and auxiliary information about its staging. Children and young men are to play the roles of the angels, while the handsomest young man available is to play the role of the Virgin. The battle between the good and bad angels is to take place in total darkness. The sermon also indicates that certain passages that are transcribed in the extant text of the play as spoken dialogue were originally intended to be sung.

Ferrario de Orduna (*525*) has published Bartolomé Aparicio's *Obra del pecador* from the 1611 edition. (The first printed edition, now lost, is thought to date from around 1560.) In this Christmas play, the Sinner is accused by

Justice, but defended by Mercy. Solace and Hope announce the Birth of Christ. Since the Sinner's salvation is now assured, he joins the biblical shepherds in the adoration scene that ends the play. Ferrario de Orduna's complementary study (*527*) addresses questions of language, theme and so on.

The plays of Juan López de Ubeda can now be read in Volume II of Rodríguez-Moñino's edition (*518*) of the author's *Cancionero general de la doctrina cristiana* (1579). The dramatic works include: *Comedia de San Alexo* (written in collaboration with Cornejo de Rojas), *Comedia de virtudes contra los vicios* and *Auto de la Esposa en los Cantares*. Unfortunately, the editor's brief introduction addresses only bibliographical questions, and the texts have no notes.

Dexeus de Moll (*519*) has edited five plays by the Mercedarian friar Jaime Torres based on the only extant printed copy of the author's works (1579). Three of the plays were composed for performance at Christmas: *Lucha alegórica para la noche de la Navidad de Cristo* in which the sibyl Eritrea interprets the wrestling match between two of the Nativity shepherds as an allegory of the Redemption; *Juego de la argolla para la noche de Navidad* in which Memory, Intellect and Will engage in an allegorical game and then worship the new-born Child; and *Coloquio moral, intitulado Labor del alma*, whose allegorical figures illustrate the duties pertinent to various types of believers. The *Desafío moral* is a Corpus Christi play in which Man is challenged to combat by the World, the Flesh and the Devil. Finally, the *Lorentina* was composed to celebrate the translation of the relics of St Lawrence to Huesca. In her introduction Dexeus de Moll evaluates Torres' place in the evolution of the sixteenth-century Castilian religious theatre.

Final considerations

The usual term for the medieval and sixteenth-century Castilian theatre, the *teatro prelopista*, that is to say the theatre prior to Lope de Vega, reflects the teleological bias that has long characterised literary histories. Works tended to be judged according to the extent to which they prefigured the seventeenth-century *comedia*. One of the significant trends of the past twenty years is the shift from such a teleological view to one which considers a given play in terms of its own internal coherence and its public's horizon of expectations.

The publication of a considerable number of previously unedited or otherwise hard-to-find texts has resulted in a more accurate picture of dramatic activity in late-medieval Castile. Plays previously available only in manuscript or in sixteenth- or seventeenth-century imprints can now be read in modern editions. Texts which had been edited in the late nineteenth or early twentieth centuries are now accessible in editions that meet modern standards of textual criticism. In general terms, such recent publications avoid the exclusively historical or linguistic commentaries so prevalent in

Ronald E. Surtz

older editions and instead at least attempt to consider the plays as literature and as theatre.

While our knowledge of the medieval dramatic tradition is still inadequate, the ever-increasing prevalence of theatrical performances in late-fifteenth-century Castile is much more clearly documented. Recent studies are more likely to be based on documentary evidence or reasonable conjecture, rather than capricious suppositions or lapidary pronouncements. New sources of information have been discovered; sources already known have enjoyed fresh readings. The shift away from the study of purely historical or linguistic questions towards the appreciation of the plays as literature is a welcome trend. The next step, their consideration as theatre, has been but tentatively taken. The need is urgent to move from a text-centred concept of theatre to one based on the notion of theatre as performance.

12

Germany and German-speaking central Europe

HANSJÜRGEN LINKE
(Edited and translated by Eckehard Simon)

When looking at the substantial corpus of medieval plays from German-speaking central Europe, it is not easy to come up with an exact tally. If we mean plays written in German – that is, in the various dialects of medieval German – the total would run to about 162 religious plays and 155 plays on secular themes, mostly short Carnival comedies. However, there are another 32 religious plays written mostly in Latin but containing passages of German verse. In addition, the area produced 53 surviving religious plays in Latin, some, like the Antichrist play of Tegernsee (c. 1160), major documents of the medieval stage. German playwrights, mainly men of the Church, were not alone, of course, in frequently writing their plays in Latin, especially during the early period (eleventh to thirteenth centuries). But the number of such plays, sung in churches, is especially large in this region. Lipphardt's comprehensive collection (43) contains about 655 liturgical Easter plays, called 'Easter offices' (Osterfeiern) by German scholars because they were performed as part of divine services. More than four-fifths of these, numbering some 528 texts, originated in religious houses of German-speaking central Europe (the old Empire or Reich), which is a fact that has been but rarely noted.

The 162 or so religious plays written in German tend to have come from cities and towns in five geographical regions: Hesse and the Frankish area along the Rhine, the Tyrol (today Austrian and Italian), Swabia and adjacent Switzerland (known as the Alemannic region) and – to a lesser extent – from southern (Austro-Bavarian) and east-central provinces.

But the plays that have survived give a somewhat misleading impression, both in numbers and distribution, of the kind of religious theatre that actually existed. This has now become quite clear with the publication in 1987 of archival records attesting to religious drama compiled by Bernd Neumann (565), the first inventory of its kind (about which more below). It shows that religious plays of some sort were staged in practically every town and certainly in many regions from which we have no texts.

Neumann's work would seem to suggest that searching town archives for evidence of secular theatre, something that still needs to be done, might lead to similar revisions in the geography of the surviving non-religious plays. Virtually all of these texts, especially Carnival plays, come to us from fifteenth-century Nuremberg or the Tyrol. But what documentation has been made available, mostly by older scholarship, shows that Carnival plays, not always comic, were staged in towns as far apart as Lübeck (on the Baltic), Eger (today Cheb in Czechoslovakia) and Deventer (on the Lower Rhine).

Judging from the texts we have, religious plays began to be written in German soon after 1250 and Carnival plays around 1430–40, although one distinct type, the so-called Neidhart play, existed by the second half of the fourteenth century. The Carnival or Shrovetide plays gave way to more modern forms in the early sixteenth century. As the Reformation came to German states at different times, it usually put a stop to the old religious theatre (see Preface, p. xvi, above). In the south and southwest regions, which remained Catholic, some religious plays, joined by newer forms like Jesuit drama, continued to be performed until the seventeenth century. In Alpine regions, religious theatre was turned into so-called *Volksschauspiele*, that is, simple folk plays put on in villages, and as such surviving until the twentieth century. The demise brought about by the Reformation was hastened by other changes: the rise of professional actors (coming at first from England), the use of new stages and theatres and the emergence of playwrights writing for publication, that is, writing drama as literature.

German medieval plays were rarely printed and virtually all the surviving texts have come down to us in manuscripts. A distinguishing feature is that religious plays, usually quite lengthy, survive mainly in single manuscripts while we often have several manuscripts – usually collections – for the shorter Carnival plays. Rolf Bergmann (559) has examined the various purposes for which religious plays were committed to writing, urging caution in speaking of a *Lesetext*, that is a copy meant only to be read. I have now given a more comprehensive typology of manuscripts (563), backing my discussion with a large set of sample pages.

While the surviving texts, as I have noted, give an incomplete picture of what was actually performed, it would seem useful to indicate briefly how many plays we have and what subjects they depict. The most up-to-date inventory of the corpus may be found in my recent survey article (564), also citing the major editions. Counted as vernacular plays will be Latin plays with German verses, ranging from a few to a substantial number.

Among religious plays, the vast majority were written for the Easter season. Passion plays (49 of them) were most popular, followed by Easter or Resurrection plays (32) and *planctus* plays called *Marienklagen* (24), featuring the lament of the Virgin under the Cross. Corpus Christi plays (10) were much less popular here than in England. Represented by very few texts are Easter season plays on individual subjects and episodes: the life of Mary Magdalene (2), the Last Supper (2), Christ's Deposition from the Cross (4), His appearance at Emmaus (the 'Peregrinus' play, 3), the Ascension (3) and the Assumption of Mary (2).

Compared to Easter, plays of the Christmas season come in a distant second. Most of them (8) depict episodes long traditional in Latin plays, called *Weihnachtsfeiern*, from the coming of the shepherds to the flight into Egypt. A feature peculiar to some German plays is the so-called *Kindelwiegen* in which players such as Joseph's maidservants sing to the Infant and even dance around the cradle. Other episodes dramatised, but infrequently, were the words of the Prophets (1), the Annunciation (2) and Mary's Purification (1).

The remaining religious plays, about one-fifth of the total, are not linked directly to Easter and Christmas and could be performed at various times of the year (although rarely in the fall). Saint and legend plays constitute the largest contingent (14), although they were far less popular here than in France. The most prominent types depict the lives of martyred saints (5), of Theophilus (3) and 'Pope Joan' (1), who both made pacts with the devil, and the discovery of a great 'relic', the Holy Cross (3). While the subject of eschatology inspired three kinds of play, only the Last Judgement plays appear to have constituted a substantial corpus (13). Of *sponsus* plays ('The Five Wise and Five Foolish Virgins') only two German versions survive, and for the Antichrist we have just a single text. Last among the minor forms are four plays dramatising various Old Testament stories and three morality plays. The latter were discovered only recently and are a typical example of how much recent research has changed the information still found in our standard texts (for example, that Germany has no morality plays).

Among plays dealing with non-religious subjects, the vast majority (148) are designated *Fastnachtspiele*, that is Carnival or Shrovetide plays. Most of them are short comic sketches, performed in houses, although heavier fare, such as political plays, was staged at Carnival as well. The typical Carnival sketch features comic types, such as the peasant, in standard revue-like situations (in verbal contest; at court), although some draw on lighter stories from literature. In terms of surviving texts, the two other types of secular plays must be regarded as minor forms. We have two pieces depicting verbal combat between May and the Harvest season (*Herbst*) and four so-called Neidhart plays. In these, the legendary court poet and knight Sir Neidhart is duped by peasants and avenges himself in turn. Neidhart plays, as I have noted, existed by the second half of the fourteenth century and appear to constitute the oldest form of secular theatre.

As we now turn to review recent research, let us cast a brief glance at the history of the field. Scholarship has traditionally concentrated on Easter, Passion and Corpus Christi plays. This was no doubt governed by the fact that these plays, as we saw, make up the bulk of extant texts. Carnival plays were, until recently, little studied because it was felt their obscenity made them improper subjects for scholarship. Although interest stirred as early as the eighteenth century, scholarly investigation of medieval drama started much later than work on lyric poetry and narrative. It seems to have run in spurts, with periods of heightened activity coming around 1840–50 (with Mone and Keller), 1880–90 (Milchsack, Lange, Froning, Wackernell,

Zingerle) and from the beginning of our century to the 1920s. Between the early thirties and the middle sixties the field lay largely fallow.

A look at publication statistics shows that work picked up very slowly at the end of World War II. Two-thirds of the roughly 600 scholarly publications produced between 1945 and the present entered the bibliography after 1965. There was also little editing and most new editions have appeared within the last twenty years.

The mid-sixties, then, marked a new beginning in the study of medieval plays, both as drama and as theatre. The rate of publication increased to double what it had been. More significant was a new kind of quality in the scholarly work being done: new areas, such as archival records, were opened up to investigation, more attention was paid to manuscripts and the research demanded greater philological skills.

Rather extensive reports on scholarship were published by Wolfgang Michael in 1957, 1973 (540), and 1988 (see the 'Recent works' section of the bibliography). The large amount of work traditionally done on Easter and Passion plays was scrutinised in detail by Karl Konrad Polheim (1972 [548]; 1975 [551]). Research and editorial work between 1978 and 1984 has now been reviewed by Bernd Neumann (1984–5 [558]) in what is planned as the first instalment of a comprehensive appraisal of recent scholarship.

Within the framework of this introduction it is, of course, not possible to mention the some 400 scholarly publications that have appeared since about 1965. We will therefore select for discussion the items most relevant for those seeking to acquaint themselves with this field. We will deal in some detail with the texts themselves: what new plays have been discovered, what editions are available. In turning to scholarship, we shall limit ourselves to highlights and make note of what still needs to be done.

NEWLY DISCOVERED PLAYS

Considering the losses sustained by central European libraries and archives in World War II, manuscripts of medieval plays fared rather well. When the inventory was complete – it took two decades – it turned out that only six manuscripts had actually perished. Luckily, five of these contained plays that had already been edited. The loss of the unpublished piece, an Annunciation play from the Tyrolean collection of Vigil Raber (no. XIX), is most regrettable because we have so few Christmas plays.

Ample compensation for our losses, however, has been provided by the twenty-four new plays that have been discovered since 1945. Some of these rather remarkable finds have been made because drama scholars are now looking more systematically through library holdings. Many, however, have come in the wake of a major German project, supported by government funds, to catalogue all medieval manuscripts.

Before mentioning some of the new plays, attention should be drawn to a second manuscript, a fragment (c. 1200) of the famed Tegernsee *Ludus de*

Antichristo, discovered by Josef Riedmann in the Tyrolean abbey of Fiecht near Schwaz. Published in an obscure regional journal, Riedmann's article (1973 [78]) has so far eluded most drama scholars, among them the latest German *Ludus* editor, Gisela Vollmann-Profe (1981 [79]), who includes a facsimile of the Munich manuscript.

Most (seventeen) of the twenty-four plays that have come to light with surprising regularity are either Easter or Passion plays. The make-up of the existing corpus would lead one to expect this. About half survive in complete copies, half as fragments. The majority come from the south, the so-called Upper German regions. Only three were written in the Low German provinces of the north. But they are remarkably older as a group, all three belonging to the fourteenth century.

One of the first finds was made in 1948 in New York's Pierpont Morgan Library where Curt Bühler and Carl Selmer came upon part of an Easter play, from the Rhenish area of Hesse (c. 1400–50), in a codex formerly owned by the Austrian abbey of Melk.[1] Prominent among more recent discoveries are stage director's sheets for an Easter play (c. 1450) which Rolf Bergmann identified in 1984 in another Austrian abbey, Göttweig (583), and Frankfurt fragments of an Easter play (c. 1300–50), recently published by Helmut Lomnitzer (see the 'Recent works' section of the bibliography), that is related to the influential Frankfurt Passion play.

Significant for its age is a fragmentary Austro-Bavarian Passion play from the first half of the fourteenth century published by Oskar Pausch in 1979 (as an 'Easter Play') from a Kremsmünster codex (581). At the other end of the time scale, Bernd Neumann will soon publish the part book for the role of Jesus (Salvator) in a two-day Passion play from Strasbourg that is closely related to the 1616 performance text of the Lucerne Passion.

A similar part sheet for a Corpus Christi play from Rothenburg (c. 1400–25) – this one containing the speeches of Kaspar, one of the Three Kings – was actually printed in a local newspaper supplement as early as 1911. But the lack of bibliographical zeal characteristic of older scholarship meant that the find did not become known until the 1970s (edited by Elizabeth Wainwright; see 608, 610).

A welcome addition to our small corpus was 'The Swabian Christmas Play' from an Augsburg miscellany now at Harvard's Houghton Library. Probably performed at Constance at the close of the famed Council (c. 1417), the piece is one of the oldest Christmas plays on record. The rubrics suggest that it was staged by choir boys, led by their Boy Bishop, both in town houses and in church (using a longer text). The play was found in 1971 by the editor of this volume, Eckehard Simon (599, 603).

Worthy of study for comparative purposes is a fragmentary Low German 'Paradise Play' from Kassel (second half of the fourteenth century) that I have recently published in the *Zeitschrift für deutsches Altertum* (1987 [620]). It has features that remind one of the twelfth-century *Jeu d'Adam*.

Most unusual among newly discovered eschatological plays is a partial text, the 'Marburger Spiel von den letzten Dingen' (c. 1450–75), to be edited by Helmut Lomnitzer. Unlike newly discovered plays from Güssing, southeast Austria (Bavarian, fifteenth-century) and from the Jantz Collection at Duke University (Alemannic, 1523), the Marburg piece differs strikingly from the standard and well-disseminated form of the Last Judgement play. Performed over two days, it features, among other things, an elaborate dramatisation of the *sponsus*, the parable of the Five Wise and Five Foolish Virgins.

The discovery of the Erfurt morality play ('Erfurter Moralität'), written before 1448, led us, as I have noted, to abandon a long-held view (see p. 209, above). Contained in a collective codex catalogued as early as 1936, the 'Erfurt Morality' is, with its nearly 18,000 verses, the lengthiest and most complex German play we have. Until the edition being prepared by Hans-Gert Roloff appears, information on the play may be found in an article by me (617). The play's length may have led some to suspect that the piece is unique and was perhaps meant only to be read. But in 1986 the fragment of a second morality, also from fifteenth-century Thuringia, came to light at Berlin (619). Textually related to the 'Erfurt Morality', it shows that moralities were in fact disseminated as stage plays.

EDITIONS AND EDITORIAL PROCEDURES

Turning to editions, let us begin our review of this field by mentioning reprints. Because many libraries were destroyed or damaged in the War, it became most necessary to reprint older editions. It is characteristic of the late-beginning new research in our field had that the majority of the eighteen or so reprints appeared after 1965. While it may be claimed that reprinting was an enterprise motivated by profit – new university libraries were all eager customers – research work could not have picked up without standard editions becoming available again.

In the period under review, several plays have been both reprinted and re-edited several times. They thus form a canon of 'favourite pieces'. In leading position with seven editions is the Tegernsee Antichrist play for which Gisela Vollmann-Profe (1981 [79]) produced the most reliable text (but see my remark on a second manuscript, above). Next in line, with five editions each, are the Easter plays of Muri and Redentin (see 569 and 574).

First mention among new editions, however, must go to those through which some thirty plays became available in print for the first time. A large number of these come from the collection of Vigil Raber, owned since his death (in 1552) by the town of Sterzing/Vipiteno in the South Tyrol. The collection disappeared during the War and did not become accessible again to scholars until the 1970s (it was returned to Sterzing in 1984). The most important single codex from Raber's library, a collection of some sixteen plays he had acquired from Benedikt Debs of Bozen (Bolzano), was edited by Walther Lipphardt (555); the flawed texts of 1981 have now been

corrected in a second edition (1986) brought out by Hans-Gert Roloff. The
'Debs-Codex' edition contains such notable pieces as three new Easter plays
(III, V, VIII), an 'Annunciation' (XIII) and two 'Depositions from the Cross'
(II and XIV) which had been edited a little earlier by Gesine Taubert (1977
[615]). Other Raber playbooks are being prepared for publication by Roloff.
The first of these volumes to appear, Volume v in the set (1980 [555]), makes
available unusual plays on such subjects as David and Goliath, and a
heavenly tribunal deciding whether Christ should die for man. The second
volume (1988) contains the Sterzing Passion plays of 1486 (compiled by
Lienhard Pfarrkircher) and 1496, the latter also performed in 1503.

Editorial work on unpublished plays continues apace. Latest to appear is
the director's copy of the Alsfeld Passion edited by Christoph Treutwein[2]
and the 'Tyrolean Ascension and Pentecost Play' brought out by Karin
Wilcke.[3] Among new editions, a special ribbon should go to those that
constitute a distinct improvement over what we had before, such as Rudolf
Schützeichel's 'St Gall (Middle Rhenish) Passion Play' (1978 [592]) and
Anthonius Touber's 'Donaueschingen Passion' (1985 [595]).

As reprints of older texts and new editions were appearing, a discussion
ensued on how best to edit medieval plays. Wolfgang Michael had addressed
this question as early as 1949.[4] Proposals made by Paul-Gerhard Völker
(1968 [544]) and Johannes Janota (in 552, pp. 76–87) about multi-layered
preparation of texts would no doubt delight specialists. But they would be
far too complex and demanding for other readers. Thus no editor has actually
followed these suggestions and what has appeared continues to be 'user-
friendly'.

One point of the debate, however, has been taken up. Recent editors no
longer engage in the time-honoured philological practice of reconstructing
archetypes in the belief that there once existed a single 'original' or *Urtext*.
Moving away from regarding plays as authorial literature, editors now
appear to agree that the original text is the one that was staged, or to put it
differently, that each performance can be said to constitute an original. When
editing the Heidelberg Passion play, Gustav Milchsack had said much the
same thing, but at a time (1880) when the philological establishment would
not tolerate such a view.

The new approach, then, is to present the texts in the manner most
appropriate to the different states in which the plays have come down to us,
an idea tried out as early as 1890–1 by Richard Froning. The aim is to
separate out layers of texts, each one having presumably been performed at
least once. The practical way to go about this has been to print the revised
and added sections parallel to the others. Karin Schneider was the first to do
this, for the two versions of the *sponsus* play (*Zehnjungfrauenspiel*) of
Thuringia (1964 [605]).[5] Peter Liebenow then used the method to come to
terms with the complex playbook of the 'Künzelsau Corpus Christi Play'
(1969 [607]) and Antje Knorr followed suit with the 'Passion Play of
Villingen' (1976 [590]).

Where the text, on the other hand, has been quite obviously corrupted in the process of copying, justifiable attempts have been made to place next to it a version that might have been staged. Hans Blosen devised such a text, quite successfully, for the 'Vienna (Silesian) Easter Play' (1979 [*580*]). Most recently, Schipke and Pensel brought out the newly discovered 'Brandenburg Easter Play' in this format (1986 [*586*]).

The striving for authenticity signalled by these editorial practices has been abetted by photographic facsimiles of the manuscripts themselves. About thirty-six plays have thus far been made available in this manner. Musicologists would benefit greatly from facsimiles of all notations found in our manuscripts, especially for the Latin plays where transcribing staffless neumes presents a special problem. In an ideal world, such facsimile editions should, of course, be produced in colour. Scribal use of various inks – black for the text, red for stage directions (rubrics), sometimes green for texts to be sung but lacking notation – is hard to detect in the black-and-white reproduction commonly used. So are diacritic marks and changes in ink shades, at times the only clue that a later hand has been at work. Only four such expensive colour facsimiles have appeared thus far, for the Easter plays of Redentin (*576*) and Brandenburg (*586*), for example, and for the Copenhagen Last Judgement play (*612*).

Much editorial work remains to be done. Our only complete edition of Carnival plays (by Adelbert von Keller, 1853, 1858) is notoriously unreliable and needs to be replaced. The same applies to some other older editions that went too far in 'improving' the text, such as those of the important Innsbruck codex 960 dated 1391 (see *575*) that contains the widely read 'Thuringian Easter Play', an Assumption of Mary and the oldest Corpus Christi play. Rapid inroads are being made in publishing the large corpus of Last Judgement plays. For six of the eight plays still unpublished, editors have been found. Their editions are coming out in such diverse formats as a full-length book (the Copenhagen Last Judgement, edited by Hans Blosen – see the 'Recent works' section of the bibliography); and an article in a yearbook (the plays of Donaueschingen and the Jantz Collection, edited by Ingeborg Henderson and Winder McConnell in the *Jahrbuch des Wiener Goethe-Vereins*). The opportunity has thus been lost, one notes with regret, to bring out a collective edition. For the *Weltgerichtspiele* do constitute a special case. It has been known since the 1906 dissertation of Rudolf Klee[6] that they are all related to each other and derive from a common Alemannic ancestor. While the 'family tree' drawn up by Klee needs to be brought up to date by the addition of some offspring unknown to him (the plays of Bern, Güssing and the Jantz Collection), it would have taught us a lot about how texts change over time and in adaptation to regional usage if the entire corpus could have been accommodated in one edition.

RECORDS

When speaking of 'sources', we used to think of the manuscripts and editions just reviewed. But newly conscious of the sociology of medieval theatre, scholars have now become keenly interested in another kind of 'source': archival records. These are entries about theatre business from local account ledgers and protocol books, the kind that since 1974 have been collected by Toronto's REED (Records of Early English Drama) project. Two years earlier, a young graduate student at Cologne, Bernd Neumann, began a similar archival project for German drama. All we had before was sporadic investigations for specific towns (Dresden, Eger/Cheb, Frankfurt-on-Main, Lübeck, Nuremberg, Vienna). Only Wackernell, in his monumental edition of the Tyrolean Passion plays (1897),[7] had tried his hand at documenting an entire region. In 1975, Neumann gave us a first sample by demonstrating that the towns along the Lower Rhine, from where we have virtually no texts, were actually alive with theatre of all kinds (550). What was published of his 1977 dissertation was limited to historical surveys and source descriptions.[8] It was not until 1987 that Neumann's entire collection, enlarged up to the last minute, was finally published in two massive volumes (565).

Neumann presents us with a whole new sociology of religious theatre in all its aspects, from financing a performance to producing masks for actors and exchanging play directors. It will take years of study to apply the new information to what we thought we knew. One of Neumann's major conclusions is mentioned in the Preface to this volume: the records show theatre active in whole regions for which not a single play survives. There was practically no town that did not have religious drama of some kind, although the intensity of thespian pursuits did vary.

The archival work is not finished, of course, and as inclusive as Neumann's annals are, they are not complete. The collection is, for one thing, limited to religious theatre. So there is now a manifest need to gather the records on secular theatre. Neumann's coverage also has some gaps. We still need to check out depositories in Switzerland and certain parts of the Low Countries, in the GDR and those Eastern Bloc countries such as Czechoslovakia, Hungary and Romania where German drama flourished in medieval times.

TRANSLATIONS, MODERN PERFORMANCES

Since medieval German plays were written in the old regional dialects, not every user of this volume will be able to read the editions here reviewed. It is unfortunate, therefore, that very few plays are available in English. Only the Tegernsee Antichrist play is today widely read (and now also performed, by the Chicago Medieval Players) in John Wright's translation (1967 [75]). The play was actually rendered into English, one notes with astonishment, as early as 1847.[9] But Latin is, of course, more accessible to students of medieval drama and Latin plays written in Germany, such as the five pieces in the *Carmina Burana* manuscript (*c.* 1230–40, now believed to come from the South Tyrol), are among the best known. David Bevington's widely used anthology (1975 [*19*]), for example, contains excellent translations of the 'Benediktbeuern' Christmas and Passion plays.

For plays written in German, English versions are available for 'The Redentin Easter Play' (by Adolf Zucker, 1941, 1961 [*566*]), 'The Saint Gall Passion Play' (by Larry West, 1976 [*591*]), and for a single Carnival play, 'The Mirthful Peasant Play' of Hans Folz.[10] An alternative may offer itself in recent editions that have modern German translations on facing pages. Chief among these are translations by Rudolf Meier (1962 [*567*]) of the Easter plays of Innsbruck and Muri, by Max Wehrli (1967 [*569*]) of Muri again, and by Brigitte Schottmann (1975 [*574*]) and Hartmut Wittkowsky (1975 [*576*]) of the Redentin Easter play. As with editions, there is clearly a canon of translation 'favourites', but a very narrow one. Work in comparative drama would obviously be aided by making many more German plays available in English.

Like Wittkowsky's Redentin Easter play, some of the older translations are in verse and were thus also intended for use by amateur groups, mainly students, wishing to perform medieval plays. Mention might be made, in this connection, of Karl Langosch's widely read anthology of Latin plays[11] and a compilation, by Carl Niessen, of the three Low German Theophilus plays into a kind of medieval *Faust*.[12]

Interest in putting on the old plays began with the Youth Movement (*Jugendbewegung*) at the start of this century, beholden to a Romanticised view of the Middle Ages. The theatre of youth groups like the Wandernde Gesellen or university students must, however, be distinguished from the so-called *Volksschauspiel*. Such folk plays, mainly religious, have medieval roots and were performed, as I have noted, in remoter rural areas, such as Alpine villages, until the first half of this century. *Volksschauspiele* are being studied extensively at Bonn by Karl Konrad Polheim, who is preparing a comprehensive bibliography. While heir to medieval theatre, such folk plays are essentially a post-medieval form of popular culture.[13]

Revival of medieval drama, however, never took on the dimensions it has assumed since the 1950s in England and North America. Local amateur performances are certainly taking place, but news of them rarely spreads beyond the town borders. No one has, at any rate, tried to gather such information. Performances on record come occasionally from public broadcasting,[14] but mainly from universities. On 10 November 1954, the Tegernsee Antichrist play was staged at Mainz University in the presence of no less a luminary than the French drama scholar Gustave Cohen.[15] At a 1986 drama conference in Bamberg (1 July), Hubert Herkommer screened a videotape of students at the University of Bern putting on the 'Bern Last Judgement Play' of 1465. The Carnival play 'Die zwen Stenndt' (1535) from the Raber collection was presented at Sterzing/Vipiteno in January 1986. What remains to be seen, however, is whether the Anglo-American movement to stage medieval plays for purposes of scholarly study will take hold in German central Europe.

Bibliographies

The field has long lacked the kind of basic tool that a comprehensive bibliography represents. A special need arises from the fact that some German theatre research is local in nature and appears in publications of limited circulation. For nearly half a century, all we had was the 1924 *Historical and Bibliographical Survey* of Maximilian Rudwin,[16] one of the few American scholars to work in this field (another was Neil C. Brooks who wrote his 1898 Harvard dissertation on 'The Frankfurt Group of Passion Plays'). For the German area, the 1954 *Bibliography of Medieval Drama* by Carl Stratman is useless even in its second edition of 1972.[17]

Rudwin's listings were limited to religious drama (though including the post-medieval period) and had quite a few gaps. In his study of Easter and Passion plays, Rolf Steinbach (1970 [*545*]) set out to complete and update Rudwin's bibliography. For secondary literature, Steinbach (who had failed to list some newer plays) was quickly surpassed by Rolf Bergmann in his 1972 study of early Passion plays (*588*). Bergmann further improved his coverage in the bibliography to his monumental 1986 *Katalog* (*561*). Started by Paul-Gerhard Völker in the 1960s and a testament to years of field work, the catalogue describes all known manuscripts of medieval religious plays in German. A companion work, Bernd Neumann's 1987 catalogue of attested performances, also contains an impressive bibliography (*565*, vol. II).

No such up-to-date bibliographies exist for secular plays. Most useful, for Carnival plays, is Gerd Simon's 1970 work (*631*), which gives reliable data about the text sources, mostly manuscript collections, some early printed editions (pp. 12–22, 87–119). Eckehard Catholy's little handbook of 1966 (*625*) can still be consulted for editions and major research. More complete – its coverage extending to sixteenth-century *Fastnachtspiele* – is the bibliography in the Carnival-play anthology of Dieter Wuttke in its second edition of 1978 (*633*, pp. 365–416).

Those seeking orientation will likely wish to read histories or surveys of the entire field. These can generally be divided into two kinds: those written before the research resurgence of the 1960s and those reflecting the radical re-ordering and rethinking of the tradition brought about by new evidence and new approaches.

The only two book-length histories of medieval German drama belong, unfortunately, to the first category. Both Wolfgang Michael's handbook of

1971 (*546*) and the two-volume survey by David Brett-Evans (1975 [*549*]), while detailed and comprehensive, are based on the scholarship of previous generations whose premises and conclusions were taken over without critical reflection. This was stated, more or less bluntly, by several reviewers of both books.[18]

Of overviews more in touch with recent work one can recommend the chapters on drama in a 1980 literary history by Max Wehrli, distinguished readings culled from a lifetime of study.[19] Wehrli sketches regional traditions with skilful strokes and adds valuable interpretations of the more significant plays. His coverage is comprehensive, extending to Latin and secular plays, failing only to do justice to the newly recognised genre of the morality.

Much useful factual and bibliographical information, most of it up-to-date, is given by Rolf Bergmann in the article on 'religious drama' written for the second edition of the *Reallexikon der deutschen Literaturgeschichte* (1984).[20] Bergmann makes concerted efforts to order the plays according to the latest information on dates and places of origin. Less successful is the article's companion piece in the *Reallexikon*, a brief article on 'secular drama' by Werner Bauer.[21] Bauer does not distinguish rigorously enough between the three types of secular theatricals (Carnival plays, the vast majority; Neidhart plays; season combat plays) and fails to render proper account of the enormous diversity of subjects the Carnival plays dramatise.

For a reliable and up-to-date introduction, the reader may wish to place alongside each other two articles (1978, 1987) and one chapter of a literary history (1987) written by me. The 1978 article in *Neues Handbuch der Literaturwissenschaft* (*553*), concluding with a section on Dutch drama, constitutes the first attempt to integrate into the chronology and typology of the texts the significant new data from archival records being gathered at Cologne by Bernd Neumann (see *565*). The article appeared in time to be used for the only introduction thus far available in English, a brief piece in the *Dictionary of the Middle Ages* written by Eckehard Simon (1984 [*557*]).

My second article (*564*) complements the first by surveying regional theatre and discussing major plays. For the entire early tradition, from the tenth century to about 1400, Latin plays included, I have given much information in my chapter in volume III, part 2 of de Boor's standard literary history, edited by Ingeborg Glier (*562*).

For regional theatre, Bernd Neumann has written well-documented surveys of the Lower Rhine (1975 [*550*]) and the Tyrol.[22] Because of the 1943 monograph by the American scholar Marshall Blakemore Evans, the local tradition best known to those outside the field is the Passion play of Lucerne. Renward Cysat's two famed sketches for the 1583 staging on the *Fischmarkt* (now *Weinmarkt*) have recently attracted the attention of the notable French theatre scholar Elie Konigson (*593*) and the British scholar John Tailby (*594*).

Those wishing to do research would be best served by going beyond these introductions to the compact and informative drama articles in the second edition of the *Verfasserlexikon*. Edited by a team of medievalists led by Kurt

Ruh (Würzburg), the new *Verfasserlexikon* (*554*) started appearing in 1978 and has by now progressed to the letter R (vol. VII). When complete, this will contain well over one hundred articles, on single plays or groups of plays, that combine meticulous basic information with original research. In articles written by various scholars (with the majority, however, coming from the Cologne team) there are bound to be differences in coverage and critical penetration. This may be seen, for instance, by comparing Norbert Richard Wolf's summary on the 'Debs-Codex' (*554*, vol. II, pp. 59–61) with Neumann's in-depth article on the play codex known as 'Erlauer Spiele' (*ibid.*, pp. 592–9). But on the whole, editorial standards are high and the data undergo rigorous checks.

As a research guide for the next generation, the new *Verfasserlexikon* will also help to introduce a standardised set of play titles developed by the Cologne group for its bibliography. Such standardisation was sorely needed. With virtually all the texts being anonymous, there has been a great deal of confusion over the names by which plays are referred to. Medieval authorities were themselves neither precise nor consistent in what they called their plays or in the terms applied to various types. For example, Lucerners always called their great medieval play 'Easter play', but to our way of classifying – since it contains both Old Testament episodes and the Crucifixion, all presented over two days – Lucerne had a 'Passion play'. Among scholars there developed over time a tendency to refer to the same piece by different names. Most annoying was the habit of naming a play for the place, usually a library, where the manuscript was found. But this is usually not identical with its home region, as indicated by the text's dialect. Thus the 'Innsbruck Easter Play' was actually written in Thuringia, the 'Vienna Easter Play' in Silesia.

The Cologne list eliminates this confusion by settling on the single name most appropriate to each piece. Some of the old titles were so well established, however, that it was advisable only to insert a 'home region' tag, as in 'Innsbruck (Thuringian) Easter Play' or 'Vienna (Silesian) Easter Play'. In the case of Carnival plays, where confusion reigned supreme, it often seemed best to coin new titles.

Rolf Bergmann was able to use the new master list in his 1986 manuscript catalogue (*561*). Minor lapses aside, the new *Verfasserlexikon* has been following it all along. When the Cologne bibliography joins these standard works, we will finally be operating with a fixed-title canon that should then find its way into new editions.

MAJOR RESEARCH

As we move on to discuss scholarly publications in the concluding section of this chapter, let us first take note of some gains that the welcome trend, mentioned above, toward studying plays from the manuscripts has brought about. Hoffmann von Fallersleben (1837), for example, had described a fragment at Göttweig Abbey as consisting of two spoken verses plus one

Hansjürgen Linke

Latin rubric. When Bergmann, as I have noted, looked at the original (1984 [*583*]), it turned out to be a bi-folio used to direct an Easter play. The unpublished fragments of what was known as the 'Berlin (Lower Rhenish) Passion Play', missing since the War from Berlin's State Library, have just been recognised as a role or part sheet for the High Priest. It gives cue words, an arrangement found otherwise only in the Jesus part book of Strasbourg mentioned above.

Codicological study has also enabled us to show, for example, that the controversial ending of the Benediktbeuern Christmas play, which Young had considered a separate piece (infelicitously labelled 'Ludus de Rege Egipti') actually belongs to the Christmas play itself.[23] By looking at the manuscripts, moreover, we have been able to correct a number of key passages in both older and newer editions.[24]

But it also sparked controversy when Werner Williams-Krapp, in a 1980 monograph (*556*), suggested that most of our manuscripts were meant to be read and that it was therefore questionable whether the 'plays' they contain were actually staged. Custodians of the field were not slow to respond. By looking closely at the page layout of some major religious plays, Rolf Bergmann (1985 [*559*]) was able to single out features directly linked to performance. I have recently given a more comprehensive response (1988 [*563*]), pointing out that codicological evidence must be combined with what the texts, especially the rubrics, say. Considering the often lengthy process of copying, I have noted, the way a text appears in a given manuscript does not necessarily tell us for what purpose it was originally written. Plays attestedly staged often come to us in copies made for reading. There are, furthermore, certain manuscripts that manifestly served two purposes: as base text for a performance and for private reading. The questions raised by Williams-Krapp have been valuable, however, in prompting us to think more critically about the 'theatrical standing' of what the manuscripts happen to preserve.

As we now take a brief look at other major scholarly contributions, we shall consider the trends they set and what remains to be done.

Of research on religious drama, about half has been devoted to Easter and Passion plays, a preference, as we saw, shared by editors. A small number of Easter plays, in fact, have received most of the attention. Thus even the few recent American contributors, like Duncan Smith and Joseph Dane, have written articles on the 'favourites', the Easter play of Redentin and the Innsbruck (Thuringian) Easter play.[25] A satirical episode virtually unique to the German Easter plays in which – after Christ releases the Patriarchs – the devils restock Hell with sinners (a town baker who weighs short, a butcher who sells spoilt meat, an amorous chaplain) has been studied in detail by Rolf Max Kully.[26] His work is one of several monographs marking the renewal of interest in medieval drama.

The best work on the Passion plays, centring on the early texts (those from the thirteenth and fourteenth centuries), has been done by Rolf Bergmann (1972 [*588*]) who brought philological expertise to bear on identifying, dating and localising the plays, often removing several layers of misinformation. The quite different ways in which German Corpus Christi plays could be performed have been outlined by Wilhelm Breuer.[27] Elizabeth Wainwright (1974 [608]) has thrown new light on how the texts of the Corpus Christi plays of Künzelsau and Freiburg im Breisgau changed over the course of many performances. In a subsequent article, she examined the unusual relationship between the long-lived Corpus Christi play of Bozen (Bolzano) (South Tyrol) and a Passion play published in 1545 by Jacob Rueff of Zurich, a convert to Protestantism.[28]

For Easter-season plays, most work remains to be done on the so-called *Marienklagen*, the *planctus* of the Virgin and others at the foot of the Cross. This was a most prolific German form and Bergmann's catalogue (561) lists some 147 texts. Yet we know so little about them that for most it has not been determined whether they were actually staged or merely sung in church. This is one of several subjects that invites participation from scholars with musicological training. One so qualified, Ulrich Mehler, has now made a significant contribution in his as yet unpublished Cologne *Habilitationsschrift* 'Marienklagen im mittelalterlichen und frühneuzeitlichen Deutschland' (1988).

Prominent among the very few publications devoted to Christmas plays is a large-scale study of the Magi plays by Norbert King (1979 [602]). Although not easy to read because of a busy system of internal references, his work is impressive in its excellent basic research and enormous range. King examines Latin, German and French plays up to 1600 on what the English called 'The Three Kings of Cologne', including Magi episodes in larger texts such as Corpus Christi plays.

After prolonged neglect, research on the Carnival plays started again in 1961 with a profound and original study by Eckehard Catholy (621) who read the plays for the first time as dramatic literature. The last serious monograph on them had appeared in 1896 (by Victor Michels). Dividing *Fastnachtspiele*, as had Michels, into revue plays (*Reihenspiele*) and story plays (*Handlungsspiele*), Catholy showed how the pieces, notably the many subtypes of revue plays, were put together and how they worked in performance. He saw them as interludes emerging from the on-going Carnival celebration. Summed up in a 1966 handbook for students (625), Catholy's work has proved lasting and influential.

In doing a morphological study of the texts, Catholy was turning against the folkloristic approach of the previous generation – including the American Maximilian Rudwin – which had regarded the Carnival plays as relics of pagan ritual and rural custom. Independent of Catholy, much the same stance was taken in the 1961 East Berlin dissertation of Werner Lenk, published in 1966 (626), which showed how familiar Carnival playwrights, most hailing from Nuremberg, must have been with late-medieval comic and didactic literature.

Carnival plays generate laughter mainly through comic obscenity, especially of the sexual kind, pursued with boundless imagination and verbal prolixity. For previous generations, this had rendered them unworthy of scholarly attention. This attitude changed radically with the student movements of the late 1960s that exorcised many a taboo. In the studies by Johannes Merkel[29] and Rüdiger Krohn (1974 [634]), the obscenity of Carnival farces is analysed and explained as an outlet (psychological and social) for the repressed artisans of Nuremberg. Beset with prejudices of their own, however, these and similar sociological studies are handicapped by the fact that the historical records on secular theatre have yet to be collected in the systematic way that Neumann has done for religious drama (565).

Next to replacing the unreliable Keller edition, retrieving archival documentation is the work that most urgently needs to be done. It would also be useful to look more closely at how the plays dramatising a story (*Handlungsspiele*) are put together, what character types they use and how they relate to the *fabliaux* (*Schwankmären*).

To see how playwrights go about their craft constitutes, in general, a promising field for future inquiry, notably for the religious plays. I have explored the scale of possibilities in composing such plays in two articles (1972 [547]; 1979 [617]).

The 'Berlin (Rhenish) Easter Play' gives rhythmic pacing to episodes strung together, but intertwined and centring on the appearance of Christ as gardener (*Hortulanus*). In his play about the female clerk who would be pope, 'Das Spiel von Frau Jutten', Dietrich Schernberg – one of very few playwrights whose name we know – manages to approximate the five-act rising and falling action of Aristotelian drama. Schernberg achieved this 'through-composed' design, as far as we know, without awareness of the classical model. In Last Judgement plays, like the 'Berner Weltgerichtspiel', the dramatic structure, falling into two parts, supports the play's theological message in a direct and manifest way. After evoking mankind's fallen state in rapidly escalating predictions of doom, a sudden trumpet (in Part Two) signals the Last Judgement. The height in complexity of plot design is achieved by the recently discovered 'Erfurt Morality' (written before 1448). It interweaves four different plot lines, all mirroring one another. Allegorical figures imparting the message are combined with 'plays' on the Ten Virgins, the Prodigal Son and the Rich Man and Lazarus. In addition, there is an overall design featuring the Virtues in the first half and the Judgement to come in the second.

Another area where much research remains to be done is that of the music of the plays. In his compendium on church-drama music, William Smoldon (1980 [93]) gives some coverage to plays of German provenance, the Wolfenbüttel Easter play, for instance, and its melodies. But the only major recent contribution is Ulrich Mehler's examination of musical terms in the rubrics of Latin and vernacular plays (1981 [95]). Mehler finds that in the range between *dicere* and *cantare* many kinds of voice performance were possible. By *dicere*, the rubrics in fact often mean 'chanting'. It will be the task of future research to probe the relationship between words and music in Latin plays with greater precision and to examine the role of music, vocal and instrumental, in the German vernacular plays, a topic which has been much neglected.

This call to scholarship is, of course, directed primarily at musicologists. And coming at the end of this chapter, it reminds us once again that medieval drama is a field that more than any other calls for and requires the participation of many specialists, from musicologists to social and art historians. With our students increasingly drawn to interdisciplinary work, medieval theatre would appear to suggest itself as an ideal subject. That is certainly the main trend in the research on German drama here reviewed, a field with excellent prospects, only now coming into its own.

NOTES

1 Curt F. Bühler and Carl Selmer, eds., 'The Melk Salbenkrämerspiel. An Unpublished Middle High German Mercator Play', *PMLA* 63 (1948): 21-63.

2 Christoph Treutwein, *Das Alsfelder Passionsspiel, Untersuchungen zur Überlieferung und Sprache, Edition der Alsfelder Dirigierrolle* (Heidelberg: Winter, 1987).

3 Karin Wilcke, ed., 'Ein unbekanntes Himmelfahrtspiel des Mittelalters', *Wirkendes Wort* 37 (1987): 187–223, 284–308.

4 Wolfgang F. Michael, 'Problems in Editing Medieval Dramas', *Germanic Review* 24 (1949): 108–15.

5 First published in 1958 in *Lebendiges Mittelalter. Festschrift für Wolfgang Stammler* (Fribourg, 1958), pp. 162–203.

6 Rudolf Klee, *Das mittelhochdeutsche Spiel vom jüngsten Tage* (Marburg: Friedrich, 1906).

7 J[oseph] E[duard] Wackernell, ed., *Altdeutsche Passionsspiele aus Tirol* (Graz, 1897; repr. Walluf: Sändig, 1972).

8 Bernd Neumann, *Zeugnisse mittelalterlicher Aufführungen im deutschen Sprachraum*, vol. 1: *Die Erforschung der Spielbelege* (Cologne: Hundt, 1979).

9 See Thomas Wright, ed., *The Chester Plays*, vol. 11 (London, 1847; repr. Wiesbaden: Kraus, 1967), pp. 227–41.

10 In Larry D. Benson and Theodore M. Andersson, trans., *The Literary Context of Chaucer's Fabliaux* (Indianapolis and New York: Bobbs-Merrill, 1971), pp. 46–59.

11 Karl Langosch, ed., *Geistliche Spiele. Lateinische Dramen des Mittelalters in deutschen Versen* (Basel and Stuttgart: Schwabe, 1957; repr. Darmstadt: Wissenschaftliche Buchgesellschaft, 1961, 1967).

12 *Theophilus, der Faust des Mittelalters. Aus den drei mittelniederdeutschen Handschriften zusammengestellt*, trans. Carl Niessen (Munich: Buchner, 1948).

13 See my 'Ist das Tiroler Schauspiel des Mittelalters Volksschauspiel?', in *552* (1975), pp. 88–109. Answering this question in the affirmative in the same volume is Polheim, 'Volksschauspiel und mittelalterliches Drama' (*552*, pp. 201–40) and 'Die Edition von Volksschauspielen', *editio* 3 (1989): 41–2.

14 In the form of radio plays. In 1976 and 1978, the Hessische Rundfunk televised the Alsfeld Passion and Hessian Christmas plays as puppet plays.

15 See Gustave Cohen, 'Der Ludus de Antichristo. Vortrag, als Einleitung gehalten zur deutschen Aufführung des "Ludus de Antichristo" im Delphischen Institut der Universität Mainz am 10. November 1954', *Beiträge zur Geschichte der*

deutschen Sprache und Literatur 79 (Halle, 1957), Sonderband: 32–6. On page 33 Cohen mentions a performance of this play in Eichstätt's cathedral square on 31 July and 1 August 1954.

16 Maximilian J. Rudwin, *A Historical and Bibliographical Survey of the German Religious Drama*, University of Pittsburgh Studies in Language and Literature 1 (Pittsburgh: University of Pittsburgh Press, 1924).

17 Carl J. Stratman, C. S. V., *Bibliography of Medieval Drama*, 2nd edn (New York: Ungar, 1972).

18 For Michael, see Hansjürgen Linke, *Anzeiger für deutsches Altertum* 84 (1973): 220–8, and Rüdiger Krohn, *Amsterdamer Beiträger zur älteren Germanistik* 6 (1974): 211–18; for Brett-Evans, see Rolf Bergmann, *Archiv für das Studium der Neueren Sprachen und Literaturen* 215 (1978): 382–8, Eckehard Simon, *Journal of English and Germanic Philology* 76 (1977): 592–5, and Hansjürgen Linke, *Anzeiger für deutsches Altertum* 88 (1977): 22–8.

19 Max Wehrli, *Geschichte der deutschen Literatur vom frühen Mittelalter bis zum Ende des 16. Jahrhunderts*, Universal-Bibliothek 10,294 (Stuttgart: Reclam, 1980), pp. 580–606, 766–802.

20 Rolf Bergmann, 'Spiele, Mittelalterliche geistliche', in *Reallexikon der deutschen Literaturgeschichte*, 2nd edn, vol. IV, ed. Klaus Kanzog and Achim Masser (Berlin, New York: de Gruyter, 1984), pp. 64–100.

21 Werner M. Bauer, 'Spiele, Mittelalterliche weltliche [Fastnachtspiel]', in *Reallexikon der deutschen Literaturgeschichte*, vol. IV, pp. 100–5.

22 Bernd Neumann, 'Das spätmittelalterliche geistliche Spiel in Tirol', in *Die österreichische Literatur. Ihr Profil von den Anfängen im Mittelalter bis ins 18. Jahrhundert (1050–1750)*, ed. Herbert Zeman (Graz: Akademische Druck- und Verlagsanstalt, 1986), pp. 521–45.

23 Hansjürgen Linke, 'Der Schluss des mittellateinischen Weihnachtsspiels aus Benediktbeuern', *Zeitschrift für deutsche Philologie* 94 (1975), Sonderheft: 1–22.

24 See, for instance, Hansjürgen Linke, 'Zum Text des Egerer Passionsspiels', *Euphorion* 78 (1984): 275–9, and 'Das missverstandene *heu*. Der verlorene und gestörte Anfang des III. Bozner Osterspiels', *Zeitschrift für deutsches Altertum* 113 (1984): 294–310.

25 Duncan Smith, 'The Role of the Priest in the Redentiner Osterspiel', *Journal of English and Germanic Philology* 68 (1969): 116–23; Joseph A. Dane, 'The Aesthetics of Myth in the Redentin Easterplay', *The Germanic Review* 53 (1978): 89–95, and 582 (1982).

26 Rolf Max Kully, *Die Ständesatire in den deutschen geistlichen Schauspielen des ausgehenden Mittelalters*, Basler Studien zur deutschen Sprache und Literatur 31 (Berne: Francke, 1966).

27 Wilhelm Breuer, 'Zur Aufführungspraxis vorreformatorischer Fronleichnamspiele in Deutschland', *Zeitschrift für deutsche Philologie* 94 (1975), Sonderheft: 50–71.

28 Elizabeth Wainwright-de Kadt, 'Das "Bozner Fronleichnamspiel" und Jacob Rueffs "Passion"'. Zur Frage der Urheberschaft', *Zeitschrift für deutsche Philologie* 99 (1980): 385–403.

29 Johannes Merkel, *Form und Funktion der Komik im Nürnberger Fastnachtspiel*, Studien zur deutschen Sprache und Literatur 1 (Freiburg im Breisgau: Schwarz, 1971).

13

The Low Countries

ELSA STRIETMAN

INTRODUCTION

The drama with which this chapter concerns itself is that of the Dutch-speaking areas of the medieval Low Countries, which in modern terms means the medieval and sixteenth-century drama of the present-day Netherlands and the provinces of Flanders, Brabant and Limburg of present-day Belgium. The interest in and the study of medieval literature in the two countries, which share their medieval heritage, did not develop at the same pace and in the same way. In Belgium, the 1830s saw the rise of an antiquarian, Romantic interest in the Middle Ages, fostered by the Flemish Movement, a cultural and later political expression of pride in the language and literature of the Dutch-speaking population.

Since the split of the Low Countries at the end of the sixteenth century, Dutch-speakers in Belgium had been a culturally and economically depressed majority. In the wake of the Romantic Movement, renewed interest in and study of what came to be perceived as a glorious era in art and literature grew rapidly. Medieval studies in the Netherlands and Belgium today draw upon the remarkably extensive collections of documents and texts which were brought to light in the process. A considerable debt of gratitude goes to German scholars, such as Hoffmann von Fallersleben,[1] for their early collections and studies concerning medieval history and literature.

There were underlying religious reasons for this cultural revival. In Belgium, where both French- and Dutch-speakers were predominantly Catholic, the pioneers of the Flemish Movement and the explorers of the Flemish past were almost by definition Catholic, and inherently sympathetic to the cultural heritage of the Middle Ages.

The Netherlands by contrast owed its existence partly to the Protestant Reformation. Since the end of the sixteenth century it had fought fiercely, first against Spain and later against England, France and various combined European powers, to achieve and then maintain a national state, identity and culture. Its survival against all odds, and its economic success and artistic glory, made the seventeenth century the Golden Age of the Netherlands. The Napoleonic Wars brought decline and foreign occupation to the Netherlands. Looking backwards for consolation, it was first and foremost to the late sixteenth and the seventeenth century that the Dutch looked and not towards the Middle Ages. The nineteenth-century Netherlands, notwith-standing its large Catholic population, especially in the Southern provinces, was spiritually a Protestant country, albeit divided into every possible nuance of Protestantism, and it identified itself more naturally with the age in which its forebears had fought to establish that religion.

The study of the medieval past and its literature came into its own somewhat later and stems from a very different heritage, that of enlightened positivism. In his authoritative 1868 history of Dutch literature W. J. A. Jonckbloet[2] stressed that the laws governing the spiritual and intellectual development of a people need to be traced from the earliest possible evidence as revealed in language and literature. The historical connections between literature and social, religious and political phenomena need to be considered and evaluated. Thus embedded in and legitimised by the much wider field of *Geisteswissenschaft*, the study of the artefacts of what were so often referred to as 'the dark Middle Ages' became respectable in the Netherlands.

Jonckbloet's own assessments of medieval literature were sometimes quite ambivalent: his *fin de siècle* aesthetic criteria made him praise above all the courtly epic and romance, but his solid liberal bourgeois convictions made him flinch from so rarefied and elitist a literature (650). This ambivalence between aesthetic and moral criteria affected other scholars as well. In terms of the drama, it had quite a lasting influence on the study of the Rhetoricians, whose literary guilds (called *Rederijkerskamers* or Chambers of Rhetoric) wrote and produced the largest number of plays in the Low Countries in the later Middle Ages. The Rhetoricians were seen on the one hand as the representatives of a nascent bourgeois self-awareness and assertion; as such their kinship with the thoroughly bourgeois culture of the Netherlands was acknowledged and credited. On the other hand, the literary products of the Chambers of Rhetoric, measured by the aesthetic criteria of the turn of the century and overshadowed by the dazzling drama of the Golden Age, could barely be considered to be art. It is quite revealing that as late as 1910, after an enormous amount of knowledge about the Rhetoricians had been gathered by both Dutch and Belgian scholars, the Dutch literary historian Knuttel would feel compelled to write an article called 'The Rehabilitation of the Rhetoricians'.[3] Even today, there is still some disparity between the two countries in that the Belgians have investigated their early drama more extensively.

I shall now turn to a discussion of the drama of the Low Countries under two main headings: the *abele spelen* ('ingenious plays') and *sotternieën* (farces) in the Van Hulthem manuscript, followed by the drama of the Chambers of Rhetoric.

The Low Countries

Introduction

The acquisition of a very large manuscript with more than 200 Middle Dutch literary texts in prose and verse, bought by the Belgian State for the Royal Library in Brussels in 1835, was an epoch-making event at a very apt moment. Interest in the medieval past and its literature, for reasons outlined above, was about to blossom. The Van Hulthem manuscript, dating from about 1410, contains four serious secular plays, the *abele spelen*, and six farces or *sotternieën*. The plays are not all grouped together in the manuscript, but each of the four serious plays is followed by a farce; the two remaining *sotternieën*, incomplete, follow each other. Each of the *abele spelen* treats a situation concerning love. The subject matter of *Esmoreit*, *Gloriant* and *Lanseloet van Denemarken* is similar to that of many romances. *Esmoreit* shows how love can overcome incompatibilities in age, religion and rank as well as repair injustice. *Gloriant* proves that love is able to defeat pride and bring together two lovers separated by distance, religion and a family feud. *Lanseloet* shows that true nobility is not achieved by birth alone but through a state of mind and a certain disposition of character. *Vanden Winter ende vanden Somer* takes the form of an elaborate debate in the *Streitgedicht* (combat poem) tradition. Winter and Summer here quarrel about which is crucial for love. Lady Venus, called in as arbiter, judges them to be of equal importance and rules that they should not disturb the balance of nature by quarrelling.

The six farces, too, are variations on a single theme: in this case, the wicked woman, a standard character in many farces and *fabliaux*. The wicked women of the farces contrast strikingly with the equally standard character of the virtuous, forbearing heroines in plays such as *Esmoreit*, *Gloriant* and *Lanseloet*, and with the power for good exercised by Venus in *Winter ende Somer*. Indeed, the farce following this *abel spel*, *Rubben*, shows a comic upsetting of the natural balance: Rubben's wife, to his naive bewilderment, gives birth to a child three months after their wedding.

The serious plays and their accompanying farces were not originally conceived as a unity, but grouped together gradually, perhaps selected for their thematic similarities. The Van Hulthem manuscript was probably used in a scriptorium as a collection from which customers could choose pieces. By the time they were incorporated into the manuscript, the plays had been welded together, *abel spel* to *sotternie*, by additions and changes in the prologues, the epilogues and the rhyme. Hoffmann von Fallersleben was the first to print these plays in 1838, aided by one of the founding fathers of the Flemish Movement, Jan Frans Willems. The most important of the succeeding editions is that of P. Leendertz Jr,[4] who edited all the *abele spelen* and *sotternieën* as well as a number of fifteenth-century plays, both religious and secular. A wealth of investigative detail is given in this edition about manu-

Elsa Strietman

scripts, incunabula and early printed editions and versions, adaptations and translations, about the stage and staging, performances, content, structure, authors, dating, place of origin, sources, language and style. A stream of editions followed which continues to this day. Particularly valuable were the editions appearing after 1945 in a Belgian series;[5] the updating and revising of these editions still continues. They are especially useful for their extensive bibliographies. In a different series, an edition of *Esmoreit* was published, with the first facsimile of the text and a very detailed, annotated bibliography, which takes into account the cumulative scholarship on the *abele spelen* in general and *Esmoreit* in particular up to 1948.[6] L. van Kammen published a diplomatic edition of all four plays and their accompanying farces in 1968 (*655*).

Notwithstanding the many editions, articles and studies, the *abele spelen* continue to be fairly elusive. Their author or authors have remained anonymous; though many attempts have been made to determine whether the plays could be the work of one man or of various specific figures, nothing has been proven. Certain specific patterns have been unearthed: a study by Stellinga[7] of their syntactical forms showed that *Esmoreit* and *Gloriant* were most closely connected and that there were a number of important similarities between these plays and *Lanseloet*, but *Vanden Winter ende vanden Somer* stands apart in this respect, as in most others.

Structural analysis, by N. Wijngaards in particular (*671*), showed the possibility that all four plays could have had, as their basic form, a kind of dramatised dialogue, possibly performed by travelling players. This is not too difficult to believe in the case of *Lanseloet* and *Winter ende Somer*. In *Lanseloet* there need never be more than two people on the stage at any one moment, even though there are six characters. *Winter ende Somer* is in effect an expanded debate, very static in form, in which two principal combatants are merely seconded by comic underlings. The names of these helpers are indicative of their nature or status, such as the *cockijn*, the vagabond or underdog. These figures do not contribute significantly to the debate; rather they represent categories of people who would be affected by the final decision, though their plight or bliss is peripheral to a more serious issue: man's dependence for his survival on the alternation of the seasons. The question 'which season is more suitable and important for love' is but a thin disguise for the universal question of whether light will follow darkness, whether life will follow death. Lady Venus shifts away in her judgement from the specific to the universal, as if to acknowledge that it is not merely love which is in the balance, but nature itself.

The two remaining *abele spelen* are of a different order. Wijngaards freely admitted that the greater number of characters and the far more complex structure of *Esmoreit* and *Gloriant* seemed to indicate that these plays, if they did derive from a dramatised dialogue, had undergone great changes. In extending his research to the farces in the Van Hulthem manuscript he nevertheless concluded that all ten plays, which he saw as very closely linked indeed, bore traces of the basic dialogue form, sometimes discernible in the one-dimensional characters, sometimes in the pattern of the dialogue, sometimes in what he saw as a lack of dramatic effectiveness, pointing towards debate rather than drama.

It is generally acknowledged that *Lanseloet* (652) is the earliest of the three and the simplest in dramatic structure. For Stellinga this is an indication of primitive beginnings. For Wijngaards, by contrast, *Lanseloet* shows the highest artistic stage of development, whereas *Esmoreit* and *Gloriant* are somewhat decadent examples, affected by the tendency in some late-medieval genres to become overburdened with irrelevant elaborations.

A different insight into the dramatic craft of the unknown author of *Gloriant* was provided by K. Iwema (672), who showed how the author created dramatic tension by means of the structure of the play, in which the real dramatic conflict in the second half is subtly announced and prepared in the first half of the play. An offshoot of this investigation was further proof of the close links between *Esmoreit* and *Gloriant*, this time in dramatic terms, whereas *Lanseloet* stands apart from the other two by reason of its simpler dramatic structure.

One of the criticisms frequently levelled at the *abele spelen* has been that they are inconsistent and illogical in their use of time and distance, requiring a suspension of disbelief on the part of their audience that does not speak well for the craftmanship of the author(s). A most illuminating piece of research with regard to their dramatic structure, and one which again grouped *Esmoreit* and *Gloriant* together, was an article by G. A. van Es about the seeming neglect of time and distance in the plays.[8] Van Es argues that, on closer inspection, these characteristics add much to the dramatic effectiveness and emotional value of the plays. A character may cover a great geographical distance within one monologue; two distant countries are dramatically but a few paces away from each other, as is apparent from the rhyme links between succeeding speeches in which time and distance have to be bridged. A principle of alternation, certainly in *Esmoreit* and *Gloriant*, less in *Lanseloet*, underlies the geographical changes. The action moves swiftly from one country to another, creating a series of rapidly alternating dramatic highlights. This suggests a simultaneous staging without changes of decor, in which chronological and geographical details are used for dramatic effect, without neo-classical regard for probability. The dramatic momentum is maintained by a series of 'snapshots', which are linked by the forward-moving impulse of the rhyme. Obeying canons of realistic decorum was not in the least a concern of the author(s); imagination was demanded of the audience, and the playwright provided dramatic tension, which carried all before it. Far-off places lent magic; people coming together or mysteries being solved after years was a source of wonder and satisfaction, not of minute calculations as to probabilities.

According to Van Es, many of the 'irregularities' in three of the *abele spelen* must be due to their various sources. *Esmoreit* is the most compli-

Elsa Strietman

cated, *Gloriant* somewhat simpler. These two plays must have been the product of a compilation of epic sources. They ring with echoes of a great number of familiar medieval themes and topics, from folk tales and religious tales to epic and romance. The author of *Lanseloet* seems to have used his material rather more independently and the play differs in its treatment of time and distance from the other two. The major conflicts in *Esmoreit* and *Gloriant* are dependent on either geographical distance or the passage of time by which the protagonists are hampered or aided. In *Lanseloet* the conflict is an inner one, that of man's struggle between the good and evil in himself. The far-off place where Lanseloet's victim, the lady Sanderijn, finds peace and happiness is symbolic: she is for ever removed from evil. The false report of her death and Lanseloet's own remorse at his treatment of her are the safeguards of her happiness: the distance is secondary.

Van Es' article was a seminal one: in dealing with this specific problem of time and distance, he raised a number of related issues, some concerning the staging of the plays, others concerning their content and interpretation.

There is no record of the performance of these plays, beyond the mention of a play of *Lanseloet* being performed in Aachen on 14 August 1412 by the company of Diest, a town in Brabant.[9] Hummelen (*681*) shows that the evidence from the texts themselves makes it likely that the actors were professionals, performing indoors for a seated audience, mixed in sex, rank and status. Unfortunately, there is no documentary evidence for the activity of professional actors in the fourteenth century, the time of the *abele spelen*. The ducal accounts in which one might have expected to find such information have yielded nothing, though a number of other performers are mentioned. Fifteenth-century town accounts frequently refer to actors, as do various annals, but it would seem that these were amateurs, either the clergy and their assistants or members of religious brotherhoods, performing liturgical or religious drama, or members of the Chambers of Rhetoric, amateur dramatic guilds, performing religious or secular drama.

Stage and stage properties for the *abele spelen* and *sotternieën* must have been fairly basic. A booth stage incorporating a curtained-off booth with two entrances and the stage front open on three sides would provide all that was needed. Hummelen (*681*) addresses himself specifically to the question of entrance and exit conventions in these plays, and the stage set-up they imply. The *abele spelen* here seem to depart from a tradition which is allegedly supposed to have existed in older religious drama in Western Europe, where the actors remained on stage throughout the play. H. H. Borcherdt[10] had already pointed out how unique the *abele spelen* seem to be in breaking with this tradition. His main argument for this was the formula with which characters are summoned in the play; the words used ('waer sidi', 'where are you?') were a mnemonic device to help the actors, as were the linking rhymes between speeches. Borcherdt states that the *waer sidi* formula implied that at the time of the *abele spelen* the older convention of simultaneous staging, whereby various locations are visible at the same time, was being abandoned in favour of a mode of staging in which the play was clearly divided into scenes and in which actors not involved left the stage. Hummelen bases his further investigation of the staging of the *abele spelen* on this formula, and also points to several instances where it is absolutely necessary to suppose that the acting space on the front stage is extended with an imagined acting space behind the curtain, a principle that will become standard practice on the Rhetoricians' stage. An example of this is the crucial moment in the farce *Lippijn* in which the cuckolded Lippijn observes his wife disporting herself with her lover the priest. The husband describes on stage the conduct of the lovers off-stage, behind the curtain or screen, in a place not further defined for the audience; whether it is field or barn or chamber is not important. Sexual activities were not allowed to be acted on stage; they had to be implied or, as is the case here, reported.

There are cases where it is clear that a character does indeed disappear from sight, for instance at a poignant moment in *Lanseloet*: Lanseloet's mother will not allow him to marry Sanderijn because she is of lower, though noble, rank, but tricks the girl into going into Lanseloet's room. The stage direction says simply 'Now she has been with him in the room' after a monologue by the mother, and before Sanderijn herself comes on stage, having just left the chamber where she has been raped by Lanseloet and lamenting her fate in a monologue not addressed to anyone; the mother must now be off-stage, or in any case out of the conventionalised acting space.

Hummelen sees the use of the *waer sidi* formula and the instances above as solid evidence of a new type of non-simultaneous staging being used in the *abele spelen* (*681*). K. Iwema (*690*) argues that the simultaneity of staging in the *abele spelen* was not totally abandoned, by analysing the use of the *waer sidi* formula. He shows that though the chief function of the formula is to call up a character, it can also be used in cases where the character is already on stage. Iwema extends his investigation to the use of this formula in later Rhetoricians' drama and finds that there indeed it was predominantly used to call up actors from behind the scenes. His conclusion for the *abele spelen*, however, is that this particular formula could well have originated in a type of staging where actors awaited their turn on stage to enter the action.

Together with the evidence of the instances where some acting is going on outside the visible acting space, such as occurs in *Lippijn*, we might conclude for the moment that the *abele spelen* at the time of their inclusion in the Van Hulthem manuscript were so to speak 'frozen' at a particular transitional phase as far as their staging was concerned. We must remember, though, that these plays survive only in this one manuscript and that the distance between the written text and the use of that text on the stage may have been considerable. Clearly, there is more work to be done here.

Staging

In 1903 H. J. E. Endepols published (in Amsterdam) his *Het decoratief en de opvoering van het Middelnederlands drama* (*The Decors and the Performance of Middle Dutch Drama*). The book is still a mine of information about stages, stage properties, machinery, masks and costumes as well as about sets, mansions and other stage compartments. Performance too is dealt with: entrances and exits of actors, prologue and epilogue speakers, intervals and music, professional actors and amateurs and much more besides. Some of his conclusions are speculative, some perhaps influenced, rightly or wrongly, by seeing contemporary performances of medieval plays, for which there existed quite a vogue in the Netherlands around the turn of the century. Endepols' considerable achievement was to have brought together much information about staging in the widest sense that could be gleaned from the major plays as they were then known.

The impressive work by J. A Worp (see note 9, this chapter) about the history of drama and the stage in the Netherlands is still invaluable, especially for its many references to sources by now obscure, and its wealth of information from primary documents. The title of the work is somewhat misleading: it most certainly does not restrict itself to the Netherlands, but deals with drama from the medieval Dutch-speaking Low Countries.

The Netherlands did not share in the revival of practical interest in the performance of medieval drama that occurred in England after World War II, partly due no doubt to the absence of big cycles such as that of York. In recent years, however, more attention has been paid to gathering knowledge about staging techniques. This is very largely due to the efforts of one man, Professor W. M. H. Hummelen, already mentioned as the author of an important article dealing with text and staging in the *abele spelen*. Hummelen's principal work, however, has concentrated on the staging of the drama of the Rhetoricians (see below).

Sources, themes and interpretations

The *abele spelen* are most obviously and immediately linked by their common theme, that of love, which naturally has generated a stream of publications. Here too, however, we have to group *Esmoreit*, *Gloriant* and *Lanseloet* together; *Vanden Winter ende vanden Somer* again stands apart. The first three plays could all be dramatised courtly romances and much of the research into their possible sources has been guided by that fact. Discussion of their content has centred on courtly literature, to the extent of trying to see the plays as influenced by Andreas Capellanus, the twelfth-century author of *De Arte Honeste Amandi*, a handbook of procedure in love. N. C. H. Wijngaards in particular (670) championed this theory but found himself strongly opposed by the Belgian scholar N. de Paepe, whose objections against Wijngaards' arguments have generally been accepted (673). He sees no need to regard the *abele spelen* as specifically determined by any particular brand of courtly literature; they can be safely acknowledged as part of that literature in its widest sense, but we must be aware of many other layers below the courtly surface. The author(s) of the *abele spelen* made free use of sources which in themselves are a panoply of Western European as well as Eastern and Far Eastern motifs.

The work of the iconoclastic historical linguist A. M. Duinhoven has in recent years undermined many sacred beliefs and cherished theories in the field of Dutch medieval studies as a whole (679). Duinhoven has set himself the task, with infinitely painstaking scholarship, of 'reconstructing' texts, by tracing interpolations, scribal errors, misunderstood syntax, in short everything that can change an 'original' text. He has been able to subvert a great number of previously unchallenged theories and assumptions, not least in the field of interpretation. The *abele spelen* too have gained from his patient and clever excavations (680), *Esmoreit* in particular (659), *Gloriant* and *Lanseloet* to a lesser degree, as yet (685, 686).

The plays: special features

In the case of *Gloriant* Duinhoven (687) casts doubt on one of the few certainties philologists had assumed about this baffling text with its many inconsistencies, namely the identity (or rather the status) of the two protagonists, Duke Gloriant and Princess Florentijn. He raises their status, via an ingenious process of reconstruction of the text, to that of respectively the son of the king of France and the daughter of a mighty sultan. Duinhoven's hypothesis is that this will be of great importance for the identification of the epic source which must have been the basis of the play and for the clarification of hitherto opaque details.

K. Iwema (672) investigated the way in which the epic subject matter was adapted by the playwright for the stage. Traditionally *Gloriant* was considered to have one basic theme: that of love triumphing over pride. Iwema's analysis of the dramatic structure of the play discloses two virtually separate dramatic tension curves which slightly overlap, in each of which a theme is contained. In the first part of the play an initial psychological conflict is resolved and love finds its fulfilment in the successful coming together of the protagonists, whereas in the second half love achieves a victory again, this time not through an inner struggle, but via a series of external difficulties. *Gloriant* shows, more than *Esmoreit* or *Lanseloet*, the epic pattern which formed the basis of its narrative. Marie Ramondt[11] had previously identified the cluster of motives in *Gloriant* as belonging to those of the 'amour lointain'. Iwema succeeded in further defining the nuances of these motives in *Gloriant*.

Even allowing for the haphazard survival of medieval plays, it seems there is enough evidence to judge *Lanseloet van Denemerken* (688) as having enjoyed great popularity.[12] *Lanseloet*'s popularity in our own times is perhaps because the story, and its hero, come close to what in our eyes is tragic. Lanseloet's inexcusable behaviour in the grip of lust and his death as a result, ultimately, of his own crime against the courtly code, make this the most 'dramatic' of the *abele spelen*. Its composition too, may be partly responsible: it succeeds in maintaining the dramatic tension and it has a coherent development which

Elsa Strietman

holds the audience in thrall better than is the case in the other, more fragmented *abele spelen*. It is the only *abel spel* of which we have a record of performance: it was shown in Aachen on 14 August 1412 by a company of actors from Diest, a town in Brabant. It is also the only *abel spel* which survived as an incunabulum and post-incunabulum. Its older printed versions range from 1486 to 1708; the story recurs in Rhetoricians' poetry and drama and the play continued to be performed as late as the end of the seventeenth or beginning of the eighteenth century in a slightly different version (*664*). *Lanseloet* was translated into German in the sixteenth century and into French, German, English and Czech in our own century.

Though it shares with the other three *abele spelen* the theme of love, *Vanden Winter ende Vanden Somer* differs from them in a number of features. It shows its debate structure clearly; it barely has a plot. The question of the debate – 'which season is more important and suitable for love?' – is not the essence of the play. The underlying theme is that of the conflict and difference between the seasons. The scene is not set at a court, nor are its characters noble. The main protagonists, Winter and Summer, though brought to life with human characteristics – such as cruelty, arrogance and harshness on the one hand, and benevolence, joyfulness and generousness on the other – are mythical characters. Their respective helpers are types: a dandy, a windbag, a chatterbox, a sluggard, a vagrant; the arbiter of the conflict is Lady Venus.

Winter ende Somer has not been edited or studied as often as the other plays (*656*), though at present there is a sudden increase in interest. H. van Dijk (*691*), in an illuminating article, deals with the composition of the play and with its adherence to, and deviation from, the traditions to which it belongs. He demonstrates how in the course of the play the expectations about its ending are radically changed. The verbal conflict between Winter and Summer cannot be resolved and, in proper chivalric fashion, it is decided that armed combat is the only way out of the deadlock. All preparations are made and a time set, but then one of the helpers suddenly realises the danger of victory or defeat for either combatant and secretly appeals to Lady Venus to negotiate a reconciliation. Venus explains the danger to mankind which the loss of any one season would entail and she does so with a number of 'scientific' arguments, derived from astronomy. This is where van Dijk sees the play as sharply departing from the popular tradition of 'seasonal conflicts' in favour of a scholarly solution.

K. van der Waerden (*693*) investigated the function of the *cockijn*, the poor anti-social vagrant, in *Winter ende Somer*. K. Iwema (*694*) has further defined the role of the *cockijn*, the least of the characters in status and significance in the play, yet who speaks the epilogue in which he rejects the scientific solution of Venus, accepted by all the other characters, in which the cosmic balance is maintained: in his stupid egocentric way he favours eternal Summer. Insisting on the last word, he paradoxically, in his insignificance, points to and strengthens the implied moral of the play: only anti-social elements such as he fail to see the importance of Venus' solution of the continuation of the natural God-given order.

Iwema deviates slightly from van Dijk's opinion that the Dutch play represents a break with the European tradition of the *Streitgedicht*; rather than a break, Iwema perceives there to be an amalgamation of two traditions: the scholarly and the popular.

Esmoreit sconincx sone van cecielien (*Esmoreit, the Son of the King of Sicily*) has received more attention than any of the other plays in the collection (*669*). *Esmoreit* contains a number of familiar literary motifs, such as that of the foundling, the search for ancestry, the accusation of a queen, the prophecy of doom because of the birth of a child and attempts to prevent its fulfilment. The search for the source of *Esmoreit* has been wide and diverse. The Christian and Islamic elements and the opposition of West versus East (the play is set in Sicily and Damascus, bulwarks of Christianity and Islam respectively) as well as the fact that the hero Esmoreit is called the son of the king of Sicily, have led to a number of articles investigating the historical and cultural background of the story (*675*). A particularly important contribution in this respect was made by L. Peeters (*682*), who identified Esmoreit's parents as having been modelled on Frederick III of Aragon, King of Sicily (1296–1337) and his wife Eleonora of Hungary; the villain of the piece seems to correspond rather well with the leader of the Guelfs, Robert of Anjou, who, as does Robbrecht in the play, tried to oust Frederick from his throne and usurp it. The Southern Netherlands were very anti-Guelf and Robert's reputation was bound to be negative there. In providing this context, Peeters also drew attention to a number of Christian elements in the text, indicating the strong influence of Franciscan spirituality. The Franciscans, too, were very prominent in the southern Low Countries and this of course also invited fresh speculation about the identity of the author or adaptor(s). The most detailed and revealing search for *Esmoreit*'s origins is once more the work of A. M. Duinhoven (*676*). His conclusion, part hypothesis, was that *Esmoreit* in its dramatic form was the last of at least five different consecutive renderings based on the Exodus story of Moses' Egyptian childhood and youth (*684*).

A fierce attack on Duinhoven's findings with regard to *Esmoreit*, the principles and methods of his approach to medieval texts in general and the value of such an approach, was launched in the mid-1970s by Herman Pleij (*678*). More than any other scholar in the Low Countries Pleij is the champion of the principles and methods of a totally different approach to medieval literature, those of reception theory and reception aesthetics. He has created a whole school of thinking which focusses on the underlying intentions, production, reception, function and effects of medieval literature in the widest sense in its contemporary context (*677*).

Pleij and his colleagues have focussed attention onto a whole range of text genres in the late-medieval period which had hitherto not been given much attention, at least not by literary scholars. These genres can be broadly arranged under the umbrella of what the Germans call *Trivialliteratur* (*683*). The title of Pleij's work speaks for itself: in translation, *The Guild of the Blue Ship. Literature, Popular Feast and Bourgeois Morality in the Late Middle Ages* (*647*). Naturally, this research into the interactions between literature and society sees drama as an important field of study. Both the drama of the Rhetoricians as well as the *abele spelen* and *sotternieën* stand to benefit from this (broadly speaking) sociological approach.

The clash between Duinhoven's method and that of Pleij found expression in Pleij's discussion of Duinhoven's *Esmoreit* edition (*689*). Pleij's main objection is to what he sees as Duinhoven's total neglect of the question of how a medieval text functioned in its society, that is, in the form in which the text survives. He also is of the opinion that Duinhoven underestimates to a serious degree the exemplary and typological aspects and function of a medieval text in general. With regard to *Esmoreit*, Pleij judges the textual reconstruction and the hunt for a source as nearly irrelevant. In his view the text as it stood in about 1410 (in the Van Hulthem manuscript) shows the technique, developed especially by the Franciscans, of demonstrating the spiritual values and truths which could be conveyed by a secular text; the audience would have picked up such references naturally, accustomed as they were to interpreting events and situations in the text or on the stage in the light of salvation history. Of course they appreciated an exciting, colourful or funny story which entertained them; at the same time they would have been well aware of the intention of the author to instruct, enlighten and edify them. An audience or readership which had been exposed to the influence of the Franciscans as much as an average audience or readership in the Low Countries (especially in the southern provinces) was likely to have been could clearly have extracted a *sermo humilis* from almost any kind of text.

As was the case in the strife between Winter and Summer, it is easy for the spectator of this scholarly strife to see that a victory or defeat of one or the other would be very much to the detriment of Dutch medieval studies. Even the somewhat acrimonious discussion has helped to illuminate not only the principles of the two different scholars, but to open the student's eyes wider for the possibilities, advantages and disadvantages of different critical approaches.

Whatever the separate origins of the four serious and six comic plays in the Van Hulthem manuscript, by the time they were included in the manuscript they were joined together, *abel spel* to *sotternie*, as a result of having been performed in combination. H. van Dijk (*692*) has shown convincingly that the *sotternieën* need not be seen only as mere appendages to the serious plays, that their composition is well thought out and that by means of the presence or absence of linking rhymes between speeches one discovers a number of implied stage directions, such as mnemonic aids for the actors, signals for stage business, exits and entrances of characters or travel from one location to another. As in the *abele spelen*, monologues in the *sotternieën* serve to cover transitions between locations, a further indication that scenery and stage properties were fairly basic; a journey or arrival had to be made clear verbally. These similarities however, as van Dijk shows, do not preclude the possibility that the plays may have had separate origins; the resemblances may be due to prevailing dramatic conventions, or to the adaptations made by a producer for specific performances.

Traditionally, farces have been held in lower esteem than serious dramas. Van Dijk's article is something of a rehabilitation of the *sotternieën* as independent plays. The stock characters, the simplicity of the plots and the often brawling endings have tended to prevent more serious investigation of their meaning and function.

N. C. H. Wijngaards (*674*) had already investigated in 1968 the structure of the farces with particular regard to their possible development from dramatised dialogue to play. Herman Pleij has shown in a number of publications the exemplary value of the farces, which he sees as having a serious moralising function underlying their seemingly superficial entertainment. He has pointed out a number of biblical allusions which, though perhaps not picked up by the audience as a whole, would have been noted by an active listener. In scholarship and criticism the farces are finally beginning to receive the attention they deserve. An excellent recent example of an edition with an extensive discussion of structure, themes, cultural-historical background, contemporary function and possible staging is that of one of the hitherto little-studied independent farces in the Van Hulthem manuscript, *Truwanten* (see *658*).

THE DRAMA OF THE RHETORICIANS

Introduction

Fifteenth- and sixteenth-century drama and literature in the Low Countries was dominated by the *Rederijkerskamers*, or Chambers of Rhetoric. These amateur literary guilds had their origin in common with non-aristocratic brotherhoods, *confréries* or guilds, which appeared in Western Europe in many places as a third estate of traders, merchants and craftsmen began to conceive of themselves as a separate order of society. The origins of the Chambers of Rhetoric go back in part to secular devotional brotherhoods which sometimes acted as assistants to the clergy in religious processions and dramatic performances. Some brotherhoods became converted into Chambers of Rhetoric. The element of mutual social and economic aid, so strong in the craft and religious guilds, can be perceived in the Chambers as well, for one of their functions was to ensure that their members were given proper funerals. Whereas in spirit the Chambers long retained the devotional element of the religious brotherhoods, in their organisation they were very akin to the

Elsa Strietman

Archers' Guilds, the powerful civic-guard guilds which every walled town in the Low Countries possessed. The Chambers developed and made independent an element that was already present in such guilds, that of dramatic activities. Important archery competitions, for instance, were accompanied by other festive events such as the performance of drama or the antics of Fools, and some members of an Archers' Guild would be involved in the performance of a mystery play, aided by members of a Chamber of Rhetoric. The literary wing of an Archers' Guild could become an independent organisation. Rhetoricians are also known to have accompanied the Archers to their great competitions.

In their activities the Chambers of Rhetoric resembled societies which were numerous in the French-speaking provinces in the Low Countries before them, the so-called *puys*. Composition and performance of poetry and drama, specifically in honour of Our Lady and the saints, were their main functions and there was a strong competitive element, just as in the case of the Chambers of Rhetoric. In the Flemish-speaking provinces in the late Middle Ages similar societies spread like wildfire. In the fifteenth century about 60 Chambers were established and the number grew to about 180 in the sixteenth century. They varied in size from as few as 16 to as many as 150 members.

Their dramatic activities involved the writing and the production of plays, religious and secular, serious and comic. The Rhetoricians played an active part in all manner of pageants and processions. In religious processions, often held on an important feast day such as Palm Sunday, Easter, Corpus Christi or Shrove Tuesday, they organised *tableaux vivants* or wagon-plays with biblical or historical subject matter, some very elaborate, with all manner of music as well as machinery. Giants, fire-breathing dragons, Trees of Jesse with small children on every branch were but a few of the wonders to be seen. On secular occasions, too, the Rhetoricians had important contributions to make and indeed were expected by their town to add lustre to such events as the celebration of peace treaties, royal or ducal entries, weddings, coronations, funerals of their immediate rulers or of members of the ducal or royal families. A very specific scenic emblem used on such occasions was the triumphal arch, which in its elaboration influenced the stage façades of the Rhetoricians. In addition to the simple platform stage with a curtained-off booth, sixteenth-century pictures show architectural façades with elaborate classically inspired decorations, with a number of entrances and compartments behind the screen, which could be incorporated into the available acting space in a number of flexible ways. The triumphal arches and the façades were often created by members of the painters' guilds which existed in various towns and maintained close links with the Rhetoricians' Chambers. In Antwerp, for instance, the Chamber of Rhetoric *De Anjelieren* (*The Gillyflower*) was part of the painters' Guild of St Luke and the pooling of all these artistic resources resulted in very elaborate decorations and staging.

The Low Countries

An important part of the Rhetoricians' activities was their participation in local or regional literary competitions and it is clear that when they travelled they were representing their town as much as their own Chamber. The most elaborate and important competitions were those between Chambers from different towns which were organised as a series of seven competitions over a number of years, the so-called *landjuweel*. This term basically indicated a trophy to be won, but came to mean any one or the complete cycle of seven competitions. The prizes grew in value and prestige in the course of the series. The winning Chamber had the duty of organising the next event, for which an invitation, a *caerte*, was sent round on which the programme and the conditions for participation were set out, both for the poetry and the drama. These competitions were not entirely typical of the activities of the Rhetoricians, but they do show to what heights they could rise and what they thought important.

Two competitions in particular have drawn perhaps excessive attention: the Ghent competition of 1539 because of the religious controversies which surrounded it and the Antwerp *landjuweel* of 1561 because of its splendour. The pictures of the stage façades in the editions have come to be seen as characteristic of the Rhetoricians' stage in general, but this view should now be modified. The Antwerp competition lives on in vivid, much quoted contemporary descriptions, thereby standing out above all other competitions in the eyes of posterity.

Judgement of the literary achievements of the Rhetoricians has been affected adversely by the printing of the complete selection of plays entered into a competition. Strict rules were laid down in respect of their length and subject matter and in particular the allegorical *spelen van sinnen* (moralities), bound as they were in these competitions to answer moral, religious, social or ethical questions, are often somewhat stiff and stilted. The *esbatementen*, however, were frequently comic and possessed verve and lively dramatic action. They were not printed, but used in exchange, copied out by other Chambers and played again, sometimes till well into the eighteenth century.

The Rhetoricians were an important social force in the life of many fifteenth- and sixteenth-century towns. A competition such as the Antwerp *landjuweel* was an occasion which involved and affected the whole town. Special provisions had to be made for the influx of crowds, streets had to be cleared, decorations had to be made and erected. Everything was turned into a spectacle: the festive entry of all the Chambers into the host town, their welcome by the resident Chambers; the presentation of their heraldic emblems; the decoration of the inns where they lodged; the *tableaux vivants* on a wagon depicting a prescribed subject such as Peace; the solemn procession to church. Then came the declamation of a Prologue on a set theme (such as the excellent contributions made by merchants to society) and in turn the actual plays: the *esbatement*, the *spel van sinnen* and the *factie* (short funny episodes of street theatre). Prizes were given for all these phases of the competition, as well as for the best actor, for the best Fool, for the most splendid celebration afterwards.

The *spelen van sinnen* exist in the greatest variety (both as competitive and independent pieces) and were the most distinctive form to be created by the Rhetoricians. Yet from the beginning of the fifteenth century there is also evidence to indicate that the guild members were producing religious dramas very similar to those of France. The Low Countries had their mystery and miracle plays and the few surviving texts are witnesses to what must have been a lively and fully developed tradition. Here too the Rhetoricians were dominant. In fact, it is not easy to find fifteenth- and sixteenth-century drama in the Low Countries without implicit or explicit involvement of the Rhetoricians.

The study of the literature and the activities of the Rhetoricians is a vast field. In the following pages I have made extensive and grateful use of a 1984 survey by D. Coigneau (648). Its bibliography lists publications about special rhetorical features, such as poetics, language, style, rhyme, imagery, themes and motifs, allegory, staging, the involvement of the Rhetoricians with the Reformation and the history of the Chambers.

At present an imbalance in the study of the Rhetoricians is being repaired: the larger part of the research so far has concentrated on the Chambers in the southern Low Countries, especially in Flanders and Brabant, undoubtedly the area where they were most widespread and influential. The Chambers in the northern Low Countries, except for some very long-lived and famous ones such as those in Haarlem, Leiden and Amsterdam, have not received the same attention, for the reasons I outlined in the introduction to this chapter. Gradually new documentary research is being undertaken and most recently the Chambers of Delft and the surrounding region, the Westland, have been excavated from obscurity by F. C. van Boheemen and T. C. J. van der Heijden (710, 717). At first sight the wealth of detail they discovered and evaluated may seem purely parochial, but from it the authors have drawn a wider picture of characteristic developments in the cultural, specifically dramatic, activities of the northern Chambers. An older, very useful account of the Rhetoricians in the northern Low Countries was that of G. A. van Es, literary historian and editor of various Rhetorician plays.[13] A. van Elslander's list of Chambers in the Low Countries is invaluable for both north and south (643), as is J. J. Mak's comprehensive work *De Rederijkers* (Amsterdam, 1944). Some southern Chambers have received new attention recently, namely those of 's-Hertogenbosch (now in the Netherlands) and Antwerp.

The Ghent Chamber of Rhetoric *De Fonteine* (The Fountain) (founded in 1448 and still in existence) publishes a Yearbook[14] with articles, monographs, text editions and surveys of research, which covers the whole field of Rhetorician literature studies. One of the comic genres of Rhetoricians' drama, the *tafelspel* (dinner-play), is the subject of a study by P. Lammens-Pikhaus.[15]

A major landmark in the study of the Rhetoricians was W. M. H. Hummelen's 1958 study of the *Sinnekens*, demonic tempters of mankind and important figures in the *spelen van sinnen* and other Rhetoricians' drama.[16] A second and even more influential book by Hummelen (who is based at the University of Nijmegen) has become the standard work for all those interested in Rhetoricians' drama. This *Repertorium van het Rederijkersdrama* (*644*) lists all the original plays in Dutch, over 600 of them, in manuscript or print, written between 1500 and 1620. An addition to the *Repertorium*, including the *abele spelen* and *sotternieën*, other farces, mystery plays and a number of plays discovered after the completion of the *Repertorium*, was published in the proceedings of the 1983 Cambridge colloquium on Medieval Drama in the Low Countries (*649*).

A great number of articles on the staging and performance practices of the Rhetoricians, often taking into account the visual evidence in engravings, etchings and paintings, are also Hummelen's work (for example, *697*). In this respect too he is doing pioneering work. Moreover, a steady increase in editions of plays is due to him and his colleagues at Nijmegen. The comic drama, subject of articles by (amongst others) Herman Pleij (*703*), is as a genre the subject of a study by W. N. M. Hüsken (*718*). A foretaste of his research was given as a paper at the Cambridge colloquium in 1983. The competitions and the activities of the Rhetoricians on public occasions and at feasts, secular or religious, have been the subject of valuable recent research (*706*). The involvement of the Rhetoricians in the religious issues of the sixteenth century is discussed in several publications, but it is still a field with many unanswered questions. Recently a revised edition appeared of the plays performed at a competition in Ghent in 1539, which had caused considerable religious controversy (*661*). The historian J. Decavele must also be mentioned. His massive study (*645*) of the beginnings of the Reformation in Flanders is very informative with regard to the Rhetoricians; he gives, amongst other things, lists of Rhetoricians who came to the notice of the authorities in connection with their alleged heretical beliefs and activities. Apart from the specifically religious context, this study also provides much information about the professions, status and education of the members of the Chambers of Rhetoric. New work on the interpretation of religious morality plays has also been done by J. B. Drewes (*704*). Finally, and very crucially with respect to the insufficiently understood connections between the Rhetoricians and their society, their political, moral and social ideology, Herman Pleij has done important pioneering work (*702*, *711*, *715*).

Mystery and miracle plays

The Rhetoricians' Chambers produced a great deal of religious drama and they are connected with the performing of the only surviving mystery plays in the Low Countries (*716*). *Die Eerste Bliscap van Maria* (*The First Joy of Mary*) and *Die Sevenste Bliscap van Onser Vrouwen* (*The Seventh Joy of Our*

Lady) are the only remnants of a cycle of seven plays which relate respectively the events leading up to the Annunciation and the Death and Assumption of Our Lady. The first recorded performance of *Die Eerste Bliscap* took place in Brussels in 1448; the last known performance of *Die Sevenste Bliscap* occurred in 1566. In 1556 *Die Vierde Bliscap* (*The Fourth Joy*) was staged, as we know from an eyewitness account by a member of the retinue of the Emperor Charles V. These mystery plays were part of the celebration of a local legendary event linked with Our Lady, which was commemorated by a very elaborate procession or *Ommeganc* (705). It took place on the Sunday before Pentecost and was organised by the Guild of the Crossbowmen who, possibly aided by members of the Chambers of Rhetoric in the town, also took part in the organisation and performance of the mystery plays. Much more is known about this procession, due to the meticulous description given by the courtier mentioned above, than about the mystery plays. Preceded by companies of archers, drummers, pipers and fifty-two craft guilds, no fewer than fourteen triumphal wagons rolled through the town, followed by all the important citizens, by monastic orders, the clergy and important prelates. On the fourteen wagons were depicted the most significant events in the life of Christ and Our Lady, by means of *tableaux vivants*, with singing and music (646).

This elaborate affair took place in the morning. The mystery plays followed in the afternoon, one *Bliscap* every year until the cycle was completed. In 1559 and 1566 the Chamber of Rhetoric called *De Korenbloemen* (The Cornflower) was responsible for the performance of *Die Sevenste Bliscap* and the two manuscripts of *Die Eerste* and *Die Sevenste Bliscapen* are both annotated by the producer, the town poet of Brussels. The stage on that occasion was built 'in the form of the Colosseum' and we may imagine it to resemble the possibly semi-circular stage on which the Passion was performed in 1547 at Valenciennes, with separate houses, opened and closed by means of curtains. There are a number of indications in the *Bliscapen* that Heaven is raised above the rest of the stage, whereas the mouth of Hell is on the level of the rest of the platform. *Die Sevenste Bliscap* most likely had three Heavens, perhaps one for God enthroned, one for the Angels and one for the Martyrs and the Blessed. The manuscript contains a list of properties, and all that would be necessary for clothing the characters. The devils were not only costumed but also wore masks or complete false heads; the cloud which envelops and conveys the Apostles from all corners of the earth to Our Lady's deathbed is mentioned, as well as the spare hands needed to perform the miracle of the withered hands when the Jews try to disturb Our Lady's funeral procession. Further properties consisted of a pulpit, wigs, wings, a grave, a bier, a shrine, St Michael's sword, staff and harness, God's throne and crown, the Host. *Die Eerste Bliscap* contains a list of players, including two women. The players sometimes have more than one role. The texts include a number of stage directions; one frequently used is that of *pausa*, a moment when the stage is empty, although action in some cases is implied behind closed curtains and often music is played. A similar expression, '*selete*', indicates either a moment when the stage is empty or the actors are silent or acting silently. It can also indicate a change of characters or a shift to a different location, and on such occasions music often had an important place.

The *Bliscapen* have not been edited frequently; the most modern edition is that by W. H. Beuken (*657*). It gives a great deal of information about the date of origin, aspects of the production of the plays, the manuscripts, the performance of *Die Sevenste Bliscap*, the music, sources, dramatic structure,[17] language and metrical construction and modern performances.

It must be noted that *Die Eerste Bliscap* is one of the earliest[18] continental plays featuring a debate between the Four Daughters of God and the three Persons of the Trinity (*649*).

Het Spel vanden Heijlighen Sacramente vander Nyeuwervaert (*The Play of the Holy Sacrament of Nyeuwervaert*) is the oldest surviving miracle play in the Low Countries. Its author is unknown, but its date of origin must be shortly after 1463 when a 'Brotherhood of the Holy Sacrament of the Nyeuwervaert' was founded in Breda to honour the miracles performed by a Host found in a marsh in a nearby village of that name. These events are the subject of the play as well as of a chronicle and a long poem in praise of the Sacrament. Its author must have been a Rhetorician. The only known performance was organised by the Breda Chamber of Rhetoric called 'Vreuchdendael' ('Valley of Joy') on 24 June, St John's Day, in 1500. A Procession of the Sacraments was a regular event in Breda on the Sunday before St John's Day; the tradition continued into the sixteenth century and it may be that the play was performed for a number of years in the same week. That the procession was accompanied by various dramatic events and dancing, possibly *tableaux vivants*, is indicated by 'a play of St Hubert, of St George, of St Barbara, of Herod, a Shepherds' play, a play of the Four Sons of Aymon versus the King of France'. There were also sword-dancers and a Wild Man.

The performance of the play took place on a stage inside or in front of an inn in the market square in Breda, and required only six players. It is no more than a description of the discovery of the Host and its miraculous property of bleeding if touched by anyone other than a priest. The miracles it performs are reported. The play required a Hell-mouth and is set in three different places; Nyeuwervaert with its church and immediate surroundings occurs five times. The liveliness and the dramatic tension are entirely due to the *Sinnekens*, devilish tempters of mankind, here called Sinful Temptation and Prevention of Virtue, who do their utmost to undo the good brought about by the Sacrament and in their failure, of course, emphasise the unconquerable powers of goodness. Their plotting and planning, their despair when failing and their fear of Lucifer, the Prince of Hell, provide comedy and movement in an otherwise static play. In this it is very typical of the drama of the Rhetoricians as it had evolved by the end of the fifteenth century and would continue until the end of the sixteenth century.

The only modern edition of *Nyeuwervaert* is that of W. J. M. A. Asselbergs and A. P. Huysmans.[19] It is very detailed and contains an extensive description of the codex and a discussion of all the texts connected with the Brotherhood and of the play itself, its editions, authorship, content, structure and performances. Most of the publications about or connected with *Nyeuwervaert* are of regional interest and few deal with its so far unidentified author,[20] with its structure or with interpretation of the text.[21]

Possibly dating from the end of the fifteenth century is the only other mystery play surviving from the Low Countries, *Het Spel van de V. Vroede ende van de V. Dwaeze Maeghden (The Play of the Five Wise and the Five Foolish Virgins)*. Both the Old and the New Testament, the parables in particular, became very popular subject matter in the drama of the Rhetoricians, especially in the sixteenth century. A characteristic feature of *The Play of the Virgins* is its allegorical nature and didactic emphasis. The Wise Virgins are the incarnations of Hope, Fear of God, Charity, Faith and Humility; the Foolish Virgins have names equally symbolic of Man's forgetfulness of the Day of Judgement: Waste of Time, Recklessness, Pride, Vainglory, Foolish Chatter.

The stage must have been similar to that used for the *Bliscapen* but with fewer locations: 'Heaven, Hell and a number of Houses', possibly arranged in such a way that Heaven was in the middle and Hell towards the right, seen from the audience. It is clear that there must have been a lot of music and singing in the intervals, but the stage directions concern mainly action and movement.

This play distinguishes itself from its French and German counterparts, the *sponsus* and the *Zehnjungfrauenspiel*, in two scenes in particular. Firstly the Foolish Virgins indulge in a waffle-eating feast, for which Waste of Time says she is making the dough. When all the Foolish Virgins are gathered, a rubric says: 'Here they put down the table with food on it.' Whether the Virgins themselves do this or special stage attendants is not clear. Banqueting is not unknown on the Dutch stage and sometimes preparations for it are part of the role of a character, as is demonstrated in the late-sixteenth-century *Esbattement van s'Menschen Sin ende Verganckelijcke Schoonheit (Comedy of Man's Desire and Fleeting Beauty)* (653). Here two *Sinnekens* fetch food and wine and thus liven up the play considerably. But at the same time, by tempting Mankind into indulgence they demonstrate their innate character. In *The Play of the Virgins*, Waste of Time has a similar function – she wastes both her own and her companions' time. Pride and Vainglory are expensively dressed and it has been noted that the description of their clothes would suggest the play's sixteenth- rather than late-fifteenth-century origin. The second scene, showing considerable originality on the part of the author, is the devil scene at the end in which the Foolish Virgins are dragged into Hell. There are no *Sinnekens* in this play but two of the devils have names very typical of these characters: Sharp Investigation and Evil Counsel. The play has a processional ending, the only one extant in Dutch drama. The stage direction reads: 'Pause. FINIS. Then they leave in joy: Our Lord with the angels and Mary after that with the virgins, and they carry her cloak.'

The manuscript of this play disappeared in the second half of the last century and the only modern edition is based on J. Ketele's text of 1846, published at Ghent. Its modern editor, Marcel Hoebeke (660), has acquitted himself well of his task. Genre and theme, the symbolism of the parable, the interpretation of the play, its dramatic and literary qualities, author, date and the Chamber of Rhetoric in which it originated are discussed. Most important is the editor's comparison of the play with its Latin and German counterparts and its sources. The text is accompanied by extensive and helpful annotations and commentary.

Die waerachtige ende seer wonderlijke historie van Mariken van Nieumeghen die meer dan seven iaren metten duvel woende ende verkeerde (*The True and Very Miraculous History of Mariken van Nieumeghen who Lived more than Seven Years with the Devil*) shows its problematic status even in its title. In subject matter it is clearly part of the literature demonstrating the miraculous powers of Our Lady as *mediatrix*. In form, it hovers between narrative and dramatic text. It survives as a printed book of c. 1515 in which the dramatic dialogues are interspersed with elaborate descriptive chapter-headings in prose. Whether the unknown author wrote it originally as a play is not at all clear. The rhymed passages may be the adaptations of a later author, who intended to liven up the text by using two different forms of narration, epic and dramatic, a technique not unknown in sixteenth-century prose novels. The language is that of the Rhetoricians and their most typical poetic product, a refrain, is recited by Mariken. It has become a classic in Dutch literature and is, ironically, the most often performed medieval Dutch 'play' in modern times.

It is an extraordinarily rich text, this *exemplum* of Mariken who was the Devil's paramour and who was yet delivered from evil and forgiven, after truly repenting, through the miraculous powers of Our Lady. It has a great deal to offer of historical, political and topical interest as well as in dramatic craft. Particularly interesting from a theatrical point of view is Mariken's moment of true insight and repentance, which occurs when she watches a play on a wagon, performed in her native town of Nijmegen, in which Our Lady pleads for forgiveness for Mankind from God and succeeds notwithstanding strong opposition from Masscheroen, the Devil's advocate. The play-within-a-play is a frequent device in the drama of the Low Countries, where a number of Rhetoricians' plays have 'inner' and 'outer' plays.

No stage directions survive, though it is clear a performance must have been demanding: there are changes in location, many properties and various tricky actions. Here, as in so many medieval and late-medieval plays, it is

Elsa Strietman

evident that the actors must have been skilled and that they were backed up by elaborate costumes, decor, machinery and properties. Doubts have been expressed about the possibility of an indoor performance, due to the many changes in location. A 1983 performance in Cambridge demonstrated that it could very satisfactorily be done in a small space. And evidence from the sixteenth century shows that very elaborate and complicated staging was possible, mostly outdoors but within the confined space of a raised platform.

One of the best editions in a long series is that of D. Coigneau (*663*). The introduction focusses on the curious text tradition of *Mariken* and the fact that it was probably not originally written for the stage, though it is, as I have noted, eminently suited for performance. Its universal appeal as a story is sufficiently proven by the many editions, adaptations and translations it has had, both contemporary and in the nineteenth and twentieth centuries. Coigneau also deals extensively with its content and function as a miracle of Our Lady.

H. van Dijk investigated Mariken's function and universal significance as a moral example and suggests that the story mirrors the history of mankind, from innocence to the Fall, then to Redemption and Salvation (*649a*). K. Iwema discusses the relationship between Mariken and the Devil figure, Moenen (*703a*). L. Peeters gives attention to the wagon play of Masscheroen in the *Mariken*; he also reveals the connections between *Mariken* and the culture of Antwerp popular printed books (*712*); he places the text in its literary and humanist background between the Rhetoricians tradition and the renewal of the Renaissance (*713*); most recently he has discussed its religious-ideological context and historical background (*714*). W. Kuiper (*717a*) has pointed out how there exists a radical change of emphasis, in the *Mariken*, from the lay devotion to Our Lady to propaganda for the role of the priest, who is in direct communion with God.

Moralities and other Rhetoricians' drama

Den Spieghel der Salicheit van Elckerlijc (*The Mirror of Bliss of Everyman*) has gained fame in world literature in its English translation *Everyman* (*698*). Its author and date of origin are unknown. It survives in three printed versions and one manuscript (*c.* 1595), but it is certainly much older than the oldest printed version of 1495 would suggest. Whether the printer, who introduced this text as 'a beautiful booklet made in the manner of a play or short play' left out any stage directions is uncertain; the four surviving versions do not contain any. One of its Latin translations, *Homulus*, claims that *Elckerlijc* was performed at a competition of the Brabant Chambers of Rhetoric in Antwerp where it won the first prize. Such competitions required moralities (*spelen van sinnen*) to be written on a theme, such as that for the great competition in Ghent in 1539: 'What is the greatest consolation for a dying man?' Though *Elckerlijc*'s allegorical presentation is entirely in keeping with the Rhetoricians' didactic mode, there is no evidence to corroborate the statement in *Homulus*.

246

Elckerlijc is an extremely sober play, which does not require much in the way of decor or properties except Elckerlijc's instruments of repentance: a cloak, a pilgrim's staff, a scourge and, of course, an entrance to a grave. Its subject matter is timeless and universal. Man's aloneness in the hour of his death, his disbelief in his own mortality, has been expressed in parables not dissimilar to *Elckerlijc*, in Buddhist, Greek, Hebrew and Islamic as well as in a host of Christian writings, as R. Vos (*654*) has demonstrated. Echoes of the Old Testament reverberate throughout the play. It is simple in style and has none of the poetic complexities often associated with the Rhetoricians, but a beautiful and restrained refrain poem and two rondels make it seem probable that its author was a Rhetorician.

The drama of the Rhetoricians shares with fifteenth-century art and literature a preoccupation with death (*707*). *Elckerlijc* however shows nothing of the macabre intensity which permeates that period: through the depth of Elckerlijc's mortal fear we are led to his acceptance and preparation. Even the unexpected horrifying desertion of his mental and physical faculties at the edge of the grave is overcome by the lasting loyalty of Duecht, a character in the play representing justice towards God and man. Elckerlijc's last words echo those of Christ on Golgotha: 'Into your hands, Father, however it be, I commend my soul in peace, I go with Duecht.' Knowledge of God's announcement of the heavenly trumpets then leads Elckerlijc, and us, straight through the valley of no return into the celestial glory. This play stresses the comfort that is yet available to mankind. More than an art of dying, it urges us to practice an art of living.

Two issues in particular have dominated the research on *Elckerlijc*: the question of the author, an as yet undecided issue, and that of the priority of *Everyman* or *Elckerlijc*, a question settled once and for all in favour of *Elckerlijc* by E. R. Tigg.[22]

An excellent survey of scholarship on *Elckerlijc* is included in the authoritative edition by R. Vos (*654*), who lists publications about the characters, structure, various cruxes in the text, themes and sources, the relation of the Dutch, English, Latin and German versions, the author and the date of origin (see also *699*). R. Vos' own contributions cover a very wide range of *Elckerlijc* studies (*709*); the bibliography in his edition speaks for itself.

More than any other Middle Dutch text, *Elckerlijc* has attracted attention from English-speaking scholars (see, for example, *695*) and several modern translations have seen or are about to see the light (for example, *666*).

For a survey of the many surviving Rhetoricians' plays, about 600 of them, one must turn to Wim Hummelen's invaluable *Repertorium van het Rederijkersdrama, 1500–c. 1620* (*644*). To give some idea of this treasure trove, a division according to subject matter, rather than genre, will be more informative. There are plays based on classical and mythological, legendary and historical material, on both ancient and contemporary subjects, on Old and New Testament stories as well as on a wide range of theological and religious, social, political and economic topics. Many of these plays are allegorical and moralistic. They are not very long; farces (see 665) vary from 300 to 600 lines, dinner-plays from 200 to 300 lines, serious plays from 1,000 to 1,500 lines. Some plays are printed, the rest in manuscript. The printed plays were often specially written for competitions and thus tied to a theme. The plays in manuscript had a longer lease on life, since they were often exchanged between Chambers searching for material to perform.

The Low Countries have left us more pictorial staging material, in engravings and paintings, than any other European country (700). The first account of the Rhetoricians' stage in English was given by George Kernodle (1944 [9a]) and his work is still a mine of information. The material he used came from printed editions of plays performed at competitions: very elaborate architectural Renaissance façade stages, strikingly similar to the decorative arches used for triumphal entries. Kernodle concluded that the architectural stage façade had the function of serving as a throne of honour and as a means of disclosing and framing didactic *tableaux vivants*, but could also itself symbolise the realistic spaces or objects evoked in the plays, such as a ship, a palace, a fountain. Hummelen, who is mainly responsible for our current knowledge of the Rhetoricians' stage (708), modified Kernodle's views. Not all Rhetoricians' plays were performed on such façade stages and the façade itself did not, in the sixteenth century, have so many different symbolic functions. The degree of realistic representation of spaces and objects was much lower than Kernodle assumes: very often the text itself suggests spaces and objects and it is left to the imagination of the audience to visualise them (701). Nevertheless the façade with three or four openings, below and above, could be used in an extraordinarily flexible way, as becomes apparent, for instance, from Willem van Haecht's *Dwerck der Apostelen* (*Acts of the Apostles*) (696).

Individual playwrights made names for themselves: the best known are the Bruges poet and playwright Anthonis de Roovere (*c.* 1430–82); the Brussels town poet Jan Smeken (*c.* 1450–1517)[23] and the Flemish Rhetorician Matthys Casteleyn (1485–1550), poet, playwright, composer and author of the first extensive *art poétique* in Dutch, *De Conste van Rhetoriken* (*The Art of Rhetoric*), written in 1548 and published in 1555.[24] His only surviving play (he is reputed to have written about 106) is the delightful *spel van sinnen Pyramus en Thisbe*, which presents the Ovidian material in an orthodox Catholic and moralistic manner (651).

The Bruges playwright Cornelis Everaert[25] collected his own thirty-five plays, written between 1509 and 1538, in a manuscript, possibly because no one else would pay much attention to his work. Reactionary in nature, his pieces are informative in reflecting the social issues of his time. Jan van den Berghe[26] (d. Brussels 1559) must be mentioned for his *spel van sinnen De Wellustighe Mensch* (*Voluptuous Man*) in which the sybaritic main character, tempted into great excesses by the *Sinnekens* Carnal Lust and Bad Faith, repents ultimately and is forgiven through God's Grace (668). The work of

the Haarlem poet Louris Jansz[27] shows him to have been a typical humanist
and liberal, tolerant, stressing the importance of reason and aware of the
evils in society, especially those brought about by war. The influence of the
Renaissance is clearly noticeable in the work of the Antwerp poet Willem van
Haecht (*fl. c.* 1530) who uses classical and mythological material. He also
wrote three plays called *The Acts of the Apostles*, remarkable for their staging:
a façade stage with three or four openings is used in an extraordinarily
flexible manner, showing numerous locations and a complete shipwreck. The
Antwerp poet and translator Cornelis van Ghistele (b. 1510) was an important interpreter of classical culture to his contemporaries. He was the *factor*
or poetic leader of one of the three Antwerp Chambers of Rhetoric, *De
Goudbloem* (The Marigold). Two of his plays were performed in May 1552
(*662*). Jacob Duym (1547–1612/20?)[28] wrote twelve plays on classical and
national historical subjects, each containing elaborate stage directions; and,
finally, one notable and in many ways representative example of sixteenth-
century Rhetoricians' drama is the already mentioned *Esbattement van
'sMenschen Sin ende Verganckelijcke Schoonheit* (*Comedy of Man's Desire
and Fleeting Beauty*) (*653*), an accomplished morality written in 1546 for a
competition in Gouda (see also *667*).

Rhetoricians' drama: what needs to be done?

An enormous amount of data has been collected, a great number of books
and articles have been written about many aspects of the drama of the
Rhetoricians. Yet there is only a comparatively small number of editions if
one considers the fact that Wim M. H. Hummelen in his *Repertorium* lists
some 600 plays and more have recently been added in an addendum to it.
Clearly, editing the available material is of great importance.

Even though much has been written about the history of the Chambers of
Rhetoric, a need identified by J. J. Mak in 1963 is still not fulfilled: there is
not yet 'an all-embracing work about the history of the Chambers of
Rhetoric based on archival material'.

We are indebted to Dirk Coigneau, who in a very thorough article (*648*)
surveyed and evaluated the field of Rhetoricians' literature and outlined a
programme of the research still to be done, a daunting task. First of all, the
widely dispersed data need to be brought together, both from primary
sources and literary documents. Secondly, Coigneau recommends what is in
effect a REED project for the literature of the Rhetoricians. Such a project
would need to explore archives and libraries in Belgium and the Netherlands.
Even though much has already been collected, a systematic investigation
would not only bring much that is new to light, but would also help to correct
and re-evaluate older transcriptions of primary sources and texts. Much is still
unclear about the literary and official organisation of the Chambers, and
even more about the social status and professions of its members.

This information would need to be ordered in a systematic chronological and geographical way and statistically processed in order to answer questions about the origins of the Chambers, their connection with the French *puys*, the background of their members and the nature and frequency of their activities, literary, public, social and political – and about their religion: be it as devout believers and helpers of the Church, as in the fifteenth century, or as participants in the turmoil of the Reformation and Counter-Reformation in the sixteenth century and later. There are still many questions to be answered about relations between the Chambers and their influence on each other, about the links between officially recognised and unofficial Chambers and between those in towns and in villages. The social layers within the Chambers and the role of women will need to be investigated, as well as the social standing of the Chambers compared with each other. Naturally the most powerful Chambers and those most important from a literary point of view have coloured our present image of the Rhetoricians as a whole, and this image needs correction through research into lesser-known Chambers.

Their literary production, repertory, religious and secular festivities, all aspects of their performance of drama need to be studied. Estimating their reception by the public and the authorities is a field of study which in itself is a large project. The Rhetoricians themselves frequently complained, often in their plays, about the low regard in which the noble art of Rhetoric was held. But the many instances in which the authorities, both for better and for worse, with support or with repression, involved themselves with the Chambers, show beyond a doubt that their social, political, religious and ideological ideas, their power as societies, the influence of their literature in general and their drama in particular were seen as a social force to be reckoned with. What is still rather obscure is the appreciation of their products as literary works. Coigneau suggests that this might be clarified by collecting and analysing the most popular surviving material, copied, printed or adapted. The printing of *spelen van sinnen* (moralities) specially written for competitions on a given theme, is not a standard for popularity in itself. Such plays would often have had little interest for other Chambers as they were tailor-made for the particular occasion. A far better measuring-stick in this respect is whether the work of a particular author was printed and reprinted, or whether plays were copied by other Chambers. There are examples of Rhetoricians' plays turning up in the eighteenth century, performed by some small town or village dramatic society.

Comparisons between prize-winning and non-prize-winning plays could tell us much about the taste of the jury, if not of the audience as a whole, though factors other than the literary and ideological played a role: actors and performance, rules and regulations for particular genres all had a part in the ultimate judgement.

The Rhetoricians' involvement, as borne out by the subject matter of their plays, in the religious issues of the sixteenth century have already made them the object of research which considers the texts as bearers of a particular mentality or ideology. There is however still much to be done to bring some clarity into the question of the function of many controversial religious plays, which have sometimes been identified with a startling array of theological positions.

Herman Pleij in particular has opened up a whole new field of studies dealing with the relationship between changes in ideology and texts, including Rhetoricians' plays. Pleij's view of sixteenth-century Rhetoricians' literature as exclusive and elitist will have to be followed up by an investigation in detail of more plays to discover whether this elitist character is an inherent feature or whether it is prevalent only on particular events or occasions.

As has been mentioned before, there is a great difference between English and Dutch research when it comes to treating dramatic texts as practical drama and it is here that, notwithstanding the many outstanding articles by Wim M. H. Hummelen on staging and all aspects of performing drama, a reorientation of scholarly thinking, and theatrical practice, is most needed.

I see as particularly important the translation of Dutch dramatic texts as a means of showing that the drama of the Low Countries was very much a part of European drama. Such translations should not only be directed towards giving an accurate text with as much background information as possible, but also towards presenting the text as a subject for performance. From my very modest experience in this respect I have already learned that it is exceedingly difficult to reconcile the demands of the scholar and of the producer, even if they are one and the same person. Accuracy of translation does not necessarily create a performable play that will convey to a non-Dutch audience the spirit of the work, and a performable text may take silent, if significant, liberties. The ideal translation-edition, in my opinion, is one which combines the original text with a literal translation and an 'artistic' representation meant for performance, accompanied by a proper introduction which besides the usual information also tries to place the play in context for a non-Dutch audience.[29]

NOTES

1 A. H. Hoffmann von Fallersleben, *Horae Belgicae. Pars Sexta* (Breslau: Grass, Barth et Soc., 1838).

2 W. J. A. Jonckbloet, *Geschiedenis der Nederlandsche Letterkunde* (Groningen: J. B. Wolters, 1868).

3 J. A. N. Knuttel, 'Rederijkers' Eerherstel', *De Gids* (1910): 433–73.

4 P. Leendertz Jr, *Middelnederlandsche Dramatische Poëzie* (Leiden: A. W. Sithoff, 1907).

5 *Klassieke Galerij* (Antwerp: De Nederlandsche Boekhandel, 1948–   ).

6 A. de Mayer and R. Roemans, eds., *Esmoreit*, Klassieke Galerij 98 (Antwerp: De Vlijt, 1948).

7 G. Stellinga, *Zinsvormen en zinsfuncties in de abele spelen* (Groningen: Wolters-Noordhoff, 1954).

8 G. A. van Es, 'Het negeren van tijd en afstand in de abele spelen', *Tijdschrift voor Nederlandse Taal- en Letterkunde* 73 (1955): 161–92.

9 J. A. Worp, *Geschiedenis van het drama en het tooneel in Nederland* (Groningen: J. B. Wolters, 1904).

10 H. H. Borcherdt, *Das europäische Theater im Mittelalter und in der Renaissance* (Leipzig: J. J. Weber, 1935), pp. 125–47.

11 Marie Ramondt, 'De bronnen van de Gloriant', *Tijdschrift voor Nederlandse Taal- en Letterkunde* 41 (1922): 33–45.

12 J. Van Mierlo, 'Het dramatische conflict in Lanseloot van Denemerken', *Verslagen en Mededelingen van de Koninklijke Vlaamsche Academie*, June 1942, 339–57.

13 G. A. van Es, 'Het Noordnederlandse rederijkersdrama in de XVIe eeuw', in *Geschiedenis van de Letterkunde der Nederlanden*, ed. F. Baur *et al.* ('s-Hertogenbosch: Teulings, 1940), vol. III, pp. 276–305.

14 *Jaarboek der Koninklijke Souvereine Kamer van Rhetorica van Vlaanderen de Fonteine* (Ghent: De Fonteine, 1943–50, 1959–).

15 P. Pikhaus, *Het Tafelspel bij de Rederijkers*, 2 vols. (Ghent: Koninklijke Academie voor Nederlandse Taal- en Letterkunde, 1988, 1989).

16 W. M. H. Hummelen, *De Sinnekens in het Rederijkersdrama* (Groningen: J. B. Wolters, 1958).

17 See also P. Minderaa, 'De compositie van *Die Sevenste Bliscap van Onser Vrouwen*', *De Nieuwe Taalgids* 49 (1956): 10–14, 65–72.

18 See G. Kazemier, 'Die datering van *Die Eerste Bliscap van Maria*', *Leuvense Bijdragen* 42 (1952): 125–36.

19 W. J. M. A. Asselbergs and A. P. Huysmans, eds., *Het spel vanden Heilighen Sacramente vander Nyeuwervaert* (Zwolle: Tjeenk Willink, 1955.)

20 J. van Mierlo, SJ, 'De Dichter vanden Sacramente vander Nyeuwervaert', in *Huldeboek Prosper Verheyden* (Antwerp: De Nederlandsche Boekhandel, 1943), 71–83.

21 J. J. Mak and P. Minderaa, 'Bij het mirakelspel van Nyeuwervaert', *Tijdschrift voor Nederlandse Taal- en Letterkunde* 74 (1956): 256–62; J. J. Mak, 'De Bloedende Hostie in het Bredase Sacramentsspel', *De Nieuwe Taalgids* 42 (1949): 297–9.

22 E. R. Tigg, 'Is *Elckerlijc* prior to *Everyman*?' *Journal of English and Germanic Philology* 38 (1939): 568–96.

23 J. Duverger, *Brussel als kunstcentrum in de XIVe en XVe eeuw* (Antwerp: De Sikkel, 1935).

24 J. van Leeuwen, *Mathys de Castelein en zijn Const van Rhetoriken* (Utrecht: J. L. Beijers, 1894).

25 J. W. Muller and L. Scharpé, *Spelen van Cornelis Everaert* (Leiden: E. J. Brill, 1920).

26 C. Kruyskamp, *Dichten en spelen van Jan van den Berghe* (The Hague: Martinus Nijhoff, 1950).

27 N. van der Laan, *Noordnederlandse Rederijkersspelen uit de zestiende eeuw* (Amsterdam: Elsevier, 1941).

28 K. L. Poll, *Over de toneelspelen van de Leidschen Rederijker Jacob Duym* (Groningen: J. B. Huber, 1898).

29 I would like to express my warmest thanks to Professor R. A. Potter, for the very generous help he has given me in preparing this chapter.

Bibliography

EUROPEAN DRAMA

Collections of articles

1 Dunn, E. Catherine, *et al.*, eds. *The Medieval Drama and Its Claudelian Revival.* Washington, DC: Catholic University of America Press, 1970.
2 Sticca, Sandro, ed. *The Medieval Drama.* Albany: State University of New York Press, 1972.
3 Denny, Neville, ed. *Medieval Drama.* Stratford-upon-Avon Studies 16. London: Arnold, 1973.
4 Muller, Gari R., ed. *Le Théâtre au Moyen Age. Actes du deuxiéme colloque de la Société Internationale pour l'Etude du Théâtre Médiéval.* Montreal: L'Aurore/ Univers, 1981.
5 Davidson, Clifford, *et al.*, eds. *The Drama of the Middle Ages: Comparative and Critical Essays.* New York: AMS Press, 1982.
6 Doglio, Federico, ed. *Atti del IV° Colloquio della Société Internationale pour l'Etude du Théâtre Médiéval, Viterbo 1983.* Viterbo: Centro Studi sul Teatro Medioevale et Rinascimentale, 1984.
7 Braet, Herman, *et al.*, eds. *The Theatre in the Middle Ages.* Louvain: Louvain University Press, 1985.
8 Davidson, Clifford, ed. *The Saint Play in Medieval Europe.* Kalamazoo: Western Michigan University, Medieval Institute Publications, 1987.

Surveys, general

9 Chambers, E. K. *The Mediaeval Stage.* 2 vols. Oxford and London: Oxford University Press, Clarendon, 1903.
9a Kernodle, George R. *From Art to Theatre: Form and Convention in the Renaissance.* Chicago: University of Chicago Press, 1944.
10 Mancini, Valentino. 'Publique et espace scénique dans le théâtre du moyen-âge'. *Revue de la Société d'Histoire du Théâtre* 4 (1965): 387–403.
11 D'Amico, Silvio. *Storia del teatro drammatico*, Vol. I: *Grecia e Roma–Medioevo.* Milan: Garzanti Editore, 1968.
12 Stemmler, Theo. *Liturgische Feiern und Geistliche Spiele. Studien zu Erscheinungsformen des Dramatischen im Mittelalter.* Buchreihe der Anglia, Zeitschrift für englische Philologie 15. Tübingen: Niemeyer, 1970.
13 Rey-Flaud, Henri. *Le Cercle magique: Essai sur le théâtre en rond à la fin du Moyen Age.* Paris: Gallimard, 1973.
14 Sticca, Sandro. 'Drama and Spirituality in the Middle Ages'. *Mediaevalia et Humanistica* 4 (1973): 69–87.

Bibliography

15 Aichele, Klaus. *Das Antichristdrama des Mittelalters, der Reformation und der Gegenreformation*. The Hague: Nijhoff, 1974.

16 Warning, Rainer. *Funktion und Struktur. Die Ambivalenzen des geistlichen Spiels*. Munich: Fink, 1974.

17 Wickham, Glynne. *The Medieval Theatre*. London: Weidenfeld and Nicolson, 1974. 3rd edn, Cambridge and New York: Cambridge University Press, 1987.

18 Axton, Richard. *European Drama of the Early Middle Ages*. London: Hutchinson, 1974; Pittsburgh: University of Pittsburgh Press, 1975.

19 Bevington, David, ed. and trans. *Medieval Drama*. Boston: Houghton Mifflin Co., 1975.

20 Fichte, Jörg O. *Expository Voices in Medieval Drama: Essays on the Mode and Function of Dramatic Exposition*. Nuremberg: Hans Carl, 1975.

21 Konigson, Elie. *L'Espace théâtral médiéval*. Paris: Centre National de la Recherche Scientifique, 1975.

22 Leeds Graduate Centre for Medieval Studies, ed. *The Drama of Medieval Europe*. Leeds Medieval Studies 1. Leeds: Leeds University Press, 1975.

23 Schmid, Rainer H. *Raum, Zeit und Publikum des geistlichen Spiels. Aussage und Absicht eines mittelalterlichen Massenmediums*. Munich: tuduv, 1975.

24 Nagler, A. M. *The Medieval Religious Stage: Shapes and Phantoms*. New Haven: Yale University Press, 1976.

25 Tydeman, William. *The Theatre in the Middle Ages*. Cambridge: Cambridge University Press, 1978.

26 Warning, Rainer. 'On the Alterity of Medieval Religious Drama'. *New Literary History* 10 (1979): 265–92.

27 Kindermann, Heinz. *Das Theaterpublikum des Mittelalters*. Salzburg: Müller, 1980.

28 Meredith, Peter, and John E. Tailby, eds. and trans. *The Staging of Religious Drama in Europe in the Later Middle Ages: Texts and Documents in English Translation*. Early Drama, Art and Music: Monograph Series 4. Kalamazoo: Western Michigan University, Medieval Institute Publications, 1983.

29 Bevington, David, Huston Diehl, *et al. Homo, Memento Finis: The Iconography of Just Judgment in Medieval Art and Drama*. Kalamazoo: Western Michigan University, Medieval Institute Publications, 1985.

30 Wickham, Glynne. *A History of the Theatre*. Cambridge: Cambridge University Press, 1985.

LATIN CHURCH DRAMA

Surveys, general

31 Young, Karl. *The Drama of the Medieval Church*. 2 vols. Oxford and London: Oxford University Press, Clarendon, 1933 (repr. 1951, 1962, 1967).

32 Guiette, Robert. 'Réflexions sur le drame liturgique'. *Mélanges offerts à René Crozet*, ed. Pierre Gallais and Ives-Jean Riou (Poitiers: Société d'Études Médiévales, 1966), vol. I, 197–202.

33 Donovan, Richard B. 'Two Celebrated Centers of Medieval Liturgical Drama: Fleury and Ripoll'. In *1*, 41–51.

34 Collins, Fletcher, Jr. *The Production of Medieval Church Music-Drama*. Charlottesville: University Press of Virginia, 1972.

35 Dunn, E. Catherine. 'Voice Structure in the Liturgical Drama: Sepet Reconsidered'. In *100*, 44–63.

36 Flanigan, C. Clifford. 'The Liturgical Drama and Its Tradition: A Review of Scholarship 1965–75'. *RORD* 18 (1975): 81–102; 19 (1976): 109–36.

Bibliography

37 Cattaneo, Enrico. 'Lo spazio ecclesiale: pratica liturgica'. In *Pievi e parrochie in Italia nel Basso Medioevo (Sec. XIII–IV)* (Italia Sacra 36. Rome: Herder Editrice e Libreria, 1984), 469–92.

38 Flanigan, C. Clifford. 'Karl Young and the Drama of the Medieval Church: An Anniversary Appraisal'. *RORD* 27 (1984): 157–66.

39 Campbell, Thomas P., and Clifford Davidson, eds. *The Fleury Playbook: Essays and Studies*. Early Drama, Art and Music: Monograph Series 7. Kalamazoo: Western Michigan University, Medieval Institute Publications, 1985.

40 Flanigan, C. Clifford. 'The Fleury Playbook and the Traditions of Medieval Latin Drama and Modern Scholarship'. In *39*, 1–25.

Editions

41 Bischoff, Bernhard, ed. *Faksimile-Ausgabe der Handschrift der Carmina Burana und der Fragmenta Burana [Clm. 4660 und 4660a] der Bayerischen Staatsbibliothek in München.* Munich: Prestel, and Brooklyn, NY: Institute of Medieval Music, 1967.

42 Bischoff, Bernhard, ed. *Carmina Burana.* Vol. 1, part 3 of *Die Trink- und Spielerlieder, die geistlichen Dramen. Nachträge,* ed. Otto Schumann and Bernhard Bischoff. Heidelberg: Winter, 1970.

43 Lipphardt, Walther, ed. *Lateinische Osterfeiern und Osterspiele.* 6 vols. Ausgaben deutscher Literatur des 15.–18. Jahrhunderts 5. Berlin, New York: de Gruyter, 1975–81.

44 Collins, Fletcher, Jr, ed. *Medieval Church Music-Dramas. A Repertory of Complete Plays.* Charlottesville: University Press of Virginia, 1976.

45 Linke, Hansjürgen. Review of *43* in *Anzeiger für deutsches Altertum und deutsche Literatur* 94 (1983): 33–8.

Origins (see also LATIN CHURCH DRAMA, *Music*)

46 Hardison, O. B., Jr. *Christian Rite and Christian Drama in the Middle Ages: Essays in the Origin and Early History of Modern Drama.* Baltimore: Johns Hopkins University Press, 1965.

47 de Boor, Helmut. *Die Textgeschichte der lateinischen Osterfeiern.* Hermaea, Germanistische Forschungen n.s. 22. Tübingen: Niemeyer, 1967.

48 Drumbl, Johann. 'Drammaturgia medievale: l'origine del dramma liturgico'. *Biblioteca Teatrale* 6–7 (1973): 1–36.

49 Drumbl, Johann. 'Drammaturgia medievale (II): ricostruire la tradizione'. *Biblioteca Teatrale* 10–11 (1974): 33–76.

50 Flanigan, C. Clifford. 'The Roman Rite and the Origins of the Liturgical Drama'. *University of Toronto Quarterly* 43 (1974): 263–84.

51 Dunn, Catherine E. 'French Medievalists and the Saints Play: A Problem for American Scholarship'. *Mediaevalia et Humanistica* n.s. 6 (1975): 51–62.

52 Drumbl, Johann. 'Ursprung des liturgischen Spiels'. *Italia Medioevale e Umanistica* 22 (1979): 45–96.

53 Drumbl, Johann. *Quem Quaeritis. Teatro sacro dell'alto medioevo.* Rome: Bulzoni Editore, 1981.

54 Grano, Giovanni. 'Sull'origine del dramma liturgico pasquale'. *Rivista Internazionale di Musica Sacra* 3 (1982): 281–92.

55 Davril, Anselme. 'Johann Drumbl and the Origin of the *Quem quaeritis*: A Review Article'. *CD* 20 (1986): 65–75.

Bibliography

Liturgy

56 Corbin, Solange. *La Déposition liturgique du Christ au Vendredi Saint: Sa place dans l'histoire des rites et du théâtre religieux.* Paris: Société d'Editions 'Les Belles Lettres', 1960.

57 Heitz, Carol. *Recherches sur les rapports entre architecture et liturgie à l'époque carolingienne.* Paris: SEVPEN, 1963.

58 Jones, Charles W. *The Saint Nicholas Liturgy and its Literary Relationships (Ninth to Twelfth Centuries).* With an 'Essay on the Music' by Gilbert Reaney. English Studies 27. Berkeley: University of California Press, 1963.

59 Sticca, Sandro. 'Christian Drama and Christian Liturgy'. *Latomus* 26 (1967): 1025–34.

60 Arlt, Wulf. *Ein Festoffizium des Mittelalters aus Beauvais in seiner liturgischen und musikalischen Bedeutung.* Cologne: Volk, 1970.

61 Flanigan, C. Clifford. 'The Liturgical Context of the *Quem Quaeritis* Trope'. *CD* 8 (1974): 45–62.

62 *Dimensioni drammatiche della liturgia medioevale. Atti del I° Convegno di Studio, Viterbo, 1976.* Rome: Bulzoni Editore, 1977.

63 Gibson, James M. '*Quem Queritis in Praesepe*: Christmas Drama or Christmas Liturgy?' *CD* 15 (1981–2): 343–65.

Easter plays (see also LATIN CHURCH DRAMA, *Music*)

64 Berger, Blandine-Dominique. *Le Drame liturgique des Pâques du Xe au XIIIe siècle: Liturgie et théâtre.* Théologie historique 37. Paris: Editions Beauchesne, 1976.

65 Norton, Michael. 'Of "Stages" and "Types" in *Visitatio Sepulchri*'. *CD* 21 (1987): 34–61, 127–48.

66 Sheingorn, Pamela. *The Easter Sepulchre in England.* Early Drama, Art and Music: Reference Series 5. Kalamazoo: Western Michigan University, Medieval Institute Publications, 1987.

Passion plays

67 Inguanez, D. M. 'Un dramma della Passione del secolo XII'. *Miscellanea Cassinese* 12 (1936): 7–30; repr. with preface by Giulio Bertoni and reproduction of the Sulmona *Officium Quarti Militis* text in *Miscellanea Cassinese* 17 (1939): 7–55.

68 Jodogne, Omer. 'Le Plus Ancien Mystère de la Passion'. *Académie Royale de Belgique, Classe des lettres et des sciences morales et politiques* 50 (1964): 288–94.

69 Sticca, Sandro. *The Latin Passion Play: Its Origins and Development.* Albany: State University of New York Press, 1970.

70 Edwards, Robert R. *The Montecassino Passion and the Poetics of Medieval Drama.* Berkeley: University of California Press, 1977.

71 Sticca, Sandro. 'The Dramatic Context of the Tours *Ludus Paschalis* and the Sulmona Passion Fragment: A Study in Literary Influences'. In 4, 85–115.

72 Binkley, Thomas. 'The Greater Passionplay in the *Carmina Burana*: An Introduction'. In *Alte Musik: Praxis und Reflexion*, ed. Peter Riedemeister and Veronika Gutmann (Wintertur: Amadeus, 1982), 144–58

The planctus

73 Grano, Giovanni. '"Planctus Mariae": analisi e sviluppo di una forma prototeatrale'. *Rivista Italiana di Drammaturgia* 18 (1980): 7–63.

Bibliography

74 Sticca, Sandro. *Il Planctus Mariae nella tradizione drammatica del Medio Evo.* Sulmona: Labor, 1984. (Trans. by Joseph R. Berrigan as *The Planctus Mariae in the Dramatic Tradition of the Middle Ages.* Athens, GA, London: University of Georgia Press, 1988.)

Ludus de Antichristo

75 Wright, John, trans. *The Play of Antichrist. Translated with an Introduction.* Medieval Sources and Translations 7. Toronto: Pontifical Institute of Mediaeval Studies, 1967.
76 Engelsing, Rolf, ed. *Ludus de Antichristo. Das Spiel vom Antichrist. Lateinisch und deutsch.* Universal-Bibliothek 8561. Stuttgart: Reclam, 1968.
77 Günther, Gerhard, ed. *Der Antichrist. Der staufische Ludus de Antichristo.* Hamburg: Wittig, 1970.
78 Riedmann, Josef. 'Ein neuaufgefundenes Bruchstück des "Ludus de Antichristo". Beiträge zur Geschichte der Beziehungen zwischen St. Georgenberg in Tirol und Tegernsee'. *Zeitschrift für Bayerische Landesgeschichte* 36 (1973): 16–38.
79 Vollmann-Profe, Gisela, ed. *Ludus de Antichristo.* 2 vols. Litterae 82. Lauterburg: Kümmerle, 1981.

Other plays

80 Avalle, D'Arco Silvio. *Il teatro medievale e il ludus danielis.* Turin: G. Giappichelli Editore, 1984.
81 Ashley, Kathleen. 'The Fleury *Raising of Lazarus* and Twelfth-Century Currents of Thought'. In *39*, 1–25.

Music

82 Lipphardt, Walther. 'Liturgische Dramen'. In *Die Musik in Geschichte und Gegenwart*, vol. VIII (Kassel: Bärenreiter Verlag, 1960), cols. 1010–51.
83 Elders, Willem. 'Gregorianisches in liturgischen Dramen der Hs. Orleans 201'. *Acta Musicologica* 36 (1964): 169–77.
84 Stevens, John. 'Music in Some Early Medieval Plays'. In *Studies in the Arts: Proceedings of the St. Peter's College Literary Society*, ed. Francis Warner (Oxford: Basil Blackwell, 1968), 21–40.
85 Smoldon, William. 'The Origins of the *Quem queritis* and the Easter Sepulchre Music-Drama, as Demonstrated by their Musical Settings'. In *2*, 121–54.
86 Dolan, Diane. *Le Drame liturgique de Pâques en Normandie et en Angleterre au moyen-âge.* Publications de l'Université de Poitiers, Lettres et Sciences Humaines 16. Paris: Presses Universitaires de France, 1975.
87 Rankin, Susan. 'Shrewsbury School, Manuscript VI: a Medieval Part Book?' *Proceedings of the Royal Musical Association* 102 (1975/6): 129–43.
88 Hughes, David G. 'The First Magdalene Lament of the Tours Easter Play'. *Journal of the American Musicological Society* 29 (1976): 276–83.
89 McGee, Timothy J. 'The Liturgical Placements of the *Quem quaeritis* Dialogue'. *Journal of the American Musicological Society* 29 (1976): 1–29.
90 Planchart, Alejandro E. *The Repertory of Tropes at Winchester.* 2 vols. Princeton: Princeton University Press, 1977.
91 Brockett, Clyde. 'Easter Monday Antiphons and the *Peregrinus* Play'. *Kirchenmusikalisches Jahrbuch* 61/62 (1977/8): 29–46.

Bibliography

92 Bjork, David A. 'On the Dissemination of *Quem queritis* and the *Visitatio sepulchri* and the Chronology of their Early Sources'. *CD* 14 (1980): 46–69.
93 Smoldon, William. *The Music of the Medieval Church Dramas*, ed. Cynthia Bourgeault. Oxford and London: Oxford University Press, 1980.
94 Reviews of *93*: Hughes, Andrew, in *Speculum* 57 (1982): 663–67; McKinnon, James, in *Notes* 38 (1982): 828–9; Planchart, Alejandro E., in *Musical Quarterly* 69 (1983): 120–3.
95 Mehler, Ulrich. *dicere und cantare. Zur musikalischen Terminologie und Aufführungspraxis des mittelalterlichen geistlichen Dramas in Deutschland*. Kölner Beiträge zur Musikforschung 120. Regensburg: Bosse, 1981.
96 Rankin, Susan. 'The Mary Magdalene Scene in the "Visitatio sepulchri" Ceremonies'. *Early Music History*, vol. 1: *Studies in Medieval and Early Modern Music*. Cambridge: Cambridge University Press, 1981: 227–55.
97 Rankin, Susan. *The Music of the Medieval Liturgical Drama in France and England*. Unpublished Ph.D. dissertation, University of Cambridge, 1981.
98 Wallace, Robin. 'The Role of Music in Liturgical Drama: a Re-Evaluation'. *Music and Letters* 65 (1984): 219–28.
99 Rankin, Susan. 'Musical and Ritual Aspects of *Quem queritis*'. *Münchener Beiträge zur Mediävistik und Renaissanceforschung* 36 (1985): 181–92.

ENGLAND

Collections of articles

100 Taylor, Jerome, and Alan H. Nelson, eds. *Medieval English Drama: Essays Critical and Contextual*. Chicago: University of Chicago Press, 1972.
101 Neuss, Paula, ed. *Aspects of Early English Drama*. Cambridge: D. S. Brewer, and Totowa, NJ: Barnes and Noble, 1983.
102 Barroll, Leeds, and Paul Werstine, eds. *Medieval and Renaissance Drama in England*, vol. 1. New York: AMS Press, 1984 (now appearing annually as a periodical; see also *132*).
103 Riggio, Milla Cozart, ed. *The 'Wisdom' Symposium. Papers from the Trinity College Medieval Festival*. New York: AMS Press, 1986.

Surveys, general

104 Gardiner, Harold C. *Mysteries' End*. New Haven: Yale University Press, 1946.
105 Craig, Hardin. *English Religious Drama of the Middle Ages*. Oxford and London: Oxford University Press, Clarendon, 1955.
106 Woolf, Rosemary. 'The Effect of Typology on the English Mediaeval Plays of Abraham and Isaac'. *Speculum* 32 (1957): 805–25.
107 Wickham, Glynne. *Early English Stages 1300 to 1660*. Vol. 1 [1300–1576]. London: Routledge and Kegan Paul, 1959.
108 Williams, Arnold. *The Drama of Medieval England*. East Lansing: Michigan State University Press, 1961.
109 Pächt, Otto. *The Rise of Pictorial Narrative in Twelfth-Century England*. Oxford and London: Oxford University Press, 1962.
110 Anderson, M. D. *Drama and Imagery in English Medieval Churches*. Cambridge: Cambridge University Press, 1963.
111 Wickham, Glynne. *Early English Stages 1300 to 1660*. Vol. 11, part 1 [1576–1660]. London: Routledge and Kegan Paul, 1963.

Bibliography

112 Harbage, Alfred. *Annals of English Drama, 975–1700*, rev. S. Schoenbaum. London: Methuen, 1964.

113 Roston, Murray. *Biblical Drama in England*. Evanston, IL: Northwestern University Press, 1968.

114 Schmitt, Natalie Crohn. 'Was There a Medieval Theatre in the Round? A Re-examination of the Evidence'. *Theatre Notebook* 23 (1968–9): 130–42; 24 (1969–70): 18–25. Repr. in *100*, 292–315.

115 Mills, David. 'Approaches to Medieval Drama', *LSE* 3 (1969): 47–61.

116 Bergeron, David. *English Civic Pageantry 1558–1642*. London: Edward Arnold, 1971.

117 Wickham, Glynne. *Early English Stages 1300 to 1660*. Vol. II, part 2 [1576–1660]. London: Routledge and Kegan Paul, 1972.

118 Diller, Hans-Jürgen. *Redeformen des englischen Misterienspiels*. Munich: Fink, 1973.

119 Kahrl, Stanley J. *Traditions of Medieval English Drama*. London: Hutchinson, 1974; Pittsburgh: University of Pittsburgh Press, 1975.

120 Happé, Peter, ed. *English Mystery Plays: A Selection*. Harmondsworth: Penguin Books, 1975.

121 Leyerle, John. 'Medièval Drama'. In *English Drama: Select Bibliographical Guides*, ed. Stanley Wells (Oxford: Oxford University Press, 1975), 19–28.

122 Southern, Richard. *The Medieval Theatre in the Round*. London: Faber and Faber, 1957; 2nd edn, rev. and expanded, 1975.

123 Davidson, Clifford. *Drama and Art: An Introduction to the Use of Evidence from the Visual Arts for the Study of Early Drama*. Kalamazoo: Western Michigan University, Medieval Institute Publications, 1977.

124 Lancashire, Ian. 'Medieval Drama'. In *Editing Medieval Texts: English, French and Latin Written in England*, ed. A. G. Rigg (New York: Garland Publishing, 1977), 58–85.

125 Dutka, JoAnna. *Music in English Mystery Plays*. Early Drama, Art and Music, Reference Series 2. Kalamazoo: Western Michigan University, Medieval Institute Publications, 1980.

126 Wickham, Glynne. *Early English Stages 1300–1660*. Vol. III: *Plays and Their Makers*. London: Routledge and Kegan Paul, and New York: Columbia University Press, 1981.

127 Cawley, A. C., Marion Jones, Peter F. McDonald and David Mills, eds. *The Revels History of Drama in English*, vol. I: *Medieval Drama*. London: Methuen, 1983.

128 Meredith, Peter. 'Scribes, Texts and Performance'. In *101*, 13–29.

129 Davidson, Clifford. *From Creation to Doom*. New York: AMS Press, 1984.

130 Lancashire, Ian. *Dramatic Texts and Records of Britain: A Chronological Topography*. Toronto: University of Toronto Press, 1984.

131 Wasson, John. 'Professional Actors in the Middle Ages and Early Renaissance'. In *102*, 1–11.

132 Barroll, Leeds, ed. *Medieval and Renaissance Drama in England*, vol. II. New York: AMS Press, 1985.

133 Kahrl, Stanley J. 'Secular Life and Popular Piety in Medieval English Drama'. In *The Popular Literature of Medieval England*, ed. Thomas J. Heffernan (Knoxville: University of Tennessee Press, 1985), 85–107.

134 Wickham, Glynne. 'English Religious Drama of the Twelfth, Thirteenth and Fourteenth Centuries: Transition Revisited'. *Sewanee Medieval Colloquium Occasional Papers* 2 (1985): 101–15.

135 Tydeman, William. *English Medieval Theatre 1400–1500*. London: Routledge and Kegan Paul, 1986.

Bibliography

136 Elliott, John R., Jr. *Playing God. Medieval Mysteries on the Modern Stage.* Studies in Early English Drama 2. Toronto: University of Toronto Press, 1989.

Documentation

137 Cook, David, and F. P. Wilson, eds. *Dramatic Records in the Declared Accounts of the Treasurer of the Chamber, 1558–1642.* Malone Collections 6. London: Malone Society, 1962.

138 Dawson, Giles, ed. *Records of Plays and Players in Kent 1450–1642.* Malone Collections 7. London: Malone Society, 1965.

139 Kahrl, Stanley J., ed. *Records of Plays and Players in Lincolnshire 1300–1585.* Malone Collections 8. London: Malone Society, 1974.

140 Wilson, F. P., and R. F. Hill, eds. *Dramatic Records in the Declared Accounts of the Office of Works, 1560–1640.* Malone Collections 10. London: Malone Society, 1977.

141 Clopper, Lawrence M., ed. *Records of Early English Drama: Chester.* Toronto: University of Toronto Press, 1979.

142 Johnston, Alexandra F., and Margaret Rogerson, eds. *Records of Early English Drama: York.* 2 vols. Toronto: University of Toronto Press, 1979.

143 Somerset, J. A. B., ed. *Halliwell-Philipps Scrapbooks: An Index.* Toronto: REED, 1979.

144 Galloway, David, and John Wasson, eds. *Records of Plays and Players in Norfolk and Suffolk 1330–1642.* Malone Collections 11. London: Malone Society, 1980.

145 Ingram, R. W., ed. *Records of Early English Drama: Coventry.* Toronto: University of Toronto Press, 1981.

146 Anderson, John J., ed. *Records of Early English Drama: Newcastle Upon Tyne.* Toronto: University of Toronto Press, 1982.

147 Galloway, David, ed. *Records of Early English Drama: Norwich 1540–1642.* Toronto: University of Toronto Press, 1984.

148 Douglas, Audrey, and Peter Greenfield, eds. *Records of Early English Drama: Cumberland / Westmorland / Gloucestershire.* Toronto: University of Toronto Press, 1986.

148a Wasson, John, ed. *Records of Early English Drama: Devon.* Toronto: University of Toronto Press, 1987.

Cycle plays

149 Prosser, Eleanor. *Drama and Religion in the English Mystery Plays: A Re-Evaluation.* Stanford: Stanford University Press, 1961.

150 Taylor, Jerome. 'The Dramatic Structure of the Middle English Corpus Christi, or Cycle, Plays'. In *Literature and Society*, ed. Bernice Slote (Lincoln: University of Nebraska Press, 1964), 175–86.

151 Kolve, V. A. *The Play Called Corpus Christi.* Stanford: Stanford University Press, 1966.

152 Williams, Arnold. 'Typology and the Cycle Plays: Some Criteria'. *Speculum* 43 (1968): 677–84.

153 Woolf, Rosemary. *The English Mystery Plays.* Berkeley and Los Angeles: University of California Press, 1972.

154 Nelson, Alan. *The Medieval English Stage: Corpus Christi Pageants and Plays.* Chicago: University of Chicago Press, 1974.

155 Stevens, Martin. *Four Middle English Mystery Cycles. Textual, Contextual, and Critical Interpretations.* Princeton: Princeton University Press, 1987.

Bibliography

York
156 Robinson, J. W. 'The Art of the York Realist'. *MP* 60 (1963): 241–51.
157 Nelson, Alan. 'Principles of Processional Staging: York Cycle'. *MP* 67 (1970): 303–20.
158 Johnston, Alexandra F., and Margaret Rogerson. 'The Doomsday Pageant of the York Mercers, 1433'. *LSE* 5 (1971): 29–34.
159 Johnston, Alexandra F., and Margaret Rogerson, 'The York Mercers and Their Pageant of Doomsday, 1433–1526'. *LSE* 6 (1972): 10–35.
160 Collier, Richard J. *Poetry and Drama in the York Corpus Christi Play*. Hamden: Archon, 1977.
161 Butterworth, Philip. 'The York Mercers' Pageant Vehicle, 1433–67: Wheels, Steering and Control'. *Medieval English Theatre* 1 (1979): 72–87.
162 Meredith, Peter. 'The Development of the York Mercers' Pageant Waggon'. *Medieval English Theatre* 1 (1979): 5–18.
163 Beadle, Richard, ed. *The York Plays*. York Medieval Texts, 2nd series. London: Edward Arnold, 1982.
164 Beadle, Richard, and Peter Meredith, eds. *The York Play: A Facsimile of British Library MS Additional 35290, together with a Facsimile of the Ordo Paginarum Section of the A/Y Memorandum Book, and a Note on the Music by Richard Rastall*. LDF 7. Leeds: University of Leeds School of English, 1983.

Wakefield/Towneley
165 England, George, ed. *The Towneley Plays. With Side-Notes and Introduction by Alfred W. Pollard*. EETS, Extra Series 88. London: K. Paul, Trench, Trübner & Co., 1897; 2nd edn, 1957.
166 Cawley, A. C., ed. *The Wakefield Pageants in the Towneley Cycle*. Manchester: Manchester University Press, 1958.
167 Rose, Martial. *The Wakefield Mystery Plays*. London: Evans Brothers, 1961.
168 Diller, Hans-Jürgen, 'The Craftsmanship of the "Wakefield Master"'. *Anglia* 83 (1965): 271–88.
169 Gardner, John. *The Construction of the Wakefield Cycle*. Carbondale: Southern Illinois University Press, 1974.
170 Cawley, A. C., and Martin Stevens, eds. *The Towneley Cycle: A Facsimile of Huntington MS HM 1*. LDF 2. Leeds: University of Leeds School of English, 1976.
171 Stevens, Martin. 'Language as Theme in the Wakefield Plays'. *Speculum* 52 (1977): 100–17.
172 Helterman, Jeffrey. *Symbolic Action in the Plays of the Wakefield Master*. Athens, GA: University of Georgia Press, 1981.
173 Preston, Michael J., and Jean D. Pfleiderer, eds. *A KWIC Concordance to the Plays of the Wakefield Master*. New York: Garland, 1982.
174 Cawley, A. C., and Martin Stevens. 'The Towneley *Processus Talentorum*: Text and Commentary'. *LSE* 17 (1986): 105–30. (See also *175*.)
175 Cawley, A. C. 'The Towneley *Processus Talentorum*: A Survey and Interpretation'. *LSE* 17 (1986): 131–9.
176 Mills, David. '"The Towneley Plays" or "The Towneley Cycle"?' *LSE* 17 (1986): 95–104.

N-Town
177 Block, K. S. *Ludus Coventriae or The Plaie Called Corpus Christi. Cotton MS Vespasian D. VIII*. EETS, Extra Series 120. Oxford and London: Oxford University Press, 1922.

178 Fry, Timothy. 'The Unity of the *Ludus Coventriae*'. *Studies in Philology* 48 (1951): 527–70.

179 Cameron, Kenneth, and Stanley J. Kahrl. 'The N-Town Plays at Lincoln'. *Theatre Notebook* 20 (1965–6): 61–72.

180 Cameron, Kenneth, and Stanley J. Kahrl. 'Staging the N-Town Cycle'. *Theatre Notebook* 21 (1967): 123–38, 152–65.

181 Gauvin, Claude. *Un Cycle du théâtre religieux anglais au moyen âge.* Paris: Editions du Centre National de la Recherche Scientifique, 1973.

182 Meredith, Peter, and Stanley J. Kahrl, eds. *The N-Town Plays: A Facsimile of British Library MS Cotton Vespasian D VIII.* LDF 4. Leeds: University of Leeds School of English, 1977.

183 Ashley, Kathleen M. '"Wyt" and "Wysdam" in N-Town Cycle'. *Philological Quarterly* 58 (1979): 121–35.

184 Collins, Patrick J. *The N-Town Plays and Medieval Picture Cycles.* Kalamazoo: Western Michigan University, Medieval Institute Publications, 1979.

185 Meredith, Peter, ed. *The Mary Play from the N-Town Manuscript.* London and New York: Longman, 1987.

Chester

186 Salter, F. M. *Mediaeval Drama in Chester.* Toronto: University of Toronto Press, 1955.

187 Clopper, Lawrence M. 'The Chester Plays: Frequency of Performance'. *Theatre Survey* 14 (1973): 46–58.

188 Lumiansky, R. M., and David Mills, eds. *The Chester Mystery Cycle: A Facsimile of MS Bodley 175.* LDF 1. Leeds: University of Leeds School of English, 1973.

189 Lumiansky, R. M., and David Mills. 'The Five Cyclic Manuscripts of the Chester Cycle of Mystery Plays: A Statistical Survey of Variant Readings'. *LSE* 7 (1974): 95–107.

190 Lumiansky, R. M., and David Mills, eds. *The Chester Mystery Cycle*, vol. 1: *Text.* EETS, Supplementary Series 3. Oxford and London: Oxford University Press, 1974.

191 Mills, David. 'The Two Versions of Chester Play 5: Balaam and Balak'. In *Chaucer and Middle English: Studies in Honour of Russell Hope Robbins*, ed. Beryl Rowland (London: Allen and Unwin, 1974), 366–71.

192 Clopper, Lawrence M. 'The History and Development of the Chester Cycle'. *MP* 75 (1977–8): 219–46.

193 Ashley, Kathleen M. 'Divine Power in Chester Cycle and Later Medieval Thought'. *Journal of the History of Ideas* 39 (1978): 387–404.

194 Clopper, Lawrence M. 'The Principle of Selection of the Chester Old Testament Plays'. *Chaucer Review* 13 (1979): 272–83.

195 Marshall, John. 'The Chester Pageant Carriage: How Right Was Rogers?' *Medieval English Theatre* 1 (1979): 49–55.

196 Lumiansky, R. M., and David Mills, eds. *The Chester Mystery Cycle: A Reduced Facsimile of Huntington Library MS 2.* LDF 6. Leeds: University of Leeds School of English, 1980.

197 Pfleiderer, Jean D., and Michael J. Preston, eds. *A Complete Concordance to the Chester Mystery Plays.* New York: Garland, 1981.

198 MacLean, Sally-Beth, ed. *Chester Art.* Kalamazoo: Western Michigan University, Medieval Institute Publications, 1982.

199 Travis, Peter W. *Dramatic Design in the Chester Cycle.* Chicago: University of Chicago Press, 1982.

200 Lumiansky, R. M., and David Mills. *The Chester Mystery Cycle: Essays and*

Bibliography

Documents. With an Essay, 'Music in the Cycle', by Richard Rastall. Chapel Hill: University of North Carolina Press, 1983.

201 Mills, David, ed. *The Chester Mystery Cycle: A Facsimile of British Library MS Harley 2124.* LDF 8. Leeds: University of Leeds School of English, 1984.

202 Mills, David, ed. *Staging the Chester Cycle: Lectures Given on the Occasion of the Production of the Cycle at Leeds in 1983.* Leeds: University of Leeds School of English, 1985.

203 Lumiansky, R. M., and David Mills, eds. *The Chester Mystery Cycle*, vol. II: *Commentary and Glossary*. EETS, Supplementary Series 9. Oxford and London: Oxford University Press, 1986.

204 Mills, David. 'Theories and Practices in the Editing of the Chester Cycle'. In *Manuscripts and Texts: Editorial Problems in Later Middle English Literature*, ed. Derek Pearsall (Cambridge: Boydell and Brewer, 1987), 110–21.

Non-cycle plays

205 Davis, Norman, ed. *Non-Cycle Plays and Fragments: Edited on the Basis of the Edition by Osborn Waterhouse, with an Appendix on the Shrewsbury Music by F. Ll. Harrison.* EETS, Supplementary Series 1. Oxford and London: Oxford University Press, 1970.

206 Denny, Neville. 'Arena Staging and Dramatic Quality in the Cornish Passion Play'. In *3*, 125–53.

207 Jeffrey, D. L. 'English Saints' Plays'. In *3*, 69–89.

208 Baker, Donald C., and J. L. Murphy, eds. *The Digby Plays: Facsimiles of the Plays in Bodley MSS Digby 133 and e Museo 160.* LDF 3. Leeds: University of Leeds School of English, 1976.

209 Anderson, John, and A. C. Cawley, eds. 'The Newcastle Play of Noah's Ark'. *REED Newsletter* 1 (1977): 11–17.

210 Davis, Norman, ed. *Non-Cycle Plays and the Winchester Dialogues: Facsimiles of Plays and Fragments in Various Manuscripts and the Dialogues in Winchester College MS 33, with Introductions and a Transcript of the Dialogues.* LDF 5. Leeds: University of Leeds School of English, 1979.

211 Baker, Donald C., John L. Murphy and Louis B. Hall, eds. *The Late Medieval Plays of Bodleian MSS Digby 133 and e Museo 160.* EETS 283. Oxford and London: Oxford University Press, 1982.

212 Dutka, JoAnna. 'The Fall of Man: the Norwich Grocers' Play'. *REED Newsletter* 9:1 (1984): 1–11.

Morality plays

213 Cawley, A. C., ed. *Everyman*. Manchester: Manchester University Press, 1961.

214 Bevington, David. *From 'Mankind' to Marlowe: Growth of Structure in the Popular Drama of Tudor England.* Cambridge, MA: Harvard University Press, 1962.

215 Williams, Arnold. 'The English Moral Play before 1500'. *Annuale Medievale* 4 (1963): 5–22.

216 Fifield, Merle. *The Castle in the Circle.* Muncie, IN: Ball State University Press, 1967.

217 Eccles, Mark, ed. *The Macro Plays: The Castle of Perseverance, Wisdom, Mankind.* EETS 262. Oxford and London: Oxford University Press, 1969.

218 Fifield, Merle. 'Quod quaeritis, o discipuli'. *CD* 5 (1971): 53–69.

219 Bevington, David, ed. *The Macro Plays. The Castle of Perseverance, Wisdom,*

Bibliography

Mankind. A Facsimile Edition with Facing Transcriptions. Folger Facsimiles: Manuscript Series 1. New York: Johnson Reprint Corp., and Washington, DC: Folger Shakespeare Library, 1972.

220 Kolve, V. A. '*Everyman* and the Parable of the Talents'. In *100*, 316–40.

221 Leigh, David J. 'The Doomsday Mystery Play: An Eschatological Morality'. In *100*, 260–78.

222 Schell, Edgar T. 'On the Imitation of Life's Pilgrimage in *The Castle of Perseverance*'. In *100*, 279–91.

223 Belsey, Catherine. 'The Stage Plan of *The Castle of Perseverance*'. *Theatre Notebook* 28 (1974): 124–32.

224 Fifield, Merle. 'The Assault on the *Castle of Perseverance* – The Tradition and the Figure'. *Ball State University Forum* 16 (1975): 16–26.

225 Potter, Robert. *The English Morality Play.* London: Routledge and Kegan Paul, 1975.

226 Fifield, Merle. 'The Community of Morality Plays'. *CD* 9 (1975–6): 332–49. Repr. in *5*, 286–303.

227 Wickham, Glynne, ed. *English Moral Interludes.* London: Dent, and Totowa, NJ: Rowman and Littlefield, 1976; 2nd edn, 1985.

228 Houle, Peter J. 'A Reconstruction of the English Morality Fragment *Somebody and Others*'. *Papers of the Bibliographical Society of America* 71 (1977): 259–77.

229 Miyajima, Sumiko. *The Theatre of Man: Dramatic Technique and Stagecraft in the English Medieval Moral Plays.* Clevedon, Avon: Clevedon Printing Co., 1977.

230 Happé, Peter, ed. *Four Morality Plays: The Castle of Perseverance, Magnyfycence, King Johan, Ane Satire of the Thrie Estaitis.* Harmondsworth: Penguin Books, 1979.

231 Kelley, Michael R. *Flamboyant Drama: A Study of 'The Castle of Perseverance', 'Mankind', and 'Wisdom'.* Carbondale and Edwardsville: Southern Illinois University Press, 1979.

231a Riggio, Milla Cozart. 'The Allegory of Feudal Acquisition in *The Castle of Perseverance*'. In *Allegory, Myth and Symbol*, ed. Morton W. Bloomfield (Cambridge, MA: Harvard University Press, 1981), 187–208.

232 Davenport, William Anthony. *Fifteenth-Century English Drama: The Early Moral Plays and their Literary Relations.* Woodbridge, Suffolk: D. S. Brewer, and Totowa, NJ: Rowman and Littlefield, 1982.

233 Schmitt, Natalie Crohn. 'The Idea of a Person in Medieval Morality Plays'. *CD* 12 (1978–9): 23–34. Repr. in *5*, 304–15.

234 Davenport, Tony. '"Lusty fresche galaunts"'. In *101*, 111–28.

235 Potter, Robert. 'Divine and Human Justice'. In *101*, 127–41.

236 Proudfoot, Richard. 'The Virtue of Perseverance'. In *101*, 92–109.

237 Schell, Edgar T. *Strangers and Pilgrims.* Chicago: University of Chicago Press, 1983.

238 Baker, Donald C. 'Is *Wisdom* a "Professional" Play?' In *103*, 67–86.

239 Gibson, Gail McMurray. 'The Play of *Wisdom* and the Abbey of St. Edmunds'. In *103*, 39–66.

240 Johnston, Alexandra F. '*Wisdom* and the Records: Is There a Moral?' In *103*, 87–102.

241 Pederson, Steven I. 'The Staging of *The Castle of Perseverance*: A Re-analysis; Testing the List Theory'. *Theatre Notebook* 40 (1986): 51–62, 104–13.

Bibliography

Tudor drama

242 Craik, T. W. *The Tudor Interlude: Stage, Costume, and Acting*. Leicester: Leicester University Press, 1958.

243 Heiserman, Arthur. *Skelton and Satire*. Chicago: University of Chicago Press, 1961.

244 Dessen, Alan C. '*Volpone* and the Late Morality Tradition'. *MLQ* 25 (1964): 383–99.

245 Dessen, Alan C. 'The "Estates" Morality Play'. *Studies in Philology* 62 (1965): 121–36.

246 Habicht, Werner. 'The Wit-Interludes and the Form of Pre-Shakespearean "Romantic Comedy"'. *RD* 8 (1965): 73–88.

247 Happé, Peter. 'Tragic Themes in Three Tudor Moralities'. *Studies in English Literature* 5 (1965): 207–27.

248 Harris, William O. *Skelton's Magnyfycence and the Cardinal Virtue Tradition*. Chapel Hill: University of North Carolina Press, 1965.

249 Bevington, David. *Tudor Drama and Politics*. Cambridge, MA: Harvard University Press, 1968.

250 Velz, John W., and Carl P. Daw, Jr. 'Tradition and Originality in *Wyt and Science*'. *Studies in Philology* 65 (1968): 631–46.

251 Anglo, Sidney. *Spectacle, Pageantry and Early Tudor Policy*. Oxford and London: Oxford University Press, Clarendon, 1969.

252 Dessen, Alan C. *Jonson's Moral Comedy*. Evanston: Northwestern University Press, 1971.

253 Hosley, Richard. 'Three Kinds of Outdoor Theatre before Shakespeare'. *Theatre Survey* 12 (1971): 1–33.

254 Pineas, Rainer. *Tudor and Early Stuart Anti-Catholic Drama*. Bibliotheca humanistica et reformatorica 5. Nieuwkorp: De Graaf, 1972.

255 Bevington, David. 'Popular and Courtly Traditions on the Early Tudor Stage'. In *3*, 91–107.

256 Jones, Robert C. 'Dangerous Sport: The Audience's Engagement with Vice in the Moral Interludes'. *RD* 6 (1973): 45–64.

257 Kantrowitz, Joanne Spencer. 'Dramatic Allegory, or, Exploring the Moral Play'. *CD* 7 (1973): 668–82.

258 Kantrowitz, Joanne Spencer. *Dramatic Allegory: Lindsay's 'Ane Satyre of the Thrie Estaitis'*. Lincoln: University of Nebraska Press, 1975.

259 Yates, Frances A. *Astrea: The Imperial Theme in the Sixteenth Century*. London: Routledge and Kegan Paul, 1975.

260 Parry, David, and Kathy Pearl, eds. *Nice Wanton: A PLS Performance Text*. Toronto: PLS, 1978.

261 Diehl, Huston. 'The Iconography of Violence in English Renaissance Tragedy'. *RD* 11 (1980): 27–44.

262 Lancashire, Ian, ed. *Two Tudor Interludes: Youth and Hickscorner*. Manchester: Manchester University Press, and Baltimore: Johns Hopkins University Press, 1980.

263 Nelson, Alan H., ed. *The Plays of Henry Medwall*. Cambridge: D. S. Brewer, and Totowa, NJ: Rowman and Littlefield, 1980.

264 Diehl, Huston. '"Reduce Thy Understanding to Thine Eye": Seeing and Interpreting in *The Atheist's Tragedy*'. *Studies in Philology* 78 (1981): 47–60.

265 Axton, Marie, ed. *Three Tudor Classical Interludes*. Cambridge: D. S. Brewer, and Totowa, NJ: Rowman and Littlefield, 1982.

Bibliography

266 Diehl, Huston. 'Inversion, Parody, and Irony: The Visual Rhetoric of Renaissance English Tragedy'. *Studies in English Literature* 22 (1982): 197–209.

Influence on Elizabethan drama and Shakespeare

267 Cole, Douglas. *Suffering and Evil in the Plays of Christopher Marlowe*. Princeton: Princeton University Press, 1962.
268 Southern, Richard. 'The Contributions of the Interludes to Elizabethan Staging'. In *Essays on Shakespeare and Elizabethan Drama in Honor of Hardin Craig*, ed. Richard Hosley (Columbia: University of Missouri Press, 1962), 3–14.
269 Mack, Maynard. *King Lear in Our Time*. Berkeley: University of California Press, 1965.
270 Margeson, J. M. R. *The Origins of English Tragedy*. Oxford and London: Oxford University Press, Clarendon, 1967.
271 Wickham, Glynne. *Shakespeare's Dramatic Heritage*. London: Routledge and Kegan Paul, 1969.
272 Dessen, Alan C. 'The Morall as an Elizabethan Dramatic Kind: An Exploratory Essay'. *CD* 5 (1971): 138–58.
273 Southern, Richard. *The Staging of Plays before Shakespeare*. New York: Theatre Arts, 1973.
274 Dessen, Alan C. 'The Elizabethan Stage Jew and Christian Example: Gerontus, Barabas, and Shylock'. *MLQ* 35 (1974): 231–45.
275 Dessen, Alan C. 'The Intemperate Knight and the Politic Prince: Late Morality Structure in 1 Henry IV'. *Shakespeare Studies* 7 (1974): 147–71.
276 Bevington, David. 'Discontinuity in Medieval Acting Traditions'. In *The Elizabethan Theatre*, vol. v. Ed. George Hibbard (Hamden, CT: Archon, 1975), 1–16.
277 Creeth, Edmund. *Mankynd in Shakespeare*. Athens, GA: University of Georgia Press, 1976.
278 Dessen, Alan C. *Elizabethan Drama and the Viewer's Eye*. Chapel Hill: University of North Carolina Press, 1977.
279 Dessen, Alan C. 'Homilies and Anomalies: The Legacy of the Morality Play to the Age of Shakespeare'. *Shakespeare Studies* 11 (1978): 243–58.
280 Wasson, John. 'The Morality Play: Ancestor of Elizabethan Drama?' *CD* 13 (1979–80): 210–21. Repr. in 5, 316–27.
281 Wilson, Jean. *Entertainments for Elizabeth I*. Studies in Elizabethan and Renaissance Culture 2. Woodbridge, Suffolk: D. S. Brewer, and Totowa, NJ: Rowman & Littlefield, 1980.
282 Dessen, Alan C. *Shakespeare and the Late Moral Plays*. Lincoln: University of Nebraska Press, 1986.

FRANCE

Surveys, general

283 Frank, Grace. *The Medieval French Drama*. Oxford and London: Oxford University Press, Clarendon, 1954; 2nd edn, 1960.
284 Droz, Eugénie, ed. *Le Recueil Trepperel: Fac-similé des trente-cinq pièces de l'original*. Geneva: Slatkine Reprints [1966].
285 Lewicka, Halina, ed. *Le Recueil du British Museum: Fac-similé des soixante-quatre pièces de l'original*. Geneva: Slatkine Reprints, 1970.
286 Chocheyras, Jacques. *Le Théâtre religieux en Savoie au XVIe siècle*. Geneva: Droz, 1971.

Bibliography

287 Helmich, Werner, ed. *Manuscrit La Vallière: Fac-similé intégral du MS. 24341 de la Bibliothèque Nationale de Paris.* Geneva: Slatkine Reprints, 1972.

288 Aubailly, Jean-Claude. *Le Théâtre médiéval profane et comique.* Paris: Larousse, 1975.

289 Chocheyras, Jacques. *Le Théâtre religieux en Dauphiné du Moyen Age au XVIIIe siècle.* Geneva: Droz, 1975.

290 Schoell, Konrad. *Das komische Theater des französischen Mittelalters.* Munich: Wilhelm Fink, 1975.

291 Helmich, Werner. *Die Allegorie im französischen Theater des 15. und 16. Jahrhunderts.* Tübingen: Max Niemeyer, 1976.

292 Runnalls, Graham A. 'Medieval French Drama: A Review of Recent Scholarship. Part I: Religious Drama'. *RORD* 21 (1978): 83–90; 22 (1979): 111–36.

293 Hindley, Alan. 'Medieval French Drama: A Review of Recent Scholarship. Part II: Comic Drama'. *RORD* 23 (1980): 93–126.

294 Knight, Alan E. 'Drama and Society in Late Medieval Flanders and Picardy'. *The Chaucer Review* 14 (1980): 379–89.

295 Lewicka, Halina. *Bibliographie du théâtre profane français des XVe et XVIe siècles.* 2nd edn. Warsaw, Paris: Centre National de la Recherche Scientifique, 1980.

296 Rey-Flaud, Henri. *Pour une dramaturgie du Moyen Age.* Paris: Presses Universitaires de France, 1980.

297 Runnalls, Graham A. '"Mansion" and "Lieu": Two Technical Terms in Medieval French Staging?' *French Studies* 35 (1981): 385–93.

298 Knight, Alan E. *Aspects of Genre in Late Medieval French Drama.* Manchester: Manchester University Press, 1983.

299 Payen, Jean-Charles. 'Théâtre médiéval et culture urbaine'. *Revue d'histoire du théâtre* 35 (1983): 233–50.

The early period (1100–1300)

The *sponsus*

300 Avalle, D'Arco, and Raffaello Monterosso, eds. *Sponsus.* Milan: Riccordo Ricciardi, 1965.

301 Hunt, Tony. 'Le "sensus moralis" du *Sponsus*'. *Cahiers de civilisation médiévale* 26 (1983): 327–34.

Le Jeu d'Adam

302 Aebischer, Paul, ed. *Le Mystère d'Adam (Ordo representacionis Ade).* Geneva: Droz, 1964.

303 Noomen, Willem. 'Le Jeu d'Adam. Etude descriptive et analytique'. *Romania* 89 (1968): 145–93.

304 Sletsjöe, Leif. *Le Mystère d'Adam: Edition diplomatique.* Paris: Klincksieck, 1968.

305 Noomen, Willem, ed. *Le Jeu d'Adam (Ordo representacionis Ade).* Paris: Honoré Champion, 1971.

306 Payen, Jean-Charles. 'Idéologie et théâtralité dans l'*Ordo Representationis Adae*'. *Etudes anglaises* 25 (1972): 19–29.

307 Muir, Lynette R. *Liturgy and Drama in the Anglo-Norman Adam.* Oxford: Basil Blackwell, 1973.

308 Hunt, Tony. 'The Unity of the Play of Adam (*Ordo representacionis Ade*)'. *Romania* 96 (1975): 368–88, 497–527.

309 Nykrog, Per. '*Le Jeu d'Adam*: Une interprétation'. *Mosaic* 8 (1975): 7–16.

Bibliography

310 Accarie, Maurice. 'Théologie et morale dans le *Jeu d'Adam*'. *Revue des langues romanes* 83 (1978): 123–47.
311 Vaughan, M. F. 'The Prophets of the Anglo-Norman *Adam*'. *Traditio* 39 (1983): 81–114.
312 Bordier, Jean-Pierre. 'Le Fils et le fruit: Le *Jeu d'Adam* entre la théologie et le mythe'. In 7, 84–102.
313 Justice, Steven. 'The Authority of Ritual in the *Jeu d'Adam*'. *Speculum* 62 (1987): 851–64.

Le Jeu de Saint Nicolas
314 Henry, Albert, ed. Le *'Jeu de Saint Nicolas'* de Jean Bodel. 2nd edn. Brussels: Presses Universitaires de Bruxelles, 1965.
315 Hunt, Tony. 'The Authenticity of the Prologue of Bodel's *Jeu de Saint Nicolas*'. *Romania* 97 (1976): 252–67.

Courtois d'Arras
316 Togeby, Knud. 'Courtois d'Arras'. *Travaux de linguistique et de littérature* 11 (1973): 603–14.
317 Macrì, Giuseppe, ed. Li *'Lais de courtois'*, *commedia francese del sec. XIII*. Lecce: Adriatica Editrice Salentina, 1977.

Le Miracle de Théophile
318 Gompertz, Stéphane. 'Du Dialogue perdu au dialogue retrouvé'. *Romania* 100 (1979): 519–28.
319 Mickel, Emanuel J. 'Free Will and Antithesis in the *Miracle de Theophile*'. *Zeitschrift für romanische Philologie* 99 (1983): 304–16.

Adam de la Halle
320 Adler, Alfred. *Sens et composition du 'Jeu de la feuillée'.* Ann Arbor: University of Michigan Press, 1956.
321 Gsell, Otto, ed. *Das 'Jeu de la feuillée' von Adam de la Halle.* Würzburg, 1970.
322 Cartier, Norman R. *Le Bossu désenchanté: Etude sur le 'Jeu de la feuillée'.* Geneva: Droz, 1971.
323 Mazouer, Charles. 'Naïveté et naturel dans le *Jeu de Robin et Marion*'. *Romania* 93 (1972): 378–93.
324 Mauron, Claude. *Le 'Jeu de la feuillée': Etude psychocritique.* Paris: José Corti, 1973.
325 Dufournet, Jean. *Adam de la Halle à la recherche de lui-même.* Paris: Société d'Edition d'Enseignement Supérieur, 1974.
326 Dufournet, Jean, ed. *Adam de la Halle: Le Jeu de la feuillée.* Ghent: Editions Scientifiques, 1977.
327 Dufournet, Jean. *Sur le 'Jeu de la feuillée'.* Paris: Société d'Edition d'Enseignement Supérieur, 1977.
328 Dufournet, Jean. 'Notes complémentaires sur le *Jeu de la feuillée*'. *Romania* 99 (1978): 98–108.
329 Rousse, Michel. 'Le *Jeu de la feuillée* et les coutumes du cycle de mai'. In *Mélanges de langue et littérature françaises du Moyen Age et de la Renaissance offerts à Charles Foulon* (Rennes: Université de Haute-Bretagne, 1980), 313–27.

Other plays
330 Perry, Anne Amari. 'An Early Historical Play: The *Seinte Resureccion*'. *Indiana Social Studies Quarterly* 31 (1978): 39–45.

Bibliography

331 Dufournet, Jean, trans. *Le Garçon et l'Aveugle*. Paris: Honoré Champion, 1982.

The late period (1300–1550)

Biblical plays

332 Jodogne, Omer, ed. *Le 'Mystère de la Passion' de Jean Michel*. Gembloux: J. Duculot, 1959.

333 Jodogne, Omer, ed. *Le 'Mystère de la Passion' d'Arnoul Gréban*. 2 vols. Brussels: Palais des Académies, 1965–83.

334 Craig, Barbara, ed. *'La Creacion', 'La Transgression', and 'L'Expulsion' of the 'Mistere du Viel Testament'*. Lawrence: University of Kansas Publications [1968].

335 Konigson, Elie. *La Représentation d'un mystère de la Passion à Valenciennes en 1547*. Paris: Centre National de la Recherche Scientifique, 1969.

336 Lazar, Moshé, ed. *Le Jugement Dernier (Lo Jutgamen General): Drame provençal du XVe siècle*. Paris: Klincksieck, 1971.

337 Meiller, Albert, ed. *La Pacience de Job: Mystère anonyme du XVe siècle*. Paris: Klincksieck, 1971.

338 Bordier, Jean-Pierre. 'Lectures du *Palatinus*'. *Le Moyen Age* 80 (1974): 429–82.

339 Runnalls, Graham A., ed. *Le Mystère de la Passion Nostre Seigneur*. Geneva: Droz, 1974.

340 Gallagher, Edward J., ed. *A Critical Edition of 'La Passion Nostre Seigneur', from Manuscript 1131 from the Bibliothèque Sainte-Geneviève, Paris*. Chapel Hill: University of North Carolina Press, 1976.

341 Elliott, John R., and Graham A. Runnalls, eds. *The Baptism and Temptation of Christ*. New Haven and London: Yale University Press, 1978.

342 Gangler-Mundwiler, Dominique. 'Les diableries nécessaires'. In *Mélanges de littérature du Moyen Age au XXe siècle offerts à Mademoiselle Jeanne Lods* (2 vols.; Paris: Ecole Normale Supérieure de Jeunes Filles, 1978), vol. I, 249–68.

343 Accarie, Maurice. *Le Théâtre sacré de la fin du Moyen Age: Etude sur le sens moral de la 'Passion' de Jean Michel*. Geneva: Droz, 1979.

344 Durbin, Peter, and Lynette Muir, eds. *The 'Passion de Semur'*. Leeds: Centre for Medieval Studies, 1981.

345 Runnalls, Graham A., ed. *La Passion d'Auvergne*. Geneva: Droz, 1982.

346 Thiry, Claude. 'Une Avocate inspirée? Procula dans quelques passions françaises'. *Le Moyen français* 11 (1982): 54–88.

347 Craig, Barbara, ed. *The Evolution of a Mystery Play*. Orlando: French Literature Publications Co., 1983.

348 Runnalls, Graham A. 'The French Passion Play Fragment of the University of Leiden'. *Romania* 105 (1984): 88–110.

349 Vitale-Brovarone, Alessandro. *Il quaderno di segreti d'un regista provenzale del Medioevo: Note per la messa in scena d'una Passione*. Alessandria: Edizioni dell'Orso, 1984.

350 Bibolet, Jean-Claude, ed. *Le Mystère de la Passion de Troyes*. 2 vols. Geneva: Droz, 1987.

Miracle plays

351 Runnalls, Graham A. 'The Manuscript of the *Miracles de Nostre Dame par personnages*'. *Romance Philology* 22 (1968–9): 15–22.

352 Runnalls, Graham A. 'Mediaeval Trade Guilds and the *Miracles de Nostre Dame par personnages*'. *Medium Aevum* 39 (1970): 257–87.

353 Runnalls, Graham A. 'The *Miracles de Nostre Dame par personnages*: Erasures

Bibliography

in the MS. and the Dates of the Plays and the "Serventois"'. *Philological Quarterly* 49 (1970): 19–29.

354 Locey, Lenita, and Michael Locey, eds. *Le Mistere d'une jeune fille laquelle se voulut habandonner a peché*. Geneva: Droz, 1976.

355 Jodogne, Omer, ed. *Miracle de Saint Nicolas et d'un Juif*. Geneva: Droz, 1982.

Saint plays

356 Mills, Leonard R. *Le Mystère de saint Sébastien*. Geneva: Droz, 1965.

357 Meiller, Albert, ed. *Le Mystère du roy Advenir*. Geneva: Droz, 1970.

358 Seubert, Bernard J. *Le Geu saint Denis*. Geneva: Droz, 1974.

359 Runnalls, Graham A., ed. *Le Cycle de mystères des premiers martyrs*. Geneva: Droz, 1976.

360 Runnalls, Graham A. 'Le Théâtre à Paris et dans les provinces à la fin du Moyen Age: *Le Mystère de saint Crespin et saint Crespinien*'. *Le Moyen Age* 82 (1976): 517–38.

361 Duplat, André, ed. *Andrieu de La Vigne: Le Mystère de saint Martin*. Geneva: Droz, 1979.

362 Lalou, E. 'Les Cordonniers metteurs en scène des mystères de s. Crespin et s. Crespinien'. *Bibliothèque de l'Ecole de Chartes* 143 (1985): 91–117.

363 Schulze-Busacker, Elizabeth. 'Le Théâtre occitan au XIVe siècle: le *Jeu de sainte Agnès*'. In *7*, 130–93.

364 Chocheyras, Jacques, and Graham A. Runnalls, eds. *La Vie de Marie Magdaleine par personnages*. Geneva: Droz, 1986.

Morality plays

365 Parfondry, Max. 'La *Condamnation de Banquet*, moralité médiévale, et son auteur, Nicole de La Chesnaye'. In *Hommage au Professeur Maurice Delbouille*, special issue of *Marche Romane* (1973): 251–68.

366 Helmich, Werner, ed. 'Moralité de Pauvre Peuple'. In *Philologica romanica Erhard Lommatzsch gewidmet* (Munich: W. Fink, 1975), 145–243.

367 Beck, Jonathan, ed. *'Le Concil de Basle' (1434): Les Origines du théâtre réformiste et partisan en France*. Leiden: E. J. Brill, 1979.

368 Houle, Peter. 'Stage and Metaphor in the French Morality, *L'Homme Juste et l'Homme Mondain*'. *The Chaucer Review* 14 (1979): 1–22.

369 Helmich, Werner, ed. *Moralités françaises: Réimpression fac-similé de vingt-deux pièces allégoriques imprimées aux XVe et XVIe siècles*. 3 vols. Geneva: Editions Slatkine, 1980.

370 Macrì, Giuseppe, ed. *'L'enfant prodigue': Moralità del sec. XVI*. Lecce: Adriatica Editrice Salentina, 1982.

371 Duplat, André. 'La *Moralité de l'aveugle et du boiteux* d'Andrieu de La Vigne: Etude littéraire et édition'. *Travaux de linguistique et de littérature* 21 (1983): 41–80.

372 Knight, Alan E. 'The Condemnation of Pleasure in Late Medieval French Morality Plays'. *The French Review* 57 (1983): 1–9.

373 Beck, Jonathan, ed. *Théâtre et propagande aux débuts de la Réforme: Six pièces polémiques du Recueil La Vallière*. Geneva: Editions Slatkine, 1986.

Farces and *sotties*

374 Lewicka, Halina. *La Langue et le style du théâtre comique français des XVe et XVIe siècles*. 2 vols. Paris: Klincksieck, 1960, 1968.

375 Bowen, Barbara C. *Les Caractéristiques essentielles de la farce française et leur survivance dans les années 1550–1620*. Urbana: University of Illinois Press, 1964.

Bibliography

376 Polak, L., ed. *Le Franc Archier de Bagnolet*. Geneva: Droz, 1966.
377 Knight, Alan E. 'The Medieval Theater of the Absurd'. *PMLA* 86 (1971): 183–9.
378 Rousse, Michel. 'Le Rythme d'un spectacle médiéval: *Maître Pierre Pathelin* et la farce'. In *Missions et démarches de la critique: Mélanges offerts au Professeur J. A. Vier* (Paris: Klincksieck, 1973), 575–81.
379 Lewicka, Halina. *Etudes sur l'ancienne farce française*. Paris: Klincksieck, 1974.
380 Aubailly, Jean-Claude. *Le Monologue, le dialogue et la sottie*. Paris: Honoré Champion, 1976.
381 Aubailly, Jean-Claude, ed. *La Farce de Maistre Pathelin et ses continuations*. Paris: Société d'Edition d'Enseignement Supérieur, 1979.
382 Arden, Heather. *Fools' Plays: A Study of Satire in the Sottie*. Cambridge: Cambridge University Press, 1980.
383 Rousse, Michel. 'L'Espace scénique des farces'. In *4*, 137–46.
384 Maddox, Donald. *Semiotics of Deceit: The Pathelin Era*. Lewisburg: Bucknell University Press, 1984.
385 Rey-Flaud, Bernadette. *La Farce ou la Machine à rire: Théorie d'un genre dramatique, 1450–1550*. Geneva: Droz, 1984.
386 Tissier, André, ed. *Recueil de farces (1450–1550)*. 3 vols. Geneva: Droz, 1986–8.

Other plays
387 Jung, Marc-René. 'La Mise en scène de l'*Istoire de la destruction de Troie la grant par personnages* de Jacques Milet'. In *6*, 563–80.
388 Koopmans, Jelle, ed. *Quatre sermons joyeux*. Geneva: Droz, 1984.

ITALY

Surveys, general

389 Kennard, Joseph Spenser. *The Italian Theater*. New York: Rudge, 1932; repr. 1964.
390 Toschi, Paolo. *Origini del teatro italiano*. Turin: Einaudi, 1955.
391 Apollonio, Mario. *Storia del teatro italiano*. 2 vols. Florence: Sansoni, 1958.
392 Ghilardi, Fernando. *Storia del teatro italiano*, vol. 1. Milan: Francesco Vallardi, 1961.
393 Nagler, Alois M. *Theater Festivals of the Medici, 1539–1637*. New Haven and London: Yale University Press, 1964.
394 Lazar, Moshé. 'L'Enfer et les diables dans le théâtre médiéval italien'. In *Studi di Filologia Romanza offerti a Silvio Pellegrini* (Padua: Liviana Editrice, 1971), 233–49.
395 Ricci, Giuliana. *Teatri d'Italia*. Milan: Bramante, 1971.
396 Fagiolo, Maurizio. *La scenografia. Dalle sacre rappresentazioni al futurismo*. Florence: Sansoni, 1973.
397 Faccioli, Emilio, ed. *Il teatro italiano*, vol. 1: *Dalle origini al Quattrocento*, part 1. Turin: Einaudi, 1975.
398 Ruffini, Franco. 'Semiotica del teatro: per una epistemologia degli studi teatrali'. *Biblioteca Teatrale* 14 (1976): 1–27.
399 Zampino, Daniela M. 'Gli studi teatrali e il 'Journal of the Warburg and Courtauld Institute''. *Biblioteca Teatrale* 18 (1977): 1–44.
400 Janssen, Steen. 'Problemi dell'analisi di testi drammatici'. *Biblioteca Teatrale* 20 (1978): 14–43.
401 Sticca, Sandro. 'Italian Theater of the Middle Ages: From the *Quem quaeritis* to

Bibliography

the *Lauda*'. In *Medieval and Renaissance Theater and Spectacle*, ed. Robert J. Rodini, special issue of *Forum Italicum*, 14 (1980): 275–310.

402 *Rappresentazioni archaiche della tradizione popolare. Atti del VI° Convegno di Studio, Viterbo, 1981*. Viterbo: Union Printing, 1982.

403 Falvey, Kathleen. 'Italian Vernacular Religious Drama of the Fourteenth to Sixteenth Centuries: A Selected Bibliography on the *Lauda drammatica* and the *Sacra rappresentazione*'. *RORD* 26 (1983): 125–44.

404 *Il francescanesimo e il teatro medievale. Atti del Convegno Nazionale di Studi, San Miniato, 1982*. Castelfiorentino: Società Storica della Valdelsa, 1984.

Laude

405 *Iacopone e il suo tempo. Atti del I° Convegno del Centro di Studi sulla Spiritualità Medievale, Todi, 1957*. Todi: Accademia Tudertina, 1959.

406 Baldelli, Ignazio. 'La lauda e i Disciplinati'. *Rassegna della Letteratura Italiana* 64 (1960): 396–418.

407 Fortini, Arnaldo. *La lauda in Assisi e le origini del teatro italiano*. Assisi: Edizioni Assisi, 1961.

408 *Il movimento dei Disciplinati nel settimo Centenario dal suo inizio. (Perugia, 1260). Convegno internazionale, Perugia, 25–8 settembre 1960*. Perugia: Deputazione di Storia Patria per l'Umbria, 1962.

409 Pericoli, Mario. *La matricola dei Disciplinati della Fraternità di S. Maria Maggiore in Todi*. Res Tudertinae 1. Todi: Tipografia Tuderte, 1962.

410 Mancini, Franco. 'Saggio per un'aggiunta di due laude estravaganti alla vulgata iacoponica'. *Rassegna della Letteratura Italiana* 69 (1965): 238–353.

411 Petrocchi, Giorgio. 'La lauda'. In *Storia della letteratura italiana*. Vol. 1: *Le origini e il Duecento* (Milan: Garzanti, 1965), 656–65.

412 Barr, M. Cyrilla. 'The Popular Hymnody of Medieval Italy and its Relationship to the Pious and Penitential Confraternities'. *Studies in Medieval Culture* 3 (1970): 151–8.

413 Pasquini, Emilio. 'La lauda'. In *Il Duecento: dalle origini a Dante*, vol. 1, ed. Emilio Pasquini and Antonio Enzo Quaglio (Bari: Laterza, 1970), 481–92.

414 Varanini, Giorgio. 'La lauda sacra nel XIII secolo'. *Cultura e Scuola* 40 (1971): 12–23.

415 *Risultati e prospettive della ricerca sul Movimento dei Disciplinati, Convegno Internazionale di Studio, Perugia, 1969*. Perugia: Arti Grafiche Città di Castello, 1972.

416 Varanini, Giorgio. *Laude dugentesche*. Padua: Editrice Antenore, 1972.

417 Gasca Queirazza, Giuliano. *Laude e laudari nell'Italia settentrionale*. Turin: Giappichelli, 1974.

418 Ceruti Burgio, Anna. 'La "Passione" del Cicerchia e alcune laude dei Disciplinati senesi'. In *Studi in onore di Raffaele Spongano* (Bologna: Massimiliano Boni Editore, 1980), 49–72.

419 Baldelli, Ignazio. 'Dal "Pianto" cassinese alla lauda umbra'. *Rassegna della Letteratura Italiana* 85 (1981): 5–15.

420 *Le laudi drammatiche umbre delle origini. Atti del V° Convegno di Studio, Viterbo, 22–5 maggio 1980*. Viterbo: Union Printing Editrice, 1981.

421 Varanini, Giorgio, Luigi Banfi and Anna Ceruti Burgio, eds. *Laude cortonesi dal secolo XIII al XV*. Vols. I*, I** and II. Florence: Olschki, 1981.

422 Doglio, Federico. 'Erode furente e i Magi cristiani, dall'*Officium Stellae* alle laudi drammatiche perugine'. In 6, 275–95.

423 Magli, Adriano. 'La lauda drammatica e la funzione dei diavoli'. In 6, 215–33.

Bibliography

424 Dutschke, Dennis, and Shona Kelly. 'Un ritrovato laudario aretino'. *Italianistica* 14 (1985): 155–83.
425 Musarra, Franco. 'Strutture drammatiche della lauda'. In 7, 251–68.

The lauda jacoponica

426 Mazza, Giuseppe, ed. *Il laudario Jacoponico Delta–VII–15 della Biblioteca Civica 'Angelo Maj' di Bergamo*. Bergamo: San Marco, 1960.
427 Pericoli, Mario. *Escatologia nella lauda Jacoponica*. Res Tudertinae 2. Todi: Tipografia Porziuncola (Assisi), 1962.
428 Toschi, Paolo. *Il valore attuale ed eterno della poesia di Jacopone*. Res Tudertinae 4. Todi: Tipografia Tiberina, 1964.
429 Bettarini, Rosanna. *Iacopone e il laudario Urbinate*. Florence: Sansoni, 1969.
430 Sapegno, Natalino. *Frate Jacopone*. Naples: Libreria Scientifica Editrice, 1969.
431 Mancini, Franco, ed. *Iacopone da Todi. Laude*. Bari: Laterza, 1974.
432 Moleta, Vincent. 'Dialogues and Dramatic Poems in the *Laudario Jacoponico*'. *Italian Studies* 30 (1975): 7–29.
433 Bernardi, Lina. *Fra Jacopone da Todi. Un revisionismo di una singolarissima figura*. Res Tudertinae 16. Todi: Tipografia Tiberina, 1978.
434 Peck, George T. *The Fool of God: Jacopone da Todi*. Tuscaloosa: The University of Alabama Press, 1980.
435 Menestò, Enrico, ed. *Atti del Convegno storico iacoponico in occasione del 750° anniversario della nascita di Iacopone da Todi*. Todi, 1980; Florence: La 'Nuova Italia' Editrice, 1981.

Sacre rappresentazioni

436 Larson, Orville K. 'Bishop Abraham of Souzdal's Description of *Sacre Rappresentazioni*'. *Educational Theatre Journal* 9 (1957): 208–13.
437 Larson, Orville K. 'Vasari's Descriptions of Stage Machinery'. *Educational Theatre Journal* 9 (1957): 287–99.
438 Musumarra, Carmelo. *La sacra rappresentazione della Natività nella tradizione italiana*. Florence: Olschki Editore, 1957.
438a Newbigin, Nerida, ed. *Nuovo corpus di sacre rappresentazioni fiorentini del Quattrocento*. Bologna: Commissione per i Testi di Lingua, 1983.

Other plays

439 Cornagliotti, Anna, ed. *La Passione di Revello*. Turin: Centro Studi Piemontesi, 1976.
440 Falvey, Kathleen. 'The First Perugian Passion Play: Aspects of Structure'. *CD* 11 (1977): 127–37; repr. in 5, 63–74.
441 Falvey, Kathleen. 'Stricture and Stanza Form in the St. Andrew Deposition Play'. *Italica* 55 (1978): 179–96.
442 Falvey, Kathleen. 'The Two Judgment Scenes in the "Great" St. Andrew Advent Play'. *Italian Culture* 2 (1982): 13–38.
443 Cornagliotti, Anna. 'Il Concilio in Paradiso e gli altri Conciliaboli nella "Passione di Revello"'. In 6, 35–44.
444 Falvey, Kathleen. 'The Italian Saint Play: The Example of Perugia'. In 8, 181–204.

Bibliography

SPAIN: CATALAN DRAMA

Surveys, general

445 Donovan, Richard B. *The Liturgical Drama in Mediaeval Spain.* Toronto: Pontifical Institute of Mediaeval Studies, 1958.

446 Massot i Muntaner, Josep. 'Notes sobre la supervivència del teatre català antic'. *Estudis Romànics* 11 (1962): 49–101.

447 Romeu i Figueras, Josep. 'Els textos dramàtics sobre el Davallament de la Creu a Catalunya, i el fragment inèdit d'Ulldecona'. *Estudis Romànics* 11 (1962): 103–32.

448 Tomás Avila, Andrés. *El culto y la liturgia en la catedral de Tarragona (1300–1700).* Tarragona: Diputación Provincial de Tarragona, 1963.

449 Llompart, Gabriel. 'La fiesta del "Corpus Christi" y representaciones religiosas en Barcelona y Mallorca (Siglos XIV–XVIII)'. *Analecta Sacra Tarraconensia* 39 (1966): 25–45.

450 Shergold, N. D. *A History of the Spanish Stage From Medieval Times until the End of the Seventeenth Century.* Oxford and London: Oxford University Press (Clarendon), 1967.

451 Doñate Sebastiá, José María. 'Aportación a la historia del teatro. Siglos XIV–XV'. In *Martínez Ferrando, archivero. Miscelánea de estudios dedicados a su memoria* (Barcelona: Asociación Nacional de Bibliotecarios, Archiveros y Arqueólogos, 1968), 149–64.

452 Llompart, Gabriel. 'La fiesta del Corpus y representaciones religiosas en Zaragoza y Mallorca (Siglos XIV–XVI)'. *Analecta Sacra Tarraconensia* 42 (1969): 181–209.

453 Romano, David. 'Figurantes judíos en representaciones sacras (Villarreal, siglos XIV y XV)'. *Sefarad* 29 (1969): 75–6.

454 Bohigas, Pere. 'Lo que hoy sabemos del antiguo teatro catalán'. In *Homenaje a William L. Fichter* (Madrid: Castalia, 1971), 81–95.

455 Rubio García, Luis. 'Introducción al estudio de las representaciones sacras en Lérida'. In *Estudios sobre la Edad Media española* (Murcia: Universidad de Murcia, 1973), 13–92.

456 Fuster, Joan. *La decadència al país valencià.* Barcelona: Curial, 1976.

457 Llompart, Gabriel. 'El Davallament de Mallorca, una paralitúrgia medieval'. *Miscellània Litúrgica Catalana* 1 (1978): 109–33.

458 Bohigas, Pere. 'Més notes sobre textos de teatre català medieval'. *Iberoromania* 10 (1979): 15–29.

459 Llompart, Gabriel. 'Les representacions de teatre religiós mallorquí en temps del bisbe Diego de Arnedo'. In *Homenatge a Francesc de B. Moll* (Barcelona: Curial, 1980), vol. II, 99–105.

460 Riquer, Martín de. *Història de la literatura catalana.* 2nd edn, revised. Vol. III, 493–524. Barcelona: Ariel, 1980.

461 Díez Borque, José María, ed. *Història del teatro en España*, vol. I. Madrid: Taurus, 1983.

462 Massot i Muntaner, Josep, ed. *Teatre medieval i del Renaixement.* Barcelona: Edicions 62, 1983.

463 Vila, Pep, and Montserrat Bruget. *Festes públiques i teatre a Girona. Segles XIV–XVIII (Notícies i documents).* Girona: Ajuntament de Girona, 1983.

Bibliography

Assumption plays

464 Sanchis Guarner, M. 'El Misteri assumpcionista de la catedral de València'. *Boletín de la Real Academia de Buenas Letras de Barcelona* 32 (1967–8): 97–112.

465 Albet, Montserrat, and Roger Alier. *Bibliografía crítica de la 'Festa' o 'Misteri d'Elig'*. Alicante: Instituto de Estudios Alicantinos, 1975.

466 Lázaro Carreter, Fernando. 'Sobre el *Misteri* de Elche'. In *Estudis de llengua i literatura catalanes oferts a R. Aramon i Serra* (Barcelona: Curial, 1979), vol. I, 373–87.

467 Massip, Jesús-Francesc. *Teatre religiós medieval als països catalans*. Barcelona: Edicions 62, 1984.

468 Romeu i Figueras, Josep. 'El teatre assumpcionista de tècnica medieval als països catalans'. In *Estudis de llengua i literatura catalanes oferts a R. Aramon i Serra* (Barcelona: Curial, 1984), vol. IV, 239–78.

469 Gómez i Muntané, María Carmen, and Jesús-Francesc Massip. *Món i misteri de la Festa d'Elx: Consueta de 1709*. 3 vols. Valencia: Generalitat Valenciana, 1986.

Other religious plays

470 Romeu i Figueras, Josep, ed. *Teatre hagiogràfic*. 3 vols. Barcelona: Barcino, 1957.

471 Romeu i Figueras, Josep. 'La *Representació de la Mort*, obra dramática del siglo XVI, y la Danza de la Muerte'. *Boletín de la Real Academia de Buenas Letras de Barcelona* 27 (1957–8): 181–225.

472 Huerta i Viñas, Ferran, ed. *Teatre bíblic. Antic testament*. Barcelona: Barcino, 1976.

473 Romeu i Figueras, Josep. 'Francesc d'Olesa, autor dramàtic: una hipòtesi versemblant'. In *Homenatge a Francesc de B. Moll* (Barcelona: Curial, 1979), vol. I, 127–37.

474 Cornagliotti, Anna. 'Sobre un fragment teatral català de l'Edat mitjana'. In *Homenatge a Josep M. de Casacuberta* (Montserrat: Abadia de Montserrat, 1980), vol. I, 163–74.

475 Massot i Muntaner, Josep. 'Notes sobre el text i l'autor de la *Representació de la Mort*'. In *Serta philologica F. Lázaro Carreter* (Madrid: Cátedra, 1983), vol. II, 347–53.

476 Duran i Sanpere, Agustí, and Eulàlia Duran. *La Passió de Cervera, misteri del segle XVI*. Barcelona: Curial, 1984.

477 Cenoz i del Aguila, G., and F. Huerta i Viñas. 'La "Consueta del fill pròdich", peça núm. 13 del MS. 1139 de la Biblioteca de Catalunya'. In *Estudis de literatura catalana en honor de Josep Romeu i Figueras* (Montserrat: Abadia de Montserrat, 1986), vol. I, 259–88.

SPAIN: CASTILIAN DRAMA

Surveys, general

478 Stern, Charlotte. 'Fray Iñigo de Mendoza and Medieval Dramatic Ritual'. *Hispanic Review* 33 (1965): 197–245.

479 Stern, Charlotte. 'Some New Thoughts on the Early Spanish Drama'. *Bulletin of the Comediantes* 18 (1966): 14–19.

480 López Morales, Humberto. *Tradición y creación en los orígenes del teatro castellano*. Madrid: Alcalá, 1968.

481 Stern, Charlotte. 'The Early Spanish Drama: From Medieval Ritual to Renaissance Art'. *RD* n.s. 6 (1973): 177–201.

Bibliography

482 Pino, Enrique del. *Tres siglos de teatro malagueño (XVI–XVII–XVIII)*. Málaga: Universidad de Málaga, 1974.
483 Flecniakoska, Jean-Louis. 'Spectacles religieux dans les *pueblos* à travers les dossiers de l'Inquisition de Cuenca (1526–1588)'. *Bulletin hispanique* 77 (1975): 269–92.
484 Stern, Charlotte. 'The *Coplas de Mingo Revulgo* and the Early Spanish Drama'. *Hispanic Review* 44 (1976): 311–32.
485 Stern, Charlotte. 'The Genesis of the Spanish Pastoral: From Lyric to Drama'. *Kentucky Romance Quarterly* 25 (1978): 413–34.
486 Surtz, Ronald E. *The Birth of a Theater: Dramatic Convention in the Spanish Theater from Juan del Encina to Lope de Vega*. Madrid: Castalia, 1979.
487 Menéndez Peláez, Jesús. *El teatro en Asturias (De la Edad Media al siglo XVIII)*. Gijón: Noega, 1981.
488 Oleza Simó, Joan. 'Hipótesis sobre la génesis de la comedia barroca'. In *La génesis de la teatralidad barroca* (Valencia: Universidad de Valencia, 1981), 9–44.
489 García de la Concha, Víctor. 'Dramatizaciones litúrgicas pascuales de Aragón y Castilla en la Edad Media'. In *Homenaje a José María Lacarra de Miguel* (Saragossa, 1982), vol. v, 153–75.
490 Díez Borque, José María, ed. *Historia del teatro en España*, vol. i. Madrid: Taurus, 1983.
491 García Valdés, Celsa Carmen. *El teatro en Oviedo (1498–1700) a través de los documentos del Ayuntamiento y del Principado*. Oviedo: CSIC and Universidad de Oviedo, 1983.
492 Rubio García, Luis. *La procesión de Corpus en el siglo XV en Murcia y religiosidad medieval*. Murcia: Academia Alfonso X el Sabio, 1983.
493 Surtz, Ronald E. 'The "Franciscan Connection" in the Early Castilian Theater'. *Bulletin of the Comediantes* 35 (1983): 141–52.
494 Surtz, Ronald E. 'Plays as Play in Early Sixteenth-Century Spain'. *Kentucky Romance Quarterly* 30 (1983): 271–6.
See also Donovan (*445*) and Shergold (*450*).

Anthologies

495 García Morales, Justo, ed. *Autos, comedias y farsas de la Biblioteca Nacional*. 2 vols. Madrid: Joyas Bibliográficas, 1962–64.
496 Moll, Jaime, ed. *Dramas litúrgicos del siglo XVI: Navidad y Pascua*. Madrid: Taurus, 1969.
497 Lázaro Carreter, Fernando, ed. *Teatro medieval*. 3rd edn. Madrid: Castalia, 1970.
498 Arias, Ricardo, ed. *Autos sacramentales (El auto sacramental antes de Calderón)*. Mexico: Porrúa, 1977.
499 Surtz, Ronald E., ed. *Teatro medieval castellano*. Madrid: Taurus, 1983.

Auto de los Reyes Magos

500 Wardropper, Bruce W. 'The Dramatic Texture of the *Auto de los Reyes Magos*'. *MLN* 70 (1955): 46–50.
501 Foster, David. 'Figural Interpretation and the *Auto de los reyes magos*'. *RR* 58 (1967): 3–11.
502 Menéndez Pidal, Ramón. '*Disputa del alma y el cuerpo y Auto de los reyes magos*'. In his *Obras Completas*, vol. xii: *Textos medievales españoles* (Madrid: Espasa-Calpe, 1976), 161–77.

Bibliography

503 Senabre, Ricardo. 'Observaciones sobre el texto del *Auto de los Reyes Magos*'. In *Estudios ofrecidos a Emilio Alarcos Llorach* (Oviedo: Universidad de Oviedo, 1976), vol. I, 417–32.

504 Stebbins, Charles, ed. and trans. 'The *Auto de los Reyes Magos*: An Old Spanish Mystery Play of the Twelfth Century'. *Allegorica* 2 (1977): 118–43.

505 Hook, David, and Alan Deyermond. 'El problema de la terminación del *Auto de los Reyes Magos*'. *Anuario de Estudios Medievales* 13 (1983): 269–78.

506 Lapesa, Rafael. 'Mozárabe y catalán o gascón en el *Auto de los Reyes Magos*'. In *Miscellània Aramon i Serra* (Barcelona: Curial, 1983), vol. III, 277–94.

Fifteenth-century drama

507 Aragone, Elisa, ed. *Rodrigo de Cota, Diálogo entre el amor y un viejo*. Florence: Felice Le Monnier, 1961.

508 Sieber, Harry. 'Dramatic Symmetry in Gómez Manrique's *Representación*'. *Hispanic Review* 33 (1965): 118–35.

509 Amícola, José. 'El *Auto de la huida a Egipto*, drama anónimo del siglo XV'. *Filología* 15 (1971): 1–29.

510 López Yepes, José. 'Una *Representación de las sibilas* y un *Planctus Passionis* en el Ms. 80 de la Catedral de Córdoba. Aportaciones al estudio de los orígenes del teatro medieval castellano'. *Revista de Archivos, Bibliotecas y Museos* 80 (1977): 545–68.

511 Torroja Menéndez, Carmen, and María Rivas Palá. *Teatro en Toledo en el siglo XV: 'Auto de la Pasión' de Alonso del Campo*. Madrid: Real Academia Española, 1977.

512 Zimic, Stanislav. 'El teatro religioso de Gómez Manrique (1412–1491)'. *Boletín de la Real Academia Española* 57 (1977): 353–400.

513 Blecua, Alberto. 'La *Egloga* de Francisco de Madrid en un nuevo manuscrito del siglo XVI'. In *Serta Philologica F. Lázaro Carreter* (Madrid: Cátedra, 1983), vol. II, 39–66.

514 López Estrada, Francisco. 'La *Representación del nacimiento de Nuestro Señor* de Gómez Manrique. Estudio textual'. *Segismundo* 18 (1984): 9–30.

515 López Estrada, Francisco. 'Nueva lectura de la *Representación del Nacimiento de Nuestro Señor* de Gómez Manrique'. In 6, 423–46.

The popular religious theatre of the sixteenth century

516 Flecniakoska, Jean-Louis. *La Formation de l'"auto' religieux en Espagne avant Calderón (1550–1635)*. Montpellier: Imprimerie Paul Déhan, 1961.

517 Flecniakoska, Jean-Louis. 'Les Rôles de Satan dans les pièces du *Códice de autos viejos*'. *Revue des langues romanes* 75 (1962–3): 195–207.

518 Rodríguez-Moñino, Antonio, ed. *Juan López de Úbeda, Cancionero general de la doctrina cristiana*, vol. I. Madrid: Bibliófilos Españoles, 1964.

519 Dexeus de Moll, Mercedes. 'Cinco piezas teatrales de Jaime Torres (1579)'. *Revista de Archivos, Bibliotecas y Museos* 74 (1967): 105–79.

520 González Ollé, Fernando, ed. *Fernán López de Yanguas, Obras dramáticas*. Madrid: Espasa Calpe, 1967.

521 Wardropper, Bruce W. *Introducción al teatro religioso del Siglo de Oro (Evolución del Auto Sacramental antes de Calderón)*. Salamanca: Anaya, 1967.

522 González Ollé, Fernando. 'La *Farsa del Santísimo Sacramento*, anónimo, y su significado en el desarrollo del auto sacramental'. *Revista de Literatura* 35 (1969): 127–65.

Bibliography

523 Weber de Kurlat, Frida, ed. *Diego Sánchez de Badajoz, Recopilación en metro: Trabajo de seminario bajo la dirrección de Frida Weber de Kurlat*. Buenos Aires: Universidad de Buenos Aires, 1968.

524 Rodríguez-Puértolas, Julio. 'La transposición de la realidad en el *Códice de autos viejos*'. *Filología* 14 (1970): 105–25.

525 Ferrario de Orduna, Lilia. 'La *Obra del pecador* según la edición de 1611 (R. 12224)'. *Filología* 16 (1972): 61–83.

526 Gewecke, Frauke. *Thematische Untersuchungen zu dem vorcalderonianischen 'Auto Sacramental'*. Geneva: Droz, 1974.

527 Ferrario de Orduna, Lilia. 'La adoración de los pastores. III. La *Obra del pecador*'. In *Homenaje al Instituto de Filología y Literaturas Hispánicas 'Dr. Amado Alonso'* (Buenos Aires: Instituto de Filología, 1975), 107–16.

528 Weiner, Jack, ed. *Sebastián de Horozco, El cancionero*. Berne and Frankfurt: Lang, 1975.

529 Fothergill-Payne, Louise. *La alegoría en los autos y farsas anteriores a Calderón*. London: Tamesis, 1977.

530 Mazur, Oleh. *El teatro de Sebastián de Horozco con una breve historia del teatro español anterior a Lope de Vega: tipos, modos y temas*. Madrid: Rocana, 1977.

531 Díez Borque, José María, ed. *Diego Sánchez de Badajoz, Farsas*. Madrid: Cátedra, 1978.

532 González Ollé, Fernando, ed. *Sebastián de Horozco, Representaciones*. Madrid: Castalia, 1979.

533 Arias, Ricardo. *The Spanish Sacramental Plays*. Boston: Twayne, 1980.

534 Vitse, Marc. 'Sobre las *Representaciones* de Sebastián de Horozco'. *Criticón* 10 (1980): 75–92.

535 Surtz, Ronald E., ed. *Juan Pastor, Aucto nuevo del santo nacimiento de Christo Nuestro Señor*. Valencia: Albatros-Hispanófila, 1981.

536 Pérez Priego, Miguel Angel. *El teatro de Diego Sánchez de Badajoz*. Cáceres: Universidad de Extremadura, 1982.

537 Surtz, Ronald E. *'El libro del Conorte' (1509) and the Early Castilian Theater*. Barcelona: Puvill, 1982.

538 Ferrer Valls, Teresa. 'Jaime Ferruz en la tradición del teatro religioso'. In *Teatros y prácticas escénicas*, vol. I: *El quinientos valenciano*, ed. Joan Oleza Simó (Valencia: Institució Alfons el Magnànim, 1984), 109–36.

539 Pérez Priego, Miguel Angel, ed. *Diego Sánchez de Badajoz, Farsas*. Madrid: Cátedra, 1985.

GERMANY

Surveys, general

540 Michael, Wolfgang F. 'Das deutsche Drama und Theater vor der Reformation. Ein Forschungsbericht'. *Deutsche Vierteljahrsschrift* 31 (1957): 106–53; 47 (1973): Sonderheft 1*–47*.

541 Christ-Kutter, Friederike, ed. *Frühe Schweizerspiele*. Altdeutsche Übungstexte 19. Berne: Francke, 1963.

542 Werner, Wilfried. *Studien zu den Passions- und Osterspielen des deutschen Mittelalters in ihrem Übergang vom Latein zur Volkssprache*. Philologische Studien und Quellen 18. Berlin: Erich Schmidt, 1963.

543 Hölzl, Norbert, ed. *Theatergeschichte des östlichen Tirol. Vom Mittelalter bis zur Gegenwart*. Part 2: *Sammlung der Spieltexte und der zeitgenössischen Zeugnisse*. Theatergeschichte Österreichs II, 2. Vienna: Böhlau, 1967.

Bibliography

544 Völker, Paul-Gerhard. 'Schwierigkeiten bei der Edition geistlicher Spiele des Mittelalters'. In *Kolloquium über Probleme altgermanistischer Editionen, Marbach am Neckar, 26. und 27. April 1966. Referate und Diskussionsbeiträge*, ed. Hugo Kuhn *et al.* (Wiesbaden: Steiner, 1968), 160–8.

545 Steinbach, Rolf. *Die deutschen Oster- und Passionsspiele des Mittelalters. Versuch einer Darstellung und Wesensbestimmung nebst einer Bibliographie zum deutschen geistlichen Spiel des Mittelalters*. Kölner germanistische Studien 4. Cologne and Vienna: Böhlau, 1970.

546 Michael, Wolfgang F. *Das deutsche Drama des Mittelalters*. Grundriss der germanischen Philologie 20. Berlin and New York: de Gruyter, 1971.

547 Linke, Hansjürgen. 'Bauformen geistlicher Dramen des späten Mittelalters'. In *Zeiten und Formen in Sprache und Dichtung. Festschrift für Fritz Tschirch zum 70. Geburtstag*, ed. Karl-Heinz Schirmer and Bernhard Sowinski (Cologne and Vienna: Böhlau, 1972), 203–25.

548 Polheim, Karl Konrad. 'Neue Forschungen zu den Oster- und Passionsspielen des deutschen Mittelalters'. *Zeitschrift für Volkskunde* 68 (1972): 242–56.

549 Brett-Evans, David. *Von Hrotsvit bis Folz und Gengenbach. Eine Geschichte des mittelalterlichen deutschen Dramas*. 2 vols. Grundlagen der Germanistik 15, 18. Berlin: Schmidt, 1975.

550 Neumann, Bernd. 'Mittelalterliches Schauspiel am Niederrhein'. In *Zeitschrift für deutsche Philologie* 94 (1975): Sonderheft *Mittelalterliches deutsches Drama*: 147–94.

551 Polheim, Karl Konrad. 'Weitere Forschungen zu den Oster- und Passionsspielen des deutschen Mittelalters. Ein Bericht'. In *Zeitschrift für deutsche Philologie* 94 (1975): Sonderheft *Mittelalterliches deutsches Drama*: 194–212.

552 Kühebacher, Egon, ed. *Tiroler Volksschauspiel. Beiträge zur Theatergeschichte des Alpenraumes*. Schriftenreihe des Südtiroler Kulturinstitutes 3. Bolzano: Athesia, 1976.

553 Linke, Hansjürgen. 'Das volkssprachige Drama und Theater im deutschen und niederländischen Sprachbereich'. In *Neues Handbuch der Literaturwissenschaft*, vol. VIII: *Europäisches Spätmittelalter*, ed. Willi Erzgräber (Wiesbaden: Athenaion, 1978), 733–63.

554 Ruh, Kurt, ed. *Die deutsche Literatur des Mittelalters: Verfasserlexikon*, revised 2nd edn, vols. I–VII. Berlin and New York: de Gruyter, 1978–90 (in progress, articles for virtually all German plays).

555 Lipphardt, Walther, and Hans-Gert Roloff, eds. *Die geistlichen Spiele des Sterzinger Spielarchivs. Nach den Handschriften herausgegeben*, vol. V (1980), vol. I (1981; rev. 1986), vol. II (1988). Mittlere, Deutsche Literatur in Neu- und Nachdrucken 18, 14, 15. Berne and Frankfurt-am-Main: Lang.

556 Williams-Krapp, Werner. *Überlieferung und Gattung. Zur Gattung 'Spiel' im Mittelalter. Mit einer Edition von 'Sündenfall und Erlösung' aus der Berliner Handschrift mgq 496*. Untersuchungen zur deutschen Literaturgeschichte 28. Tübingen: Niemeyer, 1980.

557 Simon, Eckehard. 'Drama, German.' In *Dictionary of the Middle Ages*, ed. Joseph R. Strayer, vol. IV (New York: Scribner's [1984]), 266–72.

558 Neumann, Bernd. 'Spätmittelalterliches Drama und Theater im deutschen Sprachgebiet: Grundlagen und Editionen (1978–84)'. *Jahrbuch der Oswald von Wolkenstein Gesellschaft* 3 (1984–5): 387–419.

559 Bergmann, Rolf. 'Aufführungstext und Lesetext. Zur Funktion der Überlieferung des mittelalterlichen deutschen Dramas'. In 7, 314–51.

560 Neumann, Bernd. 'Geistliches Schauspiel als Paradigma stadtbürgerlicher Literatur im ausgehenden Mittelalter'. In *Germanistik – Forschungsstand und*

Bibliography

Perspektiven. Vorträge des Deutschen Germanistentages 1984, ed. Georg Stötzel, part 2: *Ältere Deutsche Literatur, Neuere Deutsche Literatur* (Berlin and New York: de Gruyter, 1985), 123–35.

561 Bergmann, Rolf. *Katalog der deutschsprachigen geistlichen Spiele und Marienklagen des Mittelalters*. Veröffentlichungen der Kommission für deutsche Literatur des Mittelalters der Bayerischen Akademie der Wissenschaften 1. Munich and Zurich: Artemis, 1986.

562 Linke, Hansjürgen. 'Drama und Theater'. In *Die deutsche Literatur im späten Mittelalter*, part 2: *1250–1370*, ed. Ingeborg Glier (Geschichte der deutschen Literatur von den Anfängen bis zur Gegenwart, ed. Helmut de Boor and Richard Newald, vol. III, part 2; Munich: Beck, 1987), 153–233, 471–85.

563 Linke, Hansjürgen. 'Versuch über deutsche Handschriften mittelalterlicher Spiele'. In *Deutsche Handschriften 1100–1400. Oxforder Kolloquium 1985*, ed. Volker Honemann and Nigel F. Palmer (Tübingen: Niemeyer, 1988), 527–89.

564 Linke, Hansjürgen. 'Vom Sakrament bis zum Exkrement. Ein Überblick über Drama und Theater des deutschen Mittelalters'. In *Theaterwesen und dramatische Literatur*, ed. Günter Holtus (Mainzer Forschungen zu Drama und Theater 1; Tübingen: Francke, 1987), 127–64.

565 Neumann, Bernd. *Geistliches Schauspiel im Zeugnis der Zeit. Zur Aufführung mittelalterlicher Dramen im deutschen Sprachgebiet*. 2 vols. Münchener Texte und Untersuchungen zur deutschen Literatur des Mittelalters 84, 85. Munich and Zurich: Artemis, 1987.

Easter plays

566 Zucker, Adolf, trans. *The Redentin Easter Play. Translated from the Low German of the Fifteenth Century with Introduction and Notes*. Records of Civilisation, Sources and Studies 32. New York: Octagon Books, 1941 (repr. 1961).

567 Meier, Rudolf, ed. *Das Innsbrucker Osterspiel. Das Osterspiel von Muri. Mittelhochdeutsch und neuhochdeutsch*. Universal-Bibliothek 8660/61. Stuttgart: Reclam, 1962.

568 Linke, Hansjürgen. 'Die Teufelsszenen des Redentiner Osterspiels'. *Jahrbuch des Vereins für niederdeutsche Sprachforschung* 90 (1967): 89–105.

569 Wehrli, Max, ed. *Das Osterspiel von Muri. Faksimiledruck der Fragmente und Rekonstruktion der Pergamentrolle*. Basle: Alkuin, 1967.

570 Wolff, Ludwig. 'Zu den Teufelsszenen des Redentiner Osterspiels'. In *Gedenkschrift für William Foerste*, ed. Dietrich Hofmann (Niederdeutsche Studien 18. Cologne and Vienna: Böhlau, 1970), 424–31.

571 Lipphardt, Walther, ed. 'Ein lateinisch-deutsches Osterspiel aus Augsburg (16. Jh.) in der Bibliothek des Kapuzinerklosters Feldkirch'. *Jahrbuch des Vorarlberger Landesmuseumsvereins* 1972: 14–29 (corrected reprint, 1978–9: 375–87).

572 Hennig, Ursula. 'Die Klage der Maria Magdalena in den deutschen Osterspielen. Ein Beitrag zur Textgeschichte der Spiele'. *Zeitschrift für deutsche Philologie* 94 (1975): Sonderheft *Mittelalterliches deutsches Drama*: 108–38.

573 Holtorf, Arne. 'Höfische Theologie im Osterspiel von Muri'. *Beiträge zur Geschichte der deutschen Sprache und Literatur* 97 (Tübingen, 1975): 339–64.

574 Schottmann, Brigitte, ed. *Das Redentiner Osterspiel. Mittelniederdeutsch und neuhochdeutsch*. Universal-Bibliothek 9744–9747. Stuttgart: Reclam, 1975.

575 Thurnher, Eugen, and Walter Neuhauser, eds. *Die Neustifter-Innsbrucker Spielhandschrift von 1391 (Cod. 960 der Universitätsbibliothek Innsbruck)*. Litterae 40. Göppingen: Kümmerle, 1975.

Bibliography

576 Wittkowsky, Hartmut, ed. *Das Redentiner Osterspiel.* Stuttgart: Urachhaus, 1975 (with facsimile).
577 Schmidtke, Dietrich, Ursula Hennig and Walther Lipphardt. 'Füssener Osterspiel und Füssener Marienklage'. *Beiträge zur Geschichte der deutschen Sprache und Literatur* 98 (Tübingen, 1976): 231–88, 395–423.
578 Thoran, Barbara. *Studien zu den österlichen Spielen des deutschen Mittelalters. (Ein Beitrag zur Klärung ihrer Abhängigkeit voneinander).* 2nd edn. Göppinger Arbeiten zur Germanistik 199. Göppingen: Kümmerle, 1976.
579 Thoran, Barbara, ed. *Das Münchner Osterspiel (Cgm 147 der Bayerischen Staatsbibliothek München).* Litterae 43. Göppingen: Kümmerle, 1977.
580 Blosen, Hans, ed. *Das Wiener Osterspiel. Abdruck der Handschrift und Leseausgabe.* Texte des späten Mittelalters und der frühen Neuzeit 33. Berlin: Schmidt, 1979.
581 Pausch, Oskar, ed. 'Das Kremsmünsterer Osterspiel. Ein Fragment aus dem 14. Jahrhundert'. *Zeitschrift für deutsches Altertum und deutsche Literatur* 108 (1979): 51–7 [fragment of a Passion play].
582 Dane, Joseph A. 'Manuscript, Text, Allusion: The Critical Description of Medieval Drama with Particular Reference to the Innsbruck Easterplay (1391)'. *The Germanic Review* 57 (1982): 157–62.
583 Bergmann, Rolf, ed. 'Die Göttweiger Dirigierrolle eines Osterspiels'. In *Festschrift für Siegfried Grosse zum 60. Geburtstag,* ed. Werner Besch *et al.* (Göppinger Arbeiten zur Germanistik 423; Göppingen: Kümmerle, 1984), 325–35.
584 Bergmann, Rolf. 'Überlieferung, Interpretation und literaturgeschichtliche Stellung des Osterspiels von Muri'. *Internationales Archiv für Sozialgeschichte der Literatur* 9 (1984): 1–21.
585 Linke, Hansjürgen. 'Die Osterspiele des Debs-Codex'. *Zeitschrift für deutsche Philologie* 104 (1985): 104–29.
586 Schipke, Renate, and Franzjosef Pensel, eds. *Das Brandenburger Osterspiel. Fragmente eines neuentdeckten mittelalterlichen geistlichen Osterspiels aus dem Domarchiv in Brandenburg/Havel.* Beiträge aus der Deutschen Staatsbibliothek 4. Berlin: Deutsche Staatsbibliothek, 1986.

Passion plays

587 Wyss, Heinz, ed. *Das Luzerner Passionsspiel.* 3 vols. Schriften herausgegeben unter dem Patronat der Schweizerischen geisteswissenschaftlichen Gesellschaft 7. Berne: Francke, 1967.
588 Bergmann, Rolf. *Studien zur Entstehung und Geschichte der deutschen Passionsspiele des 13. und 14. Jahrhunderts.* Münstersche Mittelalter-Schriften 14. Munich: Fink, 1972.
589 Polheim, Karl Konrad, ed. *Das Admonter Passionsspiel. Textausgabe, Faksimileausgabe, Untersuchungen.* 3 vols. Munich, Paderborn and Vienna: Schöningh, 1972, 1980.
590 Knorr, Antje, ed. *Villinger Passion. Literaturhistorische Einordnung und erstmalige Herausgabe des Urtextes und der Überarbeitungen.* Göppinger Arbeiten zur Germanistik 187. Göppingen: Kümmerle, 1976.
591 West, Larry E., trans. *The Saint Gall Passion Play. With an Introduction and Notes.* Medieval Classics: Texts and Studies 6. Brookline and Leiden: Classical Folia Editions, 1976.
592 Schützeichel, Rudolf, ed. *Das mittelrheinische Passionsspiel der St. Galler Handschrift 919.* Tübingen: Niemeyer, 1978.
593 Konigson, Elie. 'La Place du Weinmarkt à Lucerne. Remarques sur l'organisation d'un espace dramatisé'. In *Recherches sur les textes dramatiques et les*

Bibliography

spectacles du XVe siècle, ed. Elie Konigson (Les voies de la création théâtrale 8; Paris: Centre National de la Recherche Scientifique, 1980), 43–90.

594 Tailby, John E. 'Die Luzerner Passionsspielaufführung des Jahres 1583: Zur Deutung der Bühnenpläne Renward Cysats'. In 7, 352–61.

595 Touber, Anthonius H., ed. *Das Donaueschinger Passionsspiel. Nach der Handschrift mit Einleitung und Kommentar.* Universal-Bibliothek 8046. Stuttgart: Reclam, 1985.

596 Hennig, Ursula, ed. *Das Wiener Passionsspiel. Cod. 12887 (Suppl. 561) der Österreichischen Nationalbibliothek zu Wien mit Einleitung und Textabdruck in Abbildung.* Litterae 92. Göppingen: Kümmerle, 1986.

597 Klammer, Bruno, ed. *Bozner Passion 1495. Die Spielhandschriften A und B.* Mittlere Deutsche Literatur in Neu- und Nachdrucken 20. Berne, Frankfurt and New York: Lang, 1986.

Christmas plays

598 Lipphardt, Walther, ed. 'Das hessische Weihnachtsspiel'. *Die Weihnachtsgeschichte.* Convivium Symbolicum 2. [Bremen:] Dorn [1958]: 27–48, 66–7.

599 Simon, Eckehard, ed. 'Das Schwäbische Weihnachtsspiel. Ein neu entdecktes Weihnachtsspiel aus der Zeit 1417–1431'. *Zeitschrift für deutsche Philologie* 94 (1975): Sonderheft *Mittelalterliches deutsches Drama*: 30–50.

600 King, Norbert, ed. 'Das Solothurner Dreikönigsspiel des Johannes Wagner (Carpentarius) vom Jahre 1561'. *Jahrbuch für Solothurnische Geschichte* 49 (1976): 45–83.

601 Bätschmann, Emilia, ed. *Das St. Galler Weihnachtsspiel.* Altdeutsche Übungstexte 21. Berne: Francke, 1977.

602 King, Norbert. *Mittelalterliche Dreikönigsspiele. Eine Grundlagenarbeit zu den lateinischen, deutschen und französischen Dreikönigsspielen und -spielszenen bis zum Ende des 16. Jahrhunderts.* Germanistica Friburgensia, 3, A and B. Freiburg, Switzerland: Universitätsverlag, 1979.

603 Simon, Eckehard. 'The Home Town of the "Schwäbische Weihnachtsspiel" (ca. 1420) and its Original Setting'. *Euphorion* 73 (1979): 304–20.

Other religious plays

604 Stammler, Wolfgang, ed. *Berner Weltgerichtsspiel. Aus der Handschrift des 15. Jahrhundert.* Texte des späten Mittelalters und der frühen Neuzeit 15. Berlin: Schmidt, 1962.

605 Schneider, Karin, ed. *Das Eisenacher Zehnjungfrauenspiel.* Texte des späten Mittelalters und der frühen Neuzeit 17. Berlin: Schmidt, 1964.

606 Wolfsgruber, Karl, and Norbert Hölzl, eds. 'Das Emmaus-Spiel aus dem spätmittelalt. Brixen'. *Der Schlern* 42 (1968): 151–62.

607 Liebenow, Peter K., ed. *Das Künzelsauer Fronleichnamspiel.* Ausgaben deutscher Literatur des 15. bis 18. Jahrhunderts, Reihe Drama II. Berlin: de Gruyter, 1969.

608 Wainwright, Elizabeth. *Studien zum deutschen Prozessionsspiel. Die Tradition der Fronleichnamsspiele in Künzelsau und Freiburg und ihre textliche Entwicklung.* Münchner Beiträge zur Mediävistik und Renaissance-Forschung 16. Munich: Arbeo-Gesellschaft, 1974.

609 Ukena, Elke, ed. *Die deutschen Mirakelspiele des Mittelalters. Studien und Texte.* 2 vols. Europäische Hochschulschriften Series I, 115. Berne, Frankfurt-am-Main: Lang, 1975.

610 Wainwright, Elizabeth. 'Das Rothenburger Rollenbuch'. *Zeitschrift für deutsche Philologie* 94 (1975): Sonderheft *Mittelalterliches deutsches Drama*: 138–47.

Bibliography

611 Wolf, Norbert Richard, ed. 'Das erste Emmausspiel im Kodex des Benedikt Debs'. *Der Schlern* 49 (1975): 467–73; 50 (1976): 659–62.

612 Blosen, Hans, ed. 'Illustrationerne i et københavnsk manuskript af det senmiddelalderlige tyske dommedagsspil'. *Convivium. Årsskrift for humaniora kunst og forskning* [1] 1976: 108–33, 175.

613 Biermann, Heinrich. *Die deutschsprachigen Legendenspiele des späten Mittelalters und der frühen Neuzeit*. Cologne: Hundt, 1977.

614 Schneider, Karin, ed. 'Docens Marienklage'. *Zeitschrift für deutsches Altertum und deutsche Literatur* 106 (1977): 138–45.

615 Taubert, Gesine, ed. 'Zwei Kreuzabnahmespiele aus dem Debs-Kodex'. *Zeitschrift für deutsches Altertum und deutsche Literatur* 106 (1977): 32–72.

616 Bergmann, Rolf, ed. 'Die Gothaer Botenrolle'. In *Studien zur deutschen Literatur des Mittelalters*, ed. Rudolf Schützeichel (Bonn: Bouvier, 1979), 589–609.

617 Linke, Hansjürgen. 'Die Komposition der Erfurter Moralität'. In *Medium Aevum deutsch [...] Festschrift für Kurt Ruh zum 65. Geburtstag*, ed. Dietrich Huschenbett *et al.* (Tübingen: Niemeyer, 1979), 215–36.

618 Kully, Elisabeth, ed. 'Das ältere St. Ursenspiel'. *Jahrbuch für Solothurnische Geschichte* 55 (1982): 5–107.

619 Schipke, Renate, ed. 'Die "Berliner Moralität". Ein unbekanntes Fragment aus dem Bestand der Deutschen Staatsbibliothek'. In *Studien zum Buch- und Bibliothekswesen*, vol. IV, ed. Friedhilde Krause and Hans-Erich Teitge (Leipzig: VEB Bibliographisches Institut, 1986), 36–45.

620 Broszinski, Hartmut, and Hansjürgen Linke, eds. 'Kasseler (mnd.) Paradiesspiel-Fragmente'. *Zeitschrift für deutsches Altertum und deutsche Literatur* 116 (1987): 36–52.

Secular plays; Carnival plays

621 Catholy, Eckehard. *Das Fastnachtspiel des Spätmittelalters. Gestalt und Funktion*. Hermaea n.s. 8. Tübingen: Niemeyer, 1961.

622 Huschenbett, Dietrich, ed. 'Vom dem König Salomon und Markolf'. *Zeitschrift für deutsche Philologie* 84 (1965): 388–408.

623 Wuttke, Dieter, ed. 'Die Druckfassung des Fastnachtspiels "Von König Salomon und Markolf"'. *Zeitschrift für deutsches Altertum und deutsche Literatur* 94 (1965): 141–70.

624 Wuttke, Dieter. 'Zum Fastnachtspiel des Spät-Mittelalters. Eine Auseinandersetzung mit Catholys Buch'. *Zeitschrift für deutsche Philologie* 84 (1965): 247–67.

625 Catholy, Eckehard. *Fastnachtspiel*. Sammlung Metzler M56. Stuttgart: Metzler, 1966.

626 Lenk, Werner. *Das Nürnberger Fastnachtspiel des 15. Jahrhunderts. Ein Beitrag zur Theorie und zur Interpretation des Fastnachtspiels als Dichtung*. Deutsche Akademie der Wissenschaften zu Berlin, Veröffentlichungen des Instituts für deutsche Sprache und Literatur 33, Reihe C. Berlin: Akademie-Verlag, 1966.

627 Simon, Eckehard. 'The Origin of Neidhart Plays. A Reappraisal'. *Journal of English and Germanic Philology* 67 (1968): 458–74.

628 Simon, Eckehard. 'The Staging of Neidhart Plays. With Notes on Six Documented Performances'. *The Germanic Review* 44 (1969): 5–20.

629 Simon, Eckehard. 'Shrovetide Plays in Late-Medieval Switzerland. An Appraisal'. *MLN* 85 (1970): 323–31.

630 Simon, Eckehard. 'The Alemannic "Herbst und Mai" Play and Its Literary Background'. *Monatshefte* 62 (1970): 217–30.

631 Simon, Gerd. *Die erste deutsche Fastnachtspieltradition. Zur Überlieferung,*

Bibliography

Textkritik und Chronologie der Nürnberger Fastnachtspiele des 15. Jahrhunderts. Germanistische Studien 240. Lübeck and Hamburg: Matthiesen, 1970.

632 Folz, Hans. 'Mirthful Peasant Play'. In *The Literary Context of Chaucer's Fabliaux. Text and Translation,* ed. Larry D. Benson and Theodore M. Andersson (Indianapolis and New York: Bobbs-Merrill, 1971), 46–59.

633 Wuttke, Dieter, ed. *Fastnachtspiele des 15. und 16. Jahrhunderts.* Universal-Bibliothek 9415. Stuttgart: Reclam, 1973; 2nd edn 1978.

634 Krohn, Rüdiger. *Der unanständige Bürger. Untersuchungen zum Obszönen in den Nürnberger Fastnachtspielen des 15. Jahrhunderts.* Scriptor-Hochschulschriften, Literaturwissenschaft 4. Kronberg/Taunus: Scriptor, 1974.

635 Simon, Eckehard. 'Neidhart Plays as Shrovetide Plays. Twelve Additional Documented Performances'. *The Germanic Review* 52 (1977): 87–98.

636 Bauer, Werner M., ed. *Sterzinger Spiele. Die weltlichen Spiele des Sterzinger Spielarchivs nach den Originalhandschriften (1510–1535) von Vigil Raber und nach der Ausgabe Zingerles (1886).* Wiener Neudrucke [n.s.] 6. Vienna: Österreichischer Bundesverlag, 1982.

637 Margetts, John, ed. *Neidhartspiele.* Wiener Neudrucke [n.s.] 7. Graz: Akademische Druck- und Verlagsanstalt, 1982.

638 Bastian, Hagen. *Mummenschanz. Sinneslust und Gefühlsbeherrschung im Fastnachtspiel des 15. Jahrhunderts.* Frankfurt-am-Main: Syndikat, 1983.

639 Linke, Hansjürgen. 'Das Tiroler (Mittlere) Neidhartspiel und seine Dirigierrolle'. *Archiv für das Studium der neueren Sprachen und Literaturen* 222 (1985): 1–21.

640 Linke, Hansjürgen. 'Die beiden Fassungen des Tiroler Fastnachtspiels "Die zwen Stenndt"'. *Daphnis* 14 (1985): 179–218.

641 Siller, Max. 'Anmerkungen zu den Neidhartspielen'. *Zeitschrift für deutsche Philologie* 104 (1985): 380–403.

642 Margetts, John, ed. *Die mittelalterlichen Neidhart-Spiele. In Abbildungen der Handschriften herausgegeben.* Litterae 73. Göppingen: Kümmerle, 1986.

THE LOW COUNTRIES

Surveys, general

643 van Elslander, A. 'Lijst van Rederijkerskamers uit de XVe en XVIe eeuw', *Jaarboek De Fonteine* (1968): 29–60.

644 Hummelen, Wim M. H. *Repertorium van het Rederijkersdrama, c. 1620.* Assen: Van Gorcum, 1968.

645 Decavele, J. *De Dageraad van de Reformatie in Vlaanderen, 1520–1561.* 2 vols. Brussels: Koninklijke Academie van Wetenschappen, 1975.

646 Kipling, Gordon. *The Triumph of Honour. Burgundian Origins of the Elizabethan Renaissance.* Leiden: Brill, 1977.

647 Pleij, Herman. *Het Gilde van de Blauwe Schuit. Literatuur, volksfeest en burgermoraal in de late middeleeuwen.* Amsterdam: Meulenhoff, 1977.

648 Coigneau, D. 'Rederijkersliteratuur'. In *Historische Letterkunde,* ed. Marijke Spies (Groningen: Wolters-Noordhoff, 1984), 35–58.

649 van Dijk, Hans, Wim Hummelen, Wim Hüsken and Elsa Strietman. 'A Survey of Dutch Drama Before the Renaissance'. *Dutch Crossing* 22 (1984): 97–131.

649a van Dijk, Hans. '*Mariken van Nieumeghen'. Dutch Crossing* 22 (1984): 27–37.

650 Spies, Marijke. 'Van mythes en meningen: over de geschiedenis van de literatuurgeschiedenis'. In *Historische Letterkunde,* ed. Marijke Spies (Groningen: Wolters-Noordhoff, 1984), 177–93.

Bibliography

Editions

651 van Es, G. A., ed. *Pyramus en Thisbe. Twee rederijkersspelen uit de zestiende eeuw.* Zwolle: Tjeenk Willink, 1965.

652 Roemans, R., and H. van Assche, eds. *Lanseloet van Denemarken.* Amsterdam: De Nederlandse Boekhandel, 1966.

653 Members of the Dutch Institute of the State University in Groningen, eds. *Een Esbattement van 'sMenschen Sin ende Verganckelijcke Schoonheit.* Zwolle: Tjeenk Willink, 1967.

654 Vos, R., ed. *Den Spieghel der Salicheit van Elckerlijc. Hoe dat elckerlijc mensche wert gedaecht rekeninghe te doen van sinen wercken.* Groningen: Wolters-Noordhoff, 1967.

655 van Kammen, L., ed. *De abele spelen.* Amsterdam: Athenaeum, 1968.

656 Stellinga, G., ed. *Het abel spel 'Vanden Winter ende vanden Somer' ende ene sotternie 'Rubben' navolghende. Voorafgegaan door de fragmenten ene sotte boerde 'Drie Daghe Here' ende ene goede sotternie 'Truwanten'.* 2nd edn. Zutphen: Thieme, 1975.

657 Beuken, W. H., ed. *Die Eerste Bliscap van Maria en Die Sevenste Bliscap van Onser Vrouwen.* Culemborg: Tjeenk Willink, 1978.

658 Werkgroep van Brusselse en Utrechtse Neerlandici, eds. *Truwanten. Een toneeltekst uit het handschrift-Van Hulthem.* Groningen: Wolters-Noordhoff, 1978.

659 Duinhoven, A. M., ed. *Esmoreit.* Zutphen: Thieme, 1979.

660 Hoebeke, Marcel, ed. *Het Spel van de V Vroede en de V Dwaeze Maeghden.* 2nd edn. The Hague: Martinus Nijhoff, 1979.

661 Erné, B. H., and L. M. van Dis, eds. *De Gentse Spelen van 1539.* 2 vols. The Hague: Martinus Nijhoff, 1982.

662 Iwema, K., ed. 'Cornelis van Ghistele: Van Eneas en Dido'. *Jaarboek De Fonteine* 33 (1982–3): 103–242.

663 Coigneau, Dirk, ed. *Mariken van Nieumeghen.* The Hague: Martinus Nijhoff, 1982.

664 Hüsken, Wim N. M., and Frans A. M. Schaars. *Sandrijn en Lanslot. Diplomatische uitgave van twee toneelrollen uit het voormalig archief van de Rederijkerskamer De Fiolieren te 's-Gravenpolder.* Nijmegen-Grave: Uitgeverij Alfa, 1985.

Translations

665 van Dijk, Hans, Jane Fenoulhet, Tanis Guest, Theo Hermans, Elsa Strietman and Paul Vincent, trans. 'Playerwater. A Sixteenth-Century Farce, with an English Translation and Introduction'. *Dutch Crossing* 24 (1984): 32–81.

666 Conley, John, Guido de Baere, H. J. C. Schaap and W. H. Toppen, trans. *The Mirror of Everyman's Salvation. A Prose Translation of the Original Everyman. Accompanied by Elckerlijc and the English Everyman.* Amsterdam: Rodopi, 1985.

667 Potter, Robert, and Elsa Strietman, trans. 'Man's Desire and Fleeting Beauty. A Sixteenth-Century Comedy'. *Dutch Crossing* 25 (1985): 29–84.

668 King, Peter, trans. 'The Voluptuous Man'. *Dutch Crossing* 28 (1986): 53–107.

669 Oakshott, Jane, and Elsa Strietman, trans. 'Esmoreit. A Goodly Play of Esmoreit, Prince of Sicily'. *Dutch Crossing* 30 (1986): 3–39.

Bibliography

Scholarship: abele spelen *and* sotternieën

670 Wijngaards, N. C. H. 'Andreas Capellanus' *De arte honeste amandi* en de abele spelen'. *Spiegel der Letteren* 5 (1961): 219–28.
671 Wijngaards, N. C. H. 'Structuurvergelijking bij de abele spelen'. *Levende Talen* (1962): 322–7.
672 Iwema, K. 'Beschouwingen over de Gloriant'. *Spiegel der Letteren* 7 (1964): 241–52.
673 de Paepe, N. 'Kunnen onze Beatrijslegenden en abele spelen geevalueerd worden door middel van Andreas Capellanus' *De arte honeste amandi?*' *Leuvense Bijdragen* 53 (1964): 120–47.
674 Wijngaards, N. C. H. 'De oorsprong der abele spelen en sotternien'. *Handelingen van de Zuidnederlandse Maatschappij voor Taal- en Letterkunde en Geschiedenis* 22 (1968): 411–23.
675 Notermans, J. 'Mohammedaanse elementen in twee abele spelen: *Esmoreit* en *Gloriant*'. *Belgisch Tijdschrift voor Filologie en Geschiedenis* 51 (1973): 624–42.
676 Duinhoven, A. M. 'Pleidooi voor reconstructie van *Esmoreit*'. *Spiegel der Letteren* 17 (1975): 241–67.
677 Pleij, Herman. 'Volksfeest en toneel in de middeleeuwen 1'. *De Revisor* 3 (1976): 52–63.
678 Pleij, Herman. 'Hoe interpreteer je een middelnederlandse tekst?' *Spektator* 6 (1976): 337–49.
679 Duinhoven, A. M. 'Corruptie is overal'. *De Nieuwe Taalgids* 70 (1977): 97–120.
680 Duinhoven, A. M. 'De epilogen van *Die Buskenblaser*, *Esmoreit* en *Truwanten*'. In *Opstellen aangeboden aan Dr. H. C. A. Kruyskamp*, ed. H. Heestermans (The Hague: Martinus Nijhoff, 1977), 63–77.
681 Hummelen, Wim M. H. 'Tekst en toneelinrichting in de abele spelen'. *De Nieuwe Taalgids* 70 (1977): 229–42.
682 Peeters, L. '*Esmoreit* sconinx sone van Cecielien: Siciliaanse historie als abel spel'. *Spiegel der Letteren* 19 (1977): 245–79.
683 Pleij, Herman. 'Volksfeest en toneel in de middeleeuwen II: Entertainers en akteurs'. *De Revisor* 4 (1977): 34–41.
684 Duinhoven, A. M. 'De bron van *Esmoreit*', *De Nieuwe Taalgids* 72 (1979): 141–2.
685 Duinhoven, A. M. 'De bron van Lanseloet'. *Tijdschrift voor Nederlandse Taal- en Letterkunde* 95 (1979): 262–87.
686 Duinhoven, A. M. 'Mere van den Lanseloet'. *Tijdschrift voor Nederlandse Taal- en Letterkunde* 96 (1980): 12–18.
687 Duinhoven, A. M. 'Over Gloriant van Brunswijc en Florentine van Abelant!' In *Wie veel leest heeft veel te verantwoorden. Opstellen over filologie en historische letterkunde aangeboden aan Prof. Dr. F. Lulofs* (Groningen: Rijksuniversiteit Groningen, Nederlands Instituut, 1980), 81–99.
688 Kazemier, G. 'De bron van Lanseloet'. *Tijdschrift voor Nederlandse Taal- en Letterkunde* 96 (1980): 1–11.
689 Pleij, Herman. 'Over de betekenis van middelnederlandse teksten'. *Spektator* 10 (1980–1): 299–339.
690 Iwema, K. 'Waer sidi – over een middelnederlandse toneelconventie'. *De Nieuwe Taalgids* 77 (1984): 48–61.
691 van Dijk, H. 'Als ons die astronominen lesen. Over het abel spel "Vanden Winter ende vanden Somer"'. In *Tussentijds. Bundel studies aangeboden aan W. P. Gerritsen ter gelegenheid van zijn vijftigste verjaardag*, ed. A. M. J. van Buuren, H. van Dijk, O. S. H. Lie, F. P. van Oostrom (Utrecht: HES, 1985), 56–70.

Bibliography

692 van Dijk, H. 'The Structure of the Sotternieën in the Van Hulthem Manuscript'. In 7, 238–50.
693 van der Waerden, K. 'De figuur van de cockijn in het abel spel vanden Winter ende vanden Somer'. *Spektator* 15 (1985–6): 268–77.
694 Iwema, K. 'De wereld van een abel spel'. *De Nieuwe Taalgids* 80 (1987): 21–7.

Scholarship: Rhetoricians' drama

695 van Laan, Th. F. 'Everyman: A Structural Analysis'. *PMLA* 78 (1963): 465–75.
696 Steenbergen, G. J. 'De apostelspelen van Willem van Haecht'. In *Liber Alumnorum Prof. Dr. E. Rombauts* (Louvain: University of Louvain, 1968), 161–77.
697 Hummelen, Wim M. H. 'Typen van toneelinrichting bij de rederijkers'. *Studia Neerlandia* 1 (1970): 51–109.
698 Parker, John J. *The Development of the 'Everyman' Drama from 'Elckerlijc' to Hofmannsthal's 'Jedermann'.* Doetinchem: John J. Parker, 1970.
699 Sellin, Paul. 'An Instructive New Elckerlijc'. *Comitatus. A Journal of Medieval Studies* 2 (1971): 63–70.
700 Hummelen, Wim M. H. 'Illustrations of Stage Performances in the Work of Crispijn Passe the Elder'. In *Essays on Drama and Theatre. Liber Amicorum Benjamin Hunningher* (Amsterdam: Moussault, 1973), 67–84.
701 Hummelen, Wim M. H. 'Inrichting en gebruik van het toneel bij Job Gommersz (1565)'. *Jaarboek De Fonteine* (1975): 7–58.
702 Pleij, Herman. 'Geladen Vermaak. Rederijkerstoneel als politiek instrument van een elite-cultuur'. *Jaarboek De Fonteine* (1975): 75–103.
703 Pleij, Herman. 'De sociale functie van humor en trivialiteit op het rederijkerstoneel'. *Spektator* 5 (1975–6): 108–27.
703a Iwema, K. 'Kanttekeningen bij Mariken van Nieumeghen'. *Spiegel der Letteren* 20 (1976): 273–8.
704 Drewes, J. B. 'Het interpreteren van godsdienstige spelen van zinne'. *Jaarboek De Fonteine* (1978–9): 5–124.
705 Twycross, Meg. 'The Flemish Ommegang and Its Pageant Cars'. *Medieval Theatre* 2 (1980): 15–41, 80–98.
706 van Autenboer, E. *Het Brabants Landjuweel der Rederijkers (1515–1600).* Middelburg: Merlijn, 1981.
707 Best, Thomas W. 'Heralds of Death in Dutch and German Everyman Plays'. *Neophilologus* 65 (1981): 397–403.
708 Hummelen, Wim M. H. 'Types and Methods of the Dutch Rhetoricians' Theatre'. In *The Third Globe. Symposium for the Reconstruction of the Globe Playhouse. Wayne State University 1979*, ed. Cyril Walter Hodges, S. Schoenbaum and Leonard Leone (Detroit: Wayne State University Press, 1981), 164–254.
709 Vos, R. 'De volgorde van de eerste helpers in de Elckerlijc'. *De Nieuwe Taalgids* 74 (1981): 133.
710 van Boheemen, F. C., and Th. C. J. van der Heijden. *De Delftse Rederijkers 'Wij rapen gheneucht'.* Amsterdam: Huis aan de Drie Grachten, 1982.
711 Pleij, Herman. *De wereld volgens Thomas van der Noot, Boekdrukker en uitgever te Brussel in het eerste kwart van de zestiende eeuw.* Muiderberg: Coutinho, 1982.
712 Peeters, L. 'Mariken van Nieumeghen en de Antwerpse volksboekcultuur'. *Spiegel der Letteren* 25 (1983): 81–97.
713 Peeters, L. 'De Historie van Mariken van Nieumeghen. Historia-Rhetorica-Ethica'. *Spiegel der Letteren* 26 (1984): 179–97.

Bibliography

714 Peeters, L. 'Mariken van Nieumeghen. Bourgondische politiek en dominicaanse vroomheid'. In *Ic ga daer ic hebbe te doene. Een bundel opstellen voor F. Lulofs* (Groningen: Wolters-Noordhoff, 1984), 167–78.
715 Pleij, Herman. 'De laat-middeleeuwse rederijkersliteratuur als vroeghumanistische overtuigingskunst'. *Jaarboek De Fonteine* (1984): 65–95.
716 Strietman, Elsa. 'Two Dutch Dramatic Explorations of the Quality of Mercy'. In 6, 179–200.
717 van Boheemen, F. C., and Th. C. J. van der Heijden. *De Westlandse Rederijkerskamers in de 16e en 17e eeuw.* Amsterdam: Rodopi, 1985.
717a Kuiper, W. 'Een Gerenoveerd Mariamirakel'. *Spektator* 15:4 (1985–6): 249–67.
718 Hüsken, Wilhelmus Norbertus Maria. *Noyt meerder vreucht. Compositie en structuur van het komische toneel in de Nederlanden voor de Renaissance.* Deventer Studiën 3. Deventer: Uitgeverij Sub Rosa, 1987.

RECENT WORKS

Here are a few major titles that have appeared since the bibliography was compiled.

EUROPEAN DRAMA

Surveys, general

Tricomi, Albert H. *Early Drama to 1600.* Acta 13. Binghamton: Center for Medieval and Early Renaissance Studies, 1987.
Andersen, Flemming G., Julia McGrew, Tom Pettitt and Reinhold Schröder, eds. *Popular Drama in Northern Europe in the Later Middle Ages: A Symposium.* Odense: Odense University Press, 1988.
Aubailly, Jean-Claude, and Edelgard E. DuBruck, eds. *Le Théâtre et la cité dans l'Europe médiévale: Actes du Vème colloque international de la Société Internationale pour l'Étude du Théâtre Médiéval,* special issue of *Fifteenth-Century Studies* 13 (1988).
Vince, Ronald M. *A Companion to the Medieval Theatre.* New York and Westport CT: Greenwood Press, 1989.
Wright, Stephen K. *The Vengeance of Our Lord. Medieval Dramatizations of the Destruction of Jerusalem.* Studies and Texts 89. Toronto: Pontifical Institute of Mediaeval Studies, 1989.

LATIN CHURCH DRAMA

Wright, Stephen K. 'The Manuscript of *Sanctus Tewdricus*: Rediscovery of a "Lost Miracle Play" from St. Omer'. *Studies in Bibliography* 42 (1989): 236–45.

ENGLAND

Surveys, general

Johnston, Alexandra F., ed. *Editing Early English Drama: Special Problems and New Directions.* New York: AMS Press, 1987.
Emmerson, Richard K. 'Dramatic Developments: Some Recent Scholarship on Medieval Drama'. *envoi. A Review Journal of Medieval Literature* 1 (1988): 23–40.
Berger, Sidney E. *Medieval English Drama. An Annotated Bibliography of Recent Criticism.* New York and London: Garland Publishing, 1990.

Bibliography

Briscoe, Marianne G., and John C. Coldewey, eds. *Contexts for Early English Drama*. Bloomington: Indiana University Press, 1989. [13 essays.]

Carroll, Virginia Schaefer. *The 'Noble Gyn' of Comedy in the Middle English Cycle Plays*. American University Studies, Series IV, English Language and Literature 79. New York and Berne: Peter Lang, 1989.

Gibson, Gail McMurray. *The Theater of Devotion. East Anglian Drama and Society in the Late Middle Ages*. Chicago: University of Chicago Press, 1989.

Jack, R. D. S. *Patterns of Divine Comedy. A Study of Mediaeval English Drama*. Cambridge: D. S. Brewer, and Woodbridge, Suffolk and Wolfeboro, NH: Boydell & Brewer, 1989.

Documentation

Cawley, A. C., Jean Forrester and John Goodchild. 'References to the Corpus Christi Play in the Wakefield Burgess Court Rolls: the Originals Rediscovered', *LSE*, n.s. 19 (1988): 85–104.

Nelson, Alan, ed. *Cambridge*. 2 vols. Records of Early English Drama 8. Toronto: University of Toronto Press, 1989.

Cycle plays

Kinneavy, Gerald Byron. *A Concordance to The York Plays*. New York: Garland, 1986.

Burns, Edward. *The Chester Mystery Cycle: A New Staging Text*. Liverpool: Liverpool University Press, 1987.

Morality plays

Davidson, Clifford. *Visualizing the Moral Life. Medieval Iconography and the Macro Morality Plays*. New York: AMS Press, 1989.

FRANCE

Johnston, Alexandra F. "Lille: The External Evidence. An Analysis'. *RORD* 30 (1988): 167–72.

Knight, Alan E. 'The Image of the City in the Processional Theater of Lille'. *RORD* 30 (1988): 153–65.

Sheingorn, Pamela. 'Illustrations in the Manuscript of the Lille Plays', *RORD* 30 (1988): 173–6.

ITALY

Diderichs, Elisabeth. *Die Anfänge der mehrstimmigen Lauda*. Tutzing: Hans Schneider, 1986.

Allegri, Luigi. *Teatro e spettacolo nel medioevo*. Bari: Editore Laterza, 1988.

Barr, M. Cyrilla. *The Monophonic Lauda and the Lay Religious Confraternities of Tuscany and Umbria in the Late Middle Ages*. Early Drama, Art and Music Monograph Series 10. Kalamazoo: Western Michigan University, Medieval Institute Publications, 1989.

Bibliography

SPAIN: CATALAN DRAMA

Quirante Santacruz, Luis. *Teatro asuncionista valenciano de los siglos XV y XVI.* Valencia: Generalitat Valenciana, 1987.

Cenoz i del Aguila, G., and F. Huerta i Viñas. '*La Consueta de Làtzer*, peca núm. 17 del ms. 1139 de la Biblioteca de Catalunya'. In *Studia in honorem prof. M. de Riquer*, vol. III, 35–59. Barcelona: Quaderns Crema, 1988.

GERMANY

Wright, Stephen K. 'Scribal Error and Textual Integrity: The Case of Innsbruck Universitätsbibliothek Cod. 960'. *Studies in Bibliography* 39 (1986): 84–7.

Blosen, Hans, and Ole Lauridsen, eds. *Das Kopenhagener Weltgerichtsspiel.* Germanische Bibliothek. Heidelberg: Carl Winter, 1988.

Lomnitzer, Helmut. 'Ein Textfund zur Frankfurter Dirigierrolle'. In *Deutsche Handschriften 1100–1400, Oxforder Kolloquium 1985*, ed. Volker Honemann and Nigel F. Palmer (Tübingen: Niemeyer, 1988), 590–608.

Michael, Wolfgang F. 'Das Drama des Mittelalters: Ein Forschungsbericht'. *Deutsche Vierteljahrsschrift für Literaturwissenschaft und Geistesgeschichte* 62 (1988): 148–95.

Zwijnenburg, Nicolette H. J. *Die Veronicagestalt in den deutschen Passionsspielen des 15. und 16. Jahrhunderts.* Amsterdamer Publikationen zur deutschen Sprache und Literatur 79. Amsterdam: Rodopi, 1988.

Linke, Hansjürgen, and Ulrich Mehler, eds. *Die österlichen Spiele der Ratschulbibliothek Zwickau. Kritischer Text und Faksimilia der Handschriften.* Altdeutsche Textbibliothek 103. Tübingen: Max Niemeyer, 1989.

THE LOW COUNTRIES

Pikhaus, P. *Het Tafelspel bij de Rederijkers*, 2 vols. Ghent: Koninklijke Academie voor Nederlandse Taal- en Letterkunde, 1988, 1989.

Author index to the bibliography

This is an alphabetical index of authors and editors whose works are listed in the bibliography, giving the internal numbers. It does not include the additional unnumbered titles in the 'Recent works' section of the bibliography.

Author index to the bibliography

Author index to the bibliography

Author index to the bibliography

Author index to the bibliography

General index

General index

General index

Droz, Eugénie 152, 168
Drumbl, Johann 27–30, 40, 173, 174
Dublin 55–6, 83
Dufournet, Jean 157–8, 166
Duinhoven, A. M. 233, 235–6
Dunn, Catherine 30
Dunstable 119, 120
Duran, Eulalia 194
Duran i Sanpere, Agustí 194–5
Durbin, Peter 159
Dutka, JoAnna 6, 117
Duverger, J. 252
Duym, Jacob 249, 252
Dymock, Sir Edward 123

Early English Text Society 2, 66–70, 72, 73, 75, 76–7, 79
Eastern Church 173, 174
Easter plays 82, 84, 189–91, 194, 199, 201, 207–14, 216, 217, 219–21
Easter sepulchres 31
Eccles, Mark 17, 72, 101
Ecclesiastical Commission of the North 122
editing medieval plays 213–14, 223
Edwards, Robert 38, 174
Eerste Bliscap van Maria, Die 241–3, 252
Eger 208, 224
Elche Assumption play 190, 191–2
Elckerlijc 71, 246–7, 252
Elizabeth I, Queen of England 106, 125, 129
Elizabethan Stage Society 2, 8, 97
Elliott, John R., Jr xvii, 10, 160
Ellis, Colin 136
Emiliani-Giudici, Paolo 185
Encina, Juan del 196, 198, 202, 203
Endepols, H. J. E. 231–2
England, George 66
Enough Is as Good as a Feast 111
Epp, Garrett 144, 148
Erfurt morality play 212, 222
'Erlauer Spiele' 219
Ermini, Filippo 174, 185
Esbattement van s'Menschen Sin ende Verganckelijcke Schoonheit 244, 249
Esmoreit 227–30, 232–33, 235–6, 251
Essex 117, 121, 125, 129
Eton 126, 129
Eutrapelia 198

Evans, Dafydd 175
Evans, Paul 40
Everaert, Cornelis 248, 252
Everyman 8, 9, 71, 73–4, 75, 79, 81, 97, 99, 102, 114–15, 246–7, 252; see also Elckerlijc
Exeter 123, 124, 126

Fabbri, Mario 188
Fabliaux 222, 223, 227
façades 238, 239, 248, 249
Faccioli, Emilio 178, 180, 181, 188
facsimile editions 214
Fagiolo, Maurizio 183
Falvey, Kathleen 18, 177, 180
farces 154, 155, 159, 162, 163–5, 168, 194, 228, 237, 241, 248; see also sotternieën and sotties
Farmer, J. S. 71, 79
Farnham, Willard 110, 116
Farsa sacramental de 1521 199, 202
Fasani, Raniero 170, 177
Fegan, E. S. 129
Feier/Spiel distinction 32–3, 34, 35, 36
feminism 115–16
Fernández, Lucas 196, 198, 202, 203
Fernández de Heredia 195
Ferrario de Orduna, Lilia 204–5
Ferrers, Sir Humphrey 119, 120
Ferrer Valls, Teresa 204
Ferruz, Jaime 204
Fet de la Sibilla i l'enperador 190
Fêtes de la Renaissance I 7
Fifield, Merle 102, 108, 114
flagellanti 170, 177, 178, 180, 184
Flanigan, C. Clifford xiv, 26, 30, 36, 37, 38, 40, 42, 52, 61
Flecniakoska, Jean-Louis 200, 202, 204
Flemish Movement 225, 227
Fleury Playbook 31, 35, 37, 45, 52
  Herod 37
  Lazarus 37
  Saint Nicholas 37, 45
  Slaughter of the Innocents 35, 37
Florence 169, 170, 172, 180, 181, 182, 187, 188
Florence manuscript 163
Folger Shakespeare Library 71–2, 128, 193
folk drama 99, 106, 107, 208, 216, 223
folklore 200, 221
Folz, Hans 216

General index

fools 165, 238, 240
Fortini, Arnaldo 177
Foster, David 201
Fothergill-Payne, Louise 202, 204
Fouquet, Jean 102, 153, 157
France Archier de Bagnolet, Le 165
France 172, 187, 189, 201
Francesc d'Olesa 195
Franceschini, Ezio 173, 175, 176, 185
Francis I, King of France 151
Franciscans 170, 171, 177–8, 179, 186,
 187, 202, 235, 236
Francisco de Madrid 199, 202
Francis of Assisi, St 169, 177–8, 180,
 182, 186, 194
Frank, Grace 17, 152
Frankfurt Passion play 211, 217
friars, *see* Dominicans; Franciscans
Froning, Richard 209, 213
Fry, Timothy 87
Furnivall, F. J. 66, 67, 68–9, 78, 79, 95
Fuster, Joan 190

Galli, Giuseppe 177, 186
Galloway, David 117, 118, 139
Gamer, Helena 24, 40
Gangler-Mundwiler, Dominique 160
García de la Concha, Victor 196
García Morales, Justo 199
García Valdés, Celsa Carmen 198
Garçon et l'Aveugle, Le 158
Gardiner, Harold C. 5, 15, 16, 17, 85
Gardiner, Stephen 122
Gardner, John 90, 91
Gauvin, Claude 87
genre 155, 157
George, St 194, 197
Gerona 190, 191
gestures 112, 113, 114, 115, 183
Geu saint Denis 162
Gewecke, Frauke 202
Ghent 239, 240, 241, 246
Ghilardi, Fernando 173, 186, 188
Gibson, Gail 103, 114, 115, 141
Gibson, James M. 34
giullari 174, 175
Glier, Ingeborg 218
Globe Theatre 133, 146
Gloriant 227–30, 232–3, 252
Gloucester 124, 126
Goldstein, Leonard 30, 40
Gómez i Muntané, María Carmen 193

Gómez Manrique 195, 196, 198, 199,
 201, 202
Gompertz, Stéphane 158
Gonfalone (confraternity) 183
González Ollé, Fernando 202, 203, 204
Good Friday 176, 183, 191, 194
Gorboduc 105
Gordon, James 66, 78, 95
Göttweig Abbey 212, 219
Graduel Romain, Le, see Solesmes,
 monks of
Grano, Giovanni 174
Grantley, Darryll 148
Gréban, Arnoul and Simon 160
 Le Mystère des Actes des Apôtres 161,
 168
Greenberg, Noah 8
Greg, W. W. 67, 79
Gregorie, Edward 76
Grosseteste, Robert 101
Gsell, Otto 157
Guessard, François 168
Guiette, Robert 37
guildhalls 106, 126
Guild of the Crossbowmen 242
guilds 80, 93, 120, 121, 162, 237–8, 242
Güssing 212, 214
Guthrie, Tyrone 5, 8

Habicht, Werner 110
Hall, Edward 111
Hallinger, Dom Kassius 40
Halliwell (-Phillipps), James Orchard
 66, 78, 82, 95, 117, 128
Hamilton, Alice 129
Happé, Peter 17, 75, 107
Harbage, Alfred 16
Hardison, O. B., Jr 15, 26–7, 29, 33, 40,
 42, 45, 51, 81, 86, 87, 98, 134
Harlwood, F. W. 129
Harman, Alec 10, 16
Harris, Markham 8
Harris, William O. 98
Harrison, F. Ll. 62
Harrison, Tony 8
Hatfield, Rab 185
Hegge plays, *see* N-Town cycle
Heidelberg Passion play 213
Heiserman, Arthur 98
Heitz, Carol 30
Helmich, Werner 163, 164
Helterman, Jeffrey 90

301

General index

Henderson, Ingeborg 214
Henderson, John 184
Hennig, Ursula 40
Henry, Albert 157
Henry, Earl of Lincoln 123
Herkommer, Hubert 216
Herrtage, S. J. 68
Hesbert, René-Jean 46, 62
Hesse 207, 211, 223
Hildeburgh, W. L. 96
Hildegard of Bingen xiii
Hildesheim 37
Hill, R. F. 6
Hilton, Walter 115
Hindley, Alan 152
Hirsch, E. D. 168
history plays 155, 159, 161–2
Hodges, C. Walter 104, 116, 133, 146
Hoebeke, Marcel 245
Homulus, see *Elckerlijc*
Hone, William 2
Hook, David 201
Horestes 105
Horozco, Sebastián de 203–4
Hosley, Richard 102, 104, 105, 136
Houle, Peter 114
houses, plays performed in 127, 209, 212
Howell, Jane 8
Hrotswitha of Gandersheim xiii, 175, 176–7, 185, 186
Huerta i Viñas, Ferran 194
Hughes, Andrew xiv, xvii, 52, 54, 56
Hughes, David G. 47–8, 56
Hummelen, Wim M. H. 230, 231, 232, 241, 247–8, 249, 251, 252
Hungerford, Lady 119–20
Hunningher, Benjamin 24, 39
Hunt, Tony 156, 157, 158
Hunter, G. K. 10
Hunter, J. 95
Hüsken, W. N. M. 241
Husmann, Heinrich 40
Hutton, Matthew 122
Huysmans, A. P. 244, 252
hymns 170, 181, 191, 192

iconography 100, 112–13, 114, 115, 148, 179
Il Cecca, *see* d'Angelo, Francesco
incipits 51
ingegni 172, 182

Ingram, R. W. 117, 118, 139
Innsbruck codex 960 214
Innsbruck (Thuringian) Easter play 214, 216, 219, 220
inns, inn-yards 106, 124–5, 145, 243
inquisition 200
interludes 4, 17, 75, 99, 104, 126, 221
intermezzi 183
Iwema, K. 229, 231, 233, 234–5, 246

Jacob de Voragine 192
Jacopone de Todi 179–80, 181, 187
    Donna de Paradiso 179, 180, 187
Jacquot, Jean 7
Janota, Johannes 213
Janssen, Steen 171
Jansz, Louris 249
Jantz Collection 212, 214
Jan van den Berghe 248, 252
Jauss, Hans Robert 36, 40
Jean du Prier 162
Jeffrey, David L. 16, 186, 187
Jerusalem 161, 168
Jesuit drama 202, 208
Jeu d'Adam, Le 155–6, 211
Jeu de sainte Agnès 162
Jews 191, 192
Joachim of Flora 170
Jodogne, Omer 160, 171
John of Beverley, St 119, 120
Johnston, Alexandra F. xviii, 8, 107, 115, 118, 129, 138, 139, 140, 147
John the Baptist, St 197, 201
Jonckbloet, W. J. A. 226, 251
Jones, Charles W. 37
Jones, Robert C. 114
Jonson, Ben 133
    Volpone 108, 109
Jonsson, Ritva 40, 46, 62, 184
Juana de la Cruz 204
Juan López de Ubeda 205
Juan Pastor 203
Jugement Dernier, Le 161
Jung, Marc-René 161
Justice, Steven 156

Kahrl, Stanley J. xvi, xvii, 6, 15, 91–2, 95, 106, 117, 118, 134, 145, 147, 148
Kantrowitz, Joanne 114
Kanzog, Klaus 224
Kassel Paradise play 211

302

General index

General index

Redentin Easter play 212, 214, 216, 220, 224
Rederijkerskamers xvi, 226, 230, 231, 232, 234, 236, 237–52
Reformation, Protestant xvi, 5, 85, 100, 112, 208, 225, 241, 250
Regularis Concordia 28, 29, 40
Reinhardt, Max 9
Renaissance 100, 106–7, 110–13, 116, 118, 151, 152, 200, 246, 248, 249
René duke of Anjou 162
Research Opportunities in Renaissance Drama (RORD) 10, 12, 13, 140, 147
responsories 57–9
Respublica, see Udall, Nicholas
revels 105, 111
Rey-Flaud, Bernadette 164
Rey-Flaud, Henri 153–4, 157
rhyme 229, 230, 236
Rhys, Ernest 73, 79
Ricci, Giuliana 183
Richard II, King of England 102, 109
Richard, Jules Marie 168
Riedmann, Josef 211
Riggio, Milla 103–4, 114, 115
Riguer, Martín de 190
ritual 200, 221
Rivas, Palá, María 197
Robert of Anjou 235
Robin Hood plays 118–20, 122, 123
Robinson, J. W. 96
Rodini, Robert J. 187
Rodríguez-Moñino, Antonio 205
Rodríguez-Puértolas, Julio 204
Roemans, R. 251
Rogerson, Margaret 118, 138, 139, 140, 147
Roloff, Hans-Gert 212–13
romances 82, 92–3, 227, 232
Romano, David 191
Romanticism 1, 66, 97, 151, 216, 225
Rome 171, 175, 183
Romeu i Figueras, Josep 190, 193–4, 195
Rose, Martial 136, 143–4
Rossi, Vittorio 187, 188
Roston, Murray 113
Rothschild, James de 151, 168
Rouen 55, 163
rounds 102, 124, 136, 137, 147
Rousse, Michel 158, 164, 166
Roy, Emile 168

Rubben 227
Rubio García Luis 191, 198
rubrics 48, 49, 51, 211, 214, 219, 220, 222, 244
Rudick, Michael 38, 40
Rudwin, Maximilian 217, 221, 224
Rueff, Jacob 224
Ruffini, Franco 171
Ruggeri, Franco 177
Ruggeri, Ruggero 186
Ruh, Kurt 218
Runnalls, Graham 152, 154, 159, 160, 162, 166
Rutebeuf 158
Ryan, R. P. 101, 116

sacre rappresentazioni xvi, 169, 172, 178, 181–5, 187, 188
St-Gall 44, 60–1
St Gall (Middle Rhenish) Passion play 213, 216
St-Martial 45, 60–1
saint plays 4, 107, 108, 119, 155, 159, 162, 177, 182, 194, 195, 203, 204, 209
Sak full of Newes 123
Salgo, Sandor 8
Salisbury 45, 123
Salter, F. M. 85, 91, 117, 118, 133, 136
salvation history 125, 236
Sánchez de Badajoz, Diego 199, 203
Sanchis Guarner, M. 192
Santa Maria de l'Estany 189, 193
Sarum Ordinal 45
satire 165, 220, 224
Scarpellini, Pietro 179, 180
Scawen, John 147
scenery 135
Scharpé, L. 252
Schell, Edgar T. 17, 108–9
Schernberg, Dietrich 222
Schipke, Renata 214
Schmitt, Natalie Crohn 101–2, 103, 114, 136, 143, 147
Schneider, Karin 213
Schoell, Konrad 154
Schoenbaum, Samuel 16, 147
schools 106, 107, 119, 126
Schottmann, Brigitte 216
Schuchter, J. D. 17
Schulze-Busacker, Elizabeth 162
Schützeichel, Rudolf 213

General index

Vasari, Giorgio 172
Vaticano Ghigiano 180
Vattaso, Marco 188
Vaughan, M. F. 156
Veltrusky, Jarmilla P. 18
Velz, John 110
Vengeance de Nostre Seigneur, La 161, 168
Veni Creator 192
Venus 227, 228, 234–5
Verfasserlexikon 218–19
Vérité cachée, La 114
versification 89, 90
Vice figure xv, 98, 107, 108, 111, 112, 114, 123
Vicente, Gil 202
Vich 190, 194
Vich Easter play 189, 191, 194
Victimae Paschalis Laudes 191
Vie de Marie Magdaleine 162
Vienna (Silesian) Easter play 214, 219
Vierde Bliscap [of Our Lady], *Die* 242
Villingen Passion play 213
Vinay, Gustavo 176, 185
virtues and vices 100, 101, 103, 108, 200
Visitatio Sepulchri 4, 18, 23–31, 33–5, 47, 49, 52–3
Vita Christi 199
Vitale-Brovarone, Alessandro 160
Viterbo, *see* Centro Studi sul Teatro Medioevale e Rinasciamentale
Vitse, Marc 204
Völker, Paul-Gerhard 213, 217
Volksschauspiele, see folk drama
Vollmann-Profe, Gisela 211, 212
von Fallersleben, Hoffman 219, 225, 227, 251
von Hofmannsthal, Hugo 9
Vos, R. 247
Vulgate Bible 53–4, 77

Wackernell, Joseph Eduard 209, 215, 223
waer sidi formula 230–1
Wager, Louis and William 122
wagons xiii–xiv, 80, 86, 93, 95, 118, 133, 135, 138–47, 166, 189, 197, 238, 239, 242, 245, 246
Wainwright, Thomas 129
Wainwright-de Kadt, Elizabeth 211, 221, 224

Wakefield cycle 66–8, 70–2, 74, 78, 80–3, 90, 93, 95, 122, 129, 136, 143–4, 148
'Second Shepherds' play' 81
Talents play 68, 70
Wakefield Master 70, 75, 90, 144
Wallace, Robin 52
Walsall 119, 120
Ward, A. W. 81, 84, 95
Wardropper, Bruce W. 201, 202
Warning, Rainer 24, 152–3
Wasson, John 106–7, 109, 111, 117, 118, 125
Waterhouse, Osborn 66, 79, 96
Weber de Kurlat, Frida 203
Webster, John 113
Wechssler, Eduard 174, 185
Wehrli, Max 216, 218, 224
Weihnachtsfeiern, see Christmas plays
Weiner, Jack 203
Weissman, Ronald F. E. 180, 187
Werner, Wilfried 35
Werstine, Paul 12
West, Larry 216
Whiting, B. J. 81
Whitsuntide 81, 118, 122
Wickham, Glynne xi, xii, xv, 10, 15, 18, 75, 81–2, 85, 86, 87, 98, 102, 104, 105, 125, 130–3, 136, 139, 144, 145, 146, 147, 148
Wijngaards, N. C. H. 228–9, 232, 237
Wilcke, Karin 213, 223
Willems, Jan Frans 227
Williams, Arnold 85, 86, 98, 132, 138, 146, 147
Williams-Krapp, Werner 220
Wilson, F. P. 6, 79
Wilson, Jean 16
Wilson, John Dover 111, 116
Wilson, Katharina M. 186
Winchester Troper 48, 59
Wisdom 72, 79, 102, 103–4, 110, 111, 114, 115
Wittkowsky, Hartmut 216
Wolf, Norbert Richard 219
Wolfenbüttel Easter play 222
women, roles of 227, 250
Woodstock 108–9
Woolf, Rosemary 17, 36, 88–9
Worp, J. A. 232, 252
Wright, John 215

310

General index